EAST INDIA PATRONAGE AND THE BRITISH STATE

'Tell me the auld auld story
O' hoo the Union brocht
Puir Scotland into being
As a country worth a thocht.'

From 'The Parrot Cry',
by Hugh MacDiarmid

EAST INDIA PATRONAGE AND THE BRITISH STATE

The Scottish Elite and Politics
in the Eighteenth Century

GEORGE K. MCGILVARY

Tauris Academic Studies
LONDON • NEW YORK

Published in 2008 by Tauris Academic Studies,
an imprint of I.B.Tauris & Co Ltd
6 Salem Road, London W2 4BU
175 Fifth Avenue, New York NY 10010
www.ibtauris.com

In the United States of America and Canada distributed by
Palgrave Macmillan, a division of St. Martin's Press
175 Fifth Avenue, New York NY 10010

Copyright © 2008 George K. McGilvary

The right of George K. McGilvary to be identified as author of this work has been asserted by the author in accordance with the Copyright, Designs and Patent Act 1988.

All rights reserved. Except for brief quotations in a review, this book, or any part thereof, may not be reproduced, stored in or introduced into a retrieval system, or transmitted, in any form or by any means, electronic, mechanical, photocopying, recording or otherwise, without the prior written permission of the publisher.

International Library of Historical Studies 54

ISBN: 978 1 84511 661 3

A full CIP record for this book is available from the British Library
A full CIP record for this book is available from the Library of Congress

Library of Congress catalog card: available

Printed and bound by Thomson Press India Ltd
Camera-ready copy edited and supplied by the author

In Memory of
Isa and *Geordie*
who have gone before

Contents

Preface	ix
Acknowledgements	xv
1. Drummond: Early Life 1675–1742	1
2. Political and Electoral Realities 1707–74	12
3. Company and Patronage Infrastructure 1720–74	28
4. Drummond and Management 1720–42	38
5. Drummond Network 1720–42	48
6. Operating from Scotland 1742–61	68
7. Government: Supply and Demand 1742–61	90
8. Shipping Positions 1742–61	113
9. Elections and Watersheds 1761–66	121
10. Ministries: Company and Favours 1765–74	136
11. Shipping Bounty 1765–74	153
12. Patrons and Recipients 1760–74	163
13. Military Recruitment 1720–80	177
14. Capital Accumulation 1720–80	184
15. Summary and Conclusions	203
Appendix	209
Short Titles and Abbreviations	233
Notes	234
Bibliography	251
Glossary	264
Index	266

Preface

This book seeks to establish that from the 1720s to the late 1770s a well-defined patronage system was instituted by ministries, allowing a disproportionate number of Scots to fill positions in the East India Company and its shipping. By virtue of this patronage, which became available through Company connections, grateful governments were able to proffer positions to selected individuals and families forming a large part of the Scottish elite; doing so in exchange for political support and votes.

Such posts promised enormous riches to individuals who survived the voyage and ravages of the Indian climate. In turn, the wealth from this source that flowed into Scotland was to be the salvation of many landed families. It increased largesse all round and contributed considerably to agricultural, commercial and industrial expansion north of the Tweed. Probably, through the mixture of social ease, security and sense of freedom from internal strife that was produced, it also encouraged, to some extent, factors that enabled the mid-century Scottish Enlightenment to flower.

It is argued that above all the development of this patronage went a long way towards securing the political management of Scotland, and together with the riches that accompanied Scots on their return, was of immense, perhaps vital importance to the survival and viability of the new state of Great Britain that had come into being with the Union of the Scottish and English Parliaments in 1707. There is the distinct possibility that without these favours and the spin-off from this patronage, the new realm might have become unstable and foundered.

■

The fiction of a Great Britain had been deliberately promoted by ministers, especially in the years immediately following the events of 1707, but successive administrations had struggled to find adequate support north of the border for the new state. Genuine resentment was prevalent and a deep and wide hostility to loss of sovereignty, undiluted because of what appeared to Scots as Westminster's abrupt disinterest thereafter.

The truth of the matter, however, was that although there was certainly a degree of insensitivity among many English ministers to what Scotland was enduring through loss of its independence, London was hampered by a lack of money and understanding of much that went on in the north. Nor did there appear to be any way in which to ease things, such as through sufficient patronage to purchase votes and so quieten discord among trouble-makers, and also to appease would-be supporters.

Yet the curious thing is that within twenty years of the Union, fortune and circumstance came together in such a way that ministers were allowed the opportunity to tap the unique patronage that stemmed from the East India Company.[1] Significant use of these posts by government agents dates in particular from 1725. Only a limited number fell to Scots before this. They were then used to great effect, and much earlier than Henry Dundas' direct control in the 1780s, as hereto believed.

The pool of sinecures, preferments and favours available in Scotland was enormously enlarged from around 1725 by remarkable and uniform amounts of India patronage. It was very quickly realised (perhaps anticipated) that its liberal application, together with whatever other favours might be found, could only help political management and secure elections.

Thus India patronage helped ministries to control Scotland politically, as well as ensuring governmental dominance in the Westminster arena; and together with the inflow of funds originating in India, accomplished the task of convincing Scots in general that they should set aside the unpopular events of the years from 1707 to the 1720s. Particularly important was the fact that the politically powerful elite: the aristocracy, landed gentry and lawyers in the main, had quickly become reconciled to being part of Britain – long before the end of the eighteenth century – and they in turn helped develop a general acceptance of the idea of a British state.

•

It all came to life with Walpole. When he assumed command as first minister in 1722 it was glaringly obvious to him that the situation in Scotland offered the most serious risk to the Union. Alerted to electoral realities in the north, he had to make sure that Scots would go on to enjoy an unusually high distribution of such patronage as was on offer.

However, the employment of this India patronage, to add to that of lay and ecclesiastical, came about only because of what appears at first glance to be the fortuitous appearance in the Company's Directorate of the Scot,

John Drummond of Quarrel. Through him initially, large numbers of Scots were to fill posts in the Company's civil, medical and shipping branches, while others became free-merchants in the settlements. (Recruitment to the Company's military wing followed, but only after Culloden).

It is the use of this India patronage by successive governments that explains the mystery and anomaly of why so many Scots appear in the lists of Company servants and in its shipping in the eighteenth century. Their numbers increased as the years wore on, swelled by those recruited because of the Company's territorial expansion and the military struggles that arose, and as prejudice and hostility within England died somewhat after the '45. These same Scots went on to contribute in a great way to the later establishment of empire in India and the Far East, while bringing back to their native land both much needed money and resolve.[2]

■

From Walpole's time Company patronage was used deliberately to facilitate the management of Scotland and to help merge it into the body of the new state. The ready availability of such numerous posts, together with widespread appreciation of their worth, encouraged the under-pinning and knitting-together that was necessary in commercial and landed society north and south of the border.

In England the ruling Whig plutocracy embraced the spread of Company favours among their Scottish counterparts, perceiving that this would help consolidate the privileged position they occupied themselves. Those involved were convinced their own future power and wealth would be safeguarded and enlarged within the new creation that came into being in 1707, and which they controlled. Their best interests would be preserved by its continuance, and this would be helped by the inclusion of their cousins in the north.

While building safe political majorities, this large source of employment for the 'right' people, together with the wealth remitted from India, deadened controversy and turmoil in Scotland. Such badly needed funds injected into the fabric of Scottish society stimulated the creation of even greater wealth. Internal threats were diluted, wide-spread disgruntlement faded; while cross-fertilisation with the English in all walks of life was achieved. The common interest of capital accumulation helped weave strands that bound the Scots and English elites firmly together in the Union framework, sustaining it.

It made a lot of sense to the Whig oligarchy in power, controlling things from Westminster, to secure the well-being of the state through healing and restoring internal divisions in this way, wherever and whenever possible.

India patronage helped do just that, and put substance into the Great Britain creation. It is almost certainly the case, therefore, that during these vital years, this system, using East India Company patronage and the posts on offer helped mend society, robbed Scottish nationalism of its urgency and the Jacobite cause of much of its strength.

∎

Favours from this source had thus been on stream for fifty years when the American colonists were ready to take a different path. But by that date Company posts had assumed greater significance, just when opportunities in the American colonies were becoming few and far between. Moreover, while harvesting of sugar, tobacco and cotton from America and the West Indies led to numerous slaves from Africa, relatively few recruits were required from the new Britain. There would have been fewer openings for younger sons, especially from the mid 1770s, if the road to the east had not been opened up, where ready markets were sourced and fortunes could be made.

Company patronage fitted perfectly into the scheme of things. All ministries, from Walpole in the 1720s, to Pitt the Younger in the 1780s saw clearly the line that must be followed: maintenance of the Protestant faith, a Protestant monarch, political stability, defence of the realm of Great Britain and expansion of trade and empire. They threatened all-out war against every enemy within or without the British Isles if any part of the whole should be endangered; and all patronage would be used to advantage.

A Great Britain was established as it were, with a blueprint ready and in place; and the systemised use of India patronage was one of the major strands in the design. Out of sight it under-pinned so much and contributed enormously to the survival of the Great Britain creation, enabling it to reach maturity.

∎

The spin-off from the patronage system was unexpected. Hopes of a brighter future came to many Scots, especially the elite; a sense of opportunities to be seized spread among them; undreamed of possibilities started appearing as the number of positions on offer swelled with the years. At first only a trickle of men were sent east through the agencies of the Company and its associated shipping, and wealth from the sub-continent appeared only slowly in Caledonia. However, from the 1750s onwards money began pouring into Scotland almost as rapidly as the immense numbers of Scots now going out to India.

The onset of the Seven Years War and the urgent need for massive manpower was to benefit the Scots greatly. Global conflict, together with the Company's expansion and transformation into a territorial power meant that the patronage system, now up and running, enabled Scots without number to make their way east. The flow of wealth into Scotland from the Indies increased correspondingly, providing a considerable boost to the capital needed for general expansion in all spheres and creation of an economic and social infra-structure. This capital was an unlooked for but welcome benefit – doubly so as far as governments were concerned; and brought immense satisfaction to the privileged orders.

To summarise: what is revealed here is a system deliberately designed and nurtured to control Scotland that had an effectiveness and wide-spread use far beyond what was first envisaged. This patronage unfailingly helped manage voting at elections north of the Tweed and consistently returned preferred candidates to Parliament, granting to ministries a measure of firm control both peripherally and at the centre of government. The consistency, sturdiness and stability thus given to the new state proved vital; especially during the successful struggle against other European powers for territories; and during the consolidation of empire that followed.

It cannot be emphasised enough, just how important this patronage was in securing political peace and security in the eighteenth century, especially during the '45 and its aftermath; then in the years following Pelham's death in 1754. In the 1760s, when government at Westminster was in turmoil, these favours were even more in demand. And it appears difficult to deny that during the critical years of the mid–century (even stretching to the end of the 1770s) India patronage was a major strand whereby consolidation was achieved, and the very concept of a Great Britain sustained.

So beneficial and fruitful were these political favours, they were used to a quite extraordinary degree throughout the rest of the 1700s and into the early 1800s. During the first quarter of the nineteenth century their significance can still be traced with some precision; and the combined impact of job opportunities, wealth creation and hope was felt everywhere.

The foundations of a lasting political constancy in Britain were initiated, as well as those for commercial, industrial and fiscal success. The strength for overseas expansion (on top of national security requirements) was given vital time to develop. Of course, it also meant the smothering, almost the snuffing-out of Scotland, in a political sense. As commentators like Bruce Lenman and John Shaw have said, Scottish problems were not even raised; the country was to be 'managed' for the greater good of the new state and for those at Westminster.[3]

The research for this subject was begun in the late 1970s at a time when India patronage and its importance had not been given prominence in Scotland – probably because in order to be appreciated properly it required an understanding of the workings of the English East India Company and its attendant peculiarities, as well as a scouring of Scottish repositories. A similar story applies to the economic and social factors that accompany the political dynamic involved.

The pages that follow stem from these investigations, tracing the origins and development of the East India patronage system and how it was managed. Hopefully, they demonstrate how much the Company, and the favours it conferred, contributed to the political, economic and social development of Scotland; and show that a substantial part of the capital needed to kick-start the agricultural, commercial and industrial revolutions in Scotland flowed from this source. In many ways these favours, and the manner in which they were distributed, contributed substantially to the continued well-being of the British state in the eighteenth century; while immense imperial advances were built on the back of the developments they helped shape.

Acknowledgements

As might be expected I owe an immense debt to librarians, those custodians of our national treasures, and to various people from all over Britain. They are too numerous to mention individually, but I salute them all, each and every one.

The book developed out of my doctorate with the Open University and I wish to thank my supervisors Mr John Riddy and Dr Angus Calder for the great encouragement, patience and understanding given me. I should also like to pay tribute to the labours of so many scholars, who lit the path ahead, sometimes quite unwittingly. Nothing happens in a vacuum.

Again, I thank my wife Margaret, daughter Lynn and son Kenneth, for their forbearance when faced over the years with my absence from family interaction because of the time that research and writing necessarily entails.

As might be expected, a monograph such as this will use some unusual words. These are explained in the glossary and indicated by an asterisk in the main text. The form and spelling of Indian words used are based on the *Handbook of Oriental History,* edited by C.H. Philips, 2nd edition, London, 1963. Square brackets encompass words I have introduced that were omitted in the originals, or they have been inserted to make the meaning clear.

1

Drummond: Early Life 1675–1742

1

The concentrated use of patronage available through the East India Company and its Shipping interest for the ends of Scottish political management began shortly after John Drummond was made a Director of the Company in April 1722. But a large part of the answer to how and why this rather unobtrusive man came to provide such a remarkable service, at the moment of greatest need, must be looked for in earlier years. By the time he became a Director, Drummond was very widely experienced in public affairs; and the skills and talents he had developed meant he was superbly tailored for the tasks he would have to undertake. He was the vital, necessary intermediary if the patronage system was to operate.

He was born in 1675, the second eldest of the five surviving sons and one daughter of George Drummond, fifth Laird of Blair-Drummond, and his wife Elizabeth, daughter of Sir Gilbert Ramsay of Bamffe, Perth. His immediate ancestors, through the Earls of Perth, had very strong connections with the House of Stewart.[1]

Drummond had been despatched to Amsterdam in 1693 to begin a mercantile career. His situation was similar to that of many Scots who had gone before. After his apprenticeship with a Mr. Spilman he set up in partnership with another merchant, Jan van der Heiden. He was able to put a great deal more money into the firm after marriage to Agatha van der Brent, sister of the Elector of Brandenburgh's agent in Amsterdam. The business prospered until 1712, when a series of miscalculations and Drummond's diplomatic activities caused him to neglect things, resulting in its crash that year. Parallel to this career as a businessman, Drummond was acting out a far more important role. From 1702 to 1713 he was an unofficial agent for Robert Harley (Earl of Oxford), Chancellor of the Exchequer, and for Henry St. John (Bolingbroke), Secretary of State for the North. He was useful to them in that he sent news and advice of diplomatic and financial activities on the continent during the War of the Spanish Succession (1701–1714); and was involved in direct and secret negotiations on their behalf. He established strong contacts with governments on both sides of the Channel in this period; and has been adjudged to have played a vital role in rallying political and financial support behind the new English ministry in 1710, on both sides of the Channel.

Drummond had first met Oxford, who was to become his chief patron in these early years, during a brief stay in London in 1704. The introduction to the then Secretary of State (1704 to 1708) was made by Dr William Stratford of Christ Church, Oxford, formerly Chaplain to the Speaker of the House of Commons when Oxford held that office.

Oxford was building up a network of correspondents, and from the continent Drummond sent him details of war-time financial transactions. He transmitted letters from agents in Europe to Whitehall, forwarded important news and sent reports. In exchange, he received a government contract for selling Cornish tin. It lasted until 1707 and was worth £1,000 per year. He was soon drawn into banking concerns and involved in financing some of Harley's secret agents on the continent.

It was Drummond's 'Dutchness' that in 1710 recommended him to Harley, as it had St. John; along with this was his willingness to give financial support to the new ministry. The Dutch were fooled, in that they thought he was one of them through naturalization. From 1711 to 1712 Drummond acted as a go-between for Heinsius, the Dutch Grand Pensionary, and Oxford. This was during the negotiations over the Utrecht peace terms at the end of the war. However, Oxford and Bolingbroke wanted the real dialogue kept to themselves, and unknown to Drummond he was used as a decoy.

The Scot expected pecuniary gain in exchange for this duty, and considered he would be given the post of Deputy Paymaster-General in 1712. For this office he had the backing of James Brydges (later Earl of Chandos), and of Bolingbroke. That year, however, he was struck down by bankruptcy. The financial collapse that followed, and the end of secret diplomacy for Oxford, virtually closed this stage in his career. He needed a new start and looked to friends in England for that purpose, intending to move from Holland to London. However, Oxford denied him the Deputy

Paymaster post; and despite repeated requests that help be given him, made by William Stratford and others, little happened.

2

From 1713 Drummond was in England and again friends rallied round. For example, the Albemarles offered a commission in a regiment, his Dutch friends proffered help, as did Sir Matthew Decker and Stratford. He was pitied, not blamed for the crash; but English traders and financiers in the Low Countries whipped up rumours that he was a Jacobite to ruin his reputation there. Despite the compromising position of his benefactor, Bolingbroke, these claims were groundless and the rumours were motivated by commercial rivalry.

Nevertheless, the smears caused Drummond great bitterness, primarily because the post-1715 period, one of such political uncertainty, created unwarranted suspicion. This resentment is doubly understandable since his diplomatic work in Holland during the war of the Spanish Succession had demonstrated loyalty to Parliament, to its supremacy and to British constitutionalism.

The 1707 Union had occurred against a background of war in Europe. It was followed by a split in the Tory leadership in 1713, which preceded the death of Queen Anne. All this and the rapid ascendancy of the Hanoverians and the Whigs in 1714, followed by the 1715 Jacobite rebellion, led to loss of direction in many quarters and to further political complexity. Some families were not quite sure which course of action would serve their best interests.

Fortunately for some, Hanoverian Whig ministers were ready to welcome back, as far as was possible, those among the 'erring' members of the aristocracy whose influence would possibly hurt if kept in exile or if forced to suffer too much. Particular attention was paid to pacifying those who might help keep the Jacobite cause alive. Drummond's relatives, the Earls of Perth, out in the '15, were in just such a category; as were the Earls of Kinnoul, Lord Bathurst, John Ogilvy (Lord Airlie) and many others. There is little doubt that such political complexities cast a shadow over many Scots at first. Charles Erskine, for example, later to be Solicitor-General, was cousin to the Earl of Mar, the Jacobite leader.

Help for Drummond finally arrived through Bolingbroke, who, as Secretary of State, gave him a commission in 1713 to participate in the Utrecht negotiations (on trade). This was to be followed, Drummond hoped, with the Consul's position at Ostend, and the Residency at Brussels. He promoted the British position at these meetings very successfully; but his hope of advancement was still uncertain and made more precarious when Oxford and Bolingbroke fell out. He was much closer to Oxford, who now began to pay more attention to him because of his own rivalry with Bolingbroke, and because once more the opportunity to use Drummond's skills had arisen.

On his return to London, Oxford had him presented to the Queen, in April 1714; and he was also treated well by Oxford's relations, especially by his son Edward, Lord Harley, and his cousin, Thomas Harley. With Oxford's fall from the Treasury Drummond was in a quandary. He tried to keep in touch with both Oxford and Bolingbroke (the latter was now head of the ministry) and used Decker towards these ends. It was all in vain. Efforts to land a post through Bolingbroke finished with the death of Queen Anne, the total discredit of her ministers, and the accession of George I and the Whigs.

These events seemed to dash Drummond's hopes of advancement, since Oxford and Bolingbroke no longer counted; but the ability of his friend James Brydges to cross over to the new Court rescued him. Brydges had influential friends around the new king; and used a familiarity with the monarch that dated back to their days of friendship in Hanover. He played on a former closeness, made it clear that he did not seek a political position for himself, and in the following years used his great wealth discreetly to the royal advantage. In 1718 he was created Duke of Chandos.

He helped Drummond enormously, as did Argyll, who had enjoyed the full backing of Drummond's family and relations in voting for the Union in 1707. Friends in the business and banking world were many too, and the importance of the City to the Whigs could only help. His associates, especially Decker and Stratford, rallied round the Scot and eased his entry into London business and political life from 1714. He was helped in this by continued close familiarity with the largely non-political Edward Lord Harley.

3

Drummond's finances also took a decided turn for the better from 1714. Returns from Dutch commercial concerns, activities as a commission agent and the help of Chandos, Stratford and Decker put him on his feet. Such was the change in his circumstances he was able in 1716 to pay off the debt he owed the East India Company (£3,413-7-5) from whom he received in return a gold cup inscribed 'Reward for Honesty'. In 1717 he was able to deposit £1,635 in Andrew Drummond's bank at Charing Cross; and by 1720 was again in business, trading in wines, diamonds and redwood and fully involved in the business life of the City of London.

Both John and Andrew Drummond were Proprietors of India stock by this date; and most important of all, in April 1722 John was elected a Director of the Company.[2] The ease with which he entered the Direction was due to the executive powers held by his friends of earlier years. Sir Matthew Decker was already a leading Director; he and the Duke of Chandos had been Proprietors since 1711. The strength of this group soon prevailed in the General Court and in the Direction.[3]

Drummond was to be a Director until 1733, when his own failing health and the death of his wife made him stand down, albeit reluctantly. He remained a Proprietor, however, and through his friends retained great powers of patronage. In those first eleven years he was part of a group that very nearly completely controlled the direction of the Company's affairs, and helped itself to the largest share of available patronage. It consisted of Drummond, Chandos, Decker and an ex-Governor of Madras, Edward Harrison. They were very close.

Decker had been a Director since 1714, and when he stepped down in 1732 had been Chairman four times between 1725 and 1732, and Deputy Chair twice, in 1720 and 1729. Harrison was Chairman in 1729, and Deputy Chair twice, in 1728 and 1731. With the support of fellow Directors, like Monson, Henry Lyell, and Josias Wordsworth, they remained a formidable set.

This entry to the Direction (and all that it meant) was to be the foundation for the patronage system whose importance to national and Scottish politics is under examination. But Drummond also continued to serve as a negotiator during those years. From 1731 until 1740, when failing health and the outbreak of the War of the Austrian Succession stopped him, he continued to act as the Government's Commissioner at Antwerp during the Congress called there to discuss the general grievances of the Emperor Charles VI and his Southern Netherlands subjects.

Drummond's long experience of the Low Countries made him an obvious choice for nomination. As it was, delays and postponements meant the Congress did not convene until 1737 and he would spend the years to 1740 in the Netherlands as negotiations were drawn out interminably. After the outbreak of the war in 1740 he left the Congress and gave up his Commission. He died two years later, on 20 December 1742.[4]

4

From the important diplomatic work that began during this early career and continued throughout his life, Drummond gained skills, contacts and experience useful for complex relationships with ministers and others operating patronage machinery. His activities as an intelligence agent had made him well aware of how things worked in Westminster's corridors of power. As a financier who combined merchant-banking knowledge with market speculation activities, he had a sound understanding of London and continental money markets. Also, several men, already indicated, who were very important to his first career, had opened the doors for his later one: James Brydges, Duke of Chandos; Dr William Stratford; Sir Matthew Decker; and the Duke of Argyll were the most important of these.

Drummond's friendship with James Brydges had begun in 1705 when Brydges visited the Netherlands, ostensibly on a casual visit. But he was then Paymaster-General and his concerns lay with the payment of Marlborough's troops and associated business. Drummond was secretly working for Oxford at that time and their common ministerial and financial interests involved them in conversations.

Their friendship, however, was genuine and Brydges used his post, not only to lay the foundations of his own great fortune, but to help Drummond whenever it was in his power to do so. Late in 1705 Brydges promised Drummond 'some employment in the privilege of remitting money to the forces', a promise he kept. And through him Drummond grew closer to 'the seamy side of Marlborough's wars.'[5] The Scot would give Brydges advance notice of events, especially of how peace negotiations were going, who would in turn then buy and sell stocks profitably. Brydges felt that his secret was safe with his friend, and both accumulated money.

It seems very likely that it was also in the years 1706 to 1709 that Drummond came into contact with the young Duke of Argyll, then serving under Marlborough in the continental wars. The nature of Drummond's employment on behalf of Oxford, his closeness to Brydges, the Paymaster-General, and his claim of kinship to Argyll, would point in that direction. Writing to Oxford in 1710, Drummond intimated that Argyll had offered him his interest 'some time since in his part of the country and I could not accept it.'[6] He was to have further connections with Argyll in the years 1715 to 1720 through their involvement in the South Sea Company, and with John Law, the financier, and his Mississippi schemes.[7]

Dr. William Stratford and Sir Mathew Decker, the two others who with Chandos and Argyll formed Drummond's closest circle were also important in their own right. The first was the son of Dr Nicholas Stratford, Warden of Manchester College, and later Bishop of Chester. He was also the godson of Thomas Harley, Minister to the Court of Hanover.

Stratford played a key role. He served as a common friend to the Harleys, to Drummond and Decker and to many of their friends at Court, such as Kinnoul and Errol. In the City he brought Drummond close to the businessmen Hoare, Watkins and Hill, sustained them as a group, and they in turn gave the Scot a firm base for his future activities in Court and City.

Stratford was more than just kind to Drummond. After his friend's bankruptcy in 1712 (at which event Decker acted as his banker and settled the creditors) Stratford recommended him anew to Robert Harley for some office. He referred to Drummond's qualities of integrity and faithfulness, and to his capacity. Nor did Drummond let Stratford down in this respect. He served Harley well, but, as his friend protested to everyone who would hear, 'with little in return to relieve his condition.'[8]

He was also involved with Drummond's family, and there was a certain amount of intimacy. He corresponded regularly with him and his wife when they were in Holland; cared for his family from Perthshire on their visits south; and looked after his wife Agatha when Drummond was away on business. Throughout the years 1712 to 1717 he was ceaseless in urging the Harleys to do something about Drummond's poor circumstances.[9]

Sir Matthew Decker's importance to Drummond's career can hardly be overestimated. He was born a Dutchman, but became a naturalised British subject. As a banker he was considered 'one of the six richest in the City of London.'[10] He was also a Director of the South Sea Company from July 1711 to August 1712; the London Correspondent for most Dutch banks, but especially Pels of Amsterdam; and from 1711 he was a Proprietor of the East India Company. In 1716 he was made a Baronet; and was an MP from 1719 to 1722. Prior to 1710 he corresponded with Drummond while the Scot was in Holland. It was a friendship that was encouraged by their shared Dutch experience and Decker's own banking involvement, both in London and Amsterdam. Theirs was a lifetime association.[11]

Drummond's combination of diplomatic, banking and business activities also meant that he developed solid associations with other leading figures, especially in the world of business; and he was on familiar terms with some leading bankers. For example: in Holland he was a friend of the Pels firm (which had Decker as its agent); in London, with Sir Theodore Janssen, Sir John Lambert, Richard Hoare, Edward Gibbon and others.[12]

In 1717 he had opened an account at the bank of his own young relation, Andrew Drummond, and worked hard to promote this enterprise. He introduced new clients, the Duke of Chandos in particular. Andrew Drummond was to acknowledge this debt to John; and they discovered they were to be of much use to each other in the next two decades. John Drummond also continued his links with the Marlboroughs and the Albemarles.[13]

Between 1713 and 1720 Drummond was embroiled with John Law, the Scottish adventurer, monetary theorist and banker. Law had gone to London in 1694, following his father's death. There, he killed a man called Wilson in a duel and fled to the continent. In Amsterdam he studied banking and finance; and it was there that he probably met Drummond. In 1705 he made a brief reappearance in Scotland, but was still an outlaw in England despite repeated efforts to return.

One of these efforts involved Drummond who was persuaded that he must entreat with Harley (in 1713) that his fellow Scot be pardoned for the duel. Drummond failed in this, despite his excellent argument that such a fine mind should not be lost to the British Government, and at any cost should be kept from the French or Dutch. Law also tried getting back across the Channel using the British Embassy in Paris, and friendship with Scots who were there: John Dalrymple, Earl of Stair; David Crawfurd; and James Gardiner.

Drummond had certainly been impressed by Law, yet by this same letter to Oxford it was clear that they were not intimates. Still, Drummond knew Law well enough to be able to depict the latter's close relationship with the Duke of Argyll and Lord Ilay, and to know that Law had money in England 'in Lord Ilay's name or under his direction.'[14]

Drummond's connection with John Law was even stronger between 1715 and 1720, and he continued to offer him further advice on how to get back into England. This familiarity turned into firm friendship from 1718, when Law was at the height of his fame in France, in control of the *Banque Generale* (later *Banque Royale*) and the *Compagnie d'Occident*.

It has also been suggested that John Drummond's 'casual acquaintance' with Law 'contributed to his own rehabilitation,' that is, it enabled Drummond's re-entry and acceptance into English public life following the disastrous events (for him) of 1714.[15] It is true that from February 1715 to February 1718 Argyll was a Director of the South Sea Company (together with many of Drummond's friends), while during these same years the Scot was acting for Oxford and the South Sea Company at the Hague. There is enough evidence to suggest that Drummond, Argyll and Law all had money in this Company at the same time, with Law's funds invested under Argyll's name.[16]

Further indication of the strength of this three-way partnership is suggested by the deep involvement of Drummond and Argyll with Law's schemes in France from 1717 onwards. Argyll was seen at Law's side in Paris; and from 1718 Drummond was there too, with £40,000 of Chandos' money to invest as well as his own. Paris was in the grip of massive speculation as funds poured in unchecked. Argyll, Chandos and Drummond were affected by the crash which came in 1720 - although Drummond emerged relatively unscathed compared to Chandos.

It would be plausible to suggest that Drummond and Law got to know one another through their mutual acquaintance the Duke of Argyll; and that this took place sometime during the years 1700 to 1709 when they were all in the Low Countries. They shared an interest in the financial problems of the great powers, and obviously in lining their own pockets. From a Drummond perspective, this friendship with Argyll was to be of prime importance later.

A solid understanding of colonial trade and the operation of monopolies had been extended through Drummond's many early ventures; and it probably occurred to him that his future lay in the direction of the East India Company in England. This is even more likely when his friendship with Sir Matthew Decker is considered. It is perhaps not too strange, therefore, that by 1722, soon after the demise of the *Compagnie d'Occident*, he was a Director of the 'Honourable Company'.[17]

In view of Drummond's complex diplomatic and financial activities on behalf of the Government prior to 1722, it is also difficult to resist the notion that he was deeply involved in the circumstances surrounding the South Sea Bubble and the crash suffered that very year. Evidence is flimsy, circumstantial and coincidental, but is worth mentioning because of the links it suggests did exist between Walpole, Argyll and Drummond prior to the formation of the idea of using India patronage for political management purposes in Scotland.

Drummond, Chandos, Argyll and John Law all had funds in the South Sea Company, and had also been involved in the French bourse. But apart from Chandos, they did not seem to suffer in the crash. This would suggest a link with Walpole and Jacombe, whose views were vindicated when the bubble burst. Members of the group were well-versed in London and continental money matters; and were involved with leading figures from these business communities, like the Pels and Hopes in Europe, as well as various London banks. It is feasible that they saw the crash coming, Drummond quickly slipped into directorships of the East India Company and the Royal Africa Company in 1722, and Walpole came to power. They all survived and were grateful to one another.[18]

5

Given their former intimacy it probably felt natural to Drummond in 1722 that he should co-ordinate all his connections for Walpole's benefit. These links were truly extensive, incorporating Court, Parliamentary and business contacts, powerful Company connections, and grassroots support north of the border. These were to be used to pursue Government's political interests in Scotland. In this latter part of his life he subordinated most other objectives, quite deliberately, to the political one of helping to create in his homeland an atmosphere suitable for its management by Walpole's government. His Company strength lay at the heart of all he did, and enabled him to spin a web of inter-locking interests.

Walpole had assumed office well-acquainted with the major figures of the London business world; and he had been in politics long enough to have some familiarity with Drummond's work in the period 1704 to 1722. Also, the special relationship the Government had with the East India Company meant that familiarity with its leading Directors was assured; that would include Drummond's friends Decker and Harrison, who controlled the Company at this time.

It would have been easy, therefore, for Walpole and Drummond to come together, they shared mutual ground and each could gain from the other. For Drummond a seat in Parliament and involvement at the heart of public affairs was important. As in his earlier relationships with Oxford and Bolingbroke, he would continue to operate within the corridors of power at Westminster. For Walpole, support among Scottish peers and MPs was essential, and in the Scottish countryside it was doubly so. Through Drummond he would have the means of securing his position.

The 1722 election had gone according to plan. All sixteen Scottish peers and an overwhelming number of the forty-five MPs were well-disposed to the ministry. Walpole aimed at repeating this kind of favourable return. He was helped in that the Jacobites were offering no real trouble in Scotland during those years. They had virtually disappeared at the elections; and many, like Bathurst and Ogilvy were deserting the Old Pretender. In 1722 Sunderland died, removing Walpole's biggest immediate rival, and he was able to concentrate on his Scottish problem.[19]

His policy with regard to Scotland was, at first, to keep two parties alive there, to balance the one with the other. But before 1725, for the first time, ministry began to throw all its support behind the Argyll group. This was mainly because Walpole wanted to bind Argyll to him while he worked at loosening Roxburgh's grip with the king.

It was the 1725 Shawfield riots in Glasgow over the Malt tax imposed by London that startled Walpole. The realisation that just below the surface Scotland bristled with discontent seemed to galvanise him into action. He decided he must use every scrap of leverage to put things on a firmer footing in Scotland; and since he would have known of Drummond's position in the East India Company and of his standing in Scotland, the time would have seemed right.

Walpole was made aware that more than mere annoyance at the Malt tax was involved in these riots. Nationalistic feelings and resentment at what appeared a sell-out in 1707 were simmering throughout the land, not just in Glasgow and Edinburgh. By and large, London did not seem to appreciate what was going on. For example, Dr. Stratford in Oxford referred in amazed tones to 'the Covenanters in Glasgow being riled.'[20] He did note, however, that the northern English papers presented a more violent picture of events in Scotland than the London ones. Conversely, this general complacency was not shared by Walpole, who was now awake to Scottish problems, and counted upon the Argathelians* and upon massive patronage to win the day.

The riots were also just the opportunity Walpole wanted for getting rid of Roxburgh. Power was at once taken from the Squadrone* and given to Argyll and Ilay. Argyll was also made Master General of Ordnance; and Robert Dundas (an enemy of the Argyll party) was replaced as Lord Advocate by Duncan Forbes.[21] In removing Roxburgh, with the King's consent, a main obstacle to Walpole's control was gone. Argyll, Ilay and Duncan Forbes, with their henchmen Milton and Scrope were now mobilised to 'bring in the Scottish tumults' and nullify Scotland as a 'potential centre of trouble...if not kept under proper control.'[22] That control was to be maintained by lavish dispensation of favours, from any source; and the meaningful India patronage John Drummond commanded and was able to distribute, was seen as important.

The first minister's intention in this respect runs through his message to Townshend in September 1725: 'Scotland and Ireland are quiet, if we take care to keep them so.' This he intended to do (as far as Scotland was concerned) through Argyll and allies like John Drummond, as it proved, who would 'keep the Scottish peers and representatives lined up in the ministerial support.' It was successful enough to make the Jacobite George Lockhart write in 1727 that 'the King of England' had fixed himself in power 'by procuring a parliament to be elected that consisted of as well-disciplined members as those of his powerful army.'[23]

2

Political and Electoral Realities 1707–74

1

To say that relations between Scotland and England during and immediately after the creation of the new state of Great Britain in 1707 were delicate would be an understatement. The nervousness and hostility – mainly on the Scots side – have been well documented elsewhere. Equally fragile and tense, however, were the next twenty years, and especially the 1720s and around 1725 when Drummond commenced his vital role as a Director of the East India Company, applying India favours to gathering votes north of the border.

As well as spreading this largesse in the hope of quieting or diverting discord in the Scottish political arena, there were expectations of a knock-on pacifying effect in other spheres. The process meant large-scale (though covert) manipulation of the political and constitutional features of Scottish life, and especially the electoral management arrangements then in operation. In such arenas this India patronage was to prove very useful.

Searching for other reasons that might explain why Scots came to enjoy India favours in such abundance fade quickly. Nothing is very evident. Their feasting at the table of India patronage, dating from the 1720s, cannot be explained in terms of wealth. Few Proprietors and Directors were Scots. At that time it was not possible to compete with English counterparts in the purchase of India stock. The country was poor and had been impoverished further by the failure of the Darien scheme in 1700. This catastrophe lost nearly all the £400,000 raised, amounting to some half the available Scottish coinage, and severely strained an already creaking Scottish economy. Encumbered estates and mortgages were common. Things appeared to reach rock-bottom in 1704.[1]

Nor were the high expectations that Scottish lairds and merchants attached to the 1707 Union realised. There was no financial bonanza. The general misery was made worse by the costs to the country of the 1715 Jacobite uprising. Consequently, it is no surprise that in the early 1720s the Scottish presence in Leadenhall was negligible. Some other forces had to be at work to explain why Scots were soon to be found in the East Indies in such numbers, dating from the mid 1720s.

Only the state of the new Union, the fragility of the young British state, the fact that India patronage was available, and the actions taken by Sir Robert Walpole to remove the threat that he felt stemmed from Scotland give a satisfactory answer. As well as fearing the signs of discontent among Scots, Walpole's disquiet lay in his sense of vulnerability – as noted, Scotland was still not under firm political control as late as 1722.

There were adequate grounds for the continuing disgruntlement in Scottish ranks because of what appeared as broken promises by the English and unforeseen added legislation. A chief concern was that centralised control from London of the government of Scotland had been achieved very quickly. For example, all office holders, including Justices of the Peace, were appointed after 1707 by royal warrant through the Lord Chancellor; and London influenced and controlled membership of judicial and administrative commissions, again principally through the Lord Chancellor.

The loss of political identity was not balanced by material rewards; and this looked and felt worse to Scots because all the apparatus of an independent Scottish state – Church, Law, Education system and so on – was still in existence, just as it had always been. Another factor was that the British Privy Council might have contained five Scots peers, but like the Scots Privy Council it was always filled with individuals favourable to the supremacy of Westminster. What is more, new Treasury and Exchequer commissions and the new Excise and Customs establishments effectively purveyed London-controlled patronage in addition to its prime purpose of providing an efficient basis for administration and revenue collection.

For these reasons and many more, the Union continued to be a source of intense dissatisfaction for many among the Scots elite; a feeling that would persist into the 1750s, and was even stronger among the less privileged. What was seen north of the Tweed as manipulation by the Whig Administration stimulated what was, at its best, post–1707 apathy in

Scotland among the ruling classes who resided there, and a simmering resentment among the lower orders.

Walpole realised that achieving stability in Scotland and attaining a sense of security at Westminster had to be brought about. The search for the means to do so was speeded up; and even in a general way he saw that patronage would have to be used, and liberally, if it could be found. As indicated, his unease was almost certainly heightened by the 1715 Jacobite uprising. It shook his fellow ministers out of their complacency and confirmed the belief that a careful watch had to be kept on the Scots.

The failure of the *South Sea Company* in 1722 also sent tremors of shock in all directions. Walpole realised that this financial collapse suggested ministerial incompetence and Whitehall weakness. It was a bad example and he foresaw that political turmoil could follow, particularly in a volatile Scotland. However, the impracticability of a military garrison and abhorrence of a London government that this would stimulate, further decided him upon a policy of appeasing those who mattered politically in Scotland. The wooing of those who mattered politically was to be promoted by the vigorous heaping of favours upon their heads.

2

Prior to 1707 Godolphin had demonstrated that it must be made perfectly obvious in Scotland which party enjoyed royal favour in order to achieve good political management there. This was to be made clear through the make-up of the Scottish Privy Council, the appointment of the Secretary of State, and by whoever had custody of the Signet.* But in 1708 the Privy Council (and with it the office of Secretary of State) was ended and power devolved upon the Squadrone, political enemies of the Duke of Argyll.[2] The Privy Council's disappearance then created an administrative vacuum that temporarily spoiled control over Scots patronage because of the uncertainty introduced.

From 1710 to 1713 Oxford had maintained administrative control in Scotland through Baron John Scrope; and in 1713 he revived the Scots Secretary post in the figure of John Erskine, Earl of Mar. 'Bobbing John', as he was called, was to disgrace himself in London eyes by leading the '15 rebellion; but in reality he was a mere nominee. He did not have the great magnate status and command of such as the Dukes of Argyll.

Scrope (who had advised Oxford and was to outlast Walpole) was to play an important part in all these developments. From 1714 he was extremely powerful in Scottish affairs, intimate with the Argyll group and acted in its interest. He was particularly friendly with Archibald Campbell,

Earl of Ilay and Duncan Forbes of Culloden. From 1724 to 1752, as Secretary of the Treasury, he brought great ability to the office. He was also well known to John Drummond of Quarrel who, when passing his considered opinion that Scrope retained his post for so long because he was so indispensable and too useful to discard, might just as well have been describing his own usefulness and suggesting his own history of collaboration with Scrope and Walpole.[3]

It was normal for Walpole to delegate authority over political matters north of the border to a Scottish manager who, while sometimes working independently, usually carried out orders from the ministry. The factors determining such a man's course of action were his own personality and relationship with Westminster politicians. However, as indicated the year 1725 marked a new departure. Walpole's aim seemed to be that he would make everyone subordinate to himself. He broke all previous arrangements and in 1725 exalted John Campbell, 2nd Duke of Argyll, at the expense of Roxburgh (who was friendly with his rivals Carteret and Cadogan). The office of Secretary of State for Scotland was abolished and Walpole took the whole management of Scottish affairs into his own hands – to be operated in Scotland through Argyll and his brother Archibald (Lord Ilay).

The First Minister was at his strongest in 1725, but still needed the Argathelians to administer Scotland and lend support in the Commons. Argyll and his brother Ilay rallied to him and set about ensuring that Walpole could count on the backing of two thirds of Scottish MPs.[4] As a result of their successful endeavours, on the accession of George 11 in 1727, Walpole took them both into the ministry. The Duke and Ilay were now firmly in charge in Scotland, mustering all available interest (which included India patronage) and putting into practice the agenda of strict political management Walpole favoured – in order to secure the threat from the north.

Argyll and his followers were now managers of Scottish affairs; and this regime was to last until 1765 when the political picture north of the border changed. Throughout these years, therefore, the electoral management of Scotland and all available patronage was placed in the hands of the Argyll group, although theoretically still controlled by the first minister.

3

Thus a line of 'substantial managers' commences in 1725, when Walpole handed what has been termed the 'Viceroyalty' of Scotland to Argyll and Ilay.[5] For large periods, Argyll and then Ilay in particular, had extensive control over Scots patronage – to the extent that there existed a distinctively Scottish system. Yet it would be wrong to say that Walpole gave the Argathelians a free hand. Until 1733 his grip remained firm. Those in power in London did not want an over-mighty Scottish manager who might work too much for his own and for Scottish interests and give these a higher valuation than theirs.

This was the kind of danger that Walpole would face in the l730s when, to ensure the support of all 16 Lords chosen as representative peers, he threw all the patronage at his disposal at Argyll. Divided Scottish representation among the Lords that would lead to weak Scottish influence in the Court was of little use to him. But the opposite, as in this instance, meant dependency on a strong Scottish manager. To ensure that Scotland remained safe and securely tied to the Union, Argyll, in turn, had to be bound to Westminster.

This strategy would seem to underlie what he envisaged for the future. Thus, until 1733 his policy with regard to the upper echelons in Scottish political society was: 'to let all the Scots act as individuals and consequently depend on those in power here in London' – namely himself and Newcastle. It seemed to work well.[6] At Westminster, meanwhile, he continued to count on Argyll's support and regarded him as fulfilling an advisory role. In Scotland the Campbell Chief was to continue to keep the peace and deliver the voters.

For the most part this was indeed the case. Through Argyll, Ilay and Duncan Forbes of Culloden, Walpole could continue to count on the backing of most Scottish MPs. The influence of these great magnates lay in the legal authority invested in them and in their electoral management, where every favour, including (as will be seen, India patronage) was used to dampen agitation.

In turn, Walpole helped the growth of the Argyll party. He placed its supporters in charge of affairs in the north of Scotland: men like the Earl of Morton, Hugh Rose of Kilravoch, Lord Lovat and Alexander Brodie. The risk he took was that there would be no political counter-weight in Scotland to the Argathelians such as had been provided by the Squadrone. The policy proved sound, however, in that by 1733 the Argathelians were indispensable, both to him and to the operation of the Government's administrative system.

Opposition to the first minister was inflamed, nevertheless, during the excise crisis of 1733 and this was to be reflected in the 1734 election. Walpole had also quarreled with Argyll over the Excise Bill; and there was the distinct possibility of his losing all ministerial control in the election of representative peers in Scotland due to take place. He needed the support of the Scottish peers to be sure of a majority.[7] Fortunately for him, Ilay's firm support and Argyll's abstention were negotiated; and in the 1734 election the Patriots were defeated and all the Scottish peers and nearly all the 45 MPs returned were Argyll supporters. Ilay's activity had made Walpole victorious; and his continued support vouchsafed nine further years of security at Westminster for the 'Prime Minister'.

The cost to Walpole was that in Scotland the independent position of the Duke and his brother Ilay was enhanced. Then in 1737, apparently to humble Scotland in the wake of the Porteous riots of the previous year, Walpole 'precipitated a long-threatened quarrel between himself and Argyll'.[8] In doing so he weakened government support in Scotland. Ilay stood by him, however, although like his brother and Duncan Forbes, he was opposed to Walpole's actions.

The result was an even greater swing towards the Argathelians, and from that point onwards the Duke of Argyll's opposition to Walpole grew, more so as the First Minister shifted over to the Squadrone, the Duke's main enemies in Scotland. By 1741 Walpole had identified fully with them; and this move alone reduced his well-wishers among the Scottish Members of Parliament at that year's election to only nineteen. Walpole's support elsewhere was quickly evaporating and with a House of Commons hostile to him and with no working majority, he resigned in January 1742. Nevertheless, the policy of flooding Scotland with all the favours he could muster had worked and continued to be useful, especially India patronage.

From 1725 onwards Argyll and Ilay managed Scotland for their political superiors. They 'worried over minute matters of patronage and managed elections by skilful horse-trading,' never excluding anyone of use if they could be convinced that their future lay with the Argathelian Whigs.[9] They kept Scotland quiet, remained loyal (to some degree) to political chiefs in the south, and yet built up a position of independence. Ilay was left completely in charge of Scottish matters when Walpole resigned in 1742 and his brother, the Duke of Argyll, died in October 1743.

4

To secure the political reality described above, all patronage after 1725, including that deriving from the East India Company, was put to work by the Duke and Ilay. Most sinecures or favours that might have a stipend attached came from the Treasury. They were normally given in return for political support. The national exchequer provided, for example, posts in the Customs, such as Collector of Salt Revenues at Prestonpans. The gift of a legal or ecclesiastical appointment was also in the possession of the ministry in London, to be distributed in Scotland as the political manager saw fit. There were, however, rather limited numbers of places on offer.

Prior to 1725 many Scots were persuaded to vote the 'right way' through payments from Secret Service funds. Those benefiting included Charles, 1st Earl of Hopetoun and the Earls of Leven, Orkney, Louden and Marchmont. This expenditure by government was meant to be in exchange for dependability, loyalty and in essence, keeping Scotland quiet. In many ways it was the cementing agent used to maintain support among Scottish landowners that preceded the large-scale employment of India patronage,

The added bonus that came from using India patronage, therefore, was an easing of the strain on the Government's purse. Although the Secret Service fund continued to be used after 1725, a year when it was employed very liberally indeed, along with India patronage, to secure Walpole's allies in Scotland, the amount disbursed fell: from £103,350 in 1725, to £42,024 in 1726.[10]

5

But whereas Walpole could experience some trouble in England in retaining majorities, a task left in the main to Newcastle, Scotland was 'the dreamland of eighteenth century political management.'[11] This has been readily explained. According to Dickson, 'from 1689, a mercantile bourgeoisie, part agrarian, part commercial captured power in church and state' in Scotland. And by the early eighteenth century this class was embarked upon determined collective action to safeguard its dominant position and interests in Scottish society through economic and political channels.

The attitude of this class to the 1707 Union is also explained by these developments. It 'voluntarily renounced state independence in order to survive as a bourgeoisie.' The landowning elements went along with things because of the pecuniary advantages gained from Court and government patronage stemming from London and the economic interests and other connections this gave them. It meant, therefore, that from 1707 to the 1770s and beyond, the Scottish bourgeoisie assumed a 'dependent or client status.'[12]

Acceptance of this conditional role by the Scottish ruling classes benefited them in that it led to a steady accumulation of capital, an increase that continued throughout the eighteenth century. A major mechanism allowing this to happen was the extension of money payments from London banks and from abroad. This gave rise to regional specializations in, for instance, the cattle trade and weaving industry. However, as is discussed in depth in a separate chapter, remittances from India and the return of enriched Scots 'Nabobs' must be counted here as well.

The formation of major banks, like the Bank of Scotland and the Royal Bank of Scotland; of the British Linen Bank with a more specialized function; and of local ones like the *Ayr* Bank, encouraged this wealth creation; and these moves profited from the active cooperation of the Duke of Argyll and his henchman Lord Milton. Others, like the Duke of Queensberry helped too. Much of this activity stemmed from, and was dominated by, available English-based capital. Scottish bankers in London, such as William Drummond and the Coutts brothers received, harboured, or forwarded Scottish monies.

There is also little doubt that it was because the Scots economy complemented rather than competed with the English one after the Union that its trade and commerce eventually prospered, especially in overseas traffic, such as that in tobacco. Nor can it be denied that economic measures were used to stem Scottish separatism post–1707. For example, by 1727 the Board of Trustees for Fisheries and manufactures had been set up.[13]

In the period in question, the Scottish aristocracy and landowners who were to benefit from this accumulation of capital held positions of power and influence 'unprecedented in Britain.' The laws of perpetual entail in Scotland (from 1684) had helped preserve the authority and prestige of the peerage with its large estates. Landowners in every shire were used to gather the revenue-tax on land, first imposed in 1667: 'Alongside that they carried responsibility for local government in the countryside, parallel to the entrenched burgess hierarchies in the towns.'[14]

Also helping to maintain absolute control was the fact that there were few small freeholders, and tenants generally had little security of tenure. It meant that legal power could be exerted on top of economic intimidation to bring about consolidated holdings, almost at will; and no Act of Parliament was needed. However, envy by Scots lairds of wealthier English landowners probably turned their minds to improvements and to using English models. In doing so they helped set Scottish agriculture on the road to being more prosperous.

What made the lairds' acceptance of client or dependent status tolerable after the Union, if not positively acceptable, was the fact that 'this indigenous ruling class' was 'to be involved in the exercise of political power, not only in Scotland itself but in Britain as a whole and later the Empire overseas.'[15] Through giving a minority of Scotsmen (though they were influential) a personal stake in the permanence of the Union, Scottish assimilation to the eighteenth century structure of English politics was given a boost.

6

Other purely political features combined with the submissive role of the Scottish aristocracy, landowners and bourgeoisie to make the management of Scotland even easier, and indeed a veritable 'dreamland'. Disbursement of patronage from London ministries had been made easier after 1707 because Scottish representation at Westminster reflected the post-Union shift of power to the south. Also, to facilitate management from Whitehall, Government had brought Scottish patronage in general under the supervision of Treasury Commissioners. They in turn handed these sinecures to the Argathelians, who they felt could be trusted. (This did not include India patronage, which was not under Treasury control.)

In addition, electoral realities in this period were preposterous. The right to vote in the Scottish counties was held by freeholders of land from the crown valued at forty shillings of 'auld extent' [or £400 Scots].* In the Royal burghs it was vested in the town councils, self-elected since the fifteenth century.[16] The thirty-three counties were monopolised by only 2,662 freeholders. They returned thirty MPs. Generally one MP cared for two counties, but six of the smallest counties shared three MPs. The situation was really even worse than it appears, and it has been calculated that only about forty-six men in Scotland were consulted when MPs for the counties were being chosen.

Control of the burghs was just as venal. The total voting strength of all the town councils was a mere 1,303. They appointed delegates, who in turn elected the fifteen Members returned for the sixty-six burghs. Burghs were gathered into fifteen groups. Edinburgh had one MP; the other fourteen groups had one MP per group. Only four or five delegates from any particular group of burghs or town councils chose the MP. Most of these were in turn bribed 'by the promise of custom for their trade and desirable posts for their sons.'[17]

Even by 1750 there were less than 4,000 voters in Scotland all told. The way they behaved is largely explained by electoral circumstances and pressures operating upon them; and especially by development of the control that could be exerted by managers. The 1707 Act of Union, while giving Scotland forty-five seats in the Commons and sixteen elected Lords in the Upper Chamber, had done something unforeseen: it loosened the legal controls over elections in Scotland, and a system of politics based on interest had sprung up.

7

To do their business in Scotland, Argyll and Ilay required a sort of Grand Vizier in charge of affairs there. It was a position admirably filled by Andrew Fletcher of Saltoun, Lord Milton, Lord Justice Clerk until 1748 and Keeper of the Signet until his death in 1766. He was able to tap the barrel of patronage on behalf of his political masters. To these ends Milton fully employed the power and influence of his own office; that stemming from the authority and rank of the Duke of Argyll and Ilay; and by recourse to special treatment he could derive from London. In addition, his ties with the East India Company through business and family connections were numerous.

Long before Walpole's fall in 1742, Argyll and Ilay had left things in Scotland to this able 'sous-ministre'. He became the real patronage manager there. Although Ilay was often involved in the minutiae of patronage, Milton became increasingly powerful as political manager and 'was sedulously courted by the ambitious.'[18] He attempted to balance the claims of local factions at elections, but his decisions were normally dictated by the ministry's need for influence, or upon how far pro-Government interests had to be buttressed in one locality or the other.

Generally speaking, his tools for this purpose were scanty. However, he did have control of the Signet. As Keeper, he could choose sheriff-deputes and sheriff-clerks, all of them lawyers like himself, whose roles were crucial during the preparations for elections. The sheriff-depute was a most important figure in each county, both in a judicial and administrative sense. His duties included that of returning officer for parliamentary elections. With the end of Heritable Jurisdictions* by the Act of 1747 he and his successors were given even more powers regarding the appointment of these officials.

The other powers at the manager's disposal concerned the distribution of patronage, which he used to maintain a political interest in burghs and counties. This was a permanent and taxing activity, requiring good management, great dexterity and skill, not to mention a constant stream of favours. A blend of social awareness and subtlety was required, nowhere more so than in the counties.

The county freeholders were less in the pockets of political managers than those manipulators would have liked. These gentlemen could be bought, but their social position made it imperative that they appeared to be independent. A patronage appointment came in the guise of an act of friendship; and it was the relationship that really mattered. Acts of seemingly disinterested familiarity and social contact that created a feeling of obligation, led to a powerful county interest. No suggestion of a dutiful support in return for past favours was hinted at during elections, just a re-affirmation and continuation of past familiarity.

In the burghs it was different, 'a well-publicised appointment could provide the necessary evidence to members of council that one of the potential members of parliament had the ear of government.' To be able to place friends in office and remove enemies from the same was regarded by councilors as proof of capability for membership of the Commons. Treating during an election was essential for success; 'bribery and corruption was a way of life' in the Scottish burghs; while the element of uncertainty there made cultivation of an interest both expensive and wearing. Nevertheless, elections were won by the politicians who could manage difficult voters in these burghs and counties; and without patronage, public interest withered in time. Favours were 'the cement of politics, creating and maintaining political influence.'[19]

In both burghs and counties, the mechanics of Milton's system were simple. In return for posts, such as those in customs and excise, and (as is traced below, positions in or associated with the East India Company) votes were vouchsafed and success at elections ensured. This was accomplished, to a very great extent, through the influence Milton and his associates could bring to bear on the superiorities* (lands held of the king); and upon the creation of fictitious votes.

8

In the counties the superiority was sometimes separated from the property that brought it and this title was often sold for cash: 'It was not the possession of land as such which carried the franchise, but the fact that land was held from the King – the so-called superiority'.[20] For the advantage of big landowners the practice had grown of granting life-rent superiorities, that is, of 'making votes'. The creation of fictitious votes was made easy and the abuse multiplied. New interests sprang up consisting of these 'nominal', 'fictitious' or 'faggot' votes (the terms were interchangeable). They were held by purported 'parchment barons', generally men of business.[21]

All this electoral potential was brought into operation through the hereditary sheriffs and stewards (deputes) at election time. As indicated, in Scotland the powers of the sheriff or his depute were enormous. Whereas in England he was only a minor official, in Scotland he was the 'key to the Scottish county administration.'[22] In 1700, twenty-one of the thirty-three sheriffdoms in Scotland were held by hereditary right; and since the sheriffs, or stewards, were judicial and administrative representatives of government in the counties (together with Justices of the Peace, Commissioners of Supply, and Lieutenants) they were very important men.

Sheriff deputes were men with legal training who, like their superiors had real authority: operating the legal and administrative machinery of the sheriff's office in the name of their masters, and using the influence of heritable jurisdiction enjoyed by the great landowners.[23] Ilay and Duncan Forbes were empowered to create these powerful hereditary sheriffs, Milton as well; but he also had the formidable task of keeping them under control, and others with similar political influence. He used all means (including India patronage) for this purpose.

This influence was exemplified in 1741 when Lord Lovat 'set his lawyers about creating the necessary superiorities for distribution among the Frasers.'[24] At elections, factions also made up the voters roll (or registry) containing fictitious votes and would twist it for their own benefit – as long as the support of the hereditary sheriff (or his depute) in charge of the election was assured.

The growth of great estates also meant voting power rested in the hands of fewer people, mainly landowners, who took advantage of the political influence or 'interest' they commanded. Through land purchase they bought these superiorities and bestowed them upon friends or dependants, as in Lord Lovat's case. In this way the 'purchaser, creditor or holder of a wadset* (mortgage) acquired the superiority with the land'.[25] An heiress transmitted it to her husband – she had no vote. A sub-infeudation of superiorities was developed. Control of burghs as well fell to those landed patrons who had 'split' freeholds to create votes and introduced non-resident dependents. All too often these procedures were accompanied by threats, intimidation and removal of place and pension from anyone who pondered an independent line.

A powerful landowner, therefore, was someone who could harness and hold in readiness a vast pool of influence. He would have his 'natural' interest and his 'nominal' ones (that is, control of 'fictitious' votes). He enjoyed voting obligations extracted from a web of relationships. These might embrace personal friendships, responsibilities, family ties and traditional adherence to him (be that of one family to another, or from a cadet to the head of a great house or clan). He also had the support he could gain through bribery or inducement.

Small government appointments (and India posts, as is shown) were secured in return. Such an influential landowner, therefore, exercised an inordinate amount of persuasion over the votes of others. He was gently but persistently pursued by Milton, and by able lieutenants, like John Drummond of Quarrel, when India favours were to be used. At the same time, individual voters were well aware of the bargaining power they, in turn, commanded.[26]

In London, Government was concerned that these very influential men, as well as sheriffs and landowners, should be supporters. In fact, in a vast number of cases, the office of hereditary sheriff was also held by the most powerful landowner, who usually also had the chief interest in the county. These included: the Campbells, Dukes of Argyll, who dominated Argyllshire, Ayrshire, and Dunbartonshire; the Earls of Cromarty in Cromartyshire; the Dukes of Queensberry in Dumfriesshire; and the Earls of Moray in Elginshire. The Campbells of Cawdor controlled Nairnshire; and the Earl of Morton the Orkney and Shetland islands.

These peers were immensely powerful political figures, and had to be dealt with delicately. Others, like the Abercrombies, Duffs and Ogilvies of Banffshire; Sinclairs of Ulbster in Caithness; Dalrymples in Clackmananshire; the Hopes of Kinrosshire; and the Douglases of Roxburghshire, were prominent families. Like many others, the length and breadth of Scotland, they held the balance in the political life of every locality. Government had to win and keep them.

9

In each group of burghs returning a Member (Edinburgh had its own) political realities were even more complicated. There were more voters in the combined burghs than in the counties, though the burgh councils voted normally en bloc. Each burgh within a group was more often than not under the influence of one powerful family. For example, in Linlithgow burghs, with ninety-four voters, the Earls of Hyndford controlled Lanark, and the Earls of March, Peebles. John Murray, the hereditary sheriff of Selkirkshire, held Selkirk, and the Dukes of Hamilton the town of Linlithgow itself.

The Duke of Argyll and Ilay had overwhelming support in at least three burghs: Ayr, Edinburgh and Glasgow, and dominated others almost without competition through the strength of the ministerial-Whig support in them. Aberdeen was held through John Maule; Dumfries through the Dukes of Queensberry, the Douglases and the Marquis of Annandale. Elgin was controlled through the Earls of Findlater; Haddington using the Dalrymples of Hailes; Inverness by Forbes of Culloden and Seaforth Mackenzies. Tain came under the Sinclairs of Ulbster, the Munros of Foulis and the Earls of Morton, Cromarty and Sutherland. Wigton was controlled through the Earls of Galloway and Stair.

Other burghs were completely venal and open to the best offer, such as Perth and Stirling. In Perth, which was won for government consistently, the Earl of Rothes (with his seat at Cupar) had the nearest to an 'interest'. Stirling was the same, safe for government through the ample distribution of government patronage; and by using Ilay's relatives and dependents: the Erskines (James and Thomas), Peter Halkett, and Henry Cunningham.[27]

The political reality in Scotland for much of the eighteenth century was that a finite number of election-conscious gentlemen – many of them mentioned here and referred to as having a 'natural interest' – controlled the votes held by their relations or intimate friends. They were brought into the Argathelian net by political managers like Milton, using a variety of bait. Posts in the East India Company's service were found to be particularly useful in that through such windows of opportunity many younger sons could redeem altered family fortunes.

The administration and management of Scotland meant securing the Government's position amid these political realities in the Scottish counties and burghs, as described. A clear chain of command had to be created by which the wishes of the central authority at Westminster would be carried out in the small towns and shires of Scotland; and 'loyal' Scots would be returned to Parliament. Since they did not master everyone or all patronage, managers like Ilay and Milton could not have absolute command. But on the other hand, for most freeholders independence was impossible and a politician's assistance was needed at some point.

John Drummond and his India patronage, as shown below, proved to be central to these developments; but it required Walpole's own personal form of political engineering to bring the Scot into the centre of this particular political arena. As far as Walpole was concerned, at the very least, if votes among the electoral superiorities in Scotland could be doubly assured by adding India patronage on a significant scale to the other posts made available through Crown and legal patronage, then a very valuable addition would have been made to his power base.

10

From 1725 until his death in 1742, the operation worked through John Drummond of Quarrel. He was the man in London with the skills and initial contacts at Westminster, in the Company and in commerce that guaranteed the successful harnessing of India patronage. After Drummond's death in 1742, Milton, aided by subsidiary political managers like John Mackenzie of Delvine, took the burden – only now the system would operate in the main from Scotland.

On behalf of Argyll (and then of Ilay, following his brother's death in 1743) Milton carried on with this India patronage built by his friend Drummond and so useful to Walpole and the Argyll group. He applied the system to the ministerial needs of the 1740s and onwards, despite English hostility occasioned by the '45. He managed to retain the Argathelian-controlled arrangement used extensively in Scotland from 1725 in the face of those at Westminster who favoured a military approach to 'pacification'.

Throughout the 1740 to 1765 period this India patronage continued to be used extensively by Ilay and his man of business, Milton; and latterly by Milton and the Earl of Bute. Drummond, Milton and John Mackenzie of Delvine were (successively) the powerful managers controlling this patronage, furthering the political direction of Scotland to the satisfaction of the Argathelians and their London counterparts.

The use of India patronage appeared to fizzle out with the fall of Bute in 1763, and even more so by the death of Milton in 1765. Indeed, the whole system geared specifically to Scottish interests lost momentum in the face of party warfare within India House, accompanied by a determined effort by Government in 1766–67 to grasp control of the Company's territories and its patronage.

This ministerial attack of 1766–67 would lead eventually to the Regulating Act of 1773, culminating in Pitt's India Act of 1784. However, the Parliamentary Inquiry of 1766–67 was not launched in order to further the policy of using India patronage to influence voting at Scottish elections. The motivation was greed for the potential riches now on offer from the new territorial dimensions of the East India Company that followed Plassey and the conquest of Bengal.

Nevertheless, the flow of India patronage favouring Scots and to the benefit of the political management of Scotland remained alive and discernible. The system kept going into the 1770s because of the strength of Scottish involvement in Company politics in the 1760s; and because of a well-grooved road from Scotland to the Indies via Westminster, India House and political influence.

These managers functioned as part of the political machine, operating in Scotland in obedience to their political masters at Westminster, as well as in their own interests. They acted as intermediaries and clearing agents for Scots who wanted to go to India. Their recommendations led to posts in the Company or in its shipping. But personal ties were not enough. For an application to succeed, total electoral support, unswerving loyalty to the Argathelians in Scotland and to the Whig Government in London continued to be essential. In this way India was to serve as 'the Scotsman's bread'; and the pursuit of empire that followed would fully unite Scotland and England.

3

Company and Patronage Infrastructure 1720–74

1

The East India Company was one of the eighteenth century's great monopolist organisations. It had its headquarters in Leadenhall Street, London, but was a vast, rambling and complex structure with tentacles that spread around the globe – all held together by the East Indiamen that ploughed the seas between London, the sub-continent of India, and China. That it was of considerable significance in almost every field of commercial activity is reflected in its official records, and the correspondence, public and private, of those involved in its business or engaged in its service.

It was associated in the public mind with the promise of wealth, danger and hardship. It suggested the exhilaration of sea travel, the threat of pirates and a sense of adventure, mystery and the unknown. Letters home spoke of the journeys, the excitement and enthusiasm, as well as the hardships, sickness and early deaths. The same eighteenth century correspondence also reflected the involvement of these individuals in the early development of yet another phenomenon, capitalism. The Company (and its servants) had feet firmly planted in the burgeoning, dynamic London financial market and had intricate relations with the major banking, insurance and commercial interests of the City, and with the London shipping world.

The monopoly was very important to the fabric of life in Britain. Apart from its commerce and occupation of a central position within the awakening London money market, it shared the privileged position, along with the Bank of England, of providing security for the continuance of the National Debt. Insurance, money-lending and under-writing of all varieties blossomed at this time, with the same merchants, bankers, goldsmiths and other businessmen sitting as Directors of various companies, including the East India Company.

Situated in the heart of the City of London and adjacent to the docks, this joint-stock Company had as its objectives the furtherance of successful trade and the profits that would accrue from such trade. Until 1774 each subscriber, male or female, who owned £500 of stock could vote or take part in discussions as might arise at shareholder meetings, or, as the Charter called them, 'General Courts of Proprietors'. They were held quarterly, although a special Court could be asked for by a quorum of nine Proprietors. And it was the General Court voting by ballot that chose the Company's Court of Directors.

This, the executive Court, numbered 24 Directors elected by the Proprietors out of their own body. Again, until 1774, the right to be a Director lay only with those shareholders who owned at least £2000 of stock. Tenure of office did not go further than 12 months. The Directors were elected in April every year; consequently the February and March period was always one of political bustle and activity as parties and interests jockeyed for support. Thirteen Directors formed a quorum and when assembled became a Court, with the power to adjust the annual dividend rate and enact laws and regulations. It met at least once a week as a body, but most business was done in a system of committees.

There was no bar upon who could become a Proprietor: Scots, Irish, Dutch, Huguenots, Jews and, unusual then, women, all could be shareholders if they had the necessary wealth and will. On occasion the Proprietors would overturn a decision of the Court of Directors during a General Court; and an airing of views, amid general pandemonium could, and did, take place. Regrettably, the Company was also an institution where influence could be readily purchased, leaving it open to manipulation and design. Posts in its service were on offer; and it had facilities for realising in Britain the wealth gained in India. This was achieved through a well-developed remittance system.

2

The connection between the national Government and the East India Company was, perforce, both intimate and complex. As one of the great financial institutions it acted (together with the Bank of England and until 1722 with the *South Sea Company*) in giving support to ministries. Its well-being was vital to the national economy. For example, the Company engrafted £9 million South Sea Stock in December 1720, as part of

Walpole's scheme (really Jacombe's) to surmount that Company's crisis. Allies of John Drummond of Quarrel within the Company almost certainly gained credit with Walpole for this.[1]

The Company depended upon the renewal of its Charter by Administration, and in turn paid the public purse for the grant of its monopoly. As each renewal date approached the Charter became a controversial centre-piece and was caught up in national politics. Under Walpole and later Pelham, however, Government ministers and Company Directors shared an identity of interest and had good relations that were maintained until the early 1760s. There was liaison upon Treasury loans and over maintenance of the Company's independence, although this came under increasing attack as the century wore on. Ministers upon close terms with leading Directors were admitted to shares in its patronage.

Governments and Directors generally had a good understanding and found each other useful. For instance, Company men invariably gave leverage to successive ministries in the inner politics of the City of London. Walpole was always attentive to the organisation and its powerful lobby in Parliament. As demonstrated here, the monopoly proved a very important cog in his political system; and this continued after his exit in 1742 and the death of his successor Henry Pelham in 1754.

The late Dame Lucy Sutherland described the Company as being wedded to Government, and 'part of the ministerialist monied interest...which clashed with an anti-ministerialist popular interest.' This alliance with the Company widened the scope of ministerial patronage: 'the Directors had in their bestowal several governments of much greater value than any in his majesty's gift...public men were already aware of the openings that existed for the relatives of some of their lesser supporters, and ministers were already exploiting their connections with the Company to this end.'[2]

3

In the economic and political history of the Company, the years 1740–1774 encompass the closing stages of its time as a purely trading body and transmutation into a nascent empire, especially so in the years from 1756 to 1773. From 1774 to 1784 it shared this power with successive governments – but was under increasing parliamentary pressure. From 1784 real power passed to a Board of Control dominated by the Government of William Pitt the Younger and lorded over by the powerful figure of Henry Dundas. With this its death warrant was signed and sealed, it just took a long time to die, which it finally did with the 1857 mutiny.

The perilous nature of the Mughal Empire by mid-eighteenth century, the growing strength of the Company – especially after the successful outcome of its struggles with the Portuguese, Dutch, and eventually the French – set the scene for the arrival of Britons in unprecedented numbers. The tremendous upheavals in India that began with war against the French in the 1740s, only to break-out in virulent form in the late 1750s in opposition to French and Indians alike, were to affect the Company in every way. This involved recruitment, and thus the patronage system. Everything became much more complex.

Scots in particular poured into India. This was especially apparent during and after the success of the Company's forces against the Nawab of Bengal at Plassey in 1757, and throughout the remainder of the Seven Years War conducted in the Indian theatre. Nor was there an end to hostilities, with further confrontations against such as the Marathas, Haider Ali of Mysore and his son Tipu Sahib, well into the 1780s.

The pursuit of war from 1756 and British success led to a change in role for the Company. From just one of many trading powers in the sub-continent it had become virtual ruler of large tracts of territory. This, in turn, brought about a change of function for its officials: from mere representatives of a trading body to administrators of an expansionist territorial power with imperial dimensions.

4

The spectacular events taking place in India were paralleled by equally stunning tumults in Leadenhall Street, where bitter contested elections disrupted executive control. The general anarchy in the organisation at home and within the Company's settlements affected everything, even patronage. It was a chaotic scenario.

Clive had gone home from Bengal in 1760, not empty-handed. (He was to return there in 1765 when he tried to suppress the very thing that he had really promoted, the speedy accumulation of unprecedented and dazzling wealth). In the meantime, uncontrollable indiscipline in India, and Bengal in particular, gave rise to scenes of amazing corruption where enormous fortunes were gained. These arose from internal trade (legal and illegal), present taking, contracts, money-lending and from plain confiscation. Bribery, intimidation, unfair use of the Company's *Dastak** (right to trade) were all common; and the Company's overwhelming superiority in arms was readily brought to bear when intimidation was needed. Everyone was involved: Company servants in all branches, private traders, Europeans of all description, not least among them the Scots.

In 1763 the Nawab of Bengal, Mir Qasim, rebelled against this state of affairs, partly through disgust and partly because he wanted a share of the ill-gotten gains. The poor ryots* (farmers) bore the brunt of this despoliation. The relative ease with which the Nawab was overthrown, although not without copious bloodshed, further consolidated the power of the Company, not only in the eyes of the British, but in those of the indigenous peoples.

The return of Clive to London in 1760 was also marked by his involvement in the politics of India house, using the fame and prestige gained from his exploits in India and the fabulous fortune he had accumulated. By late 1762 he was trying to oust the chairman, Laurence Sulivan, the 'Uncrowned king of Leadenhall', and assume control.

In these bitter contests between Sulivan and Clive – and their followers, dominance swung from one to the other. Their rivalry created a virtual 'civil war' in the Company (a situation that was to last until Clive's suicide in 1774 and beyond). Company elections every April were the scenes of battle between the two forces. By 'splitting' stock into £500 units, both sides created voters with the right to take part in the April ballot each year. Government and Opposition were brought into the contests, along with a whole gamut of interests, such as the Shipping interest;* speculators; groups like the Scots in the Company; or returned bodies of 'Indians' (people with service in India) who supported either Sulivan or Clive. The contests were exciting, passionate and filled the newspapers.

Clive, after having lost the opening battle in 1763 and drawn the second one in 1764, by 1765, had won the first 'war'. But there were to be many more campaigns. Sulivan came back to power in 1769 and the feud (simmering in the background) was publicly resumed. In 1773 Clive was brought before the bar of the House of Commons to answer charges of corruption brought against him, for which Sulivan was unfairly blamed. As a result, even after Clive's death in 1774, the Irishman was to feel the wrath of his late enemy's friends; and this continued until his own demise and beyond.

From 1766–67 and the first Parliamentary Inquiry, the Company had to deal with growing interference in its affairs. This was the first overture by Westminster in a not so subtle campaign that eventually led to ministerial control. That loss of executive powers by its own Proprietors should be the final outcome came about because of the Company's continued financial embarrassment and especially a major monetary crisis in 1772. Lord North's Regulating Act of 1773 was the result.

In the meantime, Warren Hastings had become Sulivan's protégé, and due to his influence had been appointed Governor of Bengal by 1772. In 1773, as a consequence of Sulivan's negotiations with Lord North, Hastings was then made Governor-General of India. But the Regulating Act that created this post, also set rules (and appointed others) with the aim of circumscribing his powers. Hastings had only a casting vote on the Board of the Supreme Council at Calcutta. The Board was split and set on a collision course. Hastings could count only on the support of Richard Barwell, and faced the undying enmity of Philip Francis, General Clavering and Colonel Monson.

Basing their strategy half upon instructions from the North Government to foil Hastings where possible and force his resignation, and partly because of personal dislike and resentment of Hastings' aura of power and authority, the last three (the 'Triumvirate') did their best to make his life impossible. They failed, however, Hastings eventually outliving or outmanoeuvring them – with the tremendous help of the party in Leadenhall led by Laurence Sulivan. The Irishman fought the hostility of the North Administration and its puppets among the Directors, and prevented Hastings' recall.

But although this success prevented the take-over of the Company for another decade, the writing was on the wall. By 1774 the ministry had effectually gained a hold that could not be shaken. Lord North's 1773 Act also marks a watershed in many ways. It was a major step on the road to Parliamentary control of the administration and government of India. Ministerial control was what counted from then on, especially with regard to the direction the Company would develop at home and abroad; and it would mean the end of the free-for-all that had been going on, virtually since 1757.

5

This picture of events home and abroad displays the non-stop, on-going nature of the problems consuming the Company in these years. Nevertheless, the patronage that it offered was increasingly sought after. Naturally, these favours were used first to place friends and relatives in a good way; but the nature of the link between a ministry and the Company dictated that posts were nearly always made available to members of the Government. Where kinship, family connection or close familiarity entered proceedings, the likelihood of this happening was enhanced.

The close ministry-Company relationship that existed also dictated that the granting of such favours was done with alacrity and grace if the ministers demonstrated publicly their regard for the Chairmen or the leading Director. Company posts and East Indiamen positions were also given in return for political favours and to particular MPs for their support when Company business came before Parliament.

Apart from these political considerations, India patronage was also available to those involved in close business transactions with individual Directors, and to the friends of particular executives who were partners in their commercial ventures, like banking, insurance and money-lending in the City. Alliances in Company politics naturally led to openings being made available to friends of one side or another in the disputes; or in return for political favours, for stock-jobbing, and for promoting the careers of friends already abroad.

'When the number of vacancies became known each year, the total was divided into thirty shares (before 1774) of which the Chair and Deputy Chair had two shares, the ordinary Director one share each.'[3] For example, if the vacancies numbered sixty, this total was divided by thirty (shares), giving two vacancies to each Director to distribute, eight to the 'Chairs' and four vacancies to be haggled over.

The figure arrived at varied annually. It took into consideration all those in the Presidencies who had died the previous year, the political situation in the settlements and the level of trade. There was tremendous competition for places at all times. Success depended upon powerful contacts. Many a gentleman considered going out as a servant or common soldier in the hope that disease might cause vacancies and he would be appointed locally and have this confirmed by the Direction afterwards.

Important benefits to a Company Director from the patronage he could offer came in tangible form, mainly pecuniary, but also in the shape of power and prestige. In the eyes of many people (not least himself) he was an important man, held in high regard because of the influence he was thought to hold. The patronage he could confer and the needs of supplicants vested him with an authority immediately recognised. Political loyalties, nonetheless, made Company Directors susceptible to changing views at Westminster, especially if they too were Members of Parliament.[4]

6

The infrastructure of East India patronage and how it functioned is reasonably clear, despite the numerous permutations, connections and fluctuating relationships that were possible among groups and individuals. What must be remembered is that it was upon these complex interconnections and ever-changing patronage interests that everything was based.

Applicants could end up in one of only three categories of occupation: Company servant; crew of an East Indiaman; or free merchant at a settlement in one or other of the Presidencies. To a seasoned veteran of the East India Company, like David Rannie, Henry Dundas' father-in-law, there was little doubt that a position in the Company proper, in its civil, medical or military branches, was much superior to any other. Such an appointment was made at India House and had security; once abroad, perquisites and trading advantages were readily available. With the favour of the Governor, or perhaps some Council members, a Company servant could quickly establish a fortune.[5]

Becoming a Company servant directly through a Director or leading Proprietor was the simple and shortest way for an individual to get to India. Occasionally, enough influence could be brought to bear to have someone carried to India on board a Company ship to set up as a free merchant there, but this was more rare.[6]

The other major way to get to India was on board an East Indiaman, as a Captain, ships mate, surgeon or purser. This normally required strong connections with those seafarers and others who made-up the Company's Shipping interest*. This body was organised in such a way that it existed separately from the Company but was linked with its executive, with the main committees and with many of the Proprietors, so that a two-way influence prevailed. Places would be found on board ship for individuals with strong connections among ship owners and Captains.[7]

For those Directors and Proprietors who had strong ties with the shippers, posts were nearly always made available; and the patronage of one of the Shipping interest's powerful ships husbands,* such as the Scot, Captain Charles Foulis, was particularly sought after. There was a close affinity among many Directors and shippers; especially with several ex-Captains serving in the Direction and almost certainly in the Committee of Shipping.

In all cases (apart from shipping) in order to become a covenanted servant permission had to be received from the Court of Directors. To succeed a petition required a promise, solicited beforehand from one of the Directors, and preferably from one of the important ones, such as the Chairman or his Deputy. The 'Chairs' were held in the highest esteem. They could dominate the Company by determining the content and timing of business brought before the Court of Directors; and through control of the most important committees, such as those of Treasury and Shipping.

Through time the relationship that developed between the Company's executive and the Shipping interest became quite intricate. For example, another Scotsman, Captain George Cumming (also a Director at various times from 1764 to 1787) was proposed for the Supervisors Commission of 1772 by his friends in the Direction, Sir George Colebrooke and Laurence Sulivan.[8]

7

With some refinements and variations it was compulsory for all who would go to India that they gain a recommendation in the manner outlined above. Variations might entail the interest of a friend or, even better, friends who were Proprietors and active shareholders, attending the General Courts and maintaining an involvement in the annual April election to the Court of Directors.

An application passed by way of a Proprietor to his friends in the Direction might have some measure of success. Sometimes one Proprietor would ask a favour of another who was on a much better footing with the leading Directors or shippers who had patronage posts to dispose of. For example, Andrew Stuart gained help (for his brother Col. James Stuart) from George Dempster; and Sir Hew Dalrymple used Alderman Baker and Mr. Chancerie to help his brother William Stair Dalrymple.[9]

For someone north of the Tweed, bereft of direct contacts within the Company or Shipping interest, the best recourse was through the patronage manager in Scotland, or via a friend who had such contact; or of anyone who was part of the Government at Westminster. The higher the political office held, Prime Minister if possible, then the greater certainty that his weight would tell.

The Earl of Bute, who in the early 1760s had an excellent understanding with the Company's powerful leader, Laurence Sulivan, is just such an example. In return for Sulivan's help, Bute – using the Paymaster-General's office, controlled by his acolyte, Lord Holland – backed Sulivan with money for the splitting of stock as qualification for votes for the April 1763 election.

In fact, in many ways the systematised use of India patronage became unavoidable with the promise of continued electoral support and the Parliamentary backing that was given in return. The Scot who could depend upon a leading member of the Commons or House of Lords had very strong leverage indeed. Alex Elliot, who could call upon his father Sir Gilbert Elliot of Minto, who was also a Proprietor, was one of many who used this route.[10]

Failing a powerful ally in Government, it was still possible to achieve success by enlisting the support of one or more pro-ministry MPs who, sure of the applicant's allegiance to king, constitution and governing establishment, would use City and Company connections on his behalf. This is exemplified by Sir Hew Dalrymple, who sought patronage for his son, for two brothers James and Robert, and for others.[11]

It was also possible for aspiring Company servants and others anxious to get to India, to use members of the Parliamentary Opposition. This is perfectly illustrated by the activities of Sir Laurence Dundas. Help from this quarter was limited, however, because the interests of Government and Company nearly always coincided.[12] Parliamentary Opposition was generally linked to those groups and individuals in Company politics opposed to the ruling figures in the Direction. Only during the contested elections of the 1760s was there more scope for the opposition groups in both Westminster and Leadenhall politics because of the rapid stream of ministries in the former and changes of control in the Company during these troubled years.

Connections were kept, because although a Proprietor was out of the Direction one year, and thus bereft of patronage, he might form one of the executive the next April and dispense favours to those friends who stayed with him through adversity. Occasionally recourse was made to an independent Member of Parliament, or one who at some stage might not be following a party line but had healthy India connections. He could go straight to a Director, perhaps an influential Proprietor, or even an important shipper. This is exemplified in George Dempster's relationship with Governor George Johnstone and Andrew Moffatt. In 1761 Dempster was also favoured by Bute, who arranged for him to have Perth Burghs.[13]

Sometimes a circuitous route through the City was used to obtain this India patronage. An intermediary was called in who was perhaps a Bank of England official, a City merchant, or a Director of one of the other monopolies on friendly terms with his equivalent in the East India Company. Again George Dempster provides illustration. He had a multitude of friends, including David Hume, Johnson, Blackstone, Goldsmith, and Reynolds who could reach out to others on his behalf.[14] Human ingenuity in all its guises can be seen in operation to secure positions in the Company and its shipping. These were the main channels. Doubtless there were others that are too deep to be traced by posterity.

4

Drummond and Management 1720–42

1

It was almost certainly clear in John Drummond's mind when he entered the East India Direction in 1722 that he would be able to serve his family and enhance their wealth through provision of positions in the Company; and this is exactly what he did. But this consideration had to take its place alongside the major reason why he was there. He knew just how useful the control of India patronage was to the Whig government, as well as for himself; a government which, from 1722 and the South Sea Bubble crash was dominated by Sir Robert Walpole.

Drummond's correspondence verifies that he deliberately began to foster extensive Scottish political connections, using the India patronage at his disposal. Members of his family in Perthshire were particularly useful: brother James, the eldest, of Blair-Drummond; William, of Grange; and his sister Mary, who had married James Haliburton of Pitcur.

He set about purchasing an estate at Quarrel, on the southern shore of the river Forth between Kincardine and Grangemouth, which cost him £7,700 (Scots).* At the same time he embarked upon the extensive and painstaking work required to establish himself at local level among the superiorities.* He involved himself in local elections for the same purpose.[1]

Drummond's friendship and the giving of India patronage in return for votes was to be for the greater ends of the Union, the stability of the new state of Britain, support of the Argathelians and of Walpole and his Whig Government. On a less grand note, self-preservation and aggrandisement among those involved in the transfer of votes and favours can never be ignored.

By this stage in his life, political friends included great pro-Union magnates like the Duke of Argyll and the Marquis of Tweeddale, both of whom had wide experience among those holding superiorities. Likewise the Earls of Morton, Leven, Hyndford and Kinnoul; Lords Elphinstone and Torphichen, all rallied to him. Most of these well-known figures and their titled successors were to make great use of Drummond's favours in the years up to 1742. Barons, such as Sir Kenneth Mackenzie and James Haliburton; burgesses like Sir Peter Halkett, John Clerk of Penicuik and Sir Hew Dalrymple did so too. These men epitomised political weight and electoral power in Scotland.

The Stewart connection in his own family's past seemed to mean little to Drummond. He was very much aware of, but appeared oblivious to, Jacobite tendencies in those he became involved with politically. He viewed followers of the Old Pretender mainly in the light of usefulness. If he could depend upon their political support then so much the better. Of those who had voted against the Union some, like Annandale, Atholl, Errol and the Earl Marischal now combined with him and in return received favours.

The Scot's steady service to influential Scottish families and to his kinsmen in sending their sons abroad using India patronage had begun in 1722, as soon as he had any influence in the East India Company Direction, and through friends; but from 1725 he was to grant patronage favours in proportion to political support and usefulness.[2]

His interest and active involvement in Scotland from around 1725 also contrasts strongly with an almost total disregard before, and marks the incorporation of India patronage into the Governmental patronage system, used overwhelmingly for the political management of Scotland. The active electioneering that Government agents (such as Drummond) were now involved in was in itself indicative of what was afoot.

Most of all, Drummond's correspondence demonstrates conclusively how important he was in creating and maintaining the docile Scottish representation at Westminster as well as a politically stable and quiet Scotland. It is exemplified very well in a letter of his to Lord Aberdour, in which he warns that Aberdour and Sir Peter Halkett must not go against Walpole's desires:

> by order, Sir R.W. is resolved that none of his friends shall countenance any candidates whatsoever for Fife other than Sir John Anstruther...if any private grudge or suspicion that Sir John is not acceptable in Fife exists, I can only answer that he is

acceptable here, and at this time that ought to satisfy every one who desires peace and quiet among the King's friends, and those who at this time will raise new candidates for Fife cannot be esteemed to be acting in concert with Sir R.W. or have any regard to the methods which he has laid down for the ease and quiet of his friends in Scotland and to those whom he has entrusted the management of affairs there.[3]

The correspondence also reveals an enormous range and number of contacts; it shows non-stop use of the India patronage he could command, and his links with London Administration and Scottish political agents alike in the years 1725 to 1742. The Abercairney and Morton manuscripts, in particular, make clear the liaison, even alliance with Walpole. They portray precisely the connection with the Argyll family; with Andrew Fletcher of Saltoun (Lord Milton) and with other friends at Court, in Government and Parliament.

By this date, his ties within the business world (added to those made in his younger years) were truly extensive. His friendships were particularly strong among Company Directors, Proprietors, the Shipping interest, and servants abroad. These communications lay bare the nature of the connections between Drummond, the government interests that he served, and the families and individuals helped. The correspondence exposes the sinews of the patronage system and its operation, when wielded by John Drummond on behalf of Government among the most influential Scottish peers and lairds.

2

Apart from hints that there were earlier links between the two, the violent events in Scotland of 1725 in themselves would have encouraged dialogue between Walpole and Drummond. There is in fact evidence, in a letter from Viscount Dupplin to him in 1727 that these ties were indeed well established by that date. The relationship was rigorously maintained throughout the years to come.

In letters to Lord Aberdour, Drummond as often as not 'went that day to Sir Robert Walpole', attending diligently to his requests.[4] In 1732 the Earl of Morton, one of Drummond's closest friends, and who exerted enormous political influence locally, while boasting of his own influence with Walpole made it plain that Drummond was more important. Both Walpole and Morton used Drummond as a middleman, channelling their letters through him.

Much of this three-way friendship reflected their political partisanship. Morton and Drummond also liked each other; and their common aims, with regard to the better political management of Scotland, were served by close unity. They were working against the 'Patriot' opposition beating at the door, especially in 1732. It was an almost unbroken law that all patronage dispensed at local level, although this might seem to concern just local issues, had a bearing on national politics.[5]

From 1733 to 1736 the direct Walpole–Drummond connection remained very strong. Governor Pitt of Madras described the relationship almost perfectly when in 1733, in a letter to Drummond, he referred to Walpole's abilities, proclaimed his fervent wish that Drummond would remain in the Direction, and outlined his own career hopes – all in the one breath. Like others inside the Company, home and abroad, he understood the power that lay concealed behind this delicate partnership.

Nor did Drummond make any secret of his friendship with Walpole. He stated it to his family, while also acknowledging that it was to Chandos that he owed his confidential position with the First Minister. Chandos had helped him get close to Walpole and kept him there; supported him in Parliament and found him favour with the King. This is corroborated in Chandos' own letters to Drummond, while other communications continually urged him to apply to Walpole for 'some mark of respect' for all the aid he had given.[6] Chandos also made reference to the combined strength of himself and Drummond in the Company's Courts, which was so important.

3

In October 1734 Drummond wrote to his brother James, 'Sir Robert Walpole told me that he had prevailed with Lord Ilay to keep Sir David Nairn's place for me'.[7] He referred to the office of Secretary to the Order of the Thistle, vacant with Nairn's death in 1734. But that it was to come through Ilay was not at all strange, considering the relationship that had been built up between Drummond and the ducal family by this date; and the fact that both the London and Scottish ends of governmental management of Scotland were involved.

From 1725 Drummond's association had been mainly with the Duke of Argyll rather than his brother Ilay. This early friendship, the small world of Scottish politics, the closeness of both to Walpole, and the need of India patronage for the better political management of Scotland, would have ensured that early contact continued. In 1732 another John Drummond, this time of Megginch, a Member of Parliament and deeply involved in Scottish politics with Drummond of Quarrel, suggested that just such a friendly state of affairs continued to exist between his friend and Argyll but also indicated the strengthening connection with Ilay.[8]

From 1733 there is no doubt at all that Ilay and Drummond of Quarrel shared a deep attachment and understanding. It is significant too that this fusion of interests coincided with Ilay's virtual take-over of the political management of Scotland from his brother, and the wresting from Walpole of a great deal of independence in the control of Scottish affairs.

In fact, as early as September 1732 Drummond is quite clear about the good terms he is on with Ilay. He informed Lord Morton's son, Aberdour: 'I cannot find Sir R. much inclined to enter into the detail of our Scots elections, leaving them very much to Lord Ilay.' In a follow-up to this revealing letter he emphasised the point again, urging Aberdour to 'use more time with Lord Ilay;' and stating that 'Sir R. Walpole. . .will not dispose of a Scots tide waiter's place without having first Lord Ilay's recommendation or approbation.' He continued: 'while Lord Ilay is with you, your Lordship and my brother [William Drummond of Grange] must solicit him for anything and everything...you will find Lord Ilay as ready to oblige my friends as he possibly can be.'[9]

Lord Aberdour served as go-between for this closer relationship; and in one of his letters to Drummond indicated some of the reasons (on both sides) for such a firm and confidential friendship. He referred to the fact that they had mutual friends and identical political interests; and that Drummond had vouchsafed that he would continue to secure his burgh constituency for the Argathelian interest and support it to the hilt in Parliament.

What was made most clear was that Ilay looked for patronage help among the voters in the shires and in the burghs through Drummond. In 1735 Drummond underlined just how deeply he had committed the patronage he controlled to the Argathelian interest in Scottish politics when he indicated that he worked only through Ilay. This applied even to kinsmen; and he advised his brother James that their cousin Laurence Drummond must gain the recommendation of both Ilay and Lord Milton (the great Lord's man of business in Scotland) before anything could happen.[10]

4

Drummond matched his friendship with Walpole, Argyll and Ilay, by offering the same to Milton, the Lord Advocate. In a series of candid letters to Milton in June and July 1727 he suggested a sort of friendship pact, promising his support and that of all his family in Scottish affairs, but particularly at elections. He, his brother William and brother-in-law James Haliburton of Pitcur would support the Argathelian political management network in Scotland and would work through Milton and Baron Scrope.

He pledged himself to use Milton's channels, despite, as he put it, being on excellent personal terms with Argyll and Ilay. What's more, he would rally his contacts in Scotland and in England, many of whom he described as 'friends of the first rank about his majesty'.[11] Such overtures would have sounded sweet to Milton and his political masters. These promises of support were the grassroots of political strength.

Drummond promised that any Scottish supporter of the Campbells in local politics would be looked after by him, especially through the provision of India posts. Nor would this only apply at election time, when those with influence would be working hard among the superiorities. He would use his power inside the Company and among his shipping friends all year round for their benefit. He backed up this promise immediately, by making special mention of Milton's particular friend Governor Macrae, then in Madras, for whom he would do 'every service in his power' and would 'serve his family' faithfully. In return, he asked for Milton's friendship, and his 'favour and assistance' in securing Perth burghs. This was granted willingly. It was done through Milton and Argyll; and as Milton's letters show, the electoral niceties involved had Walpole's wholehearted approval. Drummond became an MP on 9 September 1727.[12]

Drummond skilfully manipulated his friends and dependants and brought them into line: thus, his friend James Haliburton of Pitcur 'must submit to what Lord Milton determined'; and he wished Aberdour was 'better friends with Lord Milton for he is better heard than all of us together.' When, at his instigation, Milton and Aberdour became confidants in 1734, Drummond enthused 'it would make things easier in Scotland and in London for us all.'[13]

He and Milton continued to keep very close contact and conducted a fruitful correspondence. The main topics were always Parliamentary elections, and in particular Drummond's control of Perth burghs; patronage – that of the Company especially, and other favours. Commerce, and how Scotland could be made to benefit was generally included.

The sinews of the management system are made clear from these letters; and Drummond was instrumental in bringing together interested parties like Lord Morton, George Dempster Senior, and Milton. He was industrious in the Commons on behalf of Walpole and the Argathelians;

while his friendships with the Duke of Argyll, Ilay, Scrope, Duncan Forbes and Milton can be seen developing.

Gaining a seat in the Commons was described by Drummond as 'the first mark...of my country's regard for me.' He did not, he stressed, wish the seat for personal gain but in order to 'serve his country.'[14] His industry in Parliament and the many testimonials from others indicate the truth of this. He was skilful at capturing the most important election officials in the counties and burghs: 'The Provost of each town was the man to secure,' he related to Milton in July 1727. In other letters he urged Milton to give preferential treatment to friends of his. For instance, he suggested that Sir Alex Wedderburn's son should be made sheriff-clerk of Haddingtonshire; that Mr. Emmery should be made Town clerk of Cupar; George Millar, who was the Town clerk of Perth, should be made Registrar of Sasines for Perthshire; and he bemoaned the loss of Provost Melville at Cupar, through his own stupidity.[15]

As a merchant Drummond could speak with some confidence on most commercial matters. He remarked to Milton upon the poor sales in London of black cattle and linen goods throughout the 1720s and 1730s; and he made strenuous efforts on behalf of Scotland's linen and cloth trade. He also tried to satisfy Milton's request for a contract allowing Saltoun House to supply barley to East Indiamen. Yet, even with the help of Sir John Eyles, his great friend in the Shipping interest, Drummond could not bring this about.[16]

In this manner patronage and political management were underpinned by Drummond's constancy and availability. He never failed to say he was 'very desirous' of helping Milton, who was urged to ask for any information or service from him. He 'awaited Milton's commands' at all times. Deference, courtesy, and willingness to help were his hall-marks; and so successful was he in maintaining this attitude that it almost became a requirement that he be consulted. Thus, by 1736 he could inform Milton that in an audience with Walpole he had assured the Minister of Milton's good health; and that Scotland was quiet and to his satisfaction. The same month he dined with the Duke of Argyll and satisfied him of the same.[17]

5

The manner in which Drummond's India patronage was harnessed to government's political wishes regarding Scotland worked satisfactorily, with Drummond enjoying a large degree of autonomy in his dealings with Milton. However, following Ilay's takeover of the machinery of Scottish political management in 1733 the situation changed slightly; and although great intimacy remained, a note of formality also entered the relationship. For example, on 14 November 1734 Drummond indicated to his brother William that he was obliged to Lord Milton on all occasions; then just two days later he added, 'Lord Milton is the one to consult on these matters [patronage] because the King puts all these things in Lord Ilay's hands.' In other words, a well ordered system, from Ilay, through Milton and Drummond was now in existence.[18]

In August 1735 Drummond was exultant, 'Lord Milton is Justice-Clerk for life...I am glad of it...he has been always my friend.'[19] His exuberance reflected that he was now firmly entrenched (and perfectly happy) within a system that he helped to operate in pursuit of goals shared with Milton, the rest of the Argathelians and with Walpole. For example, he noted with relish the anguish of the 'Patriot Lords' when the King snubbed the Duke of Hamilton and hung on to every word of the Earl of Hopetoun. At all times he expressed himself happy at the defeat of political enemies in the Lords and the Commons.

In fact another delicate change in relationships took place by 1734. Drummond moved slightly away from Walpole and now served Ilay just as much as he did the first minister. It was a move dictated more by the change in association of his mentors than personal design. His loyalty and political backing for Walpole never wavered, but the patronage at his disposal was increasingly made available, first and foremost, to Ilay and Milton for the administration of Scottish business, now increasingly in their pocket.

As early as 1728 Drummond had also become an important member of the Court circle. His previous career and especially the contacts with Argyll and Chandos helped. Walpole had him presented to George II in 1728 and to Queen Caroline in 1733. He was close to Townshend, Marlborough and Lord Bathurst, and particularly to Thomas Hay, Viscount Dupplin and Earl of Kinnoul.[20] The latter was very useful: he held Walpole's confidence and served the Prime Minister faithfully. Hay was also an important and influential member of the political management structure in London that dealt with Scottish business. He worked with Walpole, John Scrope, Argyll and Ilay, informally offering advice and information. Later he was to help Walpole's successor Henry Pelham, in the management of parliamentary elections.[21]

Drummond was important to the Scottish aristocracy and landed gentry, both because he was part of the Argathelian party, with governmental and parliamentary connections, and because he had such a great deal of patronage to dispense. He was equally essential to many others: to the bourgeoisie domiciled in Scotland, to those in London, and others leading a peripatetic life between the two.[22] In Parliament he was an active figure, being described in 1734 as *fully engaged in* 'Scottish, Colonial and trade matters.' He remained firmly in the circle that clung to Walpole at Westminster. It was a group that included among its leading Scots members: Argyll, Ilay, Scrope, Morton, Kinnoul and Charles Erskine. Chandos, as in everything else, helped him find his way in the Commons.[23]

In 1722 Drummond already had many business acquaintances, but he continued to add to these. Such men were equally important to him for operation of the patronage system because of the wider cross-connections they provided. He used these contacts carefully and always on a *quid pro quo* basis. Such was the case with his relation Andrew Drummond.

Wealthy Scots, such as Queensberry were persuaded to place their money beside his own in Andrew Drummond's bank. From this John Drummond derived political gains, such as those that would stem from Queensberry's friendship, not to mention young Andrew Drummond's gratitude and help. He worked in similar fashion with Coutts the bankers in London, who were also Scottish; and was involved with another Scot, Hugh Campbell, in a side-line of remitting diamonds from India.

From 1728 onwards he was friendly with the Dutch envoy, Mr Hope. This was to be a rather important future connection for Scots in the East India Company because of the amount of stock held by this Dutch banking family with Scottish antecedents. Drummond's own directorships of the *Royal Africa Company* in 1722, and of the *Royal Exchange Assurance Company* in 1726, helped to consolidate an already considerable stature in the City, and opened out other avenues.[24]

6

At India House his influence remained strong, even after leaving the Direction in 1733. This is illustrated by Chandos' reference to them both still 'winning in the Direction.'[25] As Proprietors they were interested in dividends, but even more so in patronage. As well as Decker and Harrison, Drummond was particularly close to John Monson, Sir Gilbert Stewart and to Governor Macrae – who had returned from Madras. He kept on close terms too with the increasingly influential Chairman and Deputy Chairman, and indeed invariably these most important positions were filled by good friends. From 1725 to 1733 they were held by five men all close to Drummond: Sir Matthew Decker, Henry Lyell, John Gould, Edward Harrison and Josiah Wordsworth.

Within the important Shipping interest his network was equally impressive and formidable, with allies among the leading ships husbands, charter-parties* and Commanders. They included the influential John Durand, Benjamin and Christopher Lethieullier, Gerard Conyen, Richard du Cane, Barrington Eaton, Thomas Frederick and Captain John Shepherd.[26]

Drummond also enjoyed particularly good relationships with leading servants abroad. The help and care he poured out upon so many in the settlements ensured this. Such was his power at India House (in league with friends) that he appeared able to grant important positions to whomsoever he saw fit. The Presidency of Madras reflected this. Governors Harrison, Macrae, Pitt, Horne and Cowan all owed their command there to him and to his friends in the Direction. Other leading members of Presidential councils, such as Dr. Colt and Robert Douglas were beneficiaries too. They in turn provided openings for others who were dependent upon Drummond's generosity, and took care of his protégés when they arrived.

Drummond was very particular with individuals who were special to powerful political friends at home. For example, Milton lavished his favours on Macrae through the Drummond–Chandos channel. Governor George Morton Pitt (the particular friend of the influential Proprietor Sir Gilbert Stewart, whose help was always needed within Leadenhall and its politics) was able to feel the warmth from his friend – again operating through Drummond and Chandos.[27]

To take stock, from the mid-1720s John Drummond can be pictured in charge of a highly sophisticated patronage system; one which fitted into the Government's overall framework for the political management of Scotland; and which stretched physically from Scotland to London and to the East Indies. It involved powerful controlling figures inside India House, shipping interests, City banking and merchant circles; as well as a large body of personal friends at Court and at Westminster.

Initial dispensation of India posts to relatives and close friends in Scotland was expanded and firmly linked to the Administration's wishes with regard to Scotland and Parliamentary majorities in London. The ministry's hopes were to be realised partly through the liberal spread of India positions among families, such as those traced below. They in turn carried sufficient influence in the Scottish regions to sway the voters towards Government and to maintain loyalty.

5

Drummond Network
1720–42

1

The families helped by John Drummond were quite remarkable in terms of numbers and position in Scottish life; and those served had important political cross-connections. These people were of significance because from them government could expect unswerving support. A pattern of inter-relationships is revealed, bringing together in collaboration powerful dynasties scattered the length and breadth of Scotland.

Such families dealt with everyday matters of political life; yet these were not confined to local level and on occasion subjects of wider significance were handled. They were also firmly linked to equals in England, through marriage, by way of relatives and in the course of friendship. There were special links with fellow Scots in London, gathering there in numbers following transfer of power in 1707. Members of this Scottish elite were to be found everywhere: connected to individuals governing Scotland; present in Parliament and at the tables of those ruling from London; gathered in the committee rooms of all the big companies; and involved in insurance underwriting, banking and commerce.

The quality and spread of Drummond's connections was impressive: At least nineteen English governmental contacts can be distinguished; he patronised around one hundred and ten politically powerful Scottish families; and personally sent abroad about fifty supplicants for East India posts. He maintained intimate dealings with around forty Company figures who helped with posts; and had some eight or nine separate business friends with influence at India House.

The immense political strength of Drummond's Whig connections throughout Scotland's counties and burghs is reflected in landowning and electoral terms. A controlling interest was maintained in many by the vast majority of his friends, especially through direction of the hereditary sheriffs. This was particularly striking when in tandem with the influence exerted by a powerful magnate like the Duke of Argyll.[1]

Crucially, he remained close to these hereditary sheriffs and influential men with a 'natural' or 'nominal' interest among the superiorities. Thus, staggering numbers gained posts in India or became crew of East Indiamen through his good offices; and whose families in turn performed useful political service. Both in county and burgh, correspondents whose families and dependents had been helped to India positions were usually the most consequential figures and government supporters to a man.

These leading families provided Drummond with direct contact to some one hundred and twenty-three hereditary sheriffs – as well as other key officials. The same people had a chief interest in twenty-eight out of the forty-eight counties and burghs in Scotland during the years 1720 to 1742. Thirty-two positive identifications of politically powerful men, who were Drummond's friends and fellow collaborators, can be made in twenty-two of the thirty-three counties. They and their families were deeply caught up in electoral activity on behalf of government Whigs through Drummond and the Argathelian group; and many were in receipt of India patronage in return for support and reliability.

The same extraordinary picture emerges within the burghs. In fourteen out of the fifteen groups of burghs, nineteen positive identifications can be made connecting people Drummond helped with the most important burgh-mongers in Scotland. Five other individuals he was in touch with are almost certainly of the same influential category through association with very pro-government families. What is more, this figure excludes the Argathelian-controlled counties of Argyllshire, Ayrshire, Buteshire and Dunbartonshire.[2]

He also maintained a presence in those counties and burghs where he was weakest. For example, in Sutherland he had James Sinclair; in Stirlingshire the Haldanes; for Selkirkshire the Pringles; and in Roxburghshire the Scotts. In Aberdeen he enjoyed the support of the Arbuthnot family; for Haddington, Lord Milton; in Perth, Lord Rothes; and for Stirling, the Erskines, Halkett and Haldane families.

Generally speaking, these men were the leading landowners and wielded overwhelming electoral power in their localities. Many others, almost certainly useful for the purpose of political management, appear in his correspondence and can be regarded in such a light. The Kinloch family and Lord Aberdour, Lord Morton's son, are just such instances. They cast votes in the elections as desired by Drummond or his superiors.[3]

Among these powerful families in Scotland closely associated with Drummond, some thirty-five cross-connections and alliances can be detected. This infrastructure strengthened his position in the north, and that of the Argathelian group within the Whig party at Westminster. It followed that the Scots placed in India by Drummond, whose relations in Scotland were allied to one another and were politically useful, could only aid and abet these central and peripheral political arrangements.[4] Such statistics demonstrate the extent of Drummond's contribution to political management in the early part of the century. Application of India patronage helped create a finer mesh for trawling Scottish political waters, and ensured rich pickings, with no landowning or electoral force left undetected or unsolicited.

2

The intricate structure of his set of connections becomes clearer by separating into groups the more important of the peers and gentry he was involved with. Analysis of these in turn illuminates the effectiveness of the system in operation and its wide-spread application. There were six categories: *The London Circle* embraced those Scots (usually resident in London) close to Walpole and part of the governmental clique, who also had extensive influence in Scotland. As mentioned, these incorporated the Argyll-Ilay group: Duncan Forbes, John Scrope, Viscount Dupplin, Sir Gilbert Stewart and Charles Erskine.

Next, a cluster considered *The Foremost Scottish Peers,* among whom an order of electoral importance emerges that reflects their respective weight among the superiorities all over Scotland. Their worth is signified by the volume of India patronage showered upon them by Drummond. Thus the Earl of Hopetoun is in the first rank, as are Morton and Aberdour, closely followed by Rothes, Hyndford and Elphinstone.

The third sort comprised those *Peers in Scotland who carried unusual weight in counties and burghs.* It included Atholl, Annandale, Fortrose, Queensberry, Moray of Abercairney, Findlater, Cathcart, the Earl Marischal, Errol, Abercromby, Seaforth, Leven and Kinnoul. Next were the *most important members of the Landed Gentry,* those lairds whose influence among the voters can be well-instanced, and whose relationship with Drummond was strong. This selection too has its more important members, such as the

Munros of Foulis, Sinclairs, Haldanes, Hopes of Hope Park and Rankeillor; the Haliburtons of Pitcur and Halkett of Pitfirrane.

The *remaining members of this Scotland-wide network* included both sides of John Drummond's family, that is, the Drummonds of Perthshire and the Ramsays of Bamffe. To them can be added the Mackenzies of Delvine; the Scotts and Douglases of Gala; Stirlings of Keir; Oliphants of Gask; Dalrymples of North Berwick; Carnegies of Forfarshire; and Clerks of Penicuik. These people formed the core of the Argathelian support and of Walpole's Whig ministry. When orchestrated for elections and in support of governmental measures across the breadth of Scotland they proved to be unbeatable.

Personal friends in Parliament complete Drummond's phalanx of supporters. They mustered in the Argathelian bloc. On the whole these were the same influential men to be found in the Scottish counties and burghs, who enjoyed Drummond's patronage from time to time. They were joined at various junctures by Lords Abercromby, Queensberry, Annandale, Douglas, Rothes, Tweeddale, Morton, Hopetoun, Atholl, Cathcart and Findlater. Until Drummond's demise, Argyll and Ilay were strengthened by the distribution of his favours among such people.

In the Commons Drummond was attached to others he had favoured with India posts for relations and connections. They included Alexander Arbuthnot, MP for Inverness, Sir John Bruce of Culdraines (only until the 1732 election), and John Drummond of Megginch. Charles Erskine, Solicitor-General and then Lord Advocate, was a friend – as was his kinsman, Thomas Erskine, the eldest son of the 6th Earl of Mar.

Thomas Erskine was also firmly in the Drummond camp because his mother, Lady Margaret Hay, was the daughter of Drummond's great friend, Thomas Hay, Viscount Dupplin, 7th Earl of Kinnoul, part of the Argathelian-Walpole circle. Another supporter was James Erskine, attached to Drummond because his mother was the widow of Thomas Ramsay of Bamffe, and Drummond's relation on his mother's side.[5] These inter-connections through marriage brought with them duties and obligations, loyalties and preferments that formed the very basis of the solidarity to be found at this level of society. Upon such structures so much depended, and why the outlines of so many matrimonial associations require definition.

Others in Parliament, just as important and useful to the Argathelians and linked to them through India patronage, included Sir Hew Dalrymple, James Haliburton of Pitcur, Sir John Hope (later 2nd of Hopetoun), David Graeme, Sir Peter Halkett, Kenneth Mackenzie (later Lord Fortrose), Sir

Kenneth Mackenzie of Cromarty, Sir Robert Munro of Foulis, John and William Maule, Sir James St. Clair, William Stewart, and James Scott of Logie.

When added to Drummond's other friends at Westminster, made through business connections in London, they formed a not inconsiderable knot of supporters, giving him a formidable political interest. This latter group consisted of colleagues such as Sir Matthew Decker, Sir John Eyles and Governor Edward Harrison, who were fellow Company Directors as well as Members of Parliament.

Others included Sir Thomas Frederick, Edward Gibbon, Richard Hoare and the banker Sir Theodore Janssen. The faction also embraced: Edward, Lord Harley and Sir William Lowther of Swillington Yorkshire; Alexander and Abraham Hume, who were also Company Proprietors; John Pringle, a relative of Drummond's friend, Thomas Pringle of Selkirk; and Sir John Ramsden of Byram Yorkshire, husband of Lady Ramsden, whose son was helped to India by Drummond.[6]

This is the picture revealed by the Scot's correspondence. It demonstrates that the operation of the East India patronage system occupied a central, though largely concealed position, sustaining fusion of the ruling propertied and business classes in the two nations. As already noted, many of the politically aware among the English governing class felt a real threat emanating from Scotland and understood that greater stability was required to safeguard their own position. It was this feeling that inspired collaboration within Walpole's inner cabal, which in turn resolved upon a policy of firm Scottish stewardship.

On the other hand, little separated the banking, commercial and professional classes north and south of the border; and the social mores of the English aristocracy and landed classes were shared by the Scottish equivalent. India patronage (and the Drummond route of tapping that patronage) was welcome and encouraged. The individuals who emerge, having benefited from Drummond's inspired sponsorship, bear witness to this. By clever use of favours he achieved an interweave of political interests; and did so to an extent that fascinated as much as it satisfied the wishes of his political masters and those of desirous friends and wavering government supporters.[7]

Each individual came to an arrangement with him that depended upon the twin objectives of continued friendship and political support. An excellent example of this is seen in September 1734. Alex Binney, the son of the Provost of Forfar, was in London and had applied to his fellow Scot for a post. Drummond told Lord Aberdour, 'I propose to make him a hostage'. He meant that in return for helping his son, the Provost would use his interest in Forfar politics on Drummond's behalf.[8]

3

John Drummond carefully served the interests of his own kinsmen and, where the opportunity presented itself, did what he could for those who had supported the Jacobite cause in 1715, but now showed a change of inclination. His own Jacobite ancestry led to an unsentimental but compassionate understanding of the predicament of those who had followed the Stewarts. His grasp of the need to bring them back within the orbit of Scottish life (for Unionist ends as well as for mending the Scottish social fabric) made him pursue a policy that would allow government to permit this on the one hand, and make the Jacobites appreciative on the other. Besides, Jacobite leaders commanded influence among many voters.

It was because of these views that George Threipland, son of one of his own Jacobite relation, Sir David Threipland, was sent out by him in 1724 as a ships surgeon and placed under the protection of Governors Macrae and Pitt, Dr Colt and John Graham. In the same year, Drummond was asked by James Ogilvie (Lord Airlie) to obtain a pardon for him; and in 1728 Drummond pleaded with Lord Chesterfield to 'show mercy for Mr. Carnegie.'[9]

In April 1731 he struggled to obtain pardons for Sir James Stewart, William Stewart, a Mr. Murray and Sir David Threipland (mentioned above) all Jacobites. Sir James Stewart's political influence was still very strong in Lanarkshire and Morayshire where he was a powerful landowner. However, by 1735 Drummond was meeting with only a limited degree of success because no Jacobites were to be admitted to any position, on instructions from above.[10]

Fear among government agents and supporters was still strong; and despite a wish to bring those sympathetic to the '15 back within the fold, and thereby use their political influence, distrust prevented them from being given patronage and posts via the system proper. Nevertheless, proof that John Drummond could by-pass the usual arrangement is indicated by his patronage of George Threipland. He was also helped that in most of the years preceding the '45 much of the distrust of Jacobites who were 'out' in the '15 had faded, allowing the patronage system to be operated on their behalf as fully as possible under the skilful and sympathetic guidance in Scotland of Lord Milton.

4

Drummond's correspondence in the 1720s and 1730s overwhelmingly indicates just how much he was part of a Scottish political group that consisted of government supporters, with only here and there an independent personality. Most business with these people concerned local politics and the patronage that could be made available to them, although this could spill over into other affairs, further cementing ties. The involvement of all such parties on the Argathelian side in elections, such as those of 1727 and 1734, illustrates the point.

Within this grouping, Drummond at all times enjoyed the support of a select knot in Scotland, mainly personal friends and firmly associated with his family. They included Lord Morton, his son Lord Aberdour and his Lady; Moray of Abercairney; the Earl of Hopetoun and his wife, Lady Anne Ogilvie; Sir Peter Halkett; and James Haliburton of Pitcur.

In a letter from George Douglas to his brother Lord Morton, dated London 15 July 1729, the political support both would give John Drummond was itemised. Douglas also urged Morton to recommend Drummond to Provost Glenbervie of St. Andrews, whose influence was essential to gain Perth burghs. He added, it was but 'the price of gratitude to the memory of the worthy old Blair [John Drummond's father] and an act of favour to this honest gentleman, who takes great pleasure in serving every man of his country when it falls in his province, and has helped many of them to business.'[11] The help given by Aberdour and Haliburton at the St. Andrews election of 1732, ably helped by Lords Douglas, Dunicade and Rothes, was again typical of this back-up. They were all reliant upon one another for support and pursued the government line in Scotland. Their involvement was deliberate, with patronage in return for influence and assistance.

To these can be added close acquaintances (many already mentioned) who formed a veritable list of who was who in Scotland at that time: his father, Sir George Drummond, fifth Laird of Blair-Drummond; Lords Leven, Grange and Kinnoul; Sir James Kinloch and Thomas Hope of Hope Park, whose family Drummond helped enormously and who vehemently promised political support in return. Others included Alexander Hay, Messrs. Hamilton and Gordon, and Sir Hew Dalrymple of North Berwick. John Drummond of Megginch guaranteed his help in the 1732 election against Sir John Bruce. The Stirlings of Keir were steadfast. As well as sending many of their family to India through Drummond, they also asked his help in getting to know the Earl of Morton and other Lords of the realm.

In 1734, at Sir James Kinloch's request, Drummond gained entry for two of his sons 'into the India Service.' They were William and John, sent out as Writers. In return their father pledged his support at the approaching election:

> I hope you don't doubt my doing all for you in my power, tho' I dare not make you the compliment that this [is] entirely in return for the personal favours I've received from you, since I must own that anyone who regards the interest of the country must prefer you.[12]

For political purposes Drummond deliberately maintained friendships all over Scotland, such as with John Burn and Eden Burnett, both of Aberdeen. The latter's brother was provided with a position in the Corn business in London. Friends of Lords Abercromby and Cathcart were found places in America and the West Indies in the 1730s. In the meantime, Drummond also made another influential and powerful contact in the person of Lord Elphinstone, helped by the amicable arrangement they came to over his purchase of the Lord's Quarrel estate.

5

Sometimes Drummond was able to obtain government favours (as opposed to India patronage) for his friends. He would 'work through Ilay and after Walpole's recommendation to oblige with a post.'[13] His generosity with every form of patronage that could be mustered for the benefit of his fellow Scots is well attested by his correspondents. Thomas Hope of Hope Park described him as 'unweary, stable and well-doing' for his 'country, countrymen and friends'. He was 'the father of all our young countrymen'.[14] Stirling of Keir referred to him as 'serviceable to your countrymen'.[15] As far as John Cleland was concerned, and for whom Drummond had performed 'numberless obligations', he was 'disinterested in his service to Scots'.[16]

In return for these favours Drummond was promised all manner of support at elections. Typical was the backing of Thomas Hope of Hope Park for all the services done by Drummond for his sons; from Lord and Lady Hyndford; from William Moncrieff; and from Drummond of Megginch. In fact, Drummond was kept so busy that he is found complaining in 1734 'my own provosts of my own towns are unprovided and dunning me daily.'[17]

Of course from the start, priority for posts in India and places on board East Indiamen went to Drummond's relations. Second were friends of the family, especially those who honoured the same patrons. This was particularly so in the 1722 to 1725 period before his patronage was modified completely to what government wished. Yet always his dispensation of favours was closely interwoven with political loyalty. Needless to say, the Drummonds held several estates in Perthshire and their own 'natural' interest was significant.

Many of those favoured were friends of his father, George Drummond. Help went to their sons and connections. In like manner relations and associates of his surviving brothers, William and James were served. Those who benefited early included his Haliburton nephews, James and John; and his niece Jean, born to his sister Mary who had married James Haliburton of Pitcur. They and their relatives, together with Drummond's cousin Alexander Wedderburn, received great help, not just in getting them to India but in pursuit of fortune once there.

Others he favoured were kinsmen like George Drummond, Provost of Edinburgh, and Andrew Drummond, the London banker, who was firmly in the Walpole camp. He also sent out to Fort St. George, his cousin George Ramsay. This relation was the incompetent son of Sir Gilbert and Elizabeth Ramsay of Bamffe, related to him through his mother. Hopeless he might be, but before he died in 1726 this Ramsay managed to remit substantial sums home to Scotland through Drummond.[18]

Friends of his nephew George Drummond (brother James' son) were helped too. Another niece, Agatha (named by his brother James in honour of his wife Agatha van der Brent) married James, Lord Aberdour, son of the Earl of Morton. The Earl was Drummond's staunch friend and political ally, and a leading figure in the Argathelian group.[19]

The relationship with the Haliburtons of the Pitcur estate was particularly close and especially that with his nephew *John Haliburton*. Young John (the son of John Haliburton) entered the Company as a Writer at Madras in 1735. Andrew Drummond the banker joined John Drummond in signing his bond. This able young man became an accomplished linguist, and was made a Factor. His skills also involved him in negotiations with the French. He and his cousin Alexander Wedderburn (also out there through John Drummond) rallied to one another. The Haliburtons were landowners with considerable electoral influence in Angus, Mid Lothian, Orkney and Shetland. In the latter they came under the shelter of the Earl of Morton and enjoyed a close friendship with that family. Sadly, John Haliburton was murdered during a Sepoy* mutiny at Pondicherry in 1748.[20]

The plum jobs abroad in the 1720s were in the Company's civil service, where prospects for private trade were best. These posts went to family and relations of very close friends. Only after they were served did Drummond grant others such lucrative posts; and again only in direct accordance with friendship and usefulness to government through local political influence. The careers of Drummond's cousin Alexander Wedderburn, of Alexander Halkett, Henry Lowther, John Hope and Hugh Campbell reflect this pecking order.

Alexander Wedderburn, the son of John Wedderburn of Dundee, was sent to the Bay of Bengal in 1721 through Drummond's influence. He began as a Purser at Surat, moved to Fort St. George, and received support in the coastal trade from his fellow Scot, Governor Macrae. In 1727 he applied to Drummond to be made a Factor at Bengal. Drummond persuaded the youth's father to supply money to trade with, personally sent him books; and in September 1727 was urging Governor Pitt to help the young man make his fortune. He also received help from Bourchier, the future Governor of Madras.

By 1731 Drummond and Sir Matthew Decker had secured him the desired Factor's position in Bengal - for which he was fulsome in his thanks. Andrew Drummond and John Crawfurd stood security. Wedderburn soon combined with others in the clannish group of young Scots treasure-hunters sent out by Drummond in this period. They had in common Drummond's patronage and the urge to make money very quickly and not much else, although their Scottish heritage seemed to bring them closer together. This circle of Scots comprised Robert Douglas, Matthew Hairstanes, a John Mackenzie and Dr. Littlejohn.

Wedderburn retained contacts made in the country trade, especially with the merchant firm of *Morse and Monson*. Using his Company position he built up a lucrative private business between 1731 and 1743, accumulating great wealth. He resigned the service and returned home in 1743.[21]

Alexander Halkett was the son of Sir Peter Halkett of Pittfirrine (uncle to both John Drummond and Alexander Wedderburn) and was sent out to Bengal by his cousin John in 1724 as a Writer. In 1733 he was made a Factor at that settlement by Drummond and his friends, despite Lord Townshend's son being in contention for the post.[22]

Henry Lowther, although English, is worth mentioning in this context. He was the brother of Drummond's City friend, Sir William Lowther. With the backing of Elizabeth, Lady Hyndford, he used Drummond to get out to Bombay in 1725. There he became a bosom friend of John Hope.

By 1728 Lowther was applying to Drummond and Sir Matthew Decker for their help in securing the Chiefship at Surat; and fawned upon Governor Phipps and then Governor Cowan with the same end in view. He too maintained an interest in country trade, in which it is clear that Drummond had a personal involvement, especially in the coffee trade from Mocha.[23]

John Hope went to Bombay some time before 1725. While there he became a close friend of Henry Lowther and shared with him in Drummond's patronage.[24] *Hugh Campbell* was sent a Writer to Fort St. George in the 1720s, where he was to become Drummond's main business agent. By 1728 he was under the care of Governors Macrae and Pitt, with whom he became very friendly. In 1732 Drummond had him made a Factor.[25] From 1726 Campbell was sending diamonds home to Drummond and to Sir Thomas Brand via Commander William Monson. These were in turn sold to a Mr. Shales, through the broker Isaac Nimes, for £1,600. In 1728 a further sum, of 1,000 pagodas, (approximately £400) was remitted to Drummond, via Campbell's attorney Major Roach.[26]

While accumulating money from the remittance of diamonds, Drummond was also pushing silver out to John Haliburton; and continued to be involved in the country trade in coffee from Mocha together with Henry Lowther. Drummond also lent money to fellow Scots abroad, such as to Dr James Scott, a brother of Scott of Gowanberry. Thus, with the purchase of the Quarrel estate (£7,700 Scots), his deposits in Andrew Drummond's bank, and all his other exploits, it is clear that in the 1720s and 1730s he was financially comfortable.[27]

Four of the most competent men he sent to India (useful to himself and in forwarding the careers of his other protégés) were Drs. Colt and Littlejohn - who arrived in Bengal in 1724, followed by John Stackhouse and Matthew Hairstanes - who were sent out to Madras in 1726. There they were befriended, at Drummond's request, by Governor Pitt. Obeying Drummond's instructions these four stalwarts, collaborators as well as correspondents, looked after and organised other Scots sent out by their benefactor, giving them every assistance.

Those helped in this way included Kenneth Mackenzie, nephew of John Mackenzie of Delvine; David Graham, friend of Hugh Sommerville; Robert Baird the surgeon; and Peter and Alexander Blair, sons of Drummond's kinsman Peter Blair of Edinburgh. The Blair youths arrived at Fort St. George in 1731 and 1732 respectively. Others, like Drummond's cousin, George Ramsay, already mentioned, were sent to Bombay; and Daniel Innes friend and kinsman of Dr. Robert Innes, also went there. They were cared for, again at Drummond's request, by Governor Cowan and Henry Lowther.[28]

6

Not surprisingly, with the memory of the '15 so strong in everyone's mind, Drummond made no Scottish appointments to the Company's military service. On the other hand, a great many individuals patronised by him were given ships berths. Besides the trust this implied, it reflected the strength of his connections with the powerful shippers associated with the Company. This was especially so with the Lethieullier brothers, Christopher and Benjamin.

Drummond's care for *James Macrae*, who became a ship's Commander and then was Governor of Madras from 1725 to 1730, perfectly exemplifies these links with the Company shipping. Macrae was to play a major role in the Company. He had gone to sea around 1692 possessed with only a smattering of education. Nevertheless, he became Commander of an East Indiaman. In 1720 he escaped the clutches of the pirate Edward England, left the sea and entered the Company's service by the back door. He was probably co-opted as a Writer in Madras, his admission into the Company's service validated after the event in London. His very rapid promotion to Governor of Madras suggests, however, that friendship with Milton and subsequently with Drummond was used. He ended up a linchpin in Drummond's system.

Macrae was in regular correspondence with Drummond from the 1720s to the early 1730s when he came back to Scotland. As well as the support of Lord Milton, he enjoyed (within the Company) that of Henry Lyell, Governor Pitt and Sir Gilbert Stewart – not to mention the backing of Drummond's cohorts. In India he was supported by Drummond's cousin Alexander Wedderburn and his friend Major Roach, especially during his feud with George Pigot.[29]

Drummond's close friend, Moray of Abercairney (also a boon companion of James Haliburton of Pitcur) asked for patronage for a seafaring nephew, *John Moray*. This illustrates the drive among trained Scottish seamen and others with skills, in this post-Union period, to get out of Scotland to London and abroad because of lack of opportunity at home. But more than that it reflects the absolute necessity that then prevailed, of having a friend in Scotland (in this case Abercairney) who in turn had a powerful London associate, John Drummond.[30]

Commander George Cumming had a career that spanned the 1720s to 1780s, and provides a splendid example of how this type of patronage was exerted. He became Captain of the *Royal Drake* in 1747, and to attain this would have spent at least 10 years serving on board East Indiamen. His career, therefore, began in the late 1730s when Drummond and Walpole dispensed India patronage. Through his wife, Susanna Dow, a niece of Robert Hume of Ayton, Berwickshire, he enjoyed the considerable influence that this landowner had with Scotland's political managers. His marriage also associated him with Robert Hume's sons, Alex and Abraham Hume, Directors and ship-owners in London. Through them he gained direct access to the East India Company and its shipping. The Ayton, Berwickshire coincidence suggests solidarity among all those with this connection that is of Cumming with the Humes and Sir James Cockburn, also from Ayton.

The patronage Cumming enjoyed he in turn visited upon other Scots: Boyd Alexander and the brothers Thomas and James Graham are but three examples. And he recommended his nephew James Cumming to a Writers post in 1766, using his position as a Director to the full. From 1747 he was an important member of the Shipping interest and became a Director in 1764. For all but 2 years, between 1764 and 1776, and at times thereafter until 1787, he was a Director and an influential figure.

As did all men in his position within the Direction, he took part in the contested elections of the period. From 1763 he was consistently pro-Clive and anti-Sulivan because of Clive's friendship with Alex Hume. This put him in a minority position in the shipping world because Sulivan commanded exceptional support there. Only his alliance with Sir George Colebrooke in 1770, possibly through the Cockburn connection, brought him over to Sulivan's side. He remained with the Sulivanite–Colebrooke faction until well after the 1773 Regulating Act. He also continued to patronise fellow Scots, such as Donald Macleod of Grisernish, Kilmuir, Invernesshire. In 1770, using his powers as a Director, he had him appointed a Writer.[31]

7

There are many other instances of Drummond granting favours to seafarers during these initial years. A *Commander Gibson* was appointed following a letter in 1727 to him from Governor Pitt seeking support. Drummond was informed that 'Gibson's wife is very rich'. But his wife's riches must have been overestimated, because the lure of money was the sole reason for going east. Two or three voyages, however, guaranteed a fortune. Drummond, Sir John Eyles, and Commander John Fenton were also responsible for the appointment of *David Graham* as Ships mate on Governor Bourchier's vessel, captained by Fenton. Accompanied by his sister, Graham arrived in India to be helped, on Drummond's orders, by Dr. Littlejohn.

Commander *John Hunter* of the *Barrington*, referred to as 'a Scotsman's son', was another who benefited – appointed through Drummond. In 1728 John Stewart, of Stewartfield in Aberdeenshire, prevailed upon Drummond to get Col. Hutchinson's son to sea. Dutifully he too was helped to become Commander of an East Indiaman.[32]

The list of those helped seems endless, but the careers of 1st Mate James Rod, Midshipman Thomas Ogilvie, Ships mate James Lamb and Supercargo Mr. Naish – together with those already given – suffice to illustrate the variety of berths that Drummond's influence could command.

James Rod owed his position to William Moncrieff, landowner in Perthshire, who wrote to Drummond on his behalf in 1731, the letter being delivered by Rod himself. The connection itself was flimsy. He was the son-in-law of Moncrieff's friend Mr. Finlayson, minister of this parish. However, the importance of a voyage to India is made clear. Rod had already sailed to China; he then commanded his own ship to the West Indies where he was shipwrecked by hurricanes in 1730. He now asked to go 1st mate on an East Indiaman rather than be in charge of his own ship to the West Indies, after experience and due consideration of both trades.

The appointment of *Thomas Ogilvie* was made in 1732 by Drummond in response to the request of Lady Anne Ogilvie of Fothringham, wife of the Earl of Hopetoun. She had been to India herself. It is a clear-cut example of a favour done in return for political support. In return Drummond and his masters were assured of the Hopetoun electoral interest.

James Lamb was appointed through Drummond's good offices in 1732, but died on his first voyage. Meanwhile, Drummond had already ensured Supercargo *Naish's* passage to India in 1731. It was done in response to the wish of his brother William and of his friend Sir Matthew Decker. Naish was a brother of Dr. Naish of Rowen, an acquaintance who lived near the family home at Blair. Supercargos invariably disembarked at a Presidency and set themselves up as free-merchants.[33]

Other Scots found a route out to India as ships surgeons or surgeon's mates (posts which were usually abandoned upon arrival). The career of George Threipland from 1724 (as shown already) and that of *Commander Elliot* exemplify this method. The latter was sent to Bencoolen, Sumatra in 1727, at the request of Lord Milton and Governor Carnegie. In turn, Carnegie had been granted his Governor's post in Bencoolen through Milton's understanding with Drummond.

Sumatra was a miserable post where life expectancy was poor. Fortunately though, with luck and the type of backing Governor Carnegie could procure, Elliot made a fortune. What brought it all about, as far as Drummond and Milton were concerned, was the fact that Governor Carnegie had 'useful connections in Forfar and Aberdeen'. The Governor's own promotion and that of Elliot had followed accordingly.[34]

Free Traders who were assisted to go search for wealth in the Indies are well represented by a young accountant, *George Fothringham*. In 1725 Sir Peter Halkett of Pittfirrine recommended him to Drummond, introducing him as a man of standing. In fact, Fothringham typified countless younger sons who had to go abroad to earn a living. He had only £2,000 (Scots) but was intent upon embarking as a trader or free merchant. Halkett concluded his recommendation with the sort of flattery that Drummond was to hear very often, albeit that it was true: 'the proofs you have given of your friendship to gentlemen of this country are so well known that many are solicitous to be recommended to your favour ... you know best what can be done.'[35]

8

Drummond's powers of patronage increased in the decade 1732 to 1742. The Abercairney manuscripts alone indicate that over twenty ships surgeon and free merchant positions were found; and at least thirty posts within the Company's civil service were filled by needy Scots. Such numbers, while reflecting his continued powers of patronage, also indicate the ever-stronger political links being forged between the Scottish lairds and his own political masters through his agency.

In general Drummond's bursts of activity in distributing patronage coincided with the lead-up to elections, such as those of 1727 and 1734. But there was a steady bestowal of favours through the years, determined of course by the availability or otherwise of posts. From 1733 in particular, following his alignment with Ilay, his devotion to serving the Argathelian and ministerial interests was marked by the increased patronage he brought to bear. His formidable power inside the Company is typified by John Home, in a letter to Drummond in 1732, giving thanks for making him Governor of Bombay in succession to Governor Cowan.[36]

From 1732 Drummond commenced sending out medical graduates to the Company's Bengal Presidency in marked numbers. *Surgeons Drummond* and *Robinson* went out on the *Drake* and received Dr. Littlejohn's help when they arrived at Fort William. *Surgeon Andrew Munro* arrived in 1733. He was later to minister to the dying Charles Carmichael, Lady Hyndford's son.[37] *Dr. Robert Douglas*, a Surgeon, was to become Principal Medical Officer at Madras. He was a kinsman of the Earl of Morton (Douglases). Drummond, who was the Earl's friend, used his influence to have him promoted. Dr. Douglas became a friend of John Haliburton while at Fort St. George, returning to Scotland enriched, in 1742.[38]

Another was *Peter Oliphant*. He was the brother of Laurence Oliphant of Gask who pleaded with Drummond on his behalf. His application was also supported by the Earl of Morton and in India by Governor Cowan and John Haliburton. He was appointed to Fort St. George in 1732 and from there went to Gombroon until 1741. *William Monteith*, a Ships Surgeon was another assisted because he was a cousin of Thomas Shairp of Houston House. Monteith informed his cousin that he had help in obtaining the post through the influence of General Dalziel of the Binns.[39]

All of these appointments, on land or on board ship, exemplify the excellence of Scottish medical training and highlight the profusion of trained doctors and surgeons in Scotland searching for and finding posts abroad. In turn they reflect the dearth of openings at home and the limited choice available without connections. Only through people like John Drummond could the middle and upper classes provide for their sons, doing so in return for pledged votes.

Of course the journey east and the climate to be faced brought heavy risks. Many of those sent out by Drummond died soon after arrival, like 'young Arbuthnot' dead in 1732, the year he went out; and 'Mrs. Smith's son', who died in Fort William that same year. Others lasted a little longer. John Cleland died in 1733, after a year's residence; Henry Crawfurd after nine years. Crawfurd's connections were extensive: his brothers Gideon, John and George resided (and commanded an interest) in Scotland. In India Henry had benefited from the friendships of Governor Pitt and Commander Fasham Nairne – both close to Drummond.[40]

Another feature of Drummond's patronage was the help given to 'ladies of quality', either in their efforts to get to India or in assisting friends. Their (generally successful) pursuit of these favours was striking, reflecting the influence they commanded, directly or otherwise. For instance, as early as 1724 Lady Ramsden of Byram had managed to get him to send her son James Ramsden out to India.

In 1732 Lord Cathcart urged Drummond to find a Miss Ballantyne a passage. She was on good terms with Lady Suffolk and Lady Betty Germain, among others. The damsel arrived in 1733, the same year as a Mrs. Baird, whose desire to go out was brought to Drummond's attention by Lords Abercromby and Morton. Also, Elizabeth, Lady Hyndford (and

Sir Thomas Frederick) pressed Drummond to get her son Charles Carmichael and her nephews, (Surgeon) Michael and George Carmichael, out to good positions. They arrived in Surat in 1733 and were placed under the wing of Henry Lowther.

Charles Carmichael's case perfectly illuminates the influence of a powerful figure like Lady Hyndford. Apart from being a big landowner in her own right in East Lothian, she could influence her husband and the Lowthers, and help Drummond at elections. In the case of George Carmichael, she instructed Drummond that he was to be 'fitted out' for abroad in sea or land service, 'not too low', at Fort St. George.

Again in 1733 the Countess of Errol, writing from Slaines Castle, prevailed upon Drummond to get a Mr. Fergusson's friend, Mr. Irvine, sent out Ships surgeon's mate. Then, that same year, she and the Earl Marischal gained (through Drummond's good offices) a post for John Forbes as a crew member of the *Harrington*, commanded by Captain Jenkins. Already in 1732 Drummond had obliged the Duchess of Atholl and Lady Ann Ogilvie.

Even as early as 1713, in his first dealings with the East India Company and before he was a Director, he had been able to oblige Mrs. Patricia Stevenson of Edinburgh by ensuring her brother William was made chaplain at St Mary's church, Fort St. George. But to cap all these instances of Drummond's grace and favour towards ladies, and to illustrate further the potency of the system that operated through him, one that reached to the highest in the land, Queen Caroline contacted him in 1733 through her Secretary, John Eckersall, to obtain a Writership for a friend.[41]

In the 1730s Drummond's India patronage continued to be used extensively by leading figures in Scottish politics and society. Patrick Sandilands, son of Lord Torphicen of Calder House, is a good example. Not only did Drummond find him the command of an East Indiaman, but ensured that the young man would receive the support of Governors Cowan, Wake and Home, and of the stalwart, Henry Lowther.

In another instance, Sir Hew Dalrymple of North Berwick, and his cousin James Home of Garnelshiel asked Drummond, Sir Matthew Decker and ex-Governor Harrison to find Home's half-brother, William Rigg a Writer's post. He subsequently went to Fort St. George in 1733, and from there to Bencoolen where he died in 1746. William Rigg had pleaded, in turn, with Drummond on behalf of his friend Oliver Stewart; and the two had joined up briefly in Fort St. George in 1737. That year Drummond also despatched to Madras a Matthew Coutts of the London banking family, with whom he was on friendly terms. Governor Pitt was asked to take particular care of him.[42]

Other friends and powerful interests were very well served – such as a Mr. Alexander and the Earl of Tweeddale. The latter persuaded Drummond to send the young brother of his friend, Mr. Hay of Bolton, out to a vacancy. The same Mr. Hay used Lord Errol's good graces with Drummond to get their mutual protégé John Buchan out.

Sir John Clerk of Penicuik asked Drummond to send his friend Mr. Gabriel Rankin to Bombay as a surgeon. Upon arrival the young man was placed in the safekeeping of Governor Cowan. Then in 1741 the Earl of Morton was highly satisfied when he (and John Haliburton, at Fort St. George) joined with Drummond in establishing Captain David Robertson in the coastal trade. It was an occupation sustained until 1760. Captain Robertson – who retired to Musselburgh – met up with David Rannie (Henry Dundas' future father-in-law) who in these years was also seeking his fortune, first as a Supercargo then as a free merchant, along the same coast.[43]

In assisting the Queen's friend, Drummond's help can be seen to embrace the exalted and the unusual. He also received a letter from the celebrated poet Alexander Pope in August 1724, thanking him for providing his nephew with a third mate's berth. In 1729 he was responsible for the settlement in Leith of '21 foreigners' who were provided by him with houses and looms, and 'set to work to spin.' These entries referred to Flemish weavers who would live at (and give the name of their homeland) to Picardy Place in Edinburgh. Their spokesman with Drummond was one called M. Daseville. Sometimes Drummond even interested himself in finding posts for those not so highly placed in Scottish society. For instance, in 1738 a John McCulloch applied to him, and was successful in getting a job in the Company's warehouse in London. But this was a rare occurrence.[44]

9

To summarize, Walpole's steadfast aim was to maintain a United Kingdom and the government thereof, and all patronage (including that of the East India Company and its shipping) was administered with this in mind. The threat of a break-up of the new Britain was very real; and the coronation of George I, followed so quickly by the 1715 rebellion made the English Whig ministry realise that it needed the support of a Scottish lobby. London feared what the threat of Scottish patriotism and Jacobitism might do to that lobby; so the Scottish dimension was boosted, and all manner of favours were used as sweeteners.

In the first instance John Scrope acted as the main channel. Then, from around 1725, as traced here, with help from John Drummond, Walpole took things much further. Precedence was given to Scottish applications for patronage; and the favours that India House offered became significant in this rapid development because they were so available, useful, and frantically coveted by the Scottish landowners he wished to influence. (Later, Townshend, Stanhope and Sunderland would follow this policy rigorously).

The task of fostering such patronage and putting it into operation was placed in the hands of the Argathelians and Drummond. It was hoped this move would in time eradicate the twin threats to the Union – Scottish separatism and Jacobitism. It was not envisaged at the time, however, just how effective India patronage would be towards achieving these ends, or the jobs and wealth so created.[45]

Through Drummond, East India Company favours found their way into a great many mansion houses of the Scottish ruling classes. Yet, while recruiting voters with influence and functioning as an integral part of the governmental patronage system, he always appeared to work as a friend. Nevertheless, despite such an outward show, political influence always determined where his favours would go – favours that brought the prospect of fabulous wealth. He helped the elite of Scottish society, those who held the essential political bargaining counters. Influence among the superiorities and wadsetters was everything, this is what counted when it came to elections. The landed classes were helped by Drummond precisely because of the influence they could bring to bear among those who had votes in their respective localities.[46]

He and Administration put enormous effort into management of the political substructure of Scotland. Support for the ministry that existed among the privileged classes was pulled firmly together; and in so doing Scottish resentment of the Union was probably bereft of the leadership required to threaten the pro-Hanover Whigs.

Persuading leading Jacobites to return to the Establishment fold for the sake of family rewards was also sound policy. The southern English might have found it difficult to accept, but he understood their influence with many Scottish voters. This is illustrated by the posts given to friends and relations of suspect Jacobite families.[47] Drummond was trying to do in practical terms what the British government had accepted theoretically that the 'solution to the problem of influential Scots Jacobites was re-integration into and reconciliation with the existing Whig establishment in Church and State.'[48]

He further understood that the Whig Hanoverian government wanted to: 'conciliate the Scottish aristocracy and draw it back into the orbit of the existing political ascendancy. The last thing it wanted to do was to purge it ruthlessly from an institution of local government whose status it was anxious to enhance.'[49] Scottish nationalistic sentiments and patriotism were partially linked with Jacobitism in the 1700s; and every method (social, economic, political and finally military) was used to try and douse it. End Jacobitism, it was believed, give out rewards, and the threat to the Union would disappear.

Placing Company patronage in Scottish hands, certainly gave Caledonians opportunities to share in the riches and other spoils available in India. Moreover, these favours did stimulate support for the Union, helped its survival and continuance, and rendered the '45 rebellion impotent. In the years that followed, this patronage was further used to deliberately weaken, dampen and finally suck the heart out of Scottish Jacobitism.

Maintenance of British stability and the Union continued to be the watch-words, and India patronage continued to be useful to future ministries. Neither the favours nor the methods by which these were channelled for government use dried up, and continued to prove adaptable and expedient during future crises. The India connection was to remain one of the major stabilizing forces coursing through British society. Its importance is apparent from governmental involvement as well as from the quality and quantity of the Scottish landed classes touched by this patronage throughout most of the century.

John Drummond's contribution to Scottish politics proved as important as his earlier involvement in Anglo-Dutch relations; and was executed in a typically discreet manner. He also influenced the socio-economic development of Scotland in an indirect way. The wealth of the returned Nabobs he had helped create had begun to impact upon the fabric of the land. After 1742 he was gone and the patronage format changed slightly with new players taking the stage. But the aims and function of the system that developed with him from the early 1720s to his death remained.

Tributes flooded in. Sir Matthew Decker's was particularly moving. He had lived in friendship for forty years and upward with this 'worthy honest man'. He thought Drummond's death 'a loss to your Scotch Nation to whom (at least to many) he has been a beneficial protector, even to a fault'. And the Scottish politician Andrew Mitchell was moved to write, 'I wish I could say there were many now alive whose benevolence and generosity equalled his'.[50]

6

Operating from Scotland 1742–61

1

The regular but unobtrusive use of India patronage continued, but as the years progressed the form of London ministries and the situations faced by them determined that there would be a change in how the system worked. The Jacobite rising in 1745 would cause a new wariness among English MPs; and they also became aware of major social, economic and intellectual changes afoot in Scotland. This all added to the unease felt in the south.

Elsewhere Britain was increasingly involved in wars with her European neighbours and in a struggle for mastery in the Americas and the Indies. Unstable ministries led to the onset of political contests in Parliament, while controversy and a power struggle erupted at the India House. Yet the solidarity of the Union had to be maintained despite the gathering storms. In fact political stability was crucial at this time of global change and expansion by the British state. All methods of achieving political management had to be updated, including India patronage. Britishness still had to be stimulated in every way possible.

Drummond's death in 1742 and changing circumstances meant that the manner of operating the India patronage machine would in some respects be different. Although the basic pattern remained and the same London and Company contacts retained, the social and political milieu now demanded that a network operate from Scotland with placement determined by agents working from there. John Drummond had dispensed favours from London with the approval of Argyll and blessing of Walpole. Those not known to him or his family had been indicated by

Argyll and Ilay, and by their man of business, Lord Milton. In this manner loyal Whigs and favourites of the Argethelian leaders were served and control maintained. After 1742 all India patronage that was in the Government's hands to give was dispensed in Scotland through Ilay and Milton.

Apart from Ilay and some others at Court, Milton relied upon the support of establishment figures like Sir Gilbert Elliot, James Stuart Mackenzie (brother of the Earl of Bute) and William Mure of Caldwell. And although he had to deal with strong, independent forces in Scotland he was helped by the clamp-down following the '45.

He was aided too by the prizes on offer following the Battle of Plassey in 1757; by the clamour of Scots striving to send their sons out to India to share in the riches; not to mention the attempts made by those servants already there to help friends and relations get out. There were repercussions in the Company too, as returned servants entered Company politics in force from 1756, determined to acquire control of the Direction.

Following the '45, Ilay and Milton were soon able to add positions in the Company's army to those that Drummond had commanded in the civil and naval branches. Only the cauterizing effect of Culloden appears to have softened ministerial attitudes towards Scots and established their credibility in English eyes. Before long regiments of Scots were gathered and despatched to India to secure Company possessions against natives and rival Companies alike.

2

Given the course of events at Westminster it was probably as well for the future of the British state that the administration of Scotland, after the long period of Walpole's rule, was still on a sound footing. In this sense Ilay's control of the political management structure in Scotland and use of India patronage there serves as more than just background material. The '45 was to have no major effect upon the deployment of patronage and favours so firmly laid down in previous years; nor did the highly unsettled nature of politics at Westminster lead to the collapse of the system. It might even be argued that it was because Scotland was so peaceful that squabbling could take place elsewhere.

A result of the incoherence in English politics in the 1740s and 1750s was the degree to which Scotland fell under Ilay's control. This development was also helped by his own strength and the fact that he shared in and continued to pursue pro-Hanoverian policies regarding the management of Scotland. This meant keeping the peace, employing all the patronage he could muster, and satisfying the wishes of those in Scotland politically powerful enough to do serious damage to the status quo.

India patronage, accordingly, remained part and parcel of Ilay's hoard of bargaining counters. It was important in helping sustain his own paramount position and also for pursuit of those same pro-Hanoverian policies for Scotland. In the eyes of Westminster politicians this India patronage was now a firm part of the currency used to entwine Parliamentary wishes with those of the Scottish political and social elite.

The eighteen years, between Walpole's fall in 1742 and that of Chatham in 1761, saw power pass rapidly from one group in Westminster to another. Carteret gave way to Henry Pelham in 1744, and his death in 1754 in turn led to a number of shifting alliances and re-groupings within the Whig oligarchy. However, Newcastle's stewardship and marshalling of patronage went a long way towards determining proceedings at Court and in Parliament. Cavendish had been followed by Chatham in 1757 and his resignation had allowed the Earl of Bute, espoused by the new monarch, George 111, to form a ministry. Dislike of Bute at Westminster, English phobia of Scots and public disgust at the terms of the Seven Years War peace formula, largely negotiated by Bute, forced his resignation in 1763. Grenville's troubled ministry was short, ending in 1765.

Yet despite such a multitude of changes, the underlying attitude of Westminster politicians towards Scotland remained constant: to continue the system of political supervision there, and with it grant as much crown, legal and ecclesiastical patronage as could be spared. Favours from the East India Company were looked for and Parliamentary figures lent themselves to securing them, when and where possible. But the shifts of power in London somewhat jumbled and blurred the lines of control and responsibility for Scottish affairs. From 1742 there was a short-lived revival of the Scottish Secretary post, in the person of Tweeddale, but it came to an end with the Jacobite rebellion; and from 1746 to 1754 Newcastle, as Secretary for the North, held the responsibility entailed.

The connection between the Secretaryship for the North and ministerial responsibility for Scotland continued, but the Treasury became increasingly involved in Scottish affairs through revenue collection – although from a political and administrative standpoint this influence had already been heavily used by Walpole and his successor Pelham. Similarly, by virtue of the legal complexities involved in the day to day moulding of laws passed in Parliament for English consumption, to the distinctive

Scottish legal and administrative reality, Lord Chancellor Hardwicke's influence grew there too.

3

Nevertheless, in Scotland after Walpole's fall in 1742 and that of John, Duke of Argyll in 1743, Ilay came into his own as the fount of all patronage of importance. He was 61 years of age when he became 3rd Duke in 1743 and was one of the Scottish elected peers in every Parliament until his death in 1761, aged 79. Outside of the 16 elected Scottish Representative Peers, Scots who were created Peers of Great Britain after 1707 were excluded from the House of Lords until 1782. They were usually to be found as Lords of the Bedchamber. Ilay was able to utilise the patronage opportunities this situation offered. Also, Members could be a potential source of trouble to the ministry if not under proper control; and it was his job to ensure that they attended the House and voted with Government. Distribution of the patronage at his command was how this was paid for.[1]

Walpole's fall temporarily split the Whig phalanx, and as seen, in Scotland (from 1742) the Squadrone again enjoyed a brief period of influence, particularly with the appointments of Mar, Montrose, Roxburgh and Tweeddale as successive Secretaries of State between 1742 and 1746. They too operated from London; and like Ilay, who depended upon Milton, also kept political agents in Edinburgh to do their bidding. Baron William Mure was to perform the same duty for Bute and his brother Stuart Mackenzie.

However, by 1744 Pelham had succeeded Carteret and taken over Walpole's mantle of power. He found Ilay very acceptable, despite all Tweeddale's efforts to create a contrary impression of him. The new Duke of Argyll proved a powerful and wily ally at Westminster; and he had command of an infrastructure in Scotland that more or less guaranteed the continuance of political management there in his interest. Thus by 1744 Ilay was really in charge, and continued so throughout the rebellion and afterwards, when the last fears of Jacobitism had subsided.

4

The Jacobites were helped in that the fall of Walpole in 1742 had left a power vacuum in Scotland and England, and with Whig strength divided the scene was set. The movement was helped by the absence of strong forces in the Highlands, and by the fact that law-abiding Chiefs were in the minority.[2] Before the rebellion the Government's aim was to contain the Highlands as a hostile political region and the Dukes of Argyll were consulted in this capacity. Containment obviously did not work, however, and after the '45 ministerial intention was to integrate the Highlands with the rest of Britain. At a political and military level this policy was 'pursued extensively and with great determination', because the ministry had received a real fright.[3]

Ilay had helped subdue the rebellion, but thereafter favoured a gentle wearing away of the Jacobites from their old connections – redirecting them towards the new Hanoverian order 'with an emphasis on economic improvement rather than political repression.'[4] Pelham's willingness to use the Argathelians allowed them their opportunity to push for such assimilation; and the Pelham–Argyll link was very good for Scotland and the Jacobites, lasting until the English minister's death in 1754.[5]

One of Ilay's ideas was the formation of Highland regiments after the '45.[6] His lead was followed by lieutenants in Scotland. At the same time, Duncan Forbes of Culloden suggested that although the rebellion began in Scotland most Scots were 'well affected' and that counting them in with the rebels would cause trouble. No disadvantage, he argued, should be shown to the Scots.[7]

What happened in effect, was that the policies of liberal patronage, political management and integration prevailed, despite the '45 – although the traumatic effect of the rebellion on English statesmen was reflected in the hardening of views towards anything remotely Scottish. Fortunately, good work by Pelham, Ilay and Milton helped batten-down anti-Scots feelings to some extent; and by turning aside much of the political rancour, averted any real threat to the political stability of the kingdom.

Ilay's triumph over the Squadrone, together with his stance over the '45, where his loyalty to the Hanoverians was never in doubt (but neither was compassion for his countrymen) helped him continue as the channel to and from Westminster and as the executor of Scottish business. Until his death he was in control of immense patronage pertaining to Scotland; and contrary to former belief, used India patronage on a wide scale.[8]

By 1754 there was no real opposition to the Argathelians and Ilay continued to control Scotland on behalf of Government.[9] He was able to use £1000 from the Secret Service fund to spend in the 1754 elections; and although not a princely sum it indicated the strength of the Pelham–Ilay understanding. It was evidence of ministerial support for returning loyal voters in Scotland; and it built confidence among Ilay's henchmen: Milton, Erskine, Buccleuch, Scrope and Maule.[10]

Thus the years 1746 to 1761 constitute a period of stability in Scotland under Ilay although the Scottish electoral system was distorted further to fit the political aims of the Scottish upper classes. Burgh votes continued to be gained through bribery and patronage; county representation was vouchsafed through the creation of fictitious votes. Landed wealth enjoyed unassailable control over Scottish politics. Only in the 1760s did uncertainty and some instability appear again.

5

The Townshend MSS. and especially the letters of John Dalrymple to Townshend in the late 1750s, reflect this very tight-knit world of the leading aristocracy. The power of Ilay and Milton is given full expression. For example, John Dalrymple maintained both had managed affairs so that Andrew Stuart was given his chance in the Douglas case. He knew that 'Milton has one of his own clerks who is Secretary to the Post Office, opening letters'.[11]

Elections were of the utmost importance to the aristocracy, and the lead-up to them had the effect of developing incredible secrecy in their ranks. Quietly, even stealthily, the word was passed around and the desires of the leading superiors were made known. For example, Milton indicated to the advocate Richard Campbell of Arkinch in 1758 that Ilay preferred Provost Roseneath for the forthcoming election in his burgh, and so it came to pass.[12]

Yet, although Scottish business was in Ilay's hands he still had to deal with the jealousy of Newcastle. Such was the Duke's enmity, Ilay suspected that he was attempting to build a new Scottish management structure. In fact it was Newcastle's fear of Ilay's strength and independence in Scotland that drove him once again to stir-up enemies of the Argathelians, such as the Dundases of Arniston, Findlater and Deskford.

Robert Dundas of Arniston, a cousin of Henry Dundas, enjoyed extensive patronage of his own. No love was lost between himself and Milton and he employed Sir David Moncrieffe to spy upon the Lord-Justice Clerk. Robert Dundas also enjoyed the confidence of Hardwicke the Lord Chancellor, and held vast legal patronage in Scotland.

Until 1754 Newcastle kept up his hostility to Ilay, but by 1755 had lost control of Scotland to him. This did not mean to say, however, that they would now agree. In 1759 they were still arguing over its administration and political management; and Newcastle even tried to give Mansfield control of patronage there. This short reverse was marked by Ilay's temporary loss of control over the Scots MPs at Westminster. However, Henry Fox, Ilay's friend, gradually won Newcastle round.[13]

Such hostility meant that Ilay found it difficult at times to get Scottish business done in London. The Scots north of the border regarded him almost as a Viceroy, but they would also go over his head if they had the ear of a leading English minister. Yet despite Treasury influence, the meddling of Newcastle and the Lord Chancellor's interference, it was Ilay, until he died in 1761, who dominated Scottish affairs; and who through Lord Milton kept strong reins on the management of Scotland. However, because Ilay's system had been so personalised it could not long survive his death; and with his passing the political management of Scotland became more uncertain.[14]

It was probably visible from 1756 that control of the northern part of Britain might fall into the hands of Ilay's nephew, the Earl of Bute. This view was certainly strengthened by his growing stature with the future George III. Meanwhile, in the same period, Chatham was building bridges that brought him in touch with the field of Scottish political management. Gilbert Elliot of Minto, Bute's great friend, had secured a seat in Parliament in 1754 through Ilay. Thereafter he acted as a go-between for Chatham and Ilay in their London business and as the link man with Lord Milton, Ilay's agent in Edinburgh.[15]

6

From the 1740s to the 1760s the disposal of India patronage in Scotland on behalf of the Government was in the hands of Andrew Fletcher of Saltoun, Lord Milton, the Lord-Justice Clerk.[16] Milton's power was perhaps best described by a contemporary, Sir Hew Dalrymple of North Berwick, who in 1760 said, 'It can reflect no dishonour on me to be overpowered by Milton who has been for 20 years past the absolute dispenser of every office and every favour from the crown, and whose power over the Duke of Argyll [Ilay] has got all his Grace's interest'.[17]

It proved impossible to oust Milton from that position throughout those years, despite the efforts of the Duke of Newcastle and Lord Chancellor, Hardwicke. Sir Hew Dalrymple again makes this clear: 'Cockburn [Sir James, of Langton, Berwickshire] goes about shouting against Milton's name, but all presents come now from Milton and no way under the direction of any English minister'.[18]

In fact Milton undertook the duties of a sort of Scottish manager, a 'sous-ministre', although there was no constitutional precedent for this and it is almost impossible to generalise about functions and characteristics. Helping things along was the fact that Milton's son, Andrew Fletcher, served as Ilay's private secretary. Only the Englishman John Scrope (from 1708 to 1724) had acted in a position that was in some ways similar to Milton's, representing Westminster views in Scotland. William Mure of Caldwell would do the same for Bute's brother, James Stuart Mackenzie, in the early 1760s.[19]

Milton was an exceptional man whose energy knew no bounds. As well as acting 'as a delegate for and channel of communication with the Scottish ministers in London', he looked after Government interests in Scotland as well as those of the Argathelian group.[20] He presented suitable candidates, be they Representative Peers for the House of Lords, or for Parliamentary elections, bye-elections or town council politics, especially those in Edinburgh. He distributed patronage at all levels.

It is claimed for him that he 'awakened among men of fortune an emulation to unite in promoting industry and knowledge'; and was an 'eminent patriot who stood in the gap and saved our country from sinking into ruin'.[21] The assessment is probably correct when it is considered that he served on the Commission of Annexed Estates, promoted Scottish banking, being a founder of the British Linen Bank in 1746, and was Deputy Governor of the Royal Bank. The Directorships there were filled by his friends, like Tinwald, Drumure and Provost William Alexander, with Duncan Forbes of Culloden as a trustee.[22]

He was virtually in command of civil administration in Scotland from 1740; and it was fortunate for Jacobites, for Scotland and for political leaders in Westminster that he was there. His 'humanity and clemency' after the '45 is well attested; and he 'preserved and restored many unhappy persons and families'.[23] He presented so many pleas asking mercy for Jacobites that he was in danger of being suspected in many quarters, especially in London, of 'countenancing Jacobites too much.'[24]

He could be accused in this way despite the fact that in liaison with the Duke of Newcastle he had ensured that every Justice of the Peace in Scotland was a non-Jacobite and 'handpicked in the counties'.[25] In many cases he was quite hard in his jurisdiction, but like Drummond of Quarrel before him, Milton knew the importance of re-integration and reconciliation.

Known Jacobites who could be assimilated were treated kindly. Cumming of Pitulie, Graham of Airth the Younger, Hamilton of Reidhouse and John Hay, W.S., were in this category.[26] However, following Pelham's death in 1754, Lord Chancellor Hardwicke squeezed identifiable Jacobites off the various official Commissions, especially in

Invernesshire. He thus thwarted the original intention of allowing them to gradually fill posts, such as Justices of the Peace – in doing so being absorbed into the new political regime.

There was a need, therefore, for India patronage in this post-Culloden, and particularly, post-Pelham period. Ilay and Milton determined upon the use of Indian favours to cajole and entice Jacobite sympathisers into reconciliation and acceptance of the Hanoverians and the Union. This patronage was not conspicuous enough, however, to cause outrage elsewhere in Whig circles; and it could be managed and directed quietly and without fuss.[27]

Such 'management' is seen in the Milton–Haldane tie-up. It is almost certain that Captain Robert Haldane and his nephew, Captain James Haldane, carried Jacobite sympathisers to India. Certainly Robert Haldane was mentioned in the *Jacobite Journal* of 1748 and James became Captain of the aptly named Indiaman the *Duke of Albany*. There is no trace of Jacobitism, however, in the Haldane family, and it appears that they were fulfilling the wishes of their friend Milton in transporting them east.[28]

The appointment in 1762 to the Captaincy of the *Duke of Albany* of Alexander Stewart, eldest son of the Jacobite Stewart of Ardshiel, was certainly due to the influence of Ilay and Milton. Stewart succeeded Captain James Haldane in the post.[29]

Captain Alexander Macleod of the *Lord Mansfield* gave a similar service, providing a recognised escape route for Highland Jacobites. Although not a Jacobite himself, his father had been 'out' in the '15 and the '45, and this probably explains his sympathies. The ship's surgeon on the *Lord Mansfield*, for example, was the Jacobite Alexander Macdonald of Skye.[30] Captain William Fullarton Elphinstone provided the same kind of service. His grand-uncle was the Jacobite George Keith, 10th Earl Marischal of Scotland, who nevertheless still had influence he could bring to bear.[31]

Yet another example of this activity concerned Baillie John Stewart, a merchant in Inverness who sent one of his sons to India using Government-inspired India patronage. He was owner and part-owner of a dozen ships, skippered by highland gentlemen, kinsmen or sons-in-law. He was sympathetic to the Jacobites and used his Whig friends to help them.

Finally, there was John Stewart, son of the Jacobite Archibald Stewart, who in turn was a brother of Sir James Stewart of Allanbank. By 1759 John Stewart was a partner in his father's wine-merchant business in York Buildings, London, which had been set up after the '45. By the mid–1760s John worked hand in glove with the adventurer Lauchlin Macleane, with a cousin, John Stewart, wine merchant in the Strand, and with Sir James

Cockburn furthering the careers of his kinsmen through the East India Company. Most of this help was given in the free-for-all years of 1765–1774 and it reflects the fact that to outward appearances at least, most Jacobites had become very nearly good Whigs.[32]

India patronage, although a substantial contribution, nevertheless formed only part of an arsenal of favours at Milton's command; and his disposal of the most important posts has been well-documented elsewhere. Narrow political power, such as control over and management of elections was what mattered. Milton alone was in charge of Ilay's 'Scottish Machine', using it to 'support the candidature of friends by providing short-term election packages and long-term servicing of constituencies.'[33]

As Shaw tells us, Milton and the Argathelians monopolized the administration of all patronage in Scotland created by Government at Westminster. Besides India patronage, this meant control over the Court of Delegates, dealing with claims against the forfeited estates; the Board of Customs; the Board of Trustees for Fisheries and Manufactures; and the Annexed Estates Commission. It was the same with regard to Scottish independent institutions such as the Convention of Royal Burghs and the Royal Bank of Scotland. He also controlled Members of Parliament, when and where he could; Lords of Session and ministers of religion.

Although Milton directed and implemented policy in Scotland he was not alone. He supervised a network of Government men, keeping them in order and lined up in support. Most were personal friends and allies; and if not were in some form of vassalage to Ilay or other Argathelians. Patronage was channelled through them according to importance, rank and usefulness.

Naturally their own families were attended to first when the need arose, but always the political motive was present. More than anything else it was imperative that those powerful enough to influence the superiorities and wadsetters at elections should be served. These Government men (and supporters deliberately placed in important Scottish institutions) ensured that arrangements were manipulated to advantage. Some were greater or lesser activists according to ability, but all operated in the Argathelian interest. In Scotland control of vital institutions and management of elections for Ilay mattered; and local knowledge and influence were always important.

It was essential to have a man of Milton's calibre in Scotland. He was the 'political fixer' needed for Ilay's system to work; the 'dynamic operator' who used his connections and superior knowledge of the

Scottish situation.[34] Like his uncle, Andrew Fletcher of Saltoun, the great patriot, he was a realist and understood what the 1707 Union had done to Scotland politically. This he faced up to; and managed Scotland on behalf of Ilay and his Westminster masters because he believed that he was doing the right thing. He was also fortunate in being able to pursue a normal course of serving both himself and the public interest.[35]

7

The systematised use of India patronage, as outlined – and clearly visible in the 1720s and 1730s, under the control of Walpole and John Drummond of Quarrel – passed in the 1740s and 1750s to Ilay and Lord Milton. Just as Drummond had been the mainstay in the operation of the earlier system so Milton was in the latter.

The number of powerful people he was in touch with is staggering. Even when the scope is narrowed by identifying only those concerned with the operation of India patronage, and not even counting the young men who actually benefited from it, well over a hundred people are positively identified. A great many others too, mainly landowners, can be regarded, from meaningful evidence, as being in receipt of India patronage in return for political support. It is useful to categorise some of the most important of the people involved in the provision of this India patronage to show how far flung was Milton's web, from John o'Groats to Westminster; and by selecting various individuals demonstrate in the clearest way the operation of the system in the Ilay–Milton period, up to 1761.[36]

As indicated, subordinate to Ilay and Milton there operated an executive-cum-administrative group, one which was quite tight-knit. In England it consisted of Sir Gilbert Elliot in the Admiralty and John Scrope at the Treasury. Their knowledge was added to by those scraps of information forwarded by Milton's London spies: John Somerville, David Scott and James Oswald. Those from within the Scottish establishment included Baron Maule, Tinwald, Duncan Forbes, James Erskine, Lord Grange and John Mackenzie of Delvine. They were aided by a network of agents and spies throughout Scotland, such as George Lind, Provosts Drummond, McAuley and Lindsay, all of Edinburgh; and Quinton Crawford, George Cheape, George Irving, Alex Ross, John Home and Patrick Cumming in various burghs.

Milton's county influence was firmly based upon landed gentry connections, such as his own in East Lothian; those of the Fletcher family in Angus and Fife; his mother, Margaret Carnegie of Pittcarow, in

Kincardineshire; those of his wife, Elizabeth Kinloch of Gilmerton, in Midlothian; and other kinsmen besides. Others related to him in one way or another included: Roseberry, Caithness and Fife; Carnegie of Southesk; Kinnoul; and the families of Kingston, Halkett, Bruce-Balfour, Dalrymple, Stewart, Campbell of Burnbank, the Wedderburns of Gosford – and the Middletons, who were also related to Ilay.[37]

Others in England invaluable for the operation of his system were Colonel John Middleton (Ilay's uncle) and George Middleton the banker. Milton was also intimate with the London-based Coutts family of bankers; with *Campbell and Bruce's* bank; and with Edward Harrison, who had become Governor of the Bank of England.[38] Inside the East India Company he was familiar with some of the most powerful Directors and Proprietors, as well as shippers and Company servants from all branches.[39] In Scotland he dispensed the patronage received from Scots within the Company; from ministerial connections with that body; and favours that came from other powerful men, like the all-knowing Laurence Sulivan.

To do this properly he involved lawyers like John Mackenzie of Delvine, Maule, Erskine and Duncan Forbes – as already mentioned. They, together with John Davidson and James Burnett brought Milton up-to-the-minute information on the strength of political affiliations at the grass-roots; and in turn served as vehicles for carrying patronage to the right destinations. Members of Ilay's own entourage were used too, both as landowners with political power attached to their properties and for their connections at Westminster and within India House.[40]

Many leading figures of the day who were Milton supporters, such as Lords Grange and Belhaven enjoyed India patronage; as did William Alexander, James Campbell of Restalrig, James Osborne, James Colquhoun and Robert Montgomery, all of Edinburgh. The aid given David Rannie of Musselburgh and George Ogilvie of Cullen was typical of the way India patronage was spread within the burghs.

In the landward areas the presence and influence of this patronage is perhaps documented best of all. Milton's grasp of how the minds of the middling lairds worked was based on his own background at Saltoun, outside Haddington. John Clerk of Penicuik, Sir Hew Dalrymple of North Berwick, Sir James Foulis of Colinton would all be as much known to him in the market-place as they were in the salon. Fife lairds like Thomas Hope of Rankeillor and James Cheape of Strathyrum were friends whose political support was eased along with the use of India patronage.[41]

Probably those lairds further away geographically from Edinburgh required more attention. Among those who benefited were Thomas

Dundas of Finigask, Orkney; Alexander Abercrombie of Banffshire; Patrick Duff of Premnay and Sir John Baird of Newbyth, MP – both Aberdeenshire. Others who profited were James Burnett of Monboddo and James Allardice of Allardice, both Kincardineshire; George Dempster of Dundee; Colonel John Graham of Kinross; Sir Alexander Grant of Invernesshire; the Johnstones of Westerhall, Dumfriesshire; and Sir James Agnew of Wigtownshire. Another was John Pringle of Haining, Selkirkshire. Most of those mentioned appear as MPs, hereditary Sheriffs, or as members of a family with the greatest influence and control in the various counties and burghs of Scotland between 1740 and 1774, and are discussed further below.[42]

The manner in which family connections, Argathelian loyalty and electoral significance came together to advance a career in the Indies can be further illustrated by the lives of Sir Robert Fletcher, the Munros of Foulis and the Stirlings of Keir. Fletcher's in particular, demonstrates just how effective a direct line to Milton could prove. The other two reveal how much the Milton–Argyll machine continued the Drummond–Walpole ties of earlier years.[43]

Robert Fletcher was the eldest son of the Jacobite Robert Fletcher of Ballinshoe, by Elizabeth Lyon, daughter of William Lyon of Carse, Angus. It was his mother's connection with Lord Milton and the guardianship bestowed upon him by this man, Scotland's charge d'affaires that began his incredible career. He owed everything to Milton who, when asked, moved him from naval service to a Writership in Madras in 1757; and had him transferred, subsequently, to the East India Company army.[44]

Fletcher had a life worth recording. Shortly after he began his army career he was knighted for gallantry in action, dismissed the Company for insolence, re-instated, then Court-martialled and cashiered. Allowed back into the Company's service he rose to the rank of Colonel. By 1773 he was in trouble again. The open hostility shown towards the Governor of Madras forced him into exile from his post in the Presidency. Back home he used membership of Parliament to influence his re-appointment to the Company's service, this time as a Brigadier-General. He then helped in the kidnap of the new Governor of Madras, Lord Pigot in 1775; placed the poor unfortunate in prison where he died; then expired himself on his way home in 1776.[45]

He truly lived up to the assessment made by a friend that he was 'a hotheaded and dangerous young man who will always be young.'[46] But the help given to Fletcher illustrates the lengths to which Milton would go to reconcile old Jacobite sympathies with the new order. His help to Fletcher had the blessing of many others, such as Fletcher's friend and contemporary Sir James Johnstone of Westerhall. By 1767 Fletcher had become aligned in Company politics with the Johnstones (sons of Sir James), with Laurence Sulivan and George Dempster.

Several men with the Munro surname carved glittering careers in India. In the military field there was Sir Hector Munro of Novar, the hero of Baksar, and Major-General Sir Thomas Munro, who later in the eighteenth century became Governor of Madras and was one of the ablest of soldiers and administrators. Another, a Robert Munro from Invernesshire, captained an East Indiaman from 1762 to the mid–1770s, making himself a fortune. Others, like George Munro, who became a Writer in the Company's civil line, reached India because they could pull enough strings.[47] But perhaps the most intriguing were those members of the *Munro of Foulis* family, from near Tain who went to India.

The presence of these Munros in the east is an excellent demonstration of the patronage and nepotism Milton allowed one of Scotland's leading families because of their strong electoral influence in Ross-shire. In 1718 a younger brother of Sir Robert Munro of Foulis was in Madras. By 1724 he had been joined by a cousin from Tain. They were both surgeons. Sir Robert's brother was Dr. Duncan Munro of Obsdale, Principal Medical Officer in Madras from 1720 to 1726. The other, Dr. Andrew Munro, was a surgeon there in 1724. They were both successful and long-lived: Duncan died in Bombay in 1746, Andrew in 1757.

They always ensured that the Foulis interest backed their own influence when securing positions in India for relations. Dr. Andrew Munro's son, Robert Duncan Munro, was secured a Writer's post in Madras, as was his nephew, George Smith of Fordyce. The son of Sir Robert Munro's other brother, Captain George Munro of Foulis, was found a position in Bombay. He was Dr. John Munro of Culcairn, and was to make friends in Bombay with Laurence Sulivan, which was to be useful to him later when Sulivan became Chairman and virtual ruler of the Company.

The Munros were clannish. George Smith of Fordyce shared in his uncle Dr. Andrew Munro's estate in 1757; and John Munro of Culcairn acted as executor of the will. The same John Munro of Culcairn received a third of his uncle Duncan Munro of Obsdale's estate when he died in 1746.

But apart from the India patronage they enjoyed, the really distinctive feature about these Munros was their dedication to the medical profession. It is intriguing that Duncan, Andrew and John Munro were contemporaries of the famous Munro family, beginning with the outstanding Dr. Alexander Munro, who dominated the Edinburgh

Medical School throughout the eighteenth century; and that these illustrious medical men commenced their work in 1726, just when their kinsmen were starting in Madras. They were a branch of the same Munros of Foulis.[48]

From 1720 to 1757 all the Principal Medical Officers of Madras were Scots: from Dr. Duncan Munro to Dr. George Ramsay, Dr. Matthew Lindsay, Dr. Andrew Munro, Dr. Robert Douglas and back to Dr. Andrew Munro again. It would appear that Munros were destined to inspire Scots medical societies wherever they settled.[49]

The *Stirlings of Keir* began their India connection in 1735 when Archibald Stirling, second son of James Stirling of Keir 'the Venetian' and of his wife, Marion, eldest daughter of Alex Stuart, Lord Blantyre, went out as purser on a ship to Bengal. He did this, according to his brother, because 'it offered him opportunities of getting a considerable quantity of goods on board.'[50] He also assumed Supercargo responsibilities.

The post of purser (and the £350 that it cost) came from Dr. Fullarton of Carberry; and he was also backed by Mr. Ochterlony, both friends and political allies of John Drummond of Quarrel. His elder brother, John Stirling, gave him credit to use for trading purposes in India; and with this backing he set himself up as a free-merchant in Bengal. By 1760 he was the 'biggest speculator in salt on the Company's new lands (around Chittagong, Bengal)' and by 1763 employed 13,000 men manufacturing this.[51]

This start given to Archibald Stirling, sending him on his way to a considerable fortune was possible in itself only because of the family's political influence in Stirling. It was a venal burgh and wooed by the Argathelians. Archibald's own position and that of his brother Harry, who was appointed an East India Company military cadet in 1737, stemmed from this local political situation.

Again Dr. Fullarton was the principal agent. He stirred the Duke of Montrose to ask Lord Wilmington to use his influence with the East India Company Directors to gain a place for one of the Stirlings of Keir. Apart from Archibald and Harry, four other Stirlings went out to India in this period. They included three uncles: John (who died there in 1742); Hugh (who died at Fort St. David in 1749); Lewis; and another brother, Jamie, who went out in 1748. Only Harry held a Company position. He transferred from the military line and was Resident at Sillibar in 1742.[52]

It is certain that Archibald Stirling's own success in India opened the way for those relations and others that he helped, such as Charles Stuart, the brother of the 8th Lord Blantyre, a kinsman on his mother's side. But as demonstrated, his own chance and that of his brother Harry was due to connection and political influence with fellow Argathelians.[53]

The family had been Jacobite, Archibald's father having been locked up in Dumbarton Castle in 1715. But their connections and electoral power cancelled out any disability this offered. With a burgeoning landed estate came even more electoral significance for the Stirlings. Added to this were their many relatives. For instance, among his kinsmen Archibald could include the Stuarts (Lords Blantyre) through his mother; his aunt was Margaret Stuart, wife of Sir Hugh Hamilton of Rosehall; his sister became Lady Stuart; his first wife's father was Col. William Erskine of Torrie. His cousin through marriage was Lord John Gray; and George Murray, 6th Lord Elibank was related to him. Other friends in Scotland included the Duke of Montrose and Lord Napier; David Rannie, John Bell of Auchtermony and most significantly, the astonishing John Mackenzie of Delvine.[54]

8

Operating in Scotland on behalf of the Argathelians and Milton, pulling together the political support of innumerable families, Whig and Jacobite alike, was the most extraordinary lawyer, John Mackenzie of Delvine. He was born in 1709, the son of John Mackenzie, advocate, by his 3rd wife Margaret, daughter of Thomas Hay of Alderston, East Lothian; and he died in 1778.

One of 14 children, and starting out in practice as a lawyer with so little that he had to borrow £395 from his wife's father – Crawford of Ballingray – by 1770 he had become a formidable landowner in Scotland. His properties ranged from Edinburgh to Perthshire and on to Loch Carron in Ross and Cromarty, the stronghold of his branch of the Mackenzie clan. He became the biggest landowner there. Also, his eldest brother, Alexander, sold him the Delvine estate, situated near Dunkeld Perthshire.[55]

The wealth and property he amassed might be considered just reward for unrelenting labours on behalf of his political masters, particularly between 1757 and 1777. Mackenzie was at the heart of a huge network. He operated in the same manner as Milton, channelling patronage, forwarding requests for favours and, when possible, satisfying those he could through his own resources, if the proposed recipient was deemed to deserve it.

He had been involved politically from the outset of his career. For instance, in the Dingwall election of 1740 the Earl of Cromarty and Lord Fortrose referred to him as 'a prominent legal agent' and charged him to 'swear out criminal letters against Sir Robert Munro of Foulis', their greatest rival.[56] He continued to handle elections and voters rolls in the 1740s. And even though just married, on 3 May 1754 he acted as Sheriff-clerk and attended Seaforth.

India patronage figured to an extraordinary degree in his activities and he probably best reflects the manner in which these particular favours were disseminated in Scotland. In his political and business connections (which included acting as legal adviser for many great figures) and in his agencies, involving the remittance of fortunes from India, he was second to none. Above all he was versed in the niceties of Scottish electoral law, and as such was indispensable to his political masters.

By 1770 he had become Deputy Keeper of the Signet and followed in the footsteps of Milton who had been Keeper. As already noted, this office vested him with a great deal of electoral power. The Signet controlled Sheriff-Deputes and Sheriff Clerks who in turn officiated at elections. After 1747 and the abolition of Heritable Jurisdictions the influence of these local figures assumed an even greater importance. They determined the crucial point – whether or not a would-be elector was on the roll.

Mackenzie was one of those dependable Government supporters who, along with others, such as George Drummond, the Provost of Edinburgh, (with whom he was also in touch) formed part of Milton's most trusted network. As early as 12th August 1740 Sir Hew Dalrymple had him presented to Ilay at Leith.[57]

As testified by his correspondence, Mackenzie's parliamentary and electoral involvement was deep and widespread. Milton entrusted him with the task of 'making the application of my doctrine', that is fulfilling Argathelian political desires. He was the man with 'the most experience of electoral laws and procedures' and his skills were used to manipulate constituencies.[58]

His initial interest in India patronage probably stemmed from its usefulness in fulfilling a life-long passion: to re-integrate the great Highland families into the Union and to prevent their further ruin. The fact that one of his younger step-brothers, George Mackenzie, also an advocate, was out in the '15 and only received a pardon in 1725 probably gave an edge to this.

However his inclinations also emerge in a bitter letter sent to Sir Alexander Macdonald of Sleat in 1768, in response to a vitriolic attack on himself. It was all the worse because (as Mackenzie's correspondence reveals) the two had been very close friends and Mackenzie had been Macdonald's lawyer and protector for decades. Mackenzie wrote:

> when from the revolution downwards the Highland families, a few only excepted, who chose the worst side, were almost extinguished, and yours by being overwhelmed in debt in full as great danger as most of them, joined relations with whom I am a close connection, they [the Mackenzies] on the principle of sympathy and friendship interposed, to their own loss, to prevent the impending ruin and were successful.[59]

This example, Mackenzie maintained, influenced him to help too and he had endeavoured to do so 'for 40 years, not to gratify ambition or avarice or importance, on the contrary, insignificance has rather been my lot.'[60]

He was a Government supporter, Whig and Argathelian and used all his leverage to secure posts for those he took under his wing who were similarly inclined. He operated part of the Government's patronage system and naturally used it for his own ends too. For over 50 years, from 1728, he built up political, business and East India Company connections in Scotland and London. His legal portfolio came to include some of Scotland's most eminent families.

As the part of Mackenzie's affairs unravels that deals only with India matters and Company patronage, a picture emerges of those involved in Scotland, London and within the organisation; and how the various connections were made and maintained. His earliest successes came from being useful to his Mackenzie clan chiefs, as already noted. The East India Company did not figure prominently until 1759, by which date his ex-Jacobite brother, George Mackenzie was in business as a merchant in London.

Although they were to be unsuccessful in the first instance, Mackenzie of Delvine and his brother went out of their way to promote the career of a young cousin of theirs, the future Major-General Sir Alexander Mackenzie of Coull. This youth was recommended to a series of ministers, such as the Earl of Marchmont and to Company Proprietors like John Home, who might have secured him a place in the Company's service.[61]

Undaunted by this lack of initial success, Mackenzie of Coull (with Mackenzie of Delvine's help) had then raised a Company of thirty military recruits in the Highlands and managed 'to carry' his 'lank and thin body that's much fatigued' into England with the men.[62] There, Mackenzie of

Delvine introduced him to Generals St. Clair and Watson, Sir James Macdonald and Col. Scott. And from this meeting Mackenzie of Coull and his men became part of a regiment going to India in the Company's service. To his disappointment young Coull was only given the rank of Lieutenant; and even the double salary granted did not cheer him.

Once in India, however, he prospered, albeit slowly; and for the rest of his life was to suffer from fever and ill-health contracted there. At first he wanted to 'quit this country where we can find neither money nor employment or subaltern preferments.' The advice from Mackenzie of Delvine's wife that he should 'tie-in with a Nabob' was impracticable to execute, and he was 'even tempted to marry if it would give him money.'[63]

Introductions and references from Mackenzie of Delvine followed. The most important of these was one to Sir Gilbert Elliot, which resulted in a command of sepoys coming his way. With this and military promotion came wealth. Of his masters, the Company Directors, he came to have a very small opinion; they were, he observed, 'as miserable as their politics and couldn't solve the problems they had created abroad.'[64]

Meanwhile, in London Mackenzie of Delvine had been strengthening his hand. Added to his brother George there was now a nephew, Colin Mackenzie, who by 1761 worked as a broker at Mr. Mayne's in New Broad Street. He was pressed into aiding and abetting Delvine's protégés.[65]

As early as 1760 Mackenzie of Delvine had also decided to become thoroughly versed in India patronage and asked his friend, Commander David Rannie, for information on 'how a young man may be provided for in India.'[66] Rannie was able to give him the details he required to the last letter. He had spent thirty-five to forty years sailing to the East Indies; and was also involved in the coastal trade there. He was versed in all aspects of Company business, in shipping and Indian matters.

Rannie, who resided in Musselburgh, had been a free merchant and ship owner and had survived the 'Black Hole' of Calcutta. He had been useful to Drummond of Quarrel and was linked with Milton, explaining his readiness to help Mackenzie of Delvine. After making a fortune in India he bought the Melville estate. One of his daughters, Elizabeth, married Henry Dundas, the future Viscount Melville; the other daughter, Janet, married Cockburn of Cockpen, and was mother of the celebrated Lord Cockburn.[67]

Mackenzie of Delvine's connection with India affairs had really proliferated from this date. Yet another nephew, Kenneth Mackenzie (brother of Coull) was now in business in London under the watchful eye of his own brother George, and was about to go to India. All strings were pulled on his behalf. Through Mackenzie of Delvine and armed with letters of recommendation, he was introduced by 'Scots friends' to General Stringer Lawrence, Sir Alexander Grant and Commander Robert Haldane. These three represented the military, civil and shipping worlds of the East India Company and were powerful figures.

The young Kenneth Mackenzie also soon found out just how influential Captain David Rannie was, and informed his uncle, Mackenzie of Delvine that a letter from Rannie 'would be of great service'. Captain Robert Haldane and Sir Alex Grant also 'got Mr. Sulivan's promise' to help this young Mackenzie; and eventually in 1762 he was allowed to go out as a free-trader in Madras.[68]

Once established in India both Kenneth Mackenzie and Alex Mackenzie of Coull applied themselves successfully to accumulating fortunes. In Kenneth Mackenzie's case he attached himself to strong Scottish groups in Madras and in Patna in the 1760s. They included a relative of his, Alex Mackenzie, who later became a shipbuilder at Calcutta; John Graham; Hugh Ross, nephew of Hugh Ross, merchant in London; Commander Francis Douglas, brother of Sir John Douglas; John Davidson, son of John Davidson, saddler in London; and Commander Kenneth Mackenzie, uncle of Mackenzie of Scotsburn. Others in this group were Captains Baillie and Wedderburn; Mr. Bogle; Mr. Mudie (for whom Kenneth Mackenzie worked at Patna); and Claud Russell. Kenneth also maintained his contact with Mackenzie of Coull.[69]

Another Scot who developed his career and fortune in the East India Company through Mackenzie of Delvine's good offices was *John Cumming of Altyre*, near Forres in Morayshire. By 1770 Cumming had risen to the rank of Lt.-Colonel and had married Mary Wedderburn, daughter of Captain Wedderburn and niece of Wedderburn of Pitfirrane. He, like his brother Captain George Cumming 'in all matters of law and business' made Mackenzie of Delvine his 'oracle' and 'wholly relied' upon his 'opinion and friendship.'[70]

John Cumming made Mackenzie of Delvine his agent for remitting and investing the fortune made in India from trading exploits. Much of this money was sent home via bills of exchange. Mackenzie was given power of attorney over his affairs, and used Messrs *Sumner and Gregory* in London and their bankers, *Castels and Wheatley*. Cumming settled money on all his relations, and bought Gosford estate, East Lothian, for £8,000. Gold sent home with his children was made payable to 'Messrs. Drummond, to save you [Mackenzie of Delvine] trouble about the exchange.'

Until his own return in 1777 he continued to remit money home through Mackenzie, mostly through gold and bills of exchange, although in 1774 diamonds were despatched worth £4,300. This was done through Thomas Anderson's remittance agency in Calcutta. In turn Anderson consigned the diamonds to Delvine. In 1775 he sent more gems, worth £3,600, all transmitted via Drummonds bank in London and thence to Mackenzie of Delvine in Scotland.

That same year another two consignments of diamonds were despatched via Drummonds bank, worth £3,600 and £8,660 respectively. These were followed by a further £11,000 in bills and silver. All of this was entrusted to John Mackenzie of Delvine, and not once was Cumming disappointed. On his return home this Nabob bought houses in Edinburgh: in George Square, Abbeyhill, Easter Road, and also in Leith. He had fortune, estate and property, with more money still to come from India.[71]

Interest in India had blossomed following Clive's exploits in 1757 and Mackenzie of Delvine certainly cashed in upon the flood of applications for posts that followed. Handling the London end of his business in this respect was John Davidson of Stewartfield, Writer to the Signet. Davidson was involved, on Mackenzie's behalf, with Scottish Company servants abroad; with Scottish Nabobs like George Mackay of Skibo and Captain David Rannie; as well as with Drummond's bank.[72]

However, a great deal of Mackenzie's contacts with the Company also stemmed from his duties as man of business for many of the Scots nobility and a number of great landowners. Most of these relationships had developed into strong friendships; and a fusion of social, political and business interests had evolved through time. For example, Sir Alexander Macdonald of Sleat could, on the one hand, ask for assistance for his nephew, the future Sir John Macpherson, to get him out Purser on an East Indiaman, and on the other refer to the 'scorbutie eruption which has shown itself upon my body and hands, not unlike the Scotch fiddle.' And he could write of his wife's wish to see again 'the land of Cakes', meaning Scotland.[73]

The same relationship applied to George Dempster of Dunnichen, widely known to be an influential East India Company Director. He and Mackenzie were good friends and involved in money matters. In September 1768 Macdonald of Sleat could inform Mackenzie, from St. Andrews, of a forthcoming golf match: 'the Silver Club will be played for tomorrow – Mr. Dempster is here and great preparations are making for a Ball.'[74] Dempster brought Mackenzie into Bute's ambit and Mackenzie also became friendly with Sir Gilbert Elliot of Minto using another client/friend, Captain Charles Congalton. Through Congalton he was introduced to others with India connections, such as Lord Elibank and the Grahams.[75]

Sir John Clerk of Penicuik was another who used Mackenzie of Delvine as his agent. Anxiety for his relations, Duncan and Robert Clerk, ensured recruitment of his services. These two were active in Company politics, particularly alongside Sir Laurence Dundas in the years from 1765 to 1774. John Mackenzie was already Sir Laurence Dundas' agent together with a John Pringle.

To sum up: Mackenzie's intermediate position enabled him to fill the important roles of broker, agent and point of contact for many. These included politicians like Milton, Bute and Elliot; powerful Scottish families like the Macdonalds, Mackenzies and Clerks of Penicuik; and he acted for Company servants abroad like Mackenzie of Coull and John Cumming. Through George Dempster, Thomas Cheape, Lauchlin Macleane and John Stewart of Hampstead – all active in company circles – he got to know Laurence Sulivan, John Townson and other powerful Directors even better.

In Scotland he was friend and agent for such as the Earls of Kinnoul, Dundonald and Strathmore, all influential landowners. His worth to them is evidenced in ensuring that Strathmore's brother, Mr. Lyon, was appointed Factor at Bencoolen in 1759. For other powerful families in Scotland (some of whom have been mentioned already) whose India links through the Government's patronage system were extensive, he performed the same service. These included the Cockburns of Eyemouth and Cockpen, Sir Hector Munro of Novar and Archibald Stirling of Keir. From 1760 he was the Earl Marischal's man of business and confidant; and from 1764 performed the same service for the Duchess of Atholl.[76]

7

Government: Supply and Demand 1742–61

1

Walpole's years of influence with the Company had ended in 1742, but while his successors did not have his weight within the organisation, relations between ministries and the monopoly's executive remained close. This was vital because the systematised patronage network involving East India Company posts continued to depend upon strong Ministry–Direction links. Disorder only really set in with the first Governmental attempt to control the Company in 1766–67; and all harmony ended with the instability and financial disasters that befell the Company between 1770 and 1773, ending in governmental intervention.

Until the contested elections of 1757–58, the Company can be regarded as fairly stable in its executive functions. The same groups of merchants, London businessmen, shippers and a sprinkling of returned Company servants controlled the Court of Directors. Among ministers, individual Members of Parliament and Company officials there were strong ties; such as those in 1756–7 of Newcastle, Devonshire (and others of that ministry) with the Company Chairman, John Payne, and with John Raymond, a leading member of the Shipping interest. This was followed by the friendship of Laurence Sulivan, Deputy Chairman in 1757, with Chatham; an understanding that eventually gave way in 1761 to one with Bute that lasted until 1763 when the minister resigned.

However, there is no doubt that the many changes of Ministry from 1761 onwards, followed by mounting Parliamentary efforts by the mid 1760s to gain control of the Company and its fledgling empire in India, weakened further the clear and continuous dialogue once entertained.

Attempts to influence and eventually control India patronage meant ministries were willing at first to link with feuding parties within the Direction while creating a bloc of pro-Government Proprietors and Directors who eventually came to dominate.

Another factor was that with war in 1756, the prominence of Chatham as a war leader, and the appearance of Laurence Sulivan (a commanding figure who emerged from, and was supported by many of the returned Company servants) the character of Government–Company relations changed. Old lines of communication gave way to new ones based on the needs of both to fight a war. Sulivan had the additional problems of staunching financial hemorrhaging, controlling indiscipline abroad and political in-fighting at home.

Fortunately for the patronage system, naval and military demands necessitated close liaison between the Company and Government. Ministers and Directors working together was epitomised in the Chatham–Sulivan relationship, and this encouraged the spread of favours. Naturally enough, Directors continued to serve family and supporters first, but an increasing numbers of indulgences were given to Government MPs who were in close alliance with leading Directors.

Thus India patronage remained useful to ministers in these troubled years because war, empire building and problems in America held their attention and left little time for home affairs. It was felt necessary that Scotland be kept politically docile at a time when disruption (both in Scotland and at Westminster) was still possible; and integration of the two societies needed more time. It was fortuitous, therefore, that circumstances from 1757 were such that the number and variety of posts available through the East India Company multiplied. It was also fortunate for ministries that by 1757 there was not much fear of Jacobitism. The systematic disarming and neutering of the Highlands by Cumberland and his associates, with its accompanying atrocities, had put paid to any physical threat.

2

Writers Petitions, independent accounts and contemporary opinion suggest that by mid-century an abnormal number of Writers for India were from Scotland.[1] The presence of Scots in such measure is largely explained by the fact that the patronage system had now operated in Scotland for some 30 years. Many recipients of favours in the 1720s and 1730s from Walpole and John Drummond of Quarrel had become powerful figures in India. Some occupied important and influential positions, such as Alexander Davidson, Governor of Madras; John Hope, George Gray the Younger and George Scott, all Members of Council; Sir Robert Fletcher and Sir Archibald Campbell, in military commands.

Secretary, Agent and Resident positions were filled by other Scots, like Alex Wedderburn, Alexander Elliot and Coull Mackenzie. Enjoyment of these posts reflected strength at home, in Westminster and in the Company. Layers of Scottish 'old boy' networks were being built-up, reaching and linking India, Leadenhall, Parliament and Scotland.

Also, a great reservoir of manpower was opened-up with the breakdown of old semi-feudal loyalties in Scotland. This was particularly so in the Highlands, and especially after the end of Heritable Jurisdictions in 1747, which had fostered a medieval outlook. Following Culloden, and with the approval and active co-operation of the main authorities, men were syphoned-off. Most went to the forces of the crown, but others who were available filled the numerous openings in the East India Company's service that appeared with the commencement of war in 1756.

There is also no doubt that 'Scots in exile' with their 'innate clannishness' drew others to India. Nevertheless, these young men were eminently suited for posts in the Company, armed as most were, with a classical education and skilled in merchant accounts. Young George Gray is a good example. He was a son of George Gray, the Surgeon at Fort William, Bengal. His Writers Petition of 1754 was signed by his lecturers at Edinburgh University. Having survived the capture of Calcutta in 1756, the youth soon became a Bengal Councillor. The rapid promotion was due to his father.

On Gray Senior's return to Britain, he had extended himself in furthering his son's career. Gray was one of a group of Scottish Nabobs, all friends, who allied with one another in pursuit of favours on behalf of their connections, seeking both within the Company and in Parliament. For instance, while acting as Mansfield's agent, the Earl was manoeuvred into securing Bute's support. Gray (Senior) was also friendly with Sulivan, and advised his son to court him too. Charles Stuart (Lord Blantyre's son), the Stirlings of Keir, Capt. Robert Haldane and the Grahams of Kinross were his allies within the Company.[2]

The successful prosecution of war in India (and elsewhere) from 1757, and in particular the defeat of the French in north and south India, and of the Nawab of Bengal, led to a hectic scramble to get out there. During the years of crisis the ministries of Chatham and the Earl of Bute required massive quantities of manpower. The essential role played by the Company alongside Royal troops in fighting the French and their allies meant it too devoured great numbers of men.

These developments transformed the status accorded India patronage at home. The friendship of an East India Company Director was fought for; and to be acquainted with the Chairman for that year, or his Deputy, augured well for those seeking favours. Company figures confirm this makeover. The numbers of civil servants in Bengal rose from 70 to 250 per annum in the 16 years from 1760 to 1776, all explained by the lust for fortune and the needs of Company and Government in harness. Between 1760 and 1830 it has been calculated that Scots gained a quarter of all India patronage, which on a population basis should have amounted to an eighth or one ninth.

Nor was it lost on the authorities (in Scotland, Parliament and in the Company) that filling these positions would provide a boost to the political aim of strengthening the Union. Posts were available, there was a *modus operandi* by which they could be grasped, and this resulted in a spread of satisfaction with the new state both north and south of the Tweed.

Scottish involvement was statistically high, a phenomenon which at least from the mid 1750s to the mid 1770s can be ascribed to the assimilation of the fighting highlander into the Company's forces, as well as traditional recruitment to its civil and naval ranks. The increase in the numbers of Scottish military cadets now sent abroad was extraordinary. 'Of 16,770 military cadetships (by 1830), 4,030 (24%) went to Scots; one tenth of these were Campbells', reflecting the strength of the Argathelian influence and the way in which Scottish managers also pursued the national interest, as perceived by Westminster.[3] To a great extent much of this was attributable to the work of Ilay and Milton through the channels of the Scottish political machine, already well-versed and adept at obtaining and using India patronage.

From 1757, and with increasing pace going into the early 1760s, the volume of Company patronage grew. The political management of Scotland was helped because of this greater requirement. Posts available directly to Government were passed on north of the border. Other places reached sympathisers in Scotland via footholds already gained in the Company at home and abroad by many kinsmen. Even more benefits would come from the contested elections in the Company, which in turn allowed more positions to come Scotland's way.

3

From the beginning the patronage system engineered by Walpole and Drummond relied upon anyone who owned stock, not just Scots, as long as they were amenable (at that time) to such as Drummond, Decker,

Chandos, Governor Harrison and others of the controlling group in the Company Direction. Certainly Scots were included among the Proprietors, but that point was not crucial. What was important was how far they would use their influence in support of a ministerial nominee for a Company post.

Scots who bought India stock did so at first because it was the next best thing to a 'gilt' edged investment. However, until the middle of the eighteenth century it was the case that the Company insisted upon the presence of buyer and seller at India House to effect the transfer. This meant that for Scottish landowners who could not get to London, or for others who were further afield or were foreigners like the Dutch, access to Company shares had to be accomplished via agents exercising letters of attorney. These legal instruments (seen as early as 1702) eased the problem of having to be present, and were in almost universal use until the late 1750s. Equally, many of the funds to purchase stock were placed in the hands of relations and business contacts in the metropolis, who utilised the money, collecting dividends in their own names, although mere nominees.

From the 1720s to the 1750s this meant that would-be Scottish Proprietors almost had to be present in London. But again fortune smiled, because this was exactly where the Scottish nobility and many of the gentry were gathered in large numbers during the years that followed the Union. The failure of the Darien scheme and a lack of capital to inaugurate any similar ventures after 1707 had pushed many Scottish merchant adventurers towards the capital. They had successfully set up shop in the early years of the century as London–Scottish businessmen, not a few of them with Jacobite secrets to hide.

These Scots soon formed a distinctive business group; an extremely close-knit combination often drawing the wrath of those excluded. They seized the opportunities available through being resident in the biggest commercial conurbation of its day; and took advantage of the openings denied before 1707 when the English business world and trading concerns were largely closed to them. The East India Company was one such field of enterprise.[4]

Many of these London-based Scottish businessmen, like Sir Alex Gilmour and Sir Alex Grant, were large stockholders in the 1740s and 1750s. At the same time, their Company involvement usually formed only one part of the complex commercial world they moved in. Both epitomize this profit making type. Gilmour was involved in Company politics and Indian affairs in general; usually he was associated with fellow Scots, like

Sir James Cockburn and Sir Laurence Dundas, all mentioned elsewhere in the text. He and Grant offer excellent illustration of how India patronage was provided by this particular group of Scots.[5]

Sir Alexander Grant MP, 5th Bart of Dalvey, Elgin, was the eldest son of Sir Patrick Grant, 4th Bart. and Lydia, daughter of William MacIntosh of Borlum. A Proprietor and landowner, he was ever ready to help his own family, collateral branches of the Grants, and fellow countrymen get to India. He began these activities in 1761. By that date the impoverishment suffered due to involvement in the Jacobite rebellion of 1745 was behind him and he had made a fortune in the West Indies as a merchant. He bought lands in Elgin and Nairn; and as a City of London businessman 'his interests extended from the Mediterranean to the West Indies, America, Africa and India.'[6]

During the Seven Years War he became a friend of John Calcraft, Bute's agent, and was on familiar terms with Milton, and Bute's acolyte, Eglinton. Through Calcraft and Bute came many contracts and patronage, particularly posts to India. This was helped by the fact that from 1749 Grant was a Proprietor of India stock. Yet the fact remained, without the influence Bute had with the Company Directors, his initial success at gaining posts for friends would have been limited.

Grant's Scottish agent was John Davidson W.S. of Stewartfield, and he also numbered Captain Robert Haldane as a friend. He was useful to Bute from a political point of view, through the clan Grant control of Invernesshire, Nairn and Elgin burghs. Later he was also able to smooth the passage of shipping patronage, via himself, and the likes of Captain Haldane; or through his influence with friends cultivated among the leading Directors, such as Laurence Sulivan and Thomas Rous.

He played particular attention to the Grants of Ballindalloch, Knockando and Auchterblain, showering favours upon those recommended to him by family and friends. If asked to make a preferment for political reasons he showed no hesitation, whether the request came from Sir James Grant of Grant of Knockando in Scotland, or from Westminster.

There seems to have been no difficulty in securing posts in the naval, military or civil line. For example, in 1761, he, Captain Robert Haldane and the Director John Dorrien (one of Sulivan's henchmen) helped Commander Charles Cathcart Grant, brother of James Grant of Castle Grant and Moy. The next year John Baillie of Dunain, Invernesshire was given a military cadet's position. In 1761 Sir Ludovick Grant of Knockando was sent out to India, where he became a Captain in the Royal army's 89th Foot Regiment, returning with a £10,000 fortune.

Two others of this branch followed: Charles Grant, who died going out in 1771, and Lt. Lewis Grant, who set off in 1768 to join the Company's forces. In 1765 and then in 1768 two Grants, Henry and James, brothers of John Grant of Ballindalloch, were sent out as Writers. And in 1770 another Ludovick Grant, 'a son of Auchterblain', was helped to an ensign's position.

Sir Alexander Grant also joined forces with James Bean and Major Dow in 1770 to send Lord Grant's kinsman, McGregor Grant, out to India as a military cadet. Probably his best appointment was Charles Grant of Knockando, who arrived in India in 1767. He was to become a Director and Chairman of the Company in the 1800s, after spending a lifetime in Bengal building up a commercial community and accumulating a fortune.[7]

London-based bankers like the Scot *Andrew Drummond* also acted as agents for their brethren in the north as well as purchasing stock on their own account. Drummond, who had started the bank at Charing Cross, was a brother of William Drummond, 4th Viscount Strathallan. He appointed to the firm the Viscount's two sons, the Hon. Henry Drummond, MP and Robert Drummond. Later the third member of the family, John Drummond, joined too. As early as 1753 this John Drummond had been sent out to India as a Writer through the influence Drummond's bank had with Company Directors.

Apart from its usefulness for Scots depositors, Drummonds bank was good for making contacts. Scots businessmen in London met lairds from their homeland in a neutral environment and they combined to make money. Connections were formed involving the bank, Company Directors and those from other institutions. In 1762, for example, John Drummond, of Drummonds bank, was one of the nine Directors of the *Sun Fire Office Insurance Company*. He and most of the other Proprietors of this insurance Company were also East India Company Proprietors and invariably members of the Company's Shipping interest. This dimension was enlarged in the 1760s through the bank's involvement in the Company's contested elections. Drummond's bank joined with its Scottish subscribers in backing the Sulivan faction in these struggles, putting up much needed cash. Andrew Drummond had personal links with Company Directors John Hope and John Boyd.[8]

Another Scot, Charles Coutts (related to Coutts the bankers) was (intermittently) a Director from 1749 to 1761; and the Scottish–Dutch banking family of Hope was also involved in Company affairs by 1760.[9] Many were shareholders in the booming assurance companies, like the *Sun*

Fire Insurance Company and the *London Fire Assurance Company*. Others, such as the Moffatt brothers, Andrew and Captain James, were underwriting East Indiamen.[10]

John Stewart, of York Buildings (who is identified by his London address from others of that name) and who was involved in the importing of wines, demonstrates two developments. He typifies how Scots enmeshed in local trade in the metropolis became proprietors of India stock; and, as an ex-Jacobite, how former opponents of Hanoverian rule were being absorbed. He and his father Archibald (younger son of Sir Robert Stewart, first Baronet of Allanbank) moved to London in 1759. Through an aunt he was connected to Sir Gilbert Elliot, and he was friendly with Andrew Stuart. He was also the agent for Sir George Colebrooke, banker and powerful East India Company Director.[11]

William Fisher (of *Fisher & Younger*) was yet another London–Scottish businessman. He acted as an agent for various prominent Scots who could not openly appear to be involved in share dealing or operating in 'margins'; either because of public office, or because it was not then the gentlemanly thing to do.[12] Scottish cartels had front men like Fordyce the banker, and were thus able to invest money and keep their identities secret. Remittance of fortunes from abroad, such as through bills of exchange from India redeemable through the Company in London, required men who were skilled, such as Fordyce and Alex Forsyth. Attorneys, like Kenneth Mackenzie of Lincoln's Inn, who remitted the fortune of Major-General Sir Alexander Mackenzie of Coull, were very knowledgeable indeed about the London money market. Such a man as Mackenzie had to know the Scottish as well as London financial institutions, since he was entrusted to forward the money from London to the north.

In such a small business community these men could not avoid dabbling in Company business because it was so important and central to 'City' life. The throng of Scots congregating there was being added to by adventurers and entrepreneurs like the Moffatts, who had made fortunes abroad and now resided in London beside their invested money. Or, like the Humes, they came into the mainstream of Company and 'City' life after service in the Company or on board East Indiamen.

Others, like General Hector Munro returned home, but kept a stake in the Company. Younger sons, such as the future Major-General Sir Alexander Mackenzie of Coull, were first despatched to London to learn the secrets of the counting-house and to be near the centre of action for the East India Company and other financial institutions in the chance of speedy recruitment. He, like so many, studied mercantile accounts, geography, 'cyphering', French and fencing.

Many of these Scots scions are found in the Royal Society of Arts in the 1750s, which for a time seemed to double as a Scots club. Others, like Thomas Cheape and Sir James Cockburn entered into business in London and became caught up in Company politics. Or, like the brothers Sir William and Robert Mayne, set the scene there for their younger relations, the Graemes of Kinross.[13]

Scots located in London continued to be important, as is illustrated by the Hume brothers in their dealings with the Company. From 1731 through to 1772 they gave the patronage system extensive support. *Alexander and Abraham Hume* MP were sons of the Jacobite Robert Hume of Ayton, Berwickshire. A Scottish background, East India Company connections and stature in the City ensured their importance in the eyes of ministers caring for Scottish affairs.

The Humes were also significant landowners in Berwickshire through their father's estate, although their lives were spent in the south. Like so many with Jacobite connections or origins they started their careers in the Ostend Company. What really shaped their fortunes was that each married a daughter of Sir Thomas Frederick who (together with his brothers Sir John and Sir Charles Frederick) was eminent in the East India Company.

From March 1733 Alexander Hume, the eldest brother, held £1,000 of East India stock, a substantial sum then. And from 1737, intermittently until 1748, he served as a Company Director. Abraham Hume, as well as holding India stock was a Director of the *South Sea Company* and of the *Exchange Assurance Company*. Both men continued active in Company politics in the 1760s. Together with Sir Hew Dalrymple they formed ties with Sir William Mayne and his brother Robert Mayne who were important to later developments in the patronage system. Relations and friends were provided for, such as those belonging to Sir Hew Dalrymple. Also, Charles Suttie, William Stair Dalrymple, and in 1747 a nephew, Captain George Cumming of the *Royal Drake*, were all cared for. Cumming later became an important Director carrying on the patronage work.[14]

This period of Ilay–Milton control from 1742 to 1761 witnessed many similar instances of such patronage being dispensed. Much of it was provided by landowners, who were also Company Proprietors, and spent a peripatetic life between home and the English capital. Sir Hew Dalrymple was one, Sir John Clerk of Penicuik another, among many. John Mackenzie of Delvine was Clerk's man of business. Earlier (pre-1720) Clerk's son Henry, was apprenticed as a seaman, voyaged to India and eventually entered the Royal Navy. All was done, of course, in accordance with Milton's wishes.

4

Featuring large among Scots with Company involvement were members of the *Johnstone* family of Westerhall, Dumfriesshire, and their uncle, *Lord Elibank*. They were landowners, Proprietors, Directors and Company civil servants; carried a formidable interest at home, and were deeply involved in all that happened from 1742 to 1774 and beyond.

Sir James Johnstone of Westerhall, Dumfriesshire, 3rd Bart had seven sons and a daughter by Barbara Murray, daughter of Alexander, 4th Lord Elibank. There was a decided Jacobite taint to the family, reflected in Sir James Johnstone's own inclinations; in the marriage of his daughter Margaret to one of the Jacobite leaders, Lord David Ogilvie; and also in the tendencies of his eldest son and successor, Sir James Johnstone, 4th Bart. However, these feelings were not (overtly at least) shared by the other members of the family, who appeared stout Whigs and loyal Hanoverians.

In age order the sons were: James, Patrick, William, George, John, Gideon and Alexander. Four of the brothers became employees of the East India Company. Patrick went out to India in 1750 and met his death in 1756 in the 'Black Hole' of Calcutta. John spent 14 years in Bengal. He eventually accumulated a fortune of £300,000, one way or another – a great deal of controversy surrounded the manner in which this money was gained.

Gideon accompanied John to Bengal and he too returned safely, but with only a modest fortune. Alexander was dismissed the Company's service in 1767, but eventually became a Lt.-Colonel in the 70th Foot Regiment of the Royal Army. However, it was the other sons, William and George (3rd and 4th sons respectively) who, together with John, formed one of the most colourful and dynamic groups involved in East India Company affairs. In particular, these three took active roles as Proprietors, speculators, and participants in the contested elections that created havoc from 1761 onwards. In the years from 1769 to 1773 they again figure large, particularly because of the savage attack launched against Clive. Later, in 1784, George Johnstone was to become a Director. In all of this, their eldest brother, Sir James, along with Alexander and Gideon, took a supporting role.

Much earlier, however, these Johnstones had joined with their uncle, Patrick Murray, 5th Lord Elibank, in buying enough India stock to make themselves considerable Proprietors with voting rights, which they threw behind George, John and William. Although neither George nor William Johnstone served as Company servants or were part of the Company's shipping, for many years they were deeply involved as Proprietors.

Without doubt the need felt in the 1760s to close ranks and defend John from the wrath of his employers and superiors (first, Laurence Sulivan the Company Chairman, and then Lord Clive) engaged their full attention. But the continued hatred between them and Clive, defence of John's fortune from attempts made through the law Courts to take it from him, speculation in India stock, and a fascination with the Company's contested elections kept them actively involved throughout the 1760s and 1770s.

In the beginning, however, it was the Government patronage system, working through Ilay and Milton that determined they would have an interest in the Company. Their father, besides being a personal friend of Milton, had a commanding political influence among the superiorities in Dumfriesshire. His interest and that of Lord Elibank made Milton very amenable to requests for help for his sons; thus Patrick, John, Gideon and Alexander all benefited.

In 1760 William Johnstone married Frances, daughter and heir of Daniel Pulteney, who in turn was heir to William Pulteney, Earl of Bath. Overnight he was rich, with at least £18,000 of a fortune and over £1,000 per annum in revenues. In 1767 he and his wife inherited the estate on the Earl's death and earlier that of her father. William assumed the name of Pulteney-Johnstone. Consequently he could afford to be very particular in the political position he looked for from Milton. With the independence that came from his new-found wealth, he had less need of patronage for himself, but had his brothers to think about.

He had already made friends with George Dempster and Andrew Stuart of Craigthorn, who were then involving themselves with the Company; and he forged friendships in Edinburgh literary circles and among fellow lawyers. He had also enough connections among the Directors by this date to recommend a certain Adam Smith.

The good standing with the ministry enjoyed by the Johnstone family was also seen in 1763 when Bute provided George Johnstone with the post of Governor of West Florida. George had earlier been a merchant seaman, but transferred to the Royal Navy and served with distinction in the Seven Years War. He was a rather erratic and quarrelsome man, but his boundless energy gained him the grudging respect of ministers, Directors and Proprietors. This was soon apparent as he became the chief organiser of the Johnstone party and their allies in the Company politics of the 1760s.

Patrick Murray, 5th Lord Elibank, of Balencrieff, Haddington, uncle to these sons of Sir James Johnstone, was perceived to have a distinct Jacobite taint. Dr. Alexander Carlyle of Inveresk maintained Elibank was a member of the 'Cocoa-Tree' Club, and thus an erstwhile follower of 'the King across the water'. His India connection began in the late 1750s when he became a Proprietor; but his interest really quickened in the 1760s when the furore concerning his nephew, John Johnstone, erupted in Leadenhall. The vigorous activity of the Johnstone brothers in the contested elections guaranteed his involvement in support of them. He provided money for splitting purposes and added his considerable influence in the General Court of Proprietors.

Apart from these nephews, Elibank was also diligently forwarding the career of an illegitimate son, William Young, whom he was able to send out as a Writer in 1764. The Scottish political managers who were his friends, such as Sir Gilbert Elliot and Milton, ensured the necessary recommendations were made and the influence of the Johnstones within the Company did the rest. Elibank sent his son an unending stream of advice and extended himself financially to help his cause. In his own words, in the splitting of stock he 'adventured beyond his depth, chiefly out of a view of helping.' This he continued to do until 1775. In the hope of advancing William Young's career he approached Directors and Proprietors alike, such as Governor Rumbold, Sir George Colebrooke, Henry Vansittart and Laurence Sulivan.

Young treated his father despicably. Nevertheless, Elibank continued his exertions on his behalf, and used the influence of his own brother, General James Murray, and that of Charles Stewart, Clavering and George Ross. The latter acted as agent and manager for himself and his brother, General James Murray. Young eventually amassed a fortune, mainly from the opium trade – money (£1,000 per annum) that was sent home via his father.

Although living almost entirely in Scotland, Elibank 'took a side in India politics in hopes of being able to serve.' In 1769 he joined with his nephews and with Sulivan, Vansittart and Lauchlin Macleane in their 'Great Scheme', which was to return the Sulivanite party to power in the Direction. He was severely injured financially by the fall in India stock that almost ruined the others involved.

The Johnstones had been well-served by the Ilay–Milton–Bute patronage system and they themselves built-up ministerial contacts. Bute,

Shelburne and Holland had all made common cause with them in Company elections. Also Sir James Lowther (1st Earl of Lonsdale) was George Johnstone's intimate friend, and had him returned to Parliament for the borough of Cockermouth in 1768. William Pulteney Johnstone became MP for Cromartyshire in the same year although, as already mentioned, he had been offered a seat (Perth burghs) through the interest of his friend George Dempster.

Within the Company the Johnstone connections stretched in every direction. Besides George Dempster and Andrew Stuart they were friends and allies of countless other Scots. By siding with Sulivan from 1764 they embraced Proprietors like Hannay and James Dalrymple of Hailes, and fellow adventurers like Lauchlin Macleane. There were family ties with the Director John Hope; while Adriaan Hope, banker in Amsterdam, as well as *Coutts*, and *Goslings* banks, were all involved with them in splitting activities – as were *Grant and Fordyce*, and the *Dumfries* bank. Johnstone connections among Scots at home and in London were extensive too. They included Alex Wedderburn (Lord Loughborough), the Earls of Hopetoun, Erskine of Kellie, Sir Adam Fergusson, and James Boswell.

In many ways the careers and activities of the Johnstones epitomise what East India patronage could do for Scots. The system provided opportunities; they made fortunes using the Company, or carved out positions using it as the vehicle to do so. For fifty years Scots would be helped in this manner; and the large Scottish presence in the monopoly, among Directors, Proprietors, Shippers and Company servants was the result.[15]

Almost rivalling the Johnstones in their importance regarding Company affairs, the patronage system and propagation of a closer union of Scotland with England were the Proprietor *Andrew Stuart* W.S. of Craigthorn, Lanark and his brother *Col. James Stuart*, who entered the Company's military Service. They were the sons of Archibald Stuart of Torrance, Lanark, by Elizabeth, daughter of Sir Andrew Myreton of Gogar, Edinburgh.

Andrew Stuart was always aware of the effect Jacobitism in his family had on the London establishment. His elder brother had served Charles Edward Stuart as an officer in the Jacobite army. On the other hand, his younger brother, James Stuart, had elected to serve with the Hanoverian one. After 28 years service, which involved duty in North America and the West Indies, James was transferred (through Andrew) in 1770 to the East Indies; and then to command of the Company's forces in Madras in 1775. There he was promoted to full Colonel.

Col. James Stuart was deeply involved in the Governor Pigot scandal that erupted in the 1770s. He helped place Pigot in prison, where he died, and was subsequently court-martialled himself and (temporarily) expelled from the Company's service. These events were carefully monitored by his brother Andrew who instigated his reinstatement using all the friends he could muster.

From 1770, when Col. James Stuart had first arrived in Madras in the Royal Army, Andrew had busied himself in Company affairs as a Proprietor, politician and patronage monger. He was close to Sir George Colebrooke, as well as to the Johnstones and George Dempster. Laurence Sulivan, Edmund Burke and Lord North were his friends, Mansfield his enemy.

He is probably best remembered for his advocacy during the famous Douglas case; and as a candidate for 'Junius', thorn in the side of Governments in the 1760s. But he also figured largely in Company politics. In particular, he loaned money to his friends the Johnstones and George Dempster for the purchase of stock 'splitting' during the contested elections.

He was part of an intimate group, all Scots and all Proprietors who, besides Dempster and the Johnstones, included Sir Adam Fergusson and Alex Wedderburn. His importance in the operation of a patronage network was realised even then. He was known by many families who trusted him. The favours he commanded came through his own position as a Proprietor; but much more important patronage flowed from association with the Dukes of Hamilton. His father was a Writer to the Signet, and both father and son were law agents for the Hamiltons. Ilay and his circle confirmed his stature when he entered London society. Mure of Caldwell, the Hamilton-Argylls, Bedfords, Lords Gower, Conway, Beaufort and Hertford all backed him.

His Company connections began in earnest in 1761 when he became a Proprietor. This appears to have been stimulated by his intimate friend William Pultney Johnstone. It is also possible that an interest in India affairs had been stirred through his wife Margaret, daughter of Sir William Stirling, 4th Bart of Ardvoch, Perth and kinsman of the Stirlings of Keir.

Andrew had become Remembrancer in Exchequer by 1771 and was mentioned as a potential candidate for the Commission of Inquiry of 1772. North wanted him for the Supreme Council in Bengal in 1773. This led to an outburst against him, as Sulivan reported to Hastings: 'Being a Scotchman it gave our enemies scope for an attack, and Mr. Stuart, with many amiable qualities, the sweetest disposition, excellent understanding and an unsullied character was scoured to a most illiberal degree.' He was turned down for the post.[16]

By 1776 Andrew was also a good friend of Henry Dundas and the 'Scotch Ministry'. He later succeeded his elder brother in the Torrance estate and inherited that of Sir John Stuart of Castlemilk. He was a bridge from the organised Government patronage up to 1765, over the mayhem that lasted from 1766 to 1775, onwards to the new control exercised by Henry Dundas.[17]

5

Due to the oligarchic structure of the East India Company few men other than the most important Directors had any real influence over the policies formulated; but each of the Directors had some share in the patronage. Between 1742 and 1761 three Scots were Directors or had Scots connections: John Hope, from 1738 to 1741 and 1744 to 1752; John Boyd, from 1753 to 1764 (Deputy Chairman in 1759); and Charles Coutts, from 1749 to 1754 and 1758 to 1766.

Milton's connection with the Company was enhanced by the presence in the Direction of Hope. From 1738 to 1752 this Director acted alongside the Lord Justice Clerk's other contacts there: the Humes, Fredericks, Suttie, Baker, Chancerie, Drake and Watts. He was a distant relative of the Earls of Hopetoun and of Adriaan Hope the Amsterdam banker, who shared the same Scottish family connections, and was deeply involved in the splitting campaigns that be-devilled Company politics in the 1760s.

The John Hope referred to here might also have been a kinsman of Drummond of Quarrel's protégé, John Hope, who was in the Company's service in Bombay in 1725 and became Customs House Controller in 1751. John Hope (the Director) was aligned with Ilay politically; and friendly with Sir James Johnstone of Westerhall whose sons were also heavily involved in Company politics in the 1760s and l770s.[18]

While their connection with the Scottish business community in London was strong, these Scots Directors were by no means the only ones in the Direction open to requests for patronage that would benefit Scots. Ministerial penetration of the Direction meant that the ethnic origins of the 'Chairs' and leading Directors scarcely mattered. As indicated, Company favours to help the Government pursue its objectives regarding the political management of Scotland – and with it political consolidation of the state – could be gained from those Company servants amenable to ministerial advances.

There is evidence that the Director William Baker had links with Pelham and Newcastle and helped Scots. Thomas Rous, Frederick Pigou and Sir George Colebrooke were three English Directors with Scottish connections who favoured Scottish applicants in the 1750s; as did Henry Crabb Boulton, John Dorrien and Robert Savage, who recommended Quinton Crawford, William Flockhart and Daniel Gordon, respectively.[19]

Aside from the Johnstone of Westerhall family, *George Dempster* of Dunnichen, both a Proprietor and Director, had probably the most striking impact; one which also stretched into the 1765–1774 period. He was the eldest son of John Dempster of Dunnichen, Dundee, by Isobel Ogilvie. After marriage to Joanna Dundas, daughter of Chief Baron, Robert Dundas, he trained as a lawyer at St. Andrews and Edinburgh Universities. A member of the 'Poker' club, he was a friend for life of David Hume, William Robertson, Alexander Carlyle and Sir Adam Fergusson.

The Dempster family were strong Argathelians. In 1733 an uncle, George Dempster, in return for patronage and favours had involved himself in elections on behalf of Drummond of Quarrel. This Government connection and the patronage that flowed from it continued with young George Dempster. In 1760 he informed Milton that he had 'secured three of Mr. Leslie's buroughs' for the Argathelians, news that Milton conveyed to Argyll. In return Dempster asked Milton (and was given) a seat in Parliament 'the highest object of my ambition.'[20] In the House Dempster supported Chatham's policies, but became a follower of Bute in 1761 when the Earl inherited Ilay's support. This commitment to Bute also followed from his having persuaded Ilay in 1760 to get Atholl to swing Perth Burghs over, thus securing the seat for him.

But Dempster's attachment to Bute only lasted as long as he was Prime Minister. His own easy financial circumstances at that time and resentment at James Stuart Mackenzie's control led him, together with Daniel Campbell of Shawfield, James Murray of Broughton and Sir Alexander Gilmour, to take an independent line. However he remained an important Member of Parliament in Government eyes, because of his own landowning influence, which translated into political influence; and was enhanced by the nominal and fictitious vote (or superiority) that Sir Adam Fergusson gave to his 'intimate and life-long friend, George Dempster.'[21]

By 1764 he was one of Shelburne's cabal of close friends who included many of the leading personalities of the day: John Dunning, Chief Justice Pratt, David Hume, Johnson, Blackstone, Goldsmith and Reynolds. After 1765 he was a member of the Rockingham group in Parliament.

However, Dempster had become involved in East India Company affairs some time before 1764. Undoubtedly his position as MP for Perth Burghs, connections with Bute and Milton, and the advancement of his younger brothers accounts for this. Commander John Hamilton Dempster of the *Earl Talbot*, Company servants Charles and Philip Dempster, and Col. George Barrington, his brother-in-law, were all helped by the patronage that Dempster could provide as a Director and Proprietor. He also had the best Parliamentary connections.

It is probable too that in furtherance of his brother John's career, Dempster forged closer links with the Company's Shipping interest and with Laurence Sulivan. At India House in 1764 he sided politically with the Johnstones and Sulivan (whom he knew through the Shelburne connection); and they remained allies throughout the years and contested elections to come.

Dempster was one of the foremost among this glittering band of Scots (landowners and lawyers in the main) who lived in great and close friendship. During the years up to and straddling the 1760s they became considerable Proprietors with an active involvement in Company affairs. Most are traced in these pages: Alexander Gilmour, Andrew Stuart of Craigthorn and Alexander Wedderburn, the future Lord Loughborough, and Dempster's great friend, Sir Adam Fergusson. After 1765, John Mackenzie of Delvine was included in this list.

These men were also associates of the Johnstones, especially of William Pultney Johnstone, and of Laurence Sulivan. They were the type of influential Scots who through their Company links nourished the hopes and desires of families in Scotland who had influence in local politics and hoped to get India patronage.

Dempster's own ruinous court case in 1768 threw him even more into Company business in his (successful) attempts to recover his fortune. He rose with the Sulivanite return to power in 1769; but his independent line, thereafter, ensured that he did not tumble with them in 1772. Instead, he was 'the popular choice of the Proprietors,' when he was elected a Director that year. From 1769 he was also back in Parliament for Perth burghs, defeating a fellow Proprietor, the Clive backed William Macintosh of Auchintully; and he operated skilfully in both the national and the Company assemblies until 1790. In 1786 he bought Skibo estate (which earlier belonged to George Mackay, and later to Andrew Carnegie); planted a new village in Letham, Angus; started a fund among returned Scots–Indians of £9,000 for fisheries; and introduced agricultural improvements on a large scale.[22]

Another Proprietor and Director of substance at this time was *Sir James Cockburn* MP, son of William Cockburn, merchant of Ayton and Eyemouth, Berwickshire. He owed his advancement, in classical fashion, to family, friendship and influence. He too was active in Company affairs into the 1770s; and his contribution to the ongoing flow of patronage directed towards his fellow compatriots was substantial. He had amassed a fortune in the West Indies, in partnership with his father-in-law, Henry Douglas, a London–Scottish merchant. The next step was to regain the Langton estates in Berwickshire – family properties that were lost to their principal creditors, the Cockburns of Cockburn. Family prestige was restored.

The patronage of Bute, exercised mainly through Sir Gilbert Elliot and John Calcraft (Cockburn's close friends) guaranteed his Baronetcy and future prosperity as a Government contractor. Entry into Leadenhall affairs followed as a matter of course from his numerous commercial activities; but also from the involvement there of his cousin, John Stewart, wine merchant in the Strand. From 1763 business connections with Sir George Colebrooke involved him further; and by then he was a Proprietor of India stock.

In 1767 and 1768 and again from 1770 to 1772 he was a Director, closely linked still with Colebrooke, joining with him in his alliance with Sulivan in 1772, splitting stock and electioneering in Leadenhall and in Westminster, which he had entered in 1770 as MP for Linlithgow burghs. Typical of the Scots he patronised were George Ramsay, son of Sir James Ramsay of Banff. The brothers John and William Renton, who had already spent 3 years in London with the Scots firm of *Fordyce, Grant and Co.*, benefited too. He was also a confidante of Alex Wedderburn (Lord Loughborough) and Alex Coutts of *Coutts* Bank.[23]

6

In the appointments of John Webster and Alexander Dalrymple; and in the disappointment of Alexander Mackenzie of Coull, the patronage system at work during these years is exceptionally explicit. In 1761 *John Webster* was appointed Writer. He was the son of Alex Webster D.D., whose first step in his son's interest had been to contact Milton in Edinburgh and the Rev. Dr. Samuel Chandler of London. Both made application to Newcastle and he in turn to the Company Chairman, Laurence Sulivan. Webster's importance to Government was his relationship to the Erskine family in Scotland and to James Bogle, the 'Secretary of the New Bank'.

Operation of the system is just as clear in the case of *Alexander Dalrymple*, 5th son of Sir James Dalrymple of Hailes, who entered the Company as a Writer in 1752. The fact that his father exerted massive electoral influence in East Lothian and that 'his uncle was the Hon. General St. Clair, who in 1752 knew the Chairman' (William Baker), meant that his entry was assured. His appointment typifies the favours granted to Scotland's senior and most influential families if Argathelian and close to Milton. His promotion was rapid, pushed on by the weight of the family's political interest. By 1754 he was employed in the Secretary's office under Governor Pigot – achieved through personal recommendation from home. This power was used again in 1760 to get him on board ship; and by 1762 he had command of the *London*.

A talent then developed (or was discovered) for map-reading and exploration. With this came success in extending the possibilities of Company trade (still with the backing of powerful people in London and Scotland). He was appointed Hydrographer to the East India Company, and from there to the office especially created for him, of Hydrographer to the Admiralty.

Alexander Mackenzie of Coull, at school in London in 1757, looked to his clan chief, Lord Cromarty, for patronage; and to John Mackenzie of Delvine, such a key player in the Ilay–Milton patronage system. The young man's hopes were high since Ilay had made his father Sheriff of Morayshire, in order, young Coull deduced, to 'set up his [Ilay's] nephew once more as a candidate for the County election.' However, he learned subsequently, that Ilay had made a mistake regarding his father and by 1759 regarded him as an enemy.[24]

As earlier indicated, in that year the young man tried to get to India through the favour of the Proprietor John Home and with the influence of John Mackenzie of Delvine's brother George, a leading merchant in London. The Lord Register had tendered his support, while Lord Marchmont promised his influence with 'a leading Director'. But it was to no avail without the patronage machine working upon his behalf from Scotland. To John Mackenzie of Delvine he blasted against 'the leading Triumvirate of this country (he meant Ilay, Milton and probably Sir Gilbert Elliot) who while in friendship with you endeavoured to give you bad impressions of my father'.[25] Nor did 'his Chief' escape censure, who would do nothing 'when a wink' would have allowed the leading Proprietor, Sir Alexander Grant to have provided for him. He would never again rely on 'chiefs or mischiefs'.[26]

Even more evidence of the Government's patronage system in operation and the strands of communication from Scotland to East India

Company Directors can be extracted from Writers Petitions. For instance, in 1749 Robert Erskine, son of Robert Erskine of Carnock and Carden, Stirlingshire, was supported in his application by a relation, Thomas Erskine, MP for the county, and a firm Argathelian. The same year Robert Moffatt benefited from his namesake Captain James Moffatt being in the Company Direction – and from the backing of Alex Johnston and James Buchanan, Scottish businessmen who ran a counting-house in London.

The following year (1750) saw John, the most notorious of the Johnstones, enter the Company's service. Perhaps his birth in 1734 at 'Haddock's Hole' beside 'The Wells O' Weary' at the foot of Arthur's Seat served as some premonition of his individuality. In 1753 his brother Patrick followed him. As already seen, they used the influence their father had with Milton, who was anxious to embroil ex-Jacobites like Sir James and could do so by offering small patronage favours such as this. The fact that Sir James Johnstone had significant political influence in Dumfriesshire did not escape Milton. The family also controlled Dumfries burghs in the 1740s. Nor did the East India Company Proprietorship of their uncle, Lord Elibank, go amiss when the brothers produced their recommendations.

For similar reasons William Lindsay, son of Sir Alex Lindsay, and Lord Mansfield's nephew, found no difficulty securing a Writership to Bengal, the best posting. What was also highlighted in 1751 was the power of the Scottish legal establishment to work the patronage machine. This was reflected in the appointment of Claud Russell, son of John Russell, Writer to the Signet, of Braidslaw, Edinburgh; and again in 1752 when Robert Loch, son of William Loch, Writer to the Signet, was appointed.[27]

7

The electoral influence of families in Scotland who owned land, but broadly speaking were termed of the second rank was equally rewarded. An example was the successful petition of James Gordon, eldest son of James Gordon of Ellon, Aberdeenshire. When needed, additional weight could be put behind the petitioner's application to ensure success, such as happened to Charles Stewart, who in 1761 was vouched for by James and Thomas Coutts, London–Scottish bankers. They affirmed that the young man had served a banking apprenticeship in Edinburgh.

The youth was fulsome in his thanks: 'Mr. Stuart's humble respects to my Lord Bute and begs to present his most grateful thanks for the great honour conferred upon him by his Lordship's recommendation to Mr. Sulivan who has appointed him for a Writer for Bengal – If Lord Bute has any commands for India Mr Stuart will be heard of at Mr Coutts's any time this month and will think himself highly honoured in receiving his Lordship's orders.'[28]

In these same years the number of Scots of the landed gentry who purchased India stock grew remarkably. Some, like Andrew Stuart are mentioned above; others included Sir Hew Dalrymple; George Dempster of Dunnichen's father; Lord Elibank; and Sir James and David Dalrymple of Hailes. In Scotland these gentlemen were able to satisfy Government politically, while as Proprietors opportunities for their own reward were available. The Argathelian signal was all that was required for them to secure Company posts. Implementation of Government's wishes could also be achieved through those Directors who were Members of Parliament. Into this category and susceptible to ministerial pressure and persuasion, came Alderman Sir William Baker, Alexander Hume, George Dempster and Sir Matthew Featherstonehaugh.[29]

This depth of Scottish involvement in the Company, while signifying the entrance of Scots capital into the London money market, also seems to reflect an understanding of the benefits conferred from earlier connections with the Company during Drummond of Quarrel's years. Certainly those such as the Dalrymples, Duncan Clerk, Andrew Stuart and Sir Alex Grant; the Douglases, Erskine and Fraser were all very much involved with Argathelian control in Scotland; and are to be regarded as contributing to and benefiting from the ongoing India patronage system.

Scottish landed wealth found new vistas opening up by engaging in capitalist exploits, such as the East India Company, in banking and dealings in shares and dividends. It was perfectly obvious to them that political influence and the favour of those in power in Parliament could only enhance personal business prospects and those of associates. The Proprietor and landowner *Sir Hew Dalrymple*, MP, from North Berwick, provides a striking example of such enrichment. More than that, he demonstrates the continued use of India patronage (through Ilay and Milton) to strengthen ministerial control in the north. Sir Hew maintained that all the positions and favours he received stemmed from Lord Milton, not least of these being India favours.

From 1734 he was a virtual one man route to India for many young men. The reasons for this were manifold. The county of Haddingtonshire and Haddington burghs were held by the Dalrymples. They were some of the foremost and most influential landowners in Scotland with rich and varied connections, whose allegiance was invaluable for any would-be political manager. For example, Sir Hew's brothers included John

Dalrymple Hamilton of Bargany, William Stair Dalrymple and Robert Dalrymple. His sons were Captain Robert and Hew Dalrymple; his nephew was James Dalrymple. Among his cousins he could list the Dalrymples of Hailes, that is Sir James and his sons, who included Sir David, Lord Hailes, and Alexander Dalrymple – among others. His uncle was Captain William Stair Dalrymple.

Sir Hew was 'one of the Duke of Argyll's gang', but could also fall out with him and seek patronage from his enemies.[30] For example, in 1746 he secured favours from George Grenville, who was then connected to Pelham and to Sir Laurence Dundas' group, the latter being a particular enemy of Ilay. For most of the time, however, he was an Argathelian and did not let his independent characteristics blind him to the offices he could gain from the Ilay–Milton power base, to pass on to friends and relations.

Study of how he exerted his influence to gain posts for some of these people again uncovers how the system, in its largely personal and informal way, had to work. Charles Suttie, for example, a relation of Sir George Suttie (who was a large landowner and also an East India Proprietor and Director) acknowledged in November 1745 that Sir Hew had got him to India. He was undoubtedly referring to Dalrymple's political contacts with the Ilay–Milton systems. Even Sir George Suttie's own Company influence, although clearly important, was inferior to the weight of the patronage machine.

Later that year Charles Suttie sought more help from Sir Hew. In particular he wanted to have his civil post changed from Tellicherry to Bengal that he might engage in trade. Later there was yet another request from this Suttie. He asked, and fully expected, that Sir Hew would not only arrange his switch to Bengal, but that he would also get Alex and Abraham Hume to influence the East Indiaman's Commander, Captain Law, to allow him to sit at the Captain's table.

In 1752 the system operated perfectly to place Sir Hew's young brother William Stair Dalrymple in Fort William, Bengal, as a Writer. All the strings of connection and influence were pulled. In Scotland Sir Hew, his brother John, Laird of Bargany, and other big landowners, like Sir George Suttie mustered their forces. Their efforts were funneled through Sir Hew's London agent, a Mr. Sainthill. Armed with letters of introduction and recommendation from Sir Hew, his brother William quickly gained favour with the 'Chairs', Alderman Baker and Mr. Chancerie who 'had the whole Direction' that year.

He also had the backing of Directors, Drake and Watts, gaining letters of recommendation from both to add to that of their fellow Director, Sir

George Suttie. Taking Drake's advice William changed from the notion of going Supercargo to that of Writer; and with such formidable backing he was chosen to go to Bengal. Unfortunately the young man was not to live long. But before he died in the 'Black Hole' he was involved to the full extent of his credit in trading exploits, particularly with Governor Roger Drake and the free-merchant John Brown. His bills of exchange passed through the Scottish firm of *Innes and Clarke* in Bengal and his London agent was the Scot, David Findlay.[31]

Sir Hew Dalrymple's influence with those in control of patronage in Scotland and with the Company's Directors is reflected in several other cases. In 1748 he secured preferment for a nephew, James Dalrymple; and to please Milton's agent, James Oswald, obtained an introduction for his friend, a Mr. Reid. To satisfy two influential voters, John Buchan of Letham and James Heriot of Dirleton, he acted again, securing positions for their respective sons: Hew Buchan and James Heriot Junior.

It must have been an endless drudge; but politics (high or low) depended upon this chain of command. He understood perfectly he must give the correct favour to the politically and socially right person. Sir Hew also received as much as he gave; and as one of the ruling families, who knew from tradition, teaching and necessity what he must do, got on with it. From his point of view, and that of his fellow travellers in Westminster and north of the border, he was doing an important political job. Apart from threats or blackmail, patronage was almost the only means that could be employed to tie to himself and his cause, an individual who was socially and economically independent.[32]

8

Shipping Positions 1742–61

1

The Company Shipping interest of the 1720–1742 period that had proved very useful to John Drummond of Quarrel, remained substantially the same in structure, size and function up to 1757. Until then it was still controlled by the same families of shippers who worked in close harmony with the Company's Directors and the Committee of Shipping. Ships husbands,* owners, or Charter Parties,* Commanders, shipbuilders and insurance underwriters formed a close-knit fraternity, collaborating with the Company, attending its different Courts and functioning in the running of the Company as Directors, Proprietors or Company servants.[1]

There were few opportunities available for interference by outside forces. Even important Directors found the Shipping interest a law unto itself. However, one of the strongest levers the Chairman of the Company did have was that he allocated voyages to the owners and Commanders of East Indiamen. This endowed him with formidable power, as far as the ranks of the shippers were concerned, not to mention the Company itself.

Some voyages were better than others, such as the Bengal run, where £8,000 to £10,000 could be made by a Commander. A good return was generated from his freight at the sales in the Company warehouses. For such a run the Chairman's support was vital; and he looked for a great deal of patronage and other forms of recompense in return.

Drummond had used this avenue to gain seafaring positions, to such an extent that his own exhaustion with it even turned him viciously against his brother with his constant requests: 'I have told you once and again not to recommend any Surgeons to me, for all the East India Company ships have either Scots Surgeons or Surgeon's mates, and till some of them die I can, nor will look out for no more, for I am made the jest of mankind, plaguing all the Societys of England with Scots Surgeons.'[2]

Ships husbands were canvassed directly for commands. Those officers appointed were confirmed by the Company. Between 1720 and 1774 East Indiamen averaged 400 to 600 tons (but were officially registered at 499 tons to avoid carrying a parson). Crews numbered anything between 60 and 130. Besides the Captain they included six mates, a surgeon and surgeon's mate, a purser, supercargo and up to five midshipmen, 'all gentlemen by education and family'. This patronage source was important, independent of Government, but open to its advances and to the back-scratching of Company Directors and Proprietors.

Pay was modest, but private trade privileges for officers permitted them to export and import their own goods. The command of an East Indiaman carried such high rewards it was usually given to a relative or friend of the owners. Although in theory the crew, from the Captain to the ships cook, had the 'privilege' of cargo space, only the Captain, Chief Mate and Second Officer were able to make a substantial profit from the private trade this permitted.[3]

Just one voyage could make a Commander's fortune and set him up for life. During the years in question he was allowed 25 tons on the outward journey and 15 tons homeward, usually exceeded. (From 1772 to 1795 the allowance was larger). He was also allowed to sell wine, cheese, beer and other foodstuffs. Three voyages brought John Waddell, the Scots Commander of the *Plassey*, £18,000; and he boosted this total with £1,224 from smuggling tea; the money being paid to him by the respectable banking firm of *Walpole and Company* of Lombard Street.

Among the Commander's other perquisites was the passage money, which could be 100 guineas and included the right to sit at the Captain's table; and passengers also paid him for cabins and meals. Ordinary seamen were often abused, their pay, food and beer being purloined by Captain and purser alike.[4]

Up to 1744 Scottish Captaincies of East Indiamen were few and far between; but the energies of John Drummond of Quarrel in the 1720s and 1730s, using the Governmental patronage system to place Scots seamen, began to bear some fruit. A continental war from 1740, war with France from 1744, and a need to recruit good seafarers also helped.

It is certainly true that some Scots served on East Indiamen and reached India prior to the John Drummond of Quarrel period, but there were not very many. It also helped, as has been suggested, that the Presbyterian Scots were more acceptable to the Dissenting and Huguenot families who dominated the Company's shipping. The education, work ethic, strong sea-going traditions and skills of the Scots were matched by those of East India Company shippers and provided a basis for mutual respect.

Captain Robert Knox of the *Ann*, who became a Minister at Kandy, exemplifies these qualities. Together with Captain Alexander Hamilton, his brother, Dr William Hamilton (a surgeon from Wishaw), and Captains George Heron, William Fraser of Bengal, Francis Seaton, Daniel Clarke, Arthur Maxwell and David Thomson, he formed part of a small Scottish presence before 1707.

After the Act of Union and with the bitter memory of the failure of the Darien Scheme fading, Scottish seafaring fortunes changed for the better. Within a few years following the blending of the Scottish mercantile community with their like in the Port of London, Scots seamen were able to forge contacts with the English shipping world based on the river Thames. Marriage and business enabled families like the Humes and Moffatts, discussed in these pages, to penetrate to the highest positions within this select body. The shipping advantages from coming within the Navigation Acts were also seized upon by Scottish Commanders and ships husbands. If registered within 12 months of 1707, Scottish vessels were admitted to British shipping, and penetration of the English trading/maritime Companies followed.[5]

One of the first to benefit from these changes (and who was to reach prominence in the East India Company marine) was *Captain Charles Boddam*. He was born in 1680, possibly in the small village of Boddam, two miles south of Peterhead. He joined the Company in 1710 and became Commander of the *Charlton* in 1716, then of the *Walpole* trading to China, from 1724 to 1736.

Command of the *Walpole* was perhaps not mere coincidence, given the existence of the Walpole–Drummond India patronage system during these years and the habit developed by ships husbands of naming a ship after a benefactor. By marrying Mary, the daughter of Rawson Hart, a Councillor in Fort St. George, he established himself; and with the birth of his sons Charles Boddam and Rawson Hart Boddam, it transpired a Company and shipping dynasty was formed.

Charles Boddam (Younger) became a Company Director, and Rawson Hart Boddam would be Governor of Bombay. The latter married Frances, daughter of Nicholas Morse, very important in the Company and in shipping. Captain Charles Boddam Senior remained in Fort St. David and by 1748 had risen to 5th in Council there.

Naturally enough, most Scots seafarers in the Company's ranks did not reach captaincy. A great many, like James Bean, remained mate of a ship. Bean was patronised by Sir James Grant of Grant and acted as an informant – to him in particular. One of his observations concerned Alex Dalrymple, of whom he had a poor opinion. He accused Dalrymple of making mischief in India and 'acting Don Quixote for 7 years.'[6]

However, one or two Scots who became Commanders were prominent between 1707 and 1744; they included John Gordon of the *Montague* and John Hunter of the *Barrington*. Both gained commands in 1722. Captain William Hutchinson was in charge of the *Sutherland* in 1723, and of the *Godolphin* in 1754. By 1773 he was Dock master at Liverpool, amassing a fortune in between times. His two brothers also served in the Company.

Other seafarers voyaging on East Indiamen in the 1720s were Commander James Macrae (before he became Governor of a Presidency), William Leggatt (a ships mate) and John Fergusson. In 1732 Fergusson became a surgeon's mate on board the *Britannia*. He had departed Ayr in 1731 and spent a year in London gaining the necessary patronage and recommendations. Other Scots Commanders operated in the 'country' (or coastal)* trade in the East, such as Captains Rannie and Craig. Captain Campbell of the *Bengal Galley* (coastal trade) died in 1730 fighting the pirate Maratha Admiral Angria. His name hints at Argathelian patronage.

Those early seafarers who were already connected with governing political figures, such as Captain Gordon's links with John Drummond of Quarrel, were invaluable for later lines of patronage via the Company's Shipping interest. By the 1750s Scots had penetrated the Company in large numbers, as Directors, Proprietors and servants (home and abroad). They were familiar with its organisation and the opportunities it offered through Members of Parliament, via Scots in the banking and business world in London, and by using agents and countless other forms of contact. That they had certainly built upon early shipping connections formed because of John Drummond's manipulation of the patronage machine is testified throughout the Company's marine records in the period 1740–1761.[7]

Between 1740 and 1743 it has been calculated that the number of European-built ships in the Company's service (East Indiamen), jumped from fifty-five to sixty-three; and remained at or about this number until 1761.[8] At one time or another during the eighteen years from 1743 to 1761, twenty-five of the sixty-three East Indiamen had Scottish Captains. Eight of these received their captaincies in the 1740s: Charles Foulis, Robert Haldane, Richard Elliot and Gabriel Steward (1744); George

Cumming (1747); John Petrie and George Lindsay (1748); and Norton Hutchinson (1749).

The other seventeen appointments were spread evenly over the 1750–1760 decade: Gilbert Slater and John Watson (1750); Alex Dickson, Benjamin Fisher and William Dalrymple (1754); Robert Veitch (1756); James Haldane, Alex Hume and Cornelius Inglis (1757); Nathaniel Inglis and William Scott (1758); James Dewar and Alexander Macleod (1759); and George Baker, Charles Haggis, James Moffatt and Andrew Ross (1760).[9]

It is significant that many of these commands were given after the outbreak of war in 1744, and others after the start of the Seven Years War in 1756; and there is little doubt that such crises acted as catalysts to this recruitment. The need for experienced sailors and the increase in shipping surely accelerated developments.[10] Nevertheless, this remarkable influx, which resulted in a very strong Scottish presence within the ranks of the Company's shippers, can really only be accounted for by dint of a deliberate effort to engage Scots in this particular field – to the exclusion of other ethnic groups. Growing Scots entry elsewhere into Company business and into the running of its affairs, as already outlined, doubtless helped inspire this policy.

Such a large number of Scottish Commanders is almost certainly an indicator that influential Scottish (or pro–Scots) individuals in the governing Establishment were at work – alongside those among the charter-parties and ships husbands. This was especially noticeable among the custodians of 'hereditary bottoms'. It was the same among the owners of East Indiamen, where the privilege of appointing Commanders had become so customary it was regarded as a right or possession.

Clear instances of the mounting Scots presence in shipping and of their new found influence were the positions they in turn could now command. The appointment of John Douglas in 1754 to the position of Writer in the Company's civil branch through the patronage of the Scottish Commander of the *Lord Anson*, Charles Foulis, illustrates the point.

2

Excellent illustration of patronage and the Shipping interest at this time is found in the careers of Robert Haldane, MP and his nephew, James Haldane, both Commanders of East Indiamen; and in the exploits of Captain James Moffatt and his brother Andrew. The former became rich and important landowners in the 1742 to 1761 period from the immense wealth drawn from India. The latter were thoroughly embroiled in a massive upsurge in ships insurance and underwriting that embraced the Company's shipping.

Captain Robert Haldane, known as 'The Entailer', was the son of John Haldane of Gleneagles and his second wife Helen, daughter of Sir Charles Erskine. He became the owner of the estates of Plean, Airthrey and Gleneagles before his death in 1767. Through his landed wealth, political connection and East India shipping position he continued the network of political patronage, helping others to places on East Indiamen and also into the Company's service.

His initial entry to life on board an East Indiaman in 1725 was managed through the Erskines. He too was soon in the Argyll–Milton interest (which the Erskine tie gave him), an allegiance that was in turn transferred to Bute. He was made Captain of the *Haselingfield* in 1744; and in 1746 first the *Tryal* and then the *Prince Edward*.

By 1747 he had moved politically to an independent position, although in 1746 was in direct communication with Milton. The reason for the shift at this time was the yearning for a seat in the Commons. He was willing to put his wealth towards attaining this goal, even passing up the offer of the Governorship of Bombay in this pursuit.

By all accounts he was 'an arrogant, ambitious, purseproud man' and this probably led him, mistakenly, to oppose Milton and Argyll. But the support of Newcastle, Sir Laurence Dundas and Alex Wedderburn, not to mention all his riches, availed him nothing in his designs upon the County of Stirlingshire. The Argathelian interest defeated him; and by 1752 Milton had bought off his opposition. Part of the purchase price was the use of Milton's influence to ensure that Haldane's nephew, James Haldane, was made Captain of the *Prince Edward* that same year, in place of his uncle Robert.

Apart from links with Milton and the Erskines, especially Baron James Erskine who had become Lord Chief Justice Clerk, Robert Haldane, was a friend of John Dalrymple of Culhorn, of John Hamilton Dalrymple of Bargany (Sir Hew Dalrymple's brother), Chalmers of Errol, George Ross (Lord Mansfield's man of business), and the Stirlings of Keir. All were involved in Company shipping. Lord Anson of the Admiralty was another good friend who helped him further the career of his own cousin, Adam Duncan of Dundee who later became an Admiral of the Fleet.

Robert Haldane's allegiance to the Argathelian cause after 1752 is reflected in this list of fellow travellers; and is demonstrated clearly in his withdrawal, without reservation, from Stirling burghs in the 1760 election because Bute wanted the seat for Alex Wedderburn. In return, that same year, he was asked to be MP for Perthshire by Milton. In this he was supported by Dalziel of the Binns and John Drummond of Paisley. Meanwhile, he continued to recommend young men to posts in India, and in this pursuit met with a great deal of success, whether in the shipping line or, as was the case with the young Walter Douglas in 1760, as a Writer in the Company's service.[11]

Commander James Haldane of Airthrey, son of Col. James Haldane, was granted his original position as a seaman through John Drummond of Quarrel, and at the request of both Walpole and the Duke of Argyll. He only gained his captaincy, as already mentioned, when in 1752–1753 the Argyll–Milton political influence was brought to bear.

The importance of such an interest is emphasised by the fact that before this date James had already spent around 18 years at sea. After 12 years as Captain of the *Prince Edward* he relinquished this post in 1765 to take command of the *Duke of Albany*. He also introduced his second son, Captain James Alexander Haldane, into the Company's shipping, in so-doing carrying on a tradition. This son made a colossal fortune, trading in saltpetre and dealing with the Scots firm of *MacIntosh and Hannay*. Following his own death in 1768, James Haldane Senior was succeeded as Captain of the *Duke of Albany* by another Scotsman, Captain John Stewart.[12]

Several circumstances would seem to suggest that the *Moffatt brothers, James and Andrew,* were involved quite substantially in directing India patronage to ministries for use in Scotland. John Moffatt, the third brother involved played a less significant role. Apart from their own Scottish origins through their father, a sister, Martha, was married to Charles Bruce, the Earl of Elgin; and James was patronised by Bute via James Oswald, who was a Lord of the Treasury from 1759 to 1763.

James Moffatt was Commander of an East Indiaman before he and Andrew became ship owners and insurers. Through marriage they were linked with the Director William Freeman and the powerful Scots Commander Charles Foulis. In association they formed a major phalanx among the shippers and within the Company Shipping interest. This was important in that they were providers of Company civil service posts and shipping berths. For example, their relation Robert Moffatt was appointed a Writer in 1749. To secure this they drew upon the patronage system fully, and the young man was recommended by the Scottish Proprietors James Buchanan and Alex Johnston. Later, in 1773, when even stronger in the Direction, they ensured that their brother John was helped to a 1st mate's post on the *Hector*.

The marriage of Lord Mansfield's nephew, Sir Thomas Mills to Andrew Moffatt's daughter formed the other vital link in the Ministry–Company–Scotland connection; and Moffatt activities indicate a steady involvement in placing India patronage in ministerial hands when so desired. In the 1750s they kept a low profile, operating from Lombard Street and building-up business with other insurers and freight agents, like William Braund, and with the *Sun Fire Assurance Company*. The startling developments in the Company, at home and abroad, in the early 1760s embroiled them deeply. To their roles in the Shipping interest they added speculation in India stock and involvement on Laurence Sulivan's side in the contested elections of the period.

From 1761 to 1765 Bute's wishes and those of Sulivan were followed; and from 1765 to 1768 they remained allied with Sulivan. Together with his other backers in the shipping world they provided him with firm support up to 1768. That year James Moffatt became a Proprietor and in 1774 a Director; and during this time he faithfully executed the wishes of his relation through marriage, Lord Mansfield, increasingly following a ministerialist line in the Company.[13]

The East India Company was expanding, and its role changed throughout this period, with defence of the Presidencies, control of the shipping lanes and growth of trade all being pursued at the expense of rival trading powers, especially the French. These events were mirrored inside the Company by an increase in the various interest groups, all grasping for power and patronage. This struggle for control of the Company, involving the Shipping interest, had first surfaced in 1757 and progressed rapidly from that point to a series of bitter contested elections. These in turn, affected the flow of Company patronage to such an extent that ministerial knowledge of, and contacts with, the controlling faction(s) in the Company became vital for the systematised use of India patronage for Scottish political ends to continue. The Shipping interest was one of the most important of these groups.[14]

9

Elections and Watersheds 1761–66

1

Ilay died in 1761 but the shape of future Scottish political management was already clear. John Stuart, 3rd Earl of Bute, nephew to Ilay, had become the key figure in the entourage of the new monarch George III. Although Ilay and his nephew had fallen out in 1759 over the distribution of the Ayr burgh seats, by 1761 this had been patched up. There is little doubt, however, that the death of 'so resourceful a friend' was to foreshorten Bute's own reign of power.[1]

Bute was an Anglo–Scot who lived in Scotland only from 1739 to 1745. In 1739 he had helped heal the rift between Walpole and John, 2nd Duke of Argyll. His other appearance was as a Scottish representative peer in 1757. His was a rising star, however, and his political career and insight were helped by being a confidante of the Royal family from 1747 to 1760. Undoubtedly this provided him with his opportunity when the new king was enthroned.[2]

While Ilay was alive Bute had little control over Scottish patronage, although there was a slight overlap during the first months of George III's reign because of Bute's influence with the king. But evidence that Ilay continued his hold over affairs north of the Tweed was reflected in the fact that his old enemy, Newcastle, was pushed further out of things. It was only following his uncle's death in April 1761 that Bute became the most important figure in Scottish eyes. But his lack of personal touch and an apparent boredom with politics there continued. He 'despised the Scots patronage' and was content to leave this to adherents.

His close group of friends, advisers and ministers in Government, included Henry Fox (later Lord Holland), the Earl of Shelburne, Lord Eglinton, Sir Gilbert Elliot of Minto, William Mure of Caldwell, James Oswald and Sir Harry Erskine. They all found themselves dealing more and more with Scottish business. Bute also placed his brother, James Stuart Mackenzie, in charge of Scottish affairs. He thought (mistakenly) that this would satisfy the Argathelians, whose support he now commanded, and would dispel their fears of a Squadrone revival led by Arniston and Marchmont.[3]

Bute's own need to be in London and yet have someone controlling affairs for him in Scotland, whom he knew and could trust, had also led to the choice of his brother. Yet at the same time, at Newcastle's insistence, he had given one of Ilay's offices, Keeper of the Great Seal in Scotland, to a potential enemy, the Earl of Marchmont. This sub-division of authority in Scotland in 1761 was made more complex by the degree of control Lord Mansfield exercised over Scottish proceedings. William Murray, 1st Baron and 1st Earl of Mansfield (Lord Chief Justice in 1768) was one of Bute's closest advisers. He was an ex-Jacobite and close relative of Lord George Murray, the Jacobite military commander at Culloden. Yet he was also a friend of Duncan Forbes until the latter's death in 1747. Mansfield and his agent, George Ross, were useful, and actively manipulated support for Bute in and out of Parliament.[4]

Bute's indifference to Scottish political management and the threatened breakdown of clear lines of command was further complicated by Mackenzie's own reluctance to manage Scotland on his brother's behalf. He in turn thrust most of these duties upon Sir Gilbert Elliot 3rd Bart of Minto, former Lord of the Admiralty and now a Lord of the Treasury. Mackenzie's own insensitivity added to the frustrations in Scotland and led to difficulties in maintaining loyalty among the Scottish group of Peers and MPs who were his responsibility. What saved the day for Bute, Mackenzie and Elliot was the willingness of Milton to go on as before, running the Argathelian organisation. To him and most others: 'Scots attached to Bute and Argyll were almost indistinguishable'.[5]

The muddled manner in which the political management of Scotland was now to proceed probably helped Milton. But he had several important men and their agents to contend with besides Bute's brother and Mansfield. William Mure of Caldwell, Baron of the Exchequer was one of these. He was already an acknowledged representative of the Bute interest, acting alongside his master's man of business, John Home. Mure had been an MP until 1761. He was related to Elliot and had a family link with

Milton. Eventually he would succeed this astute master in the autumn of 1764; but from 1761 they worked side by side, with Mure learning how to handle things; and acting as 'a point of contact in Edinburgh for those who wished patronage.'[6]

Next to Milton, Sir Gilbert Elliot was by far the most important of Bute's Scottish connections, and the man relied upon when making appointments in his homeland. Elliot, an advocate, was familiar mainly with members of the legal profession in Scotland, but among them, of course, was Milton, who ensured that Elliot's friends would 'act together to support a party line, the party being Bute's and the line Milton's.'[7]

As well as participating with Milton and James Stuart Mackenzie in the management of Scottish political affairs, such as acting as a contact for Navy posts, Elliot's gifts as an orator and Parliamentarian were extremely useful; and he helped marshal Bute's Scottish support in the Commons, even after his leader's fall from grace in 1763. He was effective to the extent that in 1766 thirty Scottish MPs, whose Argathelian complexion was still evident, were identified as Bute followers.[8]

On the whole, the old Argathelian interest was happy to be harnessed to the Bute Government and to figure in its arrangements regarding Scotland. Milton's task was made easy in that clearly it was to their benefit to acclaim Bute, his friends and ministers, many of them Scotsmen, who were the King's friends and who formed his Government. The choicest patronage flowed abundant from this, the fountainhead. As a consequence, throughout Bute's ministry Milton remained the most effective politician in Scotland, as well as its chief correspondent and spokesman. However, his mental powers failed very soon after the demise of this Administration and he died early in 1766.

2

Until the contested elections broke out, the ministry's methods of extracting Company patronage followed the well-worn ways laid down in the Walpole–Drummond of Quarrel period, but now implemented by the Ilay–Milton management machine. In all of this, relationships, back-scratching and indulgence proved effective. Everything received a severe jolt, however, with the political contests. These began in late 1757 and continued sporadically but with increasing intensity until 1765 and beyond. Fortunately, the main sinews of the patronage system held firm, such as using existing ministerial connection with Company leaders; through inter-locking interests stretching from Scotland to the London business community; by way of backstairs lobbies at Westminster; and by links within the labyrinth of Company Courts and committees.

The many groups and factions that made up the Company's Court of Directors and General Court of Proprietors were open to a variety of approaches, all of which could end in India patronage for Government use in Scotland. The request for a post could be initiated in any of these quarters, as long as it got back to Westminster, or to the powers in Scotland, to be used as electoral currency there.

The years up to 1757 were ones of harmony and compromise between Government and the Company; and their need to work closely together had gained strength from the continental hostilities that began in 1740. Even closer collaboration was needed throughout the Seven Years War of 1756–1763; but with this came problems that began to stretch the Company's limited resources, fracture stability and rock it to the core.

The old commercial interest running the Company had no answer to the onset of pressures and problems (external and internal) that began in 1756. War against the French, who allied with native rulers hostile to the English Company, led to a financial drain. The expence of prosecuting these wars and the added strain of remittance bills drawn extravagantly upon the Company by servants abroad began to take its toll. All of this was made worse by Clive's victory at Plassey in 1757, which raised the Company from a trading concern to a potentially great territorial power, but brought with it a host of problems and responsibilities.

The momentous and disturbing events taking place abroad and the financial strains now placed upon the organisation were accompanied by ever intensifying struggles for power at India House. They first appeared in the lead-up to the April 1758 election of Directors. This contest, unlike those of a later date, did not involve the 'splitting' of stock into £500 units in order to create voting rights. It was the consequence of disagreements on what policies should be followed to deal with the Company's new found situation and problems in India; and also reflected the determined efforts by new forces in the Company, those returned 'Indians' (most of them from Bombay) headed by Laurence Sulivan and Stephen Law, who, in alliance with friends in the Shipping interest, challenged the old brigade in control of the Company's Courts.[9]

From April 1757 (when Sulivan became Deputy Chairman) to April 1758 the factions clashed in the Company's Courts and in public – reflected in press campaigns. Behind the struggle for control lay the glittering prizes of patronage, power and influence. Sulivan and his 'Bombay Squad' of Company servants returned from that Presidency were disenchanted at the ignorance and lack of concern in the old Direction. Backed by powerful figures in the Company's shipping, such as the Godfrey family, Timothy Tullie, Captains Thomas Lane, Samuel Hough and others, they squared up to the Chairman, John Payne and his coterie of supporters in the Direction who had no first-hand experience of India. Their success was such that Sulivan would retain an absolute control for the next six years.[10]

By the 1760s, it was very much common knowledge that power and immense riches were to be had from control of the Company; and that contesting the election of Directors offered a means of gaining both. The election in the April of each year decided who was in command at India House and who was to be given the opportunity to accumulate riches abroad. Wealth from India was realised using bills of exchange drawn upon the Company or by one of many other forms of remittance. Using carefully chosen servants, many Company officials, home and abroad, ensured that funds were remitted for their personal benefit.

The competing factions strove to control nomination of the Chairman or Deputy Chairman posts and to fill the Direction with their followers. They (and leading Proprietors sympathetic to those in power) regardless of being Scottish or not, would recommend people to posts in proportion to the backing given by individuals or their families and the finance they made available for the contested elections. These funds were used for the purchase and splitting of stock into the £500 units that carried a vote. During these troubled years this activity absorbed and sucked in every type of financier, adventurer and gambler. It also gave the General Court of Proprietors teeth, to the extent that powerful and rich shareholders, whose support would be needed at every election, were able to influence potential members of each Direction. In turn, they received the favours asked for.

The power of the Company Chairman also changed dramatically. The altered circumstances in India and the sharpened demand for patronage in London charged him with an overriding importance. What is more, the attraction of India meant that demand far outstripped supply, a situation only partly remedied by the ever-increasing supply of mercantile and military recruits, many of them from Scotland. To make a real fortune in India, however, normally called for a position in the Company's civil service, and this placed the 'Chairs' under even greater pressure. The demand for such posts was reflected in the huge increase in Writers Petitions.[11]

The ministry's renewed interest in India affairs and desire for patronage was aided by the Company's periodic need to renew its Charter. The price squeezed out of Leadenhall for its renewal also included India posts for selected individuals. Prominent figures in Parliament and leading lights in the City of London as well, were soon embroiled in Company affairs. Politicians, merchants, bankers and other monied interests rushed to become Proprietors. By the early 1760s Newcastle and Cavendish, then Chatham, Henry Fox (the Paymaster-General) and Sir Gilbert Elliot, Ilay's friend, were deeply drawn into its politics. Aspiring politicians, adventurers and speculators competed and jockeyed for position and patronage, drawn by the power the Company proclaimed, lured by the prospect of riches that its possessions overseas seemed to offer.[12]

3

Following events in Bengal from 1757, there was an even fuller flow of posts to Scotland. This is indicated by the number of Scots allocated Writerships, by the surge of captaincies and other seagoing positions, and by the military cadetships, not to mention Scots regiments forming part of the Royal forces, despatched to India. This flood of posts to Scots was even more pronounced from 1761 with the coming to power of Bute.

As individuals, groups or as part of larger factions, Scots were also profoundly implicated in the ongoing struggles for mastery within India House that commenced during the lead-up to the April 1758 election. They were ever-present during Sulivan's years of almost total control from 1758 to 1765, and involved in the skirmishes leading to Lord North's Regulating Act of 1773. They would play a part right up to Pitt's India Act of 1784 and beyond.

From the first, Sulivan exerted an authoritarian control over all aspects of Company life. This firmness came naturally to him, but was also used deliberately in the effort to correct abuses abroad, curb mischief and mismanagement there and rescue the Company from financial collapse. India presented a picture of fortunes being made, of power falling into the hands of Company servants with little or no effective restraint; of a general free-for-all. His attempts to control this from London meant he and Robert Clive (following his return in 1760), would eventually cross swords. It also meant that those servants castigated severely by him (those principally from the Bengal Presidency) would join with Clive when they returned home. The Company was to reverberate with their struggles and the turmoil had a knock-on effect upon the disbursement of India patronage.[13]

From the outset, most Scots were overwhelmingly on the side of Sulivan. They constituted both friends and allies, whether grouped as part of the Shipping interest, 'Bombay Squad', commercial interest in the City, or as servants abroad. From his Bombay days, up to 1753, Sulivan could count upon a number of them: George Scott, Accountant and Collector at Bombay, who worked beside him in the Fort; Alex Douglas, Customs Collector at Mahim; John Hope, Warehouse keeper; William Shaw, Andrew Gardner, Robert Erskine, David Seton, James Lister, John Cameron and Alex Fleming.

Like John Hope, many of these servants had returned, and were in London. Others had gone back to Scotland, but were represented in the 'City'. Captains Robert Haldane, James Dewar, John Watson (with whom Sulivan had business accounts) and Captain Forbes of the Bombay marine can be numbered in this way. On the military side he could count upon Major James Kilpatrick (who he made 3rd in Council in Bengal in 1757) and Major William Mackenzie.[14]

In London Sulivan had developed other Scottish connections among his 'natural interest', as he called the shippers. These included Captains Charles Boddam and James Moffatt, both commanders with a vested right of command, making them almost a permanent fixture in Company shipping. James Moffatt and his brother Andrew, husbands of 'permanent bottoms', also had the vested right as owners or commanders to have a ship in the Company's service. They and their brother John had added insurance-broking to their portfolio (for shipping in particular); and as well as acting as Directors and Proprietors were involved as speculators in 'change alley', gambling, through advance knowledge, upon the value of India stock.

Yet another Scot, Dr. John Munro, was a member of Sulivan's 'marine society', a syndicate put together for private trading purposes, with members operating in India and in London. To this number Sulivan added, in 1755, Scots connections from the Royal Society of Arts, who included a James Stewart and a Mr. Macpherson.[15] From within the Company this Scots caucus worked hand in glove with him, sharing in the patronage he could offer. Through Sulivan they developed close ties with ministerial agents, and despatched favours to friends in Scotland.

4

Scots, many acting as Directors or Proprietors, would constitute a formidable presence during the political contests. Some, such as the Johnstone family and their uncle, Lord Elibank, would play a major part in the dramas of these years.[16] The emergence of the Johnstones in the Company, of commanders like Charles Foulis and the Haldanes in its shipping, and of innumerable others who had been sent to India and were now in positions of power, either there or at home, wrung changes in the way that India patronage would be creamed off for purposes of Scottish political management. Indeed the Scots must be regarded at this time – as indeed they were by contemporaries – as a special entity; although a clannish disposition (abetted by English hostility) made them appear more united than was the case.[17]

Many Scots played active and vigorous roles. For example, Drummond, Fordyce and Fisher, all bankers in London, were involved in putting up money for the purchase and splitting of stock. Sir Laurence Dundas, Alex and Abraham Hume, Sir William and Robert Mayne, brought their fortunes to bear for this purpose – as well as 'dealing in the alley', buying and selling India stock. Others, such as Sir Gilbert Elliot, James and Sir John Macpherson, Andrew Stuart, Lauchlin Macleane (an Ulster Scot) and Lord Mansfield, dealt in the sometimes shady areas of back-stairs politics, bringing to bear upon Company affairs Government cash and influence, when and where ministries so desired.[18]

From 1761 to 1765 the people in Scotland to be helped would be those with close ties with Argathelian-minded ministers, as had always been the case; but satisfaction would now depend more upon personal connection with individuals, such as those above, who were involved in Company politics and contested elections, in its shipping and with the direction of affairs abroad. Failing this, some such contact would have to be made for them through ministerial connections.

5

From 1761 Bute's links with Sulivan, the leading figure at India house, were directed through Lord Shelburne and the Secretary of State, Lord Egremont. The connection was strengthened by using Egremont's Under-Secretary, Robert Wood, who had been Sulivan's friend for some considerable time. The close liaison needed in framing the clauses of the settlement to end the Seven Years War, particularly as they applied to the Indian theatre, had brought Bute and Sulivan together. They collaborated as early as 10 November 1761. In joining with Bute, Sulivan was cutting the ties he had built-up with Chatham when pursuing the war against the French in India.[19]

The April 1763 contested election was marked by the Bute ministry's wholesale (and open) participation on Sulivan's behalf. Political influence, the use of Government funds (through Lord Holland and the Pay Office) and secretariat influence, were all brought to bear; while myriads of Government dependants swarmed to his side and ensured success against Clive and his allies.

This interference in Company affairs by the head of Government, a Scotsman at that, was a clear sign to others, including his countrymen how to vote. Scots involved themselves in the purchase of India stock, splitting it for voting purposes. Of course, behind these moves lay the same greed for power, patronage and wealth in evidence at every level and among all concerned. Sulivan and his party were successfully returned at the ballot.

Meanwhile, ensconced at Leadenhall since 1761, the formidable Johnstone group, led by George, John and William Pultney Johnstone, had been quietly involved in splitting activities, raising loans from Scottish relations, like their uncle, Lord Elibank, and from Andrew Stuart of Craigthorn. In February 1763 they came to the fore on the East India Company political stage, joining Clive's 'Bengal Squad' against Sulivan at the 1763 election because John Johnstone had been castigated and finally dismissed for his alleged misdeeds in Bengal.

Following his election success, Sulivan was approached in August 1763 by Sandwich, one of Grenville's ministerial friends, in an effort to stop the feud with Clive. Sulivan was too powerful an enemy and his City support was an integral part of the backing required by Grenville's new Government. The attempt was of no avail and the arrival in England of despatches from Bengal saying that the Presidency had 'become a scene of bloodshed and confusion' ended the hopes of restraint on either side of the Company divide.

Clive then made certain of the Grenville ministry's support for the 1764 election and thus of eventual success. It was done mainly through the ministry's busy agent, Charles Jenkinson. Again the Johnstones entered the lists, in February 1764, in the attempt to get John Johnstone re-instated and his name cleared. Their political weight was significant to the extent that Sulivan admitted that 'the Scotch' working as a unit seriously affected the outcome of the election.

The ballot had resulted in a draw, Sulivan's vast reach in the City matching ministerial influence and the combined funds of Clive and the Pay Office. Sulivan, however, withdrew, his pride hurt at not being swept into the Chair, and he sensed a change for the worse. This left a clear field for the Clivites. The power of the 'Scotch' also determined that John Johnstone was re-established in 1764, thus setting an ugly precedent.

Sulivan built up a strong Scottish support in the lead-up to the April 1765 election. The Johnstones had swung over to his side. They disliked Clive's power and haughtiness, and his efforts to take John Johnstone's wealth from him in the Court of Chancery.[20] To the Johnstones and their friends, he added the powerful Proprietor John Stewart, who was against the renewal of Clive's *jagir*;* and Charles Boddam was also invited to be on his list, thus bringing in all Boddam's banking and shipping relations. Sir James Cockburn, who had a large stock holding, entered on his side, and brought with him his relation, James Stewart of Buckingham Street, London.

For this election Sulivan gained the backing of the independently-minded George Dempster, a Director and Proprietor of reputation and stature. At the time Dempster was a firm friend of Bute. In return for this support he was offered an important India post by Sulivan, which he turned down.[21] However, yet again ministerial support (by Grenville) proved decisive in settling the outcome in favour of the Clivites, although Bute worked hard for Sulivan that year.[22]

Following Clive's victory Sulivan was excluded from power, and the make-up of the Direction reflected Clive's strength. Through his agents, Luke Scrafton and John Walsh, he dictated the business of the Court of Directors from India, and controlled most Company patronage.

6

Such stirring proceedings home and abroad, between 1758 and 1765, impacted upon the patronage system and its organised use by Government for political control in Scotland. In London, ministerial figures, MPs and Scottish businessmen were now involved in Company affairs on a scale hitherto unknown. As noted, they were caught up in the Courts and Committees, in backstairs politics and in almost every facet of the Company. Its business assumed new importance.

Through such London-based intermediaries and their friends filtered the India patronage that made such involvement invaluable to Government and to Scottish political managers, north or south of the Tweed. Measurement of the success of the Scottish participation in this period is reflected in the startling numbers involved in 'splitting' stock for the contested elections, and by so many youths from north of the border receiving Writers positions. It was out of all proportion.

Operation of the patronage system in Scotland during Bute's years in office naturally received a major fillip with a Scot as the leading minister. At the Scottish end Milton and William Mure of Caldwell worked with the all-powerful Chairman Laurence Sulivan and his associates functioning within the Company. Shelburne, Holland and Eglinton all acted as Bute's subsidiaries and as alternate channels of communication with the Company, as well as for the routing of patronage north.

The complex infrastructure involving these principals, through whom patronage was given and received, can be glimpsed now and then. Boswell's diaries for example, give details of Bute's partiality for Scots and the nature of his alliance with other powerful individuals on their behalf, such as Henry Fox, 'hired by the promise of a peerage to break the power of Bute's political enemies in the House.'[23]

Nevertheless, Scottish affairs and the minutia of providing patronage for Scots had to be handled for Bute by one of his aides, so great was his distaste for this activity. In 1763 Boswell tried to get a job from the first minister through Eglinton (Alex Montgomerie), using a mass of Scottish contacts that included Lord Elibank and Sir James Macdonald, and even involved Lord Sandwich. Other intimates used were Patrick Crawford of Auchenames and, from 1757, Alex Wedderburn.

London was a hotbed of Scottish cliques in the 1760s, feting and dining one another. The Scottish aristocracy kept very much in touch and passed on favours. For example, the Duke of Queensberry, Sir Ludovick Grant, the Maxwells of Annandale, the Anstruthers of Balcakie, Erskines of Kellie, Johnstone of Grange and George Dempster of Dunnichen were all part of this ménage. They and others, including James 'Fingal' Macpherson, enjoyed Bute's friendship.[24]

Bute's principal contact with Sulivan was through Shelburne and his intermediary, Col. Scott. But he could be more direct. In 1761 he personally recommended Charles Stuart to Sulivan, who in turn appointed the youth a Writer for Bengal. Charles Stuart was vouched for by James and Thomas Coutts, in Boswell's words, 'well-known Scots bankers in London.' At this time James Coutts was in collusion with Milton. He had thanked Milton in 1760 for placing Royal Bank of Scotland business his way; and even earlier had supported Milton's scheme for the Linen Bank.[25]

The normal approach, however, is conveyed in the cases of John Graham and Alexander Hall. In Graham's case Eglinton wrote to Charles Jenkinson the following in 1763: 'The bearer is the young gentleman John Graham whom you was (sic) so good as to recommend to Mr. Rous [a Director] for a Company in the East India service. Graham waited on Rous with your letter of recommendation and Rous had agreed that he should have the Company, but this dispute coming on [the contested election] prevented the thing taking effect. Pray be so good as mention Graham to Sulivan. [The Company Chairman] He is really a fine young fellow.'[26]

Alexander Hall was the brother of Sir John Hall of Dunglass, near Berwick, an important landowner. In 1762 young Alexander was a Member of Council at Bencoolen, in Sumatra, a very unhealthy place. Through a family friend, Dr. Pringle, who was close to Shelburne, he tried to get away. Shelburne wrote to Sulivan on his behalf, but to no avail. Hall was needed there because of his experience in dealing with the Dutch and the difficulty of replacing him, so unpopular was the spot.[27]

Bute will always be remembered in the context of India patronage because he was the only man of the first rank in British Society then, to despatch his 3rd son, the Hon. Frederick Stuart, to India. A Writership was obtained for him in 1769, through Sulivan, and he remained in India until 1775. Normally such a family would not contemplate a career in India in the Company's service for one of its scions. But Frederick was a black sheep. Bute wanted him out of the way; and there was always the chance that he would return with a fortune through the help of Warren Hastings and the Nawab of Arcot.[28]

As noted, under the aegis of Bute, Sir Gilbert Elliot was certainly in an excellent position to push forward the protégés of his Scottish friends and political supporters. Close association with James Stuart Mackenzie, intimate friendship with William Mure of Caldwell, long acquaintance with Milton and the Scottish legal elite, and his family's privileged position, ensured a firm base in Scotland. His mother was a daughter of Sir Robert Stewart of Allanbank; and his wife was Agnes, daughter of Hugh Dalrymple, 2nd son of the 1st Bart of Hailes. This brought other Company connections: Sir Hew Dalrymple of North Berwick and Alex Dalrymple, Hydrographer to the Navy. He also held some important posts: Lord of the Treasury, 1761–2; Treasurer of the Chamber, 1762–70; Keeper of the Signet in Scotland and Treasurer of the Navy from 1770 to his death.

He had powerful friends in London, such as Chatham and the Grenvilles; and became the special confidant of George III. As one of the original members of the Poker Club he was an intimate of William Pultney Johnstone, with George Dempster; and with members of the Edinburgh literary circle that included David Hume and John Home. The Johnstones and Dempster consolidated his position within the East India Company. Through a leading Proprietor, John Stewart of Hampstead, he was kept well-informed upon India matters as they unfolded in the Company Courts.[29]

Elliot's correspondence indicates that during the Bute years, 1760 to 1763, he made several efforts to get posts for his countrymen, and followed this up by using Shelburne after Bute's demise. He was industrious but discreet in seeking these favours. It is clear, for example, that in 1760 he obtained a Writership to Madras for his relation Quinton Crawford. It was done through the Director Crabb Boulton. In 1770 his India connections were given fresh impetus with the entry into the Company, as a Writer, of his second son, Alexander

The backstairs dealings associated with this appointment readily reflect the way in which patronage might flow. It transpired that in 1769 Elliot was dealing in Company stock through Coutts the bankers, via an agent, Andrew Douglas. Three sums of £500, one of £600, one of £700 and one of £88 were introduced through this medium – a total of £2,888. This money was almost certainly used for the collusive transfer (splitting) of stock; and Elliot was undoubtedly acting in support of Sulivan, who made a successful bid to return to power in the Direction that year. Sulivan and his ally Colebrooke, who vouched for Alexander Elliot in his Writer's Petition, ensured that he would be cared for; and Sulivan also placed the youth under the protection of Warren Hastings in Bengal. Hastings made him his private secretary.

In Bengal young Elliot proved an excellent narrator of on-going events, conveying these observations home to his father. He also formed part of a Scots caucus that involved Bute's son, the Hon. Frederick Stuart, John Graham, John Stewart formerly of Hampstead, and from 1774, Lauchlin Macleane.[30]

7

In the 1760s an increase in the number of Company servants returning with impressive fortunes and, perhaps of more importance, the prominence given to these 'Nabobs' by a press avid for anything to do with fabulous riches from the east, naturally stimulated Scottish desires for more India posts. This played into ministerial hands in the sense that if they continued to satisfy this demand then electoral and Parliamentary support from the politically involved Scots who mattered in this context was assured.

What is more, the economic needs of the Scottish gentry, the abolition of Heritable Jurisdictions and the eclipse of 'clannish, semi-feudal elements' helped the blatant political manipulation. Nominal votes cast the right way continued to give electoral control; although 'electioneering in this period was a hazardous business without a lawyer at your elbow.'[31]

Landed family influence continued to count for much in the 1760s (and 1770s) not just because of property but through intimate connections with Government in Scotland and at Westminster. Those wadsetters (mortgagees) who held a sub-division of the superiorities and thus had a vote were equally significant.

Bute had continued the political patronage system that operated in Scotland with Milton in charge; and to win elections this master had continued to create broad-based combinations of interests, such as through family connections and traditional alliances. Increasingly the rewards given to loyal adherents included India patronage. Such India Company commanders and military men as Captain Robert Haldane, the future General Hector Munro and Sir Robert Fletcher were all drawn in.

Even after his resignation in 1763 Bute (although he had effectively muddied the waters, leaving no clear-cut chain of authority pertaining to Scotland) tried to get all Scottish political management to pass through his brother, James Stuart Mackenzie. He, by that time, was operating under the aegis of the Grenville ministry. Many of the Scots nobility who had followed Bute had also welcomed Mackenzie's continuance in office and were happy to acknowledge him, but not the Scottish politicians in London to whom he appeared both obnoxious and obstructive.

Still greater opposition came from that quarter because of Bute's efforts to make his brother the King's minister for Scotland, even though a great deal of Scottish patronage 'passed through offices which Mackenzie did not control.' For instance, many Scots in London followed Bedford, who from 1764 was also in Grenville's Government. They included Sir Laurence Dundas, the Earl of Panmure and Lord Frederick Campbell, who all expressed different views from those of James Stuart Mackenzie.[32]

Yet Mackenzie did have power. This was clearly seen in 1765 when he bragged that the Generalship of the Mint in Scotland (a sinecure worth £250 per annum) 'might possibly have fallen to the lot of a Captain of an Indiaman...if I had not strongly objected to it.'[33] Basically, however, all was still well, as far as proper political management in Scotland was concerned, while Milton was still at the helm, and because James Stuart Mackenzie depended upon him. This lasted until the autumn of 1764 when Mure of Caldwell succeeded Milton.

However, events in London were about to change everything. Before his fall in 1765, Grenville forced James Stuart Mackenzie's dismissal, and abolished the post of minister for Scottish affairs. Responsibility for Scottish business then reverted to the ancient Newcastle, who formed part of the incoming Rockingham ministry. He in turn offered the powers of management in Scotland to Robert Dundas, Lord President of the Court of Session. But Dundas' refusal, the eclipse of Mackenzie, Elliot and Mure of Caldwell, and more significantly, the senility then death in 1766 of Milton created a new situation north of the border as well.

Meanwhile, with Sulivan's defeat in the 1765 Company contested election, his Scottish allies paid the penalty; and coinciding with the senility of Milton and the ejection of James Stuart Mackenzie from office, the Argathelian use of India patronage haemorrhaged. The new relationships to be struck up would no longer be based upon unswerving loyalty to an Argathelian-dominated establishment that had been in power in Westminster and Edinburgh for so long. All that remained of this was the headless body of Argyll supporters in Scotland whose allegiance would now only be secured through indulgences.

10

Ministries: Company and Favours 1765–74

1

The ministries from 1765 to 1770 of Rockingham, Chatham and Grafton, were so short and so beset with major problems that Scottish matters scarcely troubled them. There was little from that quarter to cause dismay in Government circles anyway.[1] All this clearly suggests that there was now no need to actively pursue India patronage on behalf of Scots. Yet old habits die hard when well established; and the sheer numbers of Scots going to India in the ten years from 1765 to 1774 indicates that India patronage was still deliberately funneled by governments to the benefit of Scots.

To do this the various ministries, from that of Grenville to Lord North, followed Bute's example. They formed strong direct links with the most powerful factions in the Company competing for control of the Direction, and thus with patronage to offer when successful. By the 1760s and early 1770s the number of favours available had swollen considerably.

Meanwhile, in Scotland, following the earlier death of Ilay, then of Milton in 1765 (and within the Company the ousting of Sulivan) there existed what could only be described as a vacuum in political management north of the border. Neither the Earl of Kinnoul nor Robert Dundas would accept from Rockingham the post of minister for Scotland. General elections were held in 1754, 1761, 1768, and 1774, but nobody was given this specific portfolio until the advent of Henry Dundas in 1778.[2]

Collapse of the political management system that had been peculiar to the Argathelians created an awkward and uneasy situation, but by no means a dangerous one. The control initiated by Walpole and John, 2nd Duke of Argyll, and carried on by Ilay and Milton under a succession of

Governments had ensured the security, stability and ultimately the survival of the state after the Union. Fears with regard to its continued existence had long passed.

Also, until North's Administration in 1770, ministries were so short in duration and Scotland had been quiet for so long (since 1746 and with no signs of future disturbance) that this bred in Whitehall a casual attitude through being accustomed to the way Scottish administration and management were pursued. What is more, so many Scots were now successfully entrenched in national life – including the Company and its shipping – that Scotland was being patronised if not managed. In the meantime the Earl of Mansfield gave guidance to the various Secretaries of the North regarding Scottish legal patronage; and some Scots made overtures to 'great personages' such as Marchmont and Queensberry, thinking that they, like Ilay before them, could supply posts.[3]

In a sense the tail began to wag the dog from 1765, in that those involved in Scottish politics and patronage were so caught in the same old grooves, they scarcely needed a political pilot to show them the way. Support for Westminster governments was still assured because those political sub-agents Milton had dealt with, such as the powerful John Mackenzie of Delvine, continued to function as their master would have wished; as did those many influential leaders among the Scottish gentry who had given the Argathelians and Milton their support for so long. Mackenzie (and his lieutenants) still followed the policies formulated by Milton, giving recommendations (increasingly sought after) in favour of actual and potential Government supporters.[4]

Significantly, in 1770 Sir Gilbert Elliot and John Mackenzie of Delvine were made respectively, Keeper and Deputy Keeper of the Signet – indicators of long-established Argathelian power. This can also be interpreted as a just reward for the profession they represented. Lawyers in Scotland, probably the most active and progressive layer of the elite after the Scottish aristocracy decamped south, had remained loyal and strong in support of the Great Britain creation. Their collaboration had lasted for so long, it would not fail now.

However, in practical terms the situation the landed elite north of the Tweed now found themselves in was far from ideal. Leading families in pursuit of India patronage, Scots managers, and new ministries at Westminster strove – almost blindly – to inter-link with each other and with those in the Company who could do them a favour. If it was not to be a powerful Director one year then perhaps the would-be saviour might be found at the next election.

It was natural for those interested in procuring patronage for Scots (whether in Government, in Parliament or in Edinburgh) to look towards their countrymen in the Company. There were now many of them ensconced at India House; and with the indiscipline that accompanied the Clive–Sulivan struggle and the rapid territorial transformation of the Company's fortunes abroad, opportunities to manoeuvre abounded.

In fact, every Court of Directors from 1764 to 1775 had a Scottish member; and this regularity continued into the next century. Others in the Direction had strong Scottish ties: William George Freeman – through the Foulis family; John Boyd – using his Scottish–West Indies ties; and Sir Henry Fletcher – via his Lord Milton connection. Thereafter, from 1766 into the late 1770s, patronage would depend upon the degree of intimacy enjoyed by agents and aspirants alike; their association with members of the various administrations; and by the depth of involvement in Company politics.

Some bought and sold India stock merely as speculators; many, like the Johnstones, were involved in the Company elections and split stock on behalf of their interest group. Others, such as Lord Elibank, and the Mayne brothers, became Proprietors to gain influence and give better support to their kin.[5]

In addition, the vacuum in Scottish political management and the frequent change of ministries at Westminster allowed manoeuvring by Opposition figures. Several, like the wealthy Sir Laurence Dundas, were able to take advantage, and took command of substantial India patronage. They also benefited from the contested elections in the Company. Increasingly, however, developments in Company politics – and thus its patronage – during the years up to 1774, came to be dominated by interfering, ever-hungrier ministries as they attempted to seize the seeming wealth of the Company.

Until Sulivan's defeat in 1765, most Scots involved with the Company had enjoyed the fruits of patronage that fell from his table. A few, such as the Johnstones, their uncle Lord Elibank and supporter Andrew Stuart, had been pro-Clive until 1764, but went over to Sulivan in 1765. Thereafter, with increasing intensity, most followed the lead given by the Sulivan group and were determined to retain the Company's independence. The Government's campaign came into particular focus in 1766/67 with the first effort at State intervention in the Company's affairs via the Inquiry straddling these years.

Parallel with this, a deliberate campaign mounted by ministry to manage a majority of the Court of Directors and thus control patronage –

in so-doing subverting the Company's position – was actively resisted by Sulivan and the majority Scottish support. It was firmly understood that Governmental success would mark an end to independent management of patronage (as indeed it proved after 1773). To the very last gasp Scottish efforts were made to maintain the Company's autonomy and with it governance of its patronage. Of course, a few Directors and Proprietors were already in the ministerial pocket through bribery, family affiliation and their own opportunism. These included James and John Macpherson, Andrew and James Moffat, Thomas Cheape, John Pringle and Lord Loughborough.

Two factors dictated the flow of patronage after 1765. The first was the success of the Clive party and ostracism of Sulivan; the other was the temporary clouding of Governmental direction or leverage because of speculation and self-aggrandisement accompanying the rapid change in Company affairs abroad, and the political turmoil at India House. The fall-out from the Clive–Sulivan feud persisted, however, and those associated with Sulivan were made to suffer. However, ministerial desires came to challenge all rivals; and by 1770 Government interest was threatening everyone in the Company.

2

Apart from all else, by early 1766 Government and Parliament in general were united in desiring control of the Company and its new territories – though the issue of proprietary rights had to be handled delicately. The aim was to secure all the wealth and favours this promised. It was also intended that these India posts would continue to buy supporters among independently-minded Scottish lairds, and conclude bargains at elections.

But whereas Bute's interference in Company politics was more or less direct, his successors left the backstairs politics such liaison demanded to men of lower rank in Governmental circles. Exceptions were Charles Townshend and Lord Shelburne who, during Chatham's ministry, played leading roles in events surrounding the 1766–67 Parliamentary inquiry into Indian affairs.[6]

Because Grenville's Government was so shaky he had needed as much patronage as possible. He tried deliberately to create an 'interest' in the Company; and the years 1764–65 saw him develop 'a coordinated system of ministerial management' using followers of Clive, patronage seekers, and ministry supporters inside the organisation.[7] In so doing many Directors became dependent upon the Government. It all ended with the minister's exit from office.

Rockingham, who counted the Proprietor George Dempster among his friends, favoured the ruling majority in the Direction throughout the remainder of 1765 and into 1766. All were followers of Clive. Chatham, as indicated, employed the Parliamentary Inquiry of 1766–67 to try and squeeze money from the Company, threaten direct involvement in its internal affairs, and suggest that the ministry might not renew the all-important Charter preserving its monopoly. However, members of his ministry, such as Shelburne, foreseeing the troubles such a severe policy might create, sided with Sulivan and his Scottish allies in the Company in seeking a compromise agreement.

The Duke of Grafton in 1768 deliberately placed Government nominees within the Company Direction in an effort to construct a ministerial faction there, just as George Grenville had done earlier. Although he had the Scot William Fraser as his political agent, Grafton's main Company links were through Sandwich and his man of business, Robert Jones. He was successful to the extent that before his exit from office, ministers and leading Directors, like Sir George Colebrooke and Sir George Wombwell had been brought together.[8]

From 1770 Lord North also used lieutenants, the very able Charles Jenkinson and John Robinson, who handled all Company contacts. Sandwich helped here too, exercising his 'personal influence with the Court of Directors, solely for minor patronage', that is, for India posts.[9] The reality, however, was that North merely carried on Grafton's system. He tried to 'manage' the Company Courts and committees through Robinson and Jenkinson, who had earlier learned the ins and outs of the Leadenhall labyrinth when with the Bute and Grenville ministries.

There was also considerable influence exerted within the Company via links between individual ministers and leading Directors. For example, Wedderburn and Mansfield directed the conduct of their respective protégés, Cheape and Moffatt. Attempts were also made into the 1770s to exploit feuding in the Company's ranks.

During these years of political turmoil Parliament, like the Company, was split into many factions, which, when not in power, allied with those in the City hostile to the ministry's friends within India House. The lack of control at home and abroad made these intrusions into the organisation easy. Unfortunately, ministerial need to be involved at Leadenhall, but not to be seen to be, also brought political adventurers like Lauchlin Macleane, James and John Macpherson into affairs.

Meanwhile, Scottish feelers were out, searching for patronage; and these continued to reach into the heart of the monopoly, though lacking former direction. Many scrambled for funds with which to buy the India stock that bought votes and influence. Those so involved came to include a good cross-section of the Scottish nobility and gentry and notable business and banking groups. The firms drawn-in stretched from Scotland to London and the Continent, such as the banks of Fordyce, Fisher, Coutts and Drummond, and the Hopes of Amsterdam.

3

Until 1769 Sulivan was unsuccessful in his efforts to overcome Clive's influence, and his return to the Direction was resisted. Nevertheless, he continued to recruit Scots. For example, for the 1766 election he added George Cumming and John Stewart (who lived in Hampstead) to his list. They operated alongside George Dempster and the Johnstones, and were headed by the energetic George Johnstone. For the 1767 contest he also had Lord Elibank splitting £1000 of stock alongside his Johnstone nephews. James Macpherson and Adriaan Hope of Amsterdam joined with them; and John Stewart of Hampstead introduced Lauchlin Maclean to Sulivan.[10]

Lauchlin Macleane was to prove a vital figure in Company affairs from 1767 to 1777, ensnaring many Scots in his schemes, forging alliances with others, such as the Macphersons, James and John. He was also a political adventurer of the highest order. Born an Ulster-Scot and Jacobite, he graduated Doctor of Medicine at Edinburgh and then served in the Indian Wars in America. After his return he began meddling in Company business, and by 1766 was co-ordinating the efforts of a group of speculators in East India stock. Although on familiar terms with Sulivan he was also an intimate of Clive's friend Robert Orme.

One of the leading orators in the House, Isaac Barré, had introduced him to Shelburne, as did the Scot, General Duncan Clarke, who like Macleane was also involved at India house. Shelburne quickly realised how useful this clever man could be, and by October 1766 Macleane was made his Under-Secretary of State and 'man of business'.

From 1767 to 1770 Macleane headed various combinations, all splitting stock in favour of Sulivan's party. In particular, he drew together a cabal of Scots, recognised as such and referred to by Sulivan in distinct terms as his 'Scotch' support. Macleane's objectives were the return of Sulivan to the Direction, together with their mutual friends. He looked forward to the patronage this would bring him, and the extent to which he would line his own pocket.

In 1773, to recoup the fortunes they both lost in the financial disaster of 1769, brought about by reckless purchase of India stock for splitting purposes, Sulivan sent him east. At his request, Macleane was then befriended by Warren Hastings, who pushed money-making posts his way.

In his turn, Macleane commanded India patronage of his own. The careers of relatives like Commander Stephen Macleane of the Indiaman *Duke of Grafton*, and of Henry Macleane, sent as a Writer to Bengal in 1772, exemplify this. Macleane was to become Hastings' agent in Britain in the years 1775–6; and was simultaneously the agent for the Nawab of Arcot, succeeding John Macpherson at the *Durbar*. Bound for India once more, he died at sea in the winter of 1776/7 when his ship was lost in a gale off the Cape of Good Hope.[11]

However, in the lead-up to the 1767 Company election – long before his demise – he supported George Dempster when he headed nine Proprietors calling for a General Court to compliment Sulivan, thus demonstrating allegiance to the Irishman. Letters between George, John and William Pulteney Johnstone also show some of the financial infrastructure linking Sulivan with many of these Scots. The letters reveal transactions involving Macleane, the Johnstones themselves, the *Hope* Bank of Amsterdam and the Scottish firms of *Coutts*, *Grant* and *Fordyce* – not to mention other banks, such as *Goslings*.

Macleane, in turn, brought in Sir Gilbert Elliot, and with him the influential Wedderburn (Lord Loughborough). William Fisher, the banker, was buying stock as early as April 1766, and again joined Sulivan for the 1767 election together with two other Scots speculators, John Stewart, and Sir Robert Fletcher.

Despite his defeats in the 1767 and 1768 elections Sulivan's list of 'Scotch' supporters grew. In the General Court of Proprietors he could now count on James Johnstone and John Scott, as well as Robert and Duncan Clerk. These allies combined speculation in India Stock and splitting for the contested elections, with taking sides in the debates over the 1766–67 Parliamentary Inquiry, as well as wangling patronage for their families and friends. Dempster and the Johnstones gave particularly strong support at this time.

The Johnstones and Sir Robert Fletcher figured in another curious effort made in September 1767 to end the Clive–Sulivan feud. It was prompted by Robert Palk, formerly Governor of Madras and friend of both Sulivan and Clive. It failed, but a portion of the terms asked for by Sulivan are enlightening: 'All prosecutions against the Johnstones etc. for recovering presents to drop. Sir Robert Fletcher's indiscretion it's hoped will be forgot by his Lordship [Clive] and that he will not object to his returning to his rank in the service'.[12]

Sulivan had also harnessed the Scottish friends of his ally Robert Palk for the 1768 election: Colonel Charles Campbell, Captain Kilpatrick, Mr. A. Preston and Mr. Lind. The support of another Scot, John Russell, was important because he and thirteen others had split £13,500 of Lord Holland's stock for voting purposes. This financial strength was again increased by the backing of the same three London–Scottish bankers: *Grants*, *Fordyce* and *Coutts*, as well as the Johnstone oriented *Hope* of Amsterdam.

These Scots and Ulster Scots were responsible for Sulivan's successful return to the Direction in April 1769. Some of them changed to his side at the last moment. They split large sums and brought other influential figures over. For example, Lauchlin Macleane secured Shelburne and Lord Holland; George Dempster recruited the Burkes and Lord Rockingham. Robert and Duncan Clerk, who had been involved in India politics since 1765, split £100,000 of Sir Laurence Dundas' money on Sulivan's behalf.[13]

William Pulteney Johnstone had introduced Sir Laurence Dundas to Sulivan, who promised him, in return for his support, a Writership to dispose of and the nomination of two of the Directors on his list. The Johnstones and Hope of Amsterdam took some share of a fund of some £100,000 that stood alongside the 'Great Scheme', worth an equivalent amount, and which like it, was operated by Sulivan and Macleane. Stock was purchased at a high price using borrowed money, such as that from the Director John Boyd, thinking that it would go even higher in value, so that at the rescounter they would pay back the money borrowed and would pocket the difference. In between times the voting rights would win a place in the Direction. In fact they won the place, but suffered when the price of India stock collapsed.

Other Scots who joined in the fray in April 1769 on Sulivan's side included members of the Shipping interest, like Charles Foulis and his relation William George Freeman. It was Foulis who brought in the Director John Boyd. John Stewart of Buckingham Street, Sulivan's old friend, and ex-Jacobite wine-merchant, sided with him too.[14]

4

The relationship between Sulivan and the Scots following his return to power in 1769 was determined by his financial crash of that year. Sulivan (and his ally Vansittart) had promised to under-write the whole of the 'Grand Scheme' mentioned above, as well as other monies borrowed on their behalf. Henceforth, the aim of Scots like the Johnstones, John Boyd, the Clerks, Sir Laurence Dundas – and the *Hope* of Amsterdam bank, was to regain their money. They also demanded and received patronage. For example, the Johnstones wanted Lord Mansfield's protégé, Sir John Lindsay, to be included in the 1769 Supervision setting out for India to look into administrative abuses there.

Sulivan also displayed the strength of his link with this Scottish support during a particular incident following the April 1769 election. A contest for the Secretaryship of the Royal Society of Arts arose between John Stewart of Hampstead and William Pulteney Johnstone. Stewart was a particular friend of Sulivan's, but he was also deeply obliged to the Johnstones. He abstained from voting on the matter, but then nominated for election to the Royal Society of Arts the whole Scottish group being proposed by Johnstone, all twelve of them. Among others, the list included George Johnstone, George Dempster and John Macpherson.[15]

In his struggles to remain a Director after 1769 Sulivan continued to enjoy the support of Scottish friends. Stewart of Hampstead and Lauchlin Macleane instigated a short-lived alliance of Sulivan, Clive and Colebrooke that same year; and the same John Stewart once more lined-up the backing of Sir Gilbert Elliot and his son Alexander. But in 1770 Sulivan was ousted, due partly, he insisted, to the 'dreadful treachery and base behaviour' of the Johnstones who deserted him at the election. They did so because they knew that he did not have Government support, was certain to lose and therefore of no further use to them.[16]

However, in 1771 Sulivan was back again, due to the assistance of Lord North; and he tried (to no avail) to have one of his Scottish friends, George Dempster, brought into the Direction with him. For the 1772 election most of the 'Scotch' fully supported him, certain of a Sulivan–Colebrooke dominance in the Direction and, therefore, of patronage. Macleane, the Johnstones, John Stewart of Buckingham Street, Andrew and Col. James Stuart of Craigthorn, and all Sulivan's supporters in the Shipping interest rallied round and he was made Deputy Chairman.[17]

5

In the never-ending pursuit of patronage and power the Scots as a group and as individuals also participated in the Company's financial crisis of 1772, the parliamentary inquiry that followed and the Regulating Act of 1773. The financial crisis was the result of a variety of factors. Clive's dual system of government in Bengal was not working well; there was indiscipline and corruption among the Company's servants; and a bullion shortage in India, especially of silver. A resurrection of French hopes coincided with Haider Ali's raids on the Carnatic; and Bengal had suffered one of the world's worst disasters with the famine of 1769. The Company's revenues fell and its costs rose dramatically.

Those in power in Leadenhall were unaware of the true picture in India. Pro-Government and other Parliamentary factions ran rampant at India house, creating an atmosphere perfect for speculation and certainly not for the welfare of the Company as an institution. The papers were full of sensational attacks on Clive, stimulated by the Johnstones as they pursued their vendetta.[18]

In 1772 the crisis was sparked off by alarm at prohibitive military costs and a huge number of bills of exchange* drawn upon the Company at short notice. And while this was being digested an international credit crisis struck. The Company, already beset by self-imposed difficulties, experiencing reduced sales and delayed payments, reached breaking point when the Bank of England refused to enlarge or renew its loan beyond October 1772 and money could not be had anywhere else.

Alexander Forsyth's bank crashed, Drummond's only just survived the credit crisis. Sulivan desperately tried to stave-off the collapse. One of his schemes was to ask his friend Hope, the Scots–Dutch banker, for help using the Company's tea stores as surety; but this failed. Again the Johnstones, and particularly Governor George Johnstone, played an important role during these momentous months. In an effort to stem the build-up of ministerial control within the Court of Directors they allied with Parliamentary Opposition and tried to cancel-out Government control of the Direction by this rather circuitous and eventually doomed method.

They and Dempster also played a part in the final events leading-up to and including the Regulating Act. Dempster had urged Edmund Burke to go out as a member of the Superintending Commission to regulate the Company's affairs in the Presidencies (a plan proposed by Sulivan in July 1772). This Burke declined. Meanwhile, Maclean's friend, Andrew Stuart of Craigthorn, was proposed by Sulivan as a Supervisor, but this was scotched by Lord North in December 1772.

Dempster and the Johnstones had also backed the call for a Parliamentary Inquiry, sparked-off by Sulivan's Judicature Bill. During the debate upon Sulivan's Bill in the Commons in 1772, Wedderburn and George Dempster spoke in favour, while the Johnstones took the opportunity to launch another attack upon Clive. In this they had some success, while Sulivan's Bill failed. Blinded by their rage against Clive, the Johnstones did not foresee, nor would they have wished for, Burgoyne's successful motion to set-up a Select Committee to investigate abuses in the Company's government. It was a move that they had helped instigate, and which in turn paved the way for direct Government interference in the Company, so utterly against their own interests. In fact, from January 1773 the General Court of Proprietors, dominated by Richmond and George Johnstone, led the Company's opposition to Lord North and these proposals.

The final blow to Company hopes of retaining independence and with it control of India patronage, came with the defeat of Sulivan in the Company election of April 1773. Even then Sulivan enjoyed a strong Scottish support that included the Johnstones, Dempster, Sir Laurence Dundas and Robert Scott. Of course this backing was natural since only Sulivan's survival in the Direction could help them regain the money lost in 1769 and provide India posts to dish out to Scots friends.

For this election Sandwich organised the pro-ministry forces within the Direction against Sulivan, who was also blamed, unfairly, for the 1772 financial crisis. Sulivan's fears of direct Government control, frequently expressed, were now realized. He said, prophetically, 'the power of ministry was not to be resisted...in future they must govern the Company'; and in fact the 1773 election returned a majority of Directors amenable to this and in line with his prediction.[19]

6

The Regulating Act fashioned the first major wedge of Government control. It would lead eventually to the end of the Company's independence and place patronage in the ministry's hands. By its terms Proprietors with little political interest in the Company were forced out. £2,000 stock was required to have a vote, and the annual election returned only 6 Directors, on a rotationary basis. With these changes, only well-organised factions with long-term objectives could develop and prosper, such as the Shipping interest, and in particular, the ministerial party. Government now had its own group in the Company's Court of Directors, and statutory powers to regulate affairs alongside the Directors themselves — all of which pointed to an inevitable loss of Company independence.

'Management' was by the Treasury, with the help of experts like Robinson, Jenkinson and Henry Dundas. They operated through agents in the Supreme Council in Bengal, and by managing the Company's Court of Directors. The latter was handled in a variety of ways: alliances between ministers and Directors; between ministers and vested interests, such as the Shipping interest; or through the influence of important figures like Lord Sandwich, who had a strong following in the Company.[20]

The General Court was the only arena that could not be dominated and where some opposition remained. For the April 1774 election Sulivan rallied the resistance, which included his Scottish supporters: such as Dempster, the Johnstones and Sir James Cockburn, for a last fight against Government control. He knew, however, that this would be merely a gesture of defiance, and the election result proved him correct. The final humiliation then arrived, when North and Robinson, though not a part of the East India Company, made a list of prospective candidates for the Direction. They were vetted by Robinson and briefed by him upon their election approach. 'So daring are men grown in subversion of our liberty' raged Sulivan, 'in this country there is little honour or gratitude.'[21]

Henceforth, the flow of India patronage to Scotland would no longer be dependent simply upon ministerial ties with individual Directors or Proprietors – the actuality since the demise of the Argathelian system in 1766. Now, apart from positions at sea (still very much under the control of the shippers) the way was clear for ministry to take the major share and portion favours as it saw fit, and Henry Dundas was about to enter his kingdom.

7

The increasing ministerial control of Company patronage during these years can be illustrated by examining in detail the activities of four prominent Scots, already mentioned in passing. Alexander Wedderburn was a leading Government supporter and most of his thinking can be fathomed from this. The manipulations of the treacherous duo, James 'Fingal' Macpherson and John Macpherson, demonstrate the shift towards ministerial domination. The actions of the powerful Proprietor, Sir Laurence Dundas show how far a man of independent means could succeed alongside Opposition groups.

Alexander Wedderburn, 1st Baron Loughborough, 1st Earl of Rosslyn and Lord Chancellor, was the 1st son of Peter Wedderburn, Advocate, of Charter Hall, Haddington, by Janet, daughter of David Ogilvie. He was a schoolfellow of Henry Dundas, friend of William Robertson, David Hume and Adam Smith, and counsel for the respondents in the famous Douglas case. He was called to both the Scottish and the English Bar.

His involvement in Indian affairs began in 1761 and dated from his friendship with Bute. He took Clive's side in the Company's contested elections of the 1760s, and became his legal adviser. In Parliament he sat as MP for Ayr burghs (in Bute's interest) from 1761 to 1768; for

Richmond, Yorkshire, from 1768 to 1769; and then in the interest of Lord Clive for Bishop's Castle and Okehampton from 1769 until 1774.

In the 1760s he had been a follower of Grenville. He spoke on India business in the Commons and became closely connected with Sir Laurence Dundas. The Company Director Thomas Cheape was subject to his control in the 1768–1772 period, when Wedderburn and Mansfield tried (unsuccessfully) to assert ministerial domination over the Company's Court of Directors.

In 1772 Wedderburn supported Sulivan's Judicature Bill, then withdrew his backing and reverted to an anti-Sulivan stance following the Johnstone attack on Clive in the House.[22] However, this did not deter him, in 1773, from recommending his friend, another John Mackenzie, to the Directors (and especially to Laurence Sulivan) for a Writership in Bengal. This John Mackenzie was also a friend of James 'Fingal' Macpherson and of Samuel Hannay. He was known to Lauchlin Macleane as well, and had acted as a go-between for Wedderburn and Sulivan. Mackenzie was accordingly appointed by Sulivan to Bengal, but while posing as a friend to Hastings, he was really hostile, and worked as Wedderburn's secret prejudiced confidante.

James 'Fingal' Macpherson is probably best known as the author or translator of *The Poems of Ossian*.[23] His direct involvement with India patronage does not appear until after 1774, but through his alliance with John Macpherson, with Bute, and from friendships with East India Company officials, such as Sir Samuel Hannay, he figures much earlier.

He was born in 1736, the illegitimate son of Andrew Macpherson of Invertromie, near Ruthven in Badenoch The family was poor, with a Jacobite background. The idea of Ossianic ballads seems to have stemmed from his classical education at Marischal College, Aberdeen. Through the *Fragments* he gained entree and instant fame with the Edinburgh literati – and most important, in 1761 the patronage of Bute.

Bute paid for the publication of *Fingal*, using his agent, John Home; and also secured posts for some of his new charge's relations. He was responsible for a sinecure of £150 per annum (for life) given to Macpherson for being the Secretary and Clerk of the Council of West Florida. After an unavoidable four years there, he returned to London in 1766, where he became a newspaper hack for Bute.

He also resumed an earlier friendship with John Macpherson, and both planned to make a fortune acting together. To do this they supported any minister who could do anything for them; and James helped John when he became the Nawab of Arcot's agent in England. Company information was gleaned and officials, such as Sulivan, were used by James (as a Proprietor) solely to promote John's cause. In 1774 he and John Macpherson switched from the Duke of Grafton and his agent Bradshaw, to the patronage of North and John Robinson in order to secure John Macpherson's return to England as the Nawab's only representative.

James Macpherson's efforts to link the ministry and the Company together in pursuit of fortune for John and himself also furthered ministerial control of the Company, because ministers were all too eager to find some cause that would legitimately involve them in the Company's affairs.[24]

John Macpherson's entry into the East India Company set him upon a startling and colourful career; and the help given him demonstrates the Governmental patronage machine's easy effectiveness. He was born in 1744 the second and youngest son of the Rev. Dr. John Macpherson of Sleat, Skye, and Janet, daughter of Donald Macleod of Bernera. She was sister of Captain Alexander Macleod, commander of the Indiaman *Lord Mansfield*. Macpherson was also related to the Earls of Seaforth.

He graduated M.A. from the University of Aberdeen in 1764 then removed to Edinburgh where he was befriended by Adam Fergusson. In 1767 Shelburne and Bute asked Warwick to get him the post of Factor in the East India Company's service. Such a request demonstrates Bute's continuing patronage of Scots political connections. Unfortunately for Macpherson, Shelburne could be of little help, because he was dependent upon the Sulivanites for favours and they had been defeated by Clive and his followers in the contested election of 1765. Before Warwick's influence was brought to bear, however, Captain Alex Macleod schemed to get his nephew out to China as a Purser on board his own ship the *Lord Mansfield*.

It was in 1766, before he went to India, that John Macpherson met his namesake James – through Shelburne and Adam Fergusson. There was an immediate rapport. Nonetheless, John Macpherson was registered to sail for India in 1767 on the *Lord Mansfield,* and this he did. At Madras, however, he attended the *Durbar** of the Nawab of the Carnatic, and by dint of audacity and trickery gained the Nawab's confidence. He had introduced himself as an 'interpreter and agent' and the Nawab commissioned him to carry his grievances to the British monarch. He paid him well to do so, with £1,200 and jewels worth £3,000. But Macpherson's most important acquisition here was the credit and authority he gained, especially that of proclaiming himself the Nawab's agent.

By 1768 he was back in London plotting with James Macpherson. They set about gaining the Duke of Grafton's sympathy for the Nawab, while attacking Bute and Shelburne because of Grafton's enmity towards them. This gained them influence with the Company Directors under the minister's control. Both Macphersons argued the importance of the Nawab as an ally of the Crown; but failed to frighten the Proprietors with the suggestion that the Nawab might throw his lot in with the French. Through Grafton's influence, however, John was appointed in 1769 a Writer to Fort St. George, in the Carnatic. Part of his security was put up by the Scot, Sir Samuel Hannay.

That year the Macphersons struck up friendships with Rockingham, with Laurence Sulivan, who was back in power in the Direction, and with Lauchlin Macleane, Andrew Stuart and their associates. Before sailing in 1770, however, their schemes received a massive blow with Lord North coming to power. The letters of recommendation from Grafton would cut no ice with the Nawab, and James Macpherson had no influence with North. This forced John Macpherson to concentrate (from 1771 to 1774) upon accumulating money (as Paymaster to the Army of the Carnatic) and upon winning the friendship of Warren Hastings in Bengal and his supporters in London. He also managed to arrange a transfer to Calcutta beside Hastings. However, it was only following the arrival of Macleane and his hearty recommendation of Macpherson, endorsed by Sulivan, that Hastings took any notice of him.

In 1773 Macleane became the Nawab of Arcot's agent in London, and John Macpherson was to represent his friend at the Nawab's *Durbar*. Meanwhile, Macpherson continued to flatter Hastings and convinced him that he was a good 'Company man and a trustful friend'. At the same time he was deeply involved in the revolts in Madras centring upon the Nawab's debts to Madras Councillors; and then in the Pigot scandal. Nevertheless, the communications link he opened between Hastings and the Nawab was useful and important to both at this time; and Macpherson also sided with Hastings in the struggles for power that developed between him and the 'Triumvirate' following the implementation of the Regulating Act. In 1777 Macpherson set out for London. He had been dismissed the Company's service by Pigot, whom he had been surreptitiously undermining. However, in helping to achieve the downfall of Pigot, Macpherson found new favour in the Nawab's eyes; and was now regarded by Hastings and his supporters at home, as a true friend.

Macpherson was not slow in using Hastings and his allies in London and took advantage of this influence to secure posts for Scottish associates. From a position of trust he and his ally James Macpherson then deceived Hastings, Sulivan and their friends mercilessly in the search for wealth and power. With Macleane's death in 1778 his agencies on behalf of the Nawab and Hastings fell into their joint control. Their continued trickery led to a fortune for both, a baronetcy and the Governor-General's post for John, and even more favours for Scottish friends. But it was done at great cost to honour and integrity.[25]

Sir Laurence Dundas, MP, 1st Bart of Kerse, Stirling, was deeply involved in India patronage and Scottish political affairs in the late 1760s and early 1770s. He originated from the poorer gentry. Born in 1710, the 2nd son of Thomas Dundas of Fingask, Stirling, by Bethia, daughter of John Baillie of Castlecary, Stirlingshire, by 1772 he was a very rich man. It was wealth that did not come through inheritance. He began to make his fortune acting as a Commissary during the '45, after gaining the confidence of the Duke of Cumberland. Real riches came his way during the Seven Years War, where he accumulated around £800,000. His earlier experience and contacts during the years of the rebellion now counted. Also, the prosecution of the war involved close liaison with the East India Company and this brought him into touch with Leadenhall and its politics.[26]

In 1769, at the behest of his Parliamentary leader, Lord Rockingham, he had bought large holdings of India stock (at least £100,000) to split for the Company election in April 1770. In this manner he proved useful to the Rockingham ministry in its efforts to gain control of Company patronage; and his own political standing in Scotland was enhanced.

With Government support and Company favours at his fingertips he was able to contest the vested interest of the jealous Scottish nobility, many of whom regarded him as an upstart. These attitudes are particularly instanced in 1772 when challenged for control of Stirling burghs by a 'Colonel Campbell, a wealthy Nabob just returned from India.'[27] During this struggle, in which he was successful, Dundas tried (in vain) to obtain the support of William Graham of Airth, playing on vague claims of long friendship. He also used his political agents, John Mackenzie of Delvine and John Pringle, W.S. to gain more esteem – relying on their credibility in political circles.[28]

However, in Scotland the reality was that Henry Dundas had eclipsed Sir Laurence Dundas. The future Viscount stood for the old traditional landed classes and their values, against the new commercial ones; and especially in opposition to the increasingly important role in Scottish social and political life of what the *Mirror* called 'the "Mushroom Family" which had sprung up overnight as the result of Indian wealth'. Henry Dundas was helped in this by the 'retreat' to Scotland between 1763 and 1775 of many Scots Representative Peers alienated by English brashness in politics and much else.[29]

Dundas' wealth led to further involvement in Company matters. He was a good friend of George Dempster, and as a Proprietor acted alongside him in support of the Sulivan faction. He split stock for the Sulivanites in the 1769 contested election, linking with Duncan and Robert Clerk. Earlier, in 1765, he had downed an enemy, Sir James Cockburn, by using his weight in the Direction. Such was his recklessness at this time he lost at least £90,000 in rash speculations; but with little impact on his fortune.[30]

Throughout the years 1770–1774, Dundas was always able to reward his followers with favours. He made particular use of Company patronage. In fact, at this time he was probably more responsible for directing India patronage into Scottish hands than any other. These were years of anarchy as well as ministerial pressure at India house. Nevertheless, he was only working, in his own way, for the grander designs of both the Rockingham and Lord North ministries; and tried to implement these policies both within Parliament and in the Company. Thus he carried on the link of India patronage and Scottish management; although in no substantial part could this be compared with the patronage machine of the Argathelians, or that of Henry Dundas yet to come. He became a Baronet in 1762, and was Governor of the Royal Bank of Scotland from 1764 to 1777. With a stake of £10,000 he was also the biggest shareholder in the Forth and Clyde Canal Company. When he died in 1781 he left a fortune of £900,000 and an estate worth £160,000.[31]

11

Shipping Bounty
1765–74

1

As Company business soared with the startling developments in India of the 1760s so did the number of European-built Indiamen employed by the Company. From sixty-three such ships in 1761, to seventy in 1763 the figures rose steadily: seventy-six in 1767, eighty-five in 1769 and eighty-seven by 1771. The number of commanders to be found in the Company's Court of Directors rose significantly too: anywhere from three to six in the early 1760s to between seven and nine in the 1769 to 1774 period.

With these increases in ships commanders the shipping bloc in Company politics assumed even greater importance. Commanders had power, influence and patronage. Moreover, captaincy of an Indiaman was a prized possession and its enhanced status attracted younger sons of the landed classes. Freeholders importuned those politicians they could reach, who had influence with the Directors, for places for their friends and relations. A 'good voyage' could set one up for life.[1]

Extensive Scottish penetration of this shipping community in the 1760s and 1770s and with it the important Shipping interest, is readily witnessed. Captains George Cumming, James Moffat and later William Fullarton Elphinstone sat as Company Directors. The Hume brothers, Alex and Abraham, Sir Laurence Dundas, Captain Charles Foulis, Andrew Moffatt, Robert Preston, James Fraser and Gilbert Slater all became ships husbands.

James Moffatt enjoyed the favour of Lord Mansfield and repaid him with Company patronage. Families of Scots shippers evolved that included ships husbands, Directors, Proprietors, politicians and Company servants, home and abroad, all able to 'provide commands for scions of Scottish families of rank with whom they were connected.'[2] Through marriage and business these Scots had managed to penetrate the monopolistic Company shipping organisation with its rampant nepotism.

Commanders Boddam and Baillie, and free-merchants John Farquhar and David Scott found their way in because of their usefulness in the 'country trade' to business contacts among London shippers, and later because of their personal wealth. They helped each other with an instinctive clannishness laced with self-interest. Commanders William Fullarton Elphinstone, George Cumming and Alex Macleod of Bernera (who are looked at in some depth below) benefited in this way: Elphinstone was helped by Sir Laurence Dundas, Cumming by Alex and Abraham Hume. They also helped their confederates. Thus the Jacobite, Alexander MacDonald, who had Skye connections, was found a position as a ships surgeon on board the *Lord Mansfield* commanded by Alex Macleod.

Some, through entry into well-established shipping families, gained extensive influence and control over shipping posts: Charles Boddam, Charles Foulis and James Moffat exemplify this. Through marriage Boddam became part of the powerful Morse–Vansittart family; Foulis and Moffat in the same way with Freeman; and Foulis patronised his nephew Commander Sir Robert Preston who became part of this group.[3] Company Directors, Proprietors, politicians and businessmen all accepted that networks on such a scale, and the patronage they could offer, was both right and proper.

The fact was that Scotland, and thus the Union, continued to benefit inordinately in terms of appointments. After 1765, although the stranglehold over Scottish political life exerted by the Dukes of Argyll was no more, those in power in Scotland, in Edinburgh and the localities were still the same Whig-inclined, Union-minded great and middling landowners who had been the bulwark of the Argathelian support for so long.

Nothing really changed among Scottish political realities in the late 1760s and early 1770s; and pursuit of posts and pensions followed well-grooved paths. In fact the triple boost of having Bute as Prime Minister from 1761, a war, and the massive expansion in India led to a follow-on in the use of India patronage for political purposes, even after the demise of Argathelian direct control with the death of Milton.

Sufficient foundations had been put down to ensure the use of shipping patronage, much as it had always been, into the 1770s. Those candidates with Jacobite pasts or tendencies swallowed their feelings and became good Whigs and supporters of George III. Nor did those promoting such people see anything but sound sense in a policy of integration. For example, Captain Alex Stewart, eldest son to Ardshiel, who was forfeited in the year 1746, by 1762 had already made four voyages to the East Indies and was now going out first mate. He was Boswell's companion in a chaise from Edinburgh to London on 15 November 1762, and whom he thought 'a jolly honest plain fellow.'[4]

Lord Elibank's purchase of shares (sixteenths) in several East Indiamen typifies the twin drives of economic reality and the probability of patronage that such a move provided him with. It also seems clear that the contested elections in the Company made it easier for this Scottish penetration of the shipping bloc.

In the early 1760s the factors determining that much shipping patronage went north were as follows: a connection with Sulivan, or at least having an ally of his among the shippers; a link with the Bute Government and an interest in ensuring a successful election outcome for Sulivan; and the means of providing continued satisfaction for Scottish Government supporters. For example, in 1762 Fasham Nairne, with excellent contacts, kept his benefactor, Lord Holland informed that 'Mr. Sulivan, from your recommendation, is trying to get me a command.'[5] Nairne was to get his wish, being made commander of the *Lord Holland*. Of course, the looming political contest lay behind this particular favour.

The rise and rise of Captain Stephen Macleane also illustrates these factors, from entry to the Company's marine service in 1767 to his command of the *Duke of Grafton* in 1773. All these promotions were owed to his 1st cousin, Lauchlin Macleane, who was at the heart of Company politics.[6]

However, Scottish penetration of shipping did not rely unduly upon who controlled the Direction. The steady stream of Scots becoming commanders continued, whether Clive or Sulivan dominated, and owed as much to ships husbands like the Moffatts as to the Chairman of the Company or any great magnate. Over 30 Scots held commands in the 1762 to 1775 period. Their promotion was regular: at least six between 1762 and 1765 when Sulivan was the leading Director; a minimum of ten between 1766 and 1768 when Clive was dominant; five straddling the years 1769 to 1770 when Sulivan was back; and more than ten in the five years from 1770 to 1775 when the ministry had supplanted the two rivals and their factions in the Company's Court of Directors.[7]

2

The extraordinary careers of some exceptional seafaring men reflect this patronage. Those of Captains Charles Foulis, Sir Robert Preston, Alexander Macleod, William Fullarton Elphinstone, Burnet Abercromby, William MacIntosh, and Sir John Lindsay are both illustrative and fascinating in themselves. These men had scrambled to the top, and they enjoyed and distributed shipping patronage in a grand manner. Their careers are particularly indicative of what India patronage and Government direction of this could achieve.

Charles Foulis (and his brother *James*) were originally from the Woodhall estate, Colinton, Edinburgh. Charles, in particular, made a deep incursion into the solid, unchanging dynastic bloc of families controlling the Company's Shipping interest. In doing so he paved the way for other Scots, such as his nephew Robert Preston, and for friends like the cadet Mr. Bagshaw.

As commander of an East Indiaman he would carry out sheet-lead, copper and wool, returning with muslins, cotton goods, spices, diamonds and gold. On his last voyage in 1755, he imported, duty free, 251 ounces of gold. Eventually he retired to Harts House in Woodford Green, and became a Company Proprietor, ships husband and owner of twelve ships. He was in an excellent position to promote other Scots to command of his East Indiamen: Captain Haggis, of the *Prince Henry* in 1760 and of the *Thames* in 1764; Captain Alex Hamilton of the *Marquis of Hamilton* in 1769; and Captain John Lennox of the *Anson*.[8]

He played an important role in the contested elections of the 1760s and 1770s; and through marriage and business formed part of the substantial Scottish presence that had infiltrated the Company and its shipping by that date. He first appears in Bombay in 1744 as a commander; then in 1749 and again in 1754, standing security for his brother, Sir James Foulis, sometime Mayor of Bombay and commanding officer of the Garrison.

In 1752 Sir James had become a Bombay Councillor. He is almost certainly Sir James Foulis of Woodhall, Colinton, who succeeded to the Baronetcy in 1742 – the eldest son of Henry Foulis. It is not clear how the brothers made their way to India, but by birth and connection they would be eminently suited to receive favours via the Argathelian patronage machine.[9]

The friendship and support Charles Foulis and Laurence Sulivan gave to each other throughout the rest of their lives – vital to Sulivan in the political contests of the 1760s and early 1770s – certainly began in Bombay in the 1740s. Through Foulis' marriage this support for Sulivan became even stronger, because Mrs. Foulis' sister married Andrew Moffatt, and his own sister, Margaret Foulis, married William Freeman. Both these gentlemen were important ships husbands like himself, and firm supporters of Sulivan. They were all friends of Charles Raymond and his family, another powerful shipper. Charles Foulis lived for the rest of his life at Woodford Green.

The power and importance of the Foulis–Freeman–Moffat group was further strengthened by Lord Mansfield's connection through marriage to the Moffatts. Also, Mansfield's 'man of business', fellow Scot, George Ross of Cromarty created another cross-link through his friendship with William Pulteney Johnstone, one of the Johnstone group, in alliance with Sulivan and his faction. These are the people referred to as Mansfield's support in the Company and explain, in particular, his strength in shipping.

In Scotland in the 1760s the Foulis family had dealings with John Mackenzie of Delvine, while in the London business world in general they were also active. As well as being a Company Proprietor, ships captain, husband and owner, Charles Foulis was a manager of 'the Sun Fire Office' (as was his relation through marriage, John Moffatt). He enjoyed Mansfield's patronage and was involved through family connections with the worlds of underwriting, brokerage and finance. These contacts, and his friendships with Sulivan and Mansfield, linked Charles Foulis and his family in Scotland firmly into the patronage machinery used by Scottish political managers. He used the system himself: as mentioned already, he recommended John Douglas to a Writership in 1754.[10]

The career of Commander *Sir Robert Preston*, nephew of the Foulis brothers, is one of the best illustrations of how far riches and success could be gained from India patronage. He was born the 5th son of Sir George Preston, 4th Bart of Valleyfield, Perth. After his father's death he virtually governed his brother, Sir Charles Preston, the 5th Bart; and eventually succeeded him in 1800. It would have been difficult for Sir Charles Preston to have suppressed his brother Robert in the easiest of circumstances, but faced with financial disaster from an encumbered estate and the natural vigour of his brother, who had returned from India very quickly, and with a fortune, he soon took a back seat.

Robert Preston's success was due in nearly every way to the patronage of his uncle, Charles Foulis. In 1762 he found the young man a berth as 3rd officer on the *Clive*. By 1768 he had pushed him to his first command, the *Asia*, and then of the *Hillsborough* from 1775–1776. By 1777 Preston, aged 37, had retired from the sea and returned to Valleyfield with the fortune made from his voyages.

After setting the family's encumbered estate in order, Preston began increasing his fortune by becoming a ship owner and insurer with his uncle Charles Foulis. His uncle's friends were his, and especially the powerful Laurence Sulivan and Warren Hastings. Within the Shipping interest he joined with Foulis's other relations the Freemans and Moffatts.

Preston became manager of the Company shipping group operating in Parliament; and also a leading member of the Shipping interest management committee. As such, he was able to help others to positions. Scots who shared in ship ownership, like him, included: Sir William Forbes of Edinburgh; John and Adam Drummond of Golden Square, London, bankers; and Thomas Coutts, banker in the Strand.[11]

Alex Macleod was the 2nd son of Donald Macleod of the island of Bernera, lying off Harris in the Outer Hebrides. Donald, or the 'Old Trojan' as he was known, was a staunch Jacobite who was 'out' in the '15 and the '45. His eldest son, Captain Norman Macleod of Unish, was just as loyal a Hanoverian and hunted his own father as an outlaw after the battle of Culloden.

Almost certainly Alex Macleod followed his brother in identifying with the Hanoverians and took no part in supporting the rebellion. His advance in 1756 to a Captaincy in an East India Company ship (the *Marlborough*) could only have been achieved by such a circumstance. It is probable that he benefited from his brother's positive pro-Government moves. But also, the desire of the Argathelian authorities to re-integrate powerful families like these Macleods goes some way to explain the support he was given.

This is more understandable when it is considered that his family was related to the Earls of Seaforth (Chiefs of the Mackenzies); that he married Helen Maclean of Berneray (his cousin); while his sister married into the family of Macdonald of Sleat. These clan families, Macleods, Macleans, Mackenzies and Macdonalds exerted a combined political influence that had to be carefully nurtured by political managers like Lord Milton. In 1756 Captain Alex Macleod, while commander of the *Marlborough,* accompanied the expedition under Clive and Admiral Watson that set off from Madras to capture Calcutta. By 1767 he was Captain and owner of the *Lord Mansfield* and remained so until he retired from the captaincy in 1769 and from East India Company business in 1771.

Through his kinsman, Sir Alex Macdonald of Sleat, he was introduced to John Mackenzie of Delvine who 'managed' quite a number of returned Company servants; and from him Macleod gained the advice he sought, which was how best to invest his considerable fortune. He was succeeded as commander of the *Lord Mansfield* by another Scot, Captain Sir William Fraser.

In 1778 Macleod purchased the Barony of Harris from Norman, the Chief of Macleod, for £15,000. This included the family lands of Bernera and St. Kilda. John Mackenzie of Delvine acted as his business agent in these transactions and in the extensive improvements to farms and fisheries that he was involved in. In 1780 Macleod became MP for Honiton and died in Harrogate in 1790.

Apart from making himself a considerable fortune, Alex Macleod used his substantial power within the Shipping interest to further the careers and interests of his fellow Highlanders. As mentioned, in 1767 he and his friends were involved in getting (Sir) John Macpherson a position in the East India Company. Captaincy of the *Lord Mansfield* also suggests a strong connection between Macleod and the Earl of Mansfield. One probability is that Mansfield, although tied by marriage into the Moffat–Foulis–Freeman Shipping interest, also found time to back Alex Macleod, and the ship was named in his honour.

Alex Macleod's ample India stock was probably another factor; as were his inclinations in Company politics where he was generally in accord with Governor George Johnstone and James 'Fingal' Macpherson. All this bespoke a powerful Scottish cross-section involving ministry, shipping and the Company executive in the 1760s.[12]

William Elphinstone began life as the 3rd son of Charles, 10th Lord Elphinstone, by Lady Clementine Fleming, the daughter of John, 6th Earl of Wigtown, and niece of the Jacobite George Keith, 9th Earl Marischal. She was the real power behind his rise to fame and fortune in Company shipping.

The family owned large estates in Stirlingshire, Dunbartonshire and Lanarkshire, but they were heavily encumbered with debt. There was a large family, five sons (John, Charles, William, Lockhart, George Keith) and five daughters.[13] In the knowledge that he was Milton's henchman, Lady Clementine wrote to Lord Panmure (in November 1755) asking him to provide for William. She knew he had 'interest enough to get positions', that is, through the Argathelian political management network.[14]

The weight of William's grand-uncle, the Earl Marischal was also brought to bear; and in that year, 1755, aged 15, he entered the Royal Navy on board a ship sailing to Virginia, and commanded by his relative, Captain Mudie. In 1756 he voyaged to Gibraltar under Captain Ogilvie; then, following Clive's victory at Plassey, decided money was to be made in the East.

He attended navigation classes and, again with his mother's help and that of the Earl Marischal and 'Scottish contacts in the shipping world' was made Midshipman on the *Winchelsea,* East Indiaman, commanded by Captain Howe. He then had his mother write to Lady Stair to urge Lady Howe to persuade her son, Captain Howe, to promote him. He understood that infinite persuasion was needed, and informed his mother 'the best way is to get a Director to speak for me.' By 1758 this was being done through an intermediary, Mr. Talbot, who had the requisite influence.[15]

From 1762 William Elphinstone was 3rd officer of the *Hector* and in 1765, aged 26 and just 10 years after making his first voyage, he became commander of the East Indiaman *Triton,* succeeding another Scot, Captain Gilbert Slater. This was unusual in one so young and involved a great deal of influence and much negotiation.

William and his father had a share in the *Triton,* although it was in the name of a Mr. Farquharson. The money for this (£2,000 each) had come from the Earl Marischal. The appointment came mainly through the interest of Sir Laurence Dundas, a family friend, but also through John Hyde, Director of the *London Assurance Company* and an East India Company Proprietor, who also had great pull with the shippers.

Other influences were at work in the promotion. These included the family links between the Elphinstones, Lord Elibank and the Johnstones. As soon as William's appointment had been verified, his brother, George Keith Elphinstone, transferred from the Royal Navy to become 3rd mate aboard the *Triton.* Earlier, in 1761, before joining the Royal Navy, George had contemplated joining the East India Company proper or its shipping. His uncle, the Earl Marischal, had arranged for him to be a Writer if he wanted; and initially, when interested, he had called upon Governor George Johnstone (his relation), Lord Howe, Lady Clementine's nephew Mr. Gascoigne, and a Mr. Ramsay.

On board the *Triton* the two brothers began to accumulate great wealth. They and their family understood that 'money gained money there [in India] more than in the rest of the world.' The first of four voyages to Madras and China was a great success. The Earl Marischal had ensured this by giving them another £4,000 to use, and they made the most of this. William in particular had a remarkable capacity for business and sent his profits and other surpluses home for banking and investment.[16]

Captain William Elphinstone was extraordinary in other ways that probably had a bearing on his success. Hickey was enchanted with him – 'a most gentlemanlike and pleasing man...a great acquisition to company.' He was also daring and had smuggled 'a smart little Madras girl' disguised as a boy into the Company factory in Canton 'where the presence of women was forbidden.' He had brought her with him from Fort St. George. After a considerable furore, which stopped all trade, he was fined 500 dollars.[17]

Probably this flair for combining social graces, financial opportunity and daring led him into marriage in June 1774 to Elizabeth Fullarton, eldest daughter of William Fullarton of Carstairs and niece and heiress of John Fullarton of Carberry, Mid Lothian. On the latter's death in 1775 the estate passed to his niece and her husband, who changed his name to William Fullarton Elphinstone.[18]

William patronised others, dating from his very first command in 1765 and even after his retiral in 1777. Because of his position in Scottish political and social life countless Scots passed to India. Most voyaged with him on the *Triton*; others via ships where he had influence. One particular recipient of this patronage was Robert Simson, who serves as an excellent example. Simson always kept in touch with Lady Clementine Elphinstone, his real benefactor, and pressurised the family to move him from ship to ship until he became Surgeon on board the *Triton*.

Others who benefited from Elphinstone patronage included Thomas Irwin, of the *Royal George*; Thomas Steven, who gained a Surgeon's post; Peter Copper; Alex Gray of the *Devonshire*; Charles Lindsay, posted to Fort St. George; Captain Whyte of the *Hannah*; Captain Thomson, the *Calcutta*; and on board the *Triton* in 1770, David Oswald and John Fleming.[19]

Elphinstone's power and influence within the Company and its shipping was of great political use to managers in Scotland. As a ship's commander, ships husband, Proprietor then Director until his death in 1824, he was much in demand. As David Scott, another powerful Scottish Director said, 'any Director with this valuable patronage could command a good interest in any Scottish Constituency.'[20]

Elphinstone placed 'Stirlingshire gentlemen' in East Indiamen to an enormous degree. It has been calculated that among the Stirlingshire Freeholders, who numbered between fifty and sixty between 1707 and 1750, and between sixty and a hundred for the rest of the century, at least thirty at any one time were 'in the civil branches of the Government or the service of the East India Company.' In turn, this 'Indian patronage undoubtedly helped to support the Elphinstone interest'.[21]

Commander Burnet Abercromby was the son of George Abercromby of Tullibody, Clackmananshire and one of four sons. He was also a nephew of James Abercromby of Brucefield, Clackmananshire, whose estate passed to him. It was probably through this uncle that he obtained his seafaring post. Friendship with Clive in Bengal in 1767 led to a request from Abercromby, in that year, for 'a good voyage.' By 1768 he was Captain of the *Grenville*. Although bankrupt in 1773 the Brucefield inheritance saved him. He retained his connection with the Company's Shipping interest after his return to Scotland.[22]

'Captain' William MacIntosh, born in the West Indies of a Scottish father and a mulatto mother, was at sea from an early age before working as an overseer for Lauchlin Macleane back in his home territory in the Caribbean. In 1773 Laurence Sulivan, then Deputy Chairman of the Company, called upon Hastings to help him; then in 1777 called upon him to do so again.

Sulivan's activity on Macintosh's behalf perfectly illustrates the degree to which patronage, after 1765, depended upon support gathered from all quarters for the Company elections. Sulivan said, 'Macintosh's friends and connections I am well acquainted with and I wish much to serve.' By 1781, however, he had deserted Sulivan and Hastings and was firmly in the Francis camp. Apparently a rather disreputable character, MacIntosh was a particular friend of Macleane and John Stewart of Hampstead, both equally disreputable it was to prove.[23]

Writerships for *William, George and Robert Lindsay* were made available through the influence (partly personal, partly ministerial) that Lord Mansfield had with the Directors Sir William James, George Cumming and Daniel Weir. William Lindsay was the son of Sir Alex Lindsay, 3rd Bart of Evelich, Perth, of the Balcarres family, by Amelia, daughter of David Murray, 5th Viscount Stormont and sister of Lord Mansfield. William was helped by his uncle to a Writers post in 1750. George and Robert Lindsay, the sons of the 5th Earl of Balcarres, enjoyed Mansfield's patronage as well.

Probably the most important of these Lindsays was Sir *John Lindsay* son of Sir Alex Lindsay (brother of William Lindsay) and also a nephew of Lord Mansfield. In 1769 he was sent to Madras through the pressure of the ministerial faction in the Company, which in turn was influenced by Mansfield and others. He went out as naval commander (Royal Navy) and Minister Plenipotentiary, to treat with the Nawab of Arcot and other native rulers. These powers were given to him in a compromise agreement made by the Crown and the Company. However, in 1771 he was recalled because his autocratic behaviour exasperated Governor Du Pré of Madras and the Company Directors. He was succeeded by Admiral Harland. Warren Hastings thought Lindsay typified most of the Scots he knew: They had 'a very powerful bias to politics and a most unconquerable aversion to those who had more power than themselves.'[24]

12

Patrons and Recipients 1760–74

1

Several of the many Scottish Proprietors, Directors, London merchants, bankers, lawyers and landowners, who continued to direct patronage northwards to their homeland in the 1760s and 1770s call out for special mention – so important was their contribution. Likewise, many recipients of these favours demonstrate awareness of how important this stream of patronage was, not just for individual families in Scotland, but for fusing Britain into one coherent whole.

Among the Scottish Proprietors worth special consideration because they reflect the patronage system in operation in later years – and the wealth brought to Scotland – are Sir James Stuart, Thomas Cheape (who also became a Director) and his relation James Cheape. *Sir James Stuart* was the son of the Solicitor-General for Scotland, but also a Jacobite exile who was pardoned in 1771. He was a brilliant political economist, 'a very deep man and a universal genius' according to Laurence Sulivan, who acknowledged his help in drawing up plans for the better government of India that were to be of use to Warren Hastings. Stuart asked Sulivan and Hastings to employ their influence on behalf of his sister Peggy and other relatives in India.[1]

Thomas Cheape became an East India Company Proprietor in 1772, but not until 1777 was he successful in his efforts to become a Director. He was the eldest son of George Cheape, Collector of Customs at Prestonpans, by Mary, daughter of Alexander Wedderburn, Commissioner of Excise for Scotland. John Drummond had been instrumental in securing this post for his father. His cousin was Alex Wedderburn, the future Lord Loughborough, whose influence and patronage he was to enjoy. After Cheape had entered the Direction, he responded to Wedderburn's ministerial proddings in return for his favours.

In 1763 he married Grace, daughter of John Stuart of Blairhall, and his wife Anne, daughter of Francis Stuart, 7th Earl of Moray. This in turn brought him the backing of Andrew and Colonel James Stuart of Craigthorn, as and when they became involved with the East India Company. He was also a partner in the firm of *Scott, Pringle and Cheape,* wine merchants, supplying wine from Madeira to the Company's settlements. This brought him contacts at Leadenhall, the post of His Majesty's Consul in Madeira (from 1763–1771) and business friends in London. He was on familiar terms with members of the Company Shipping interest.

Connections with Government followed from his diplomatic post in Madeira. From 1777 he was a leading Director, deeply involved in Company politics. As one contemporary observed, he kept a 'strict' friendship with Alex Wedderburn while providing for his 'numerous family'. His father's home was Wellfield in North Fife.

One of Thomas Cheape's relations was *James Cheape,* son of James Cheape, merchant in Leith. Young James Cheape had been appointed a Writer in 1762 through Wedderburn's friendship with Bute, and the favour of William Baker, MP, who had been a Director during the Drummond of Quarrel years, and retained some influence. In 1769, while in Bombay and Broach as a Factor in the Company, James Cheape made an enduring friendship with James Beck of Damside, Fife, a fellow Company civil servant. Beck owed his own position in the Company to the Director John Manship who had befriended him. James Cheape then asked Beck to use Manship's patronage to get his brother George out to India.

James bought the estate of Strathyrum, St. Andrews, for £8,800 in 1782 (now part of the Old Course). He subsequently purchased two other farms there for a total of £7,450. As James Beck said, he had changed 'from a Broach Councillor to a Fife Laird of some consideration.'[2]

2

Two Lairds who used the system to great effect, ensuring that their offspring and relations benefited, were Sir William Baillie of Polkemet and Thomas Shairp of Houston House. On behalf of his eldest son James and second eldest, William, *Sir William Baillie of Polkemet* applied to Col. Alex Hope, the brother of Col. John Hope, MP, and a Company Proprietor, for positions abroad. Col. John Hope was in turn the friend of the powerful and rich Proprietor Sir Laurence Dundas and was thus successful. James entered the civil service, William the military. Subsequently James married the daughter of a Baillie Seton. He eventually returned from an 'unhealthy salt station' in India with £10,000 and became 'partner to a Mr. Taylor in the Landmarket.'[3]

Thomas Shairp of Houston House, Uphall, approached George Dempster to 'find a berth on a ship' for his son Walter. He was duly found one as a ships mate. Andrew Stuart of Craigthorn was in turn asked to find Company positions for Shairp's two grandsons, Thomas and John Shairp. They too were found posts, as Writers.[4]

Formidable among the politicians, lawyers and agents involved in working the system were *John Davidson*, W.S. of Stewartfield, and his brother Henry. John was the London link for Lord Milton and John Mackenzie of Delvine. As well as the transmission of patronage, he and his brother acted as middle-men for Company servants remitting fortunes home. This was done through *Drummond's* bank in London, onwards to Mackenzie of Delvine in Scotland. John Davidson's own clients embraced Lord Selkirk and George Mackay of Skibo. His Company connections included Laurence Sulivan, Sir George Colebrooke, Dr. Charles Stuart, Andrew Stuart of Craigthorn, Sir Alex and Captain Charles Grant.

It is probable that two brothers, Alex and John Davidson, sons of Mr. Davidson, saddler merchant in London, were connected to Davidson of Stewartfield. *John Davidson* went out a Writer to Madras in 1752 with Claud Russell. He befriended many Scots who followed him out, such as Kenneth Mackenzie, nephew to John Mackenzie of Delvine. He rose to 2nd in command at Vizipatam in 1768 and came home with a fortune in 1776. In 1760, while in Madras, he managed to get his brother, *Alex Davidson*, out beside him. He too prospered and also found success at Vizipatam where he became the chief Company official. Like his brother, he cared for fellow Scots, such as Captain William Fullarton Elphinstone and James Grant. His wife was with him in India when he died in 1791.[5]

'Little' John Stewart was the son of James Stewart, Attorney of the Exchequer in Edinburgh, and a cousin of John 'Jack' Stewart and of Archibald Stewart. He was inclined to be adventurous and became one of Shelburne's secret agents, working with Lauchlin Macleane in the world of backstairs politics that embraced Westminster and Leadenhall. He and Macleane were particularly active, forming connections that linked the Chatham ministry and the Company's directorate in the 1766 to 1768 period. He recruited and helped young Scots in London by introducing them to the Royal Society of Arts, which seemed almost a Caledonian Society in this period.[6]

Of course, the man who would eventually dominate and control all Scottish patronage was the politician and statesman, *Henry Dundas*, 1st Lord Melville. For twenty odd years, from 1784 to 1805, he was, as Lord Cockburn described him, the 'Pharos of Scotland.'[7] His career has been very well documented. In the mid 1760s and 1770s he was a Government agent, controlling the election of the Scottish representative peers and Scottish MPs. He was Treasurer of the Navy from 1783, and in practice, head of the Board of Control set up to manage Indian affairs by Pitt's Act of 1784. The patronage he held was enormous and was used to bring Scots MPs to the support of Government. Some evidence of his preparation for all this is visible in the years up to 1775.

By birth he had the proper connections. He was the 4th son of Robert Dundas of Arniston, Lord President of the Court of Session, by his 2nd wife, Anne, daughter of Sir William Gordon of Invergordon, Bart. He was the half-brother of Robert Dundas, who, like his father, was also to become Lord President of the Court of Session.

By 1766, aged 24, he was Solicitor-General for Scotland. Family ties helped him to this early success. Financial security came in 1765 with marriage to Elizabeth, daughter of Commander David Rannie of Melville, master of an East Indiaman. She brought with her a dowry of £10,000. Through her father he also gained knowledge of India and of the Company and its affairs. Dealing with Rannie's estate, upon his death in 1768, brought Dundas into touch with John Mackenzie of Delvine and John Davidson, both involved in Indian business. Dundas was obliged to Mackenzie 'for your delicacy with regard to the late Mr. Rannie's affairs...John Davidson knows more of all these affairs than I do.'[8]

Dundas proceeded to establish himself in the eyes of some of the most powerful Scottish figures. In 1766 he met Lord Mansfield who thought he was destined for the highest positions. By 1772 he was a friend of the Duke of Buccleuch; two years later he was MP for Midlothian; and in 1775, aged 33, was Lord Advocate in North's ministry. After moving to London his brother, Robert Dundas, the Lord President, kept him informed of Scottish affairs. With his brother's death in 1787, control of the Scottish political patronage network passed to Henry Dundas.

It was no coincidence, therefore, that Dundas became immersed in Indian affairs and that he should bend India patronage to the ends of Scottish political management. He was more aware than most contemporaries of the use made of this patronage over the previous fifty to sixty years, and better placed to exploit it again at every opportunity.[9]

3

London merchants continued to play a conspicuous part in the dispensation of India patronage in the 1760s and 1770s. *Sir William and Robert Mayne*, merchants in the capital provide excellent illustration. They took admirable care of their nephews *John, Thomas, and George Graham*, the sons of John Graham of Kernoc, a merchant in Edinburgh.

By 1770 the Grahams were in India. Two of them, full brothers, John and Thomas Graham, arrived in the 1760s, John to a military command in 1763, Thomas as a Writer in 1768. They were the offspring of their father's second marriage to Helen Mayne, daughter of William Mayne of Powie Logie, Clackmananshire. George Graham, the eldest of the three in India was a half-brother. His mother was Agnes Buchanan, John Graham of Kernock's first wife.

Sir William Mayne, MP, Bart (later Baron Newhaven) and his brother, Robert Mayne, MP, were uncles of John and Thomas Graham through their sister, Helen Mayne. Robert was a partner in the London banking firm of *Mayne and Needham*. He was married to Charlotte, the sister of Alex Pringle of Whytebank, Selkirk, who became a rich Company servant. Both brothers were members of the 'Society for the Encouragement of Arts and Sciences'.

Sir William Mayne ran the family business of *Mayne and Barn*. He had been a merchant in Lisbon and returned to London with a modest fortune in 1751. From 1757 to 1763 he was also a director of the *Royal Exchange Insurance Company*; and the chief architect in procuring the necessary patronage for his nephews.

He and his brother were firm followers of Bute. Sir William let Bute know that he desired a military command for young John Graham. Bute in turn communicated this request to the Director Thomas Rous, through Lord Eglinton and Charles Jenkinson. However, the contested elections of April 1763 intervened, by which Rous was ousted from power, to be replaced by his arch-enemy, Laurence Sulivan. The same approach, through the same channel was made to Sulivan with the certainty of success because young John Graham's wife was also, coincidentally, Laurence Sulivan's ward.

From 1770 the three brothers in India combined with but one thought in mind, to accumulate wealth. They gained contracts for supplying the troops in Bengal and engaged in private trade in association with the Maynes in London. John was transferred from the Company army and made Resident* at Burdwan in 1770. By 1774 he had remitted home at least £95,000, some of it in diamonds. With his arrival in India in 1770,

George, the eldest brother, took charge. He used all the knowledge and expertise learned in Jamaica and by 1776 had gathered a considerable fortune as well.

Besides the Maynes in London, the Grahams were involved with numerous Scottish associates. For example, they had links with the Johnstones; and many Scots in India were partners in firms they had set up. For instance, before 1766, Thomas and John were doing business with David Killican and Dr. Burnett, with John Fleming, William Duff and *Charteris and Menteith*. Other exploits involved Captain Fullerton, Thomas Motte and a 'Mr. Dangeroux'.

They traded in grain for the army and for East Indiamen; bought and sold freight in the coastal trade, and became caught up in money lending. They set up and operated a sugar mill, bringing the parts and the engineer from Britain; and they traded in China silk. In many ways David Killican was a special friend to the Grahams. They remitted their fortunes home through his agency; and it is more than likely that it was they who in 1771 asked Sulivan and Sir James Cockburn to make Killican a Factor in Bengal, where he had already operated as a free-trader for some considerable time.

With George in Midnapore and John and Thomas in Patna they covered vast territories and operated successful joint-ventures. Friendship with Sulivan brought them the support in India of a multitude of people, and in particular that of Warren Hastings and Richard Barwell in the Supreme Council of Bengal. Through them the Grahams and Killican gained the 'carriage' contract (carpentry work at Fort William). As their trading exploits expanded they ventured into opium, cloth, arrack and tobacco; in doing so introducing Scots as sub-agents and merchants, such as *Messrs Crawford and Duncanson*, and a Captain Mackenzie.

William Berrie, one of their agents in India, a fellow Scot and a chief informant, was quite explicit in his depiction of how India patronage and Scottish affairs were thoroughly entwined. His letter to George Graham in 1774 asked if a son of the Edinburgh advocate, Dr. Cullen, could be placed in the protection of Captain Mackenzie. It was thought at home that he had the chance of command of an Indiaman, and if this could be secured 'it would go down well in Scotland' where Dr. Cullen was 'well-known and highly respected by almost all the nobility.'[10]

Almost every young Scot mentioned to the Grahams by Berrie was the son of a good friend in Scotland who remained vitally interested in their welfare. It was expected at home that these Scots abroad would rally round each other; and the whole 'clan' in India could expect the unfaltering support of those at home. Thus the Grahams enjoyed the favour of the Grants, of the Fullartons and of the Elphinstones because of their friendship with Col. Grant and Commanders Fullerton and Fullarton Elphinstone.

Through them Lieutenants Buchanan, Drummond, MacIntosh and Hamilton received promotion. Medical men were introduced to each other, such as Dr. Urquhart to Dr. Hunter. At India House, apart from Sulivan, they had the patronage of Daniel Weir, Col. Alexander Dow, Sir Robert Fletcher and John Adams. The Grahams eventually managed to come back to Scotland, purchase Kinross House and by 1778 had taken control of Kinrosshire seats. They also retained their India stock and with it considerable Company influence.[11]

Another London merchant deeply involved was *Sir Samuel Hannay*, MP, 3rd Bart of Kirkdale, Kirkcudbrightshire, and of Philpot Lane, Fenchurch Street, London. He maintained the London end of a business partnership that embraced three other brothers busy making fortunes in India during the 1770s and 1780s. One of them, Ramsay Hannay, was a free merchant trading to China and involved generally in the coastal trade of India. He worked hand in glove with another brother, Col. Alexander Hannay of the Company's army, who shared with James Fraser a contract for supplying elephants to the Nawab of Oude. The third brother was John Hannay, who had been appointed a Writer in 1769. They were the sons of William Hannay of Kirkdale, and Margaret, daughter of Patrick Johnston of Girthon, Kirkcudbright.

Sir Samuel Hannay's influence was considerable. He was important at Leadenhall, as a member of the Shipping interest and as one of the City men who then predominated in the Direction. He was a close associate of John and James 'Fingal' Macpherson and was also a creditor of the Nawab of Arcot. Hannay illustrates the degree to which Scots businessmen had penetrated the 'City' of London and their involvement in India patronage.

The activities of the Maynes, Grahams, Hannays and their associates also reflect the manner in which Company patronage was to be dispensed in the 1760s and onwards. Shares would depend upon successful involvement in the annual April contested election. By the mid–1760s the phenomenal purchase of India stock had sucked in resident Scots like Lord Elibank, and London–Scots such as the Maynes; and they all went in deeper than they wished. As Robert Mayne said, 'we have, for many years, held each of us, a qualification, tho' with considerable loss, to serve our friends on your side and to enable us now and then to provide for a relation.'[12]

By the end of the 1760s patronage continued to depend upon factors such as: points of contact inside the Direction, among the shippers, the London business world, Parliament, and Scottish families with political influence. However, it also increasingly relied upon servants in the east, whose money, made in India, was used for voting purposes. Robert Mayne was able to inform John Graham that his possession of stock would give him a sway with the Direction when he returned home.[13]

4

Recognition of just how far Scottish tentacles reached into the City of London, aiding and abetting the provision of posts to Scots, is made complete with an evaluation of the role of two banking firms: Drummonds, and Hope of Amsterdam. There were many others, such as Coutts, but these two claim a special place.

By the 1760s and 1770s *Drummond's bank*, which in the 1720s and 1730s had links with John Drummond of Quarrel and Walpole, had assumed an importance beyond its purely financial dimensions. It continued, however, to care for the resources of the exiled Scots nobility in London. Links were made with legal representatives in Scotland and agents of the London-based Scots gentry and businessmen.

These legal agents, in particular, were nurtured and sustained by the bank's executives: men like John Davidson W.S. of Stewartfield and his brother Henry, who were agents for the Duke of Buccleuch, among others. This Scottish connection was relatively easy to maintain, given the strength of Drummond relations in Scotland and the services the bank could provide in remitting money or bullion north or south, as required.

As indicated earlier, the Edinburgh goldsmith, Andrew Drummond, had started his bank 'at the sign of the golden eagle' on the east side of Charing Cross in the 1720s. He had then appointed as partners, firstly the two sons of his brother William, of Strathallan, and later John the third member of this family. The business continued to be useful to Scots in London and became very successful. It handled deposits that stemmed from Scottish estates, and for securing money flowing into Britain through trade, from the East, from the West Indies and the Americas. The cash was put to good use in London or, if Scots were involved, forwarded to . Scotland as and when directed.

Success led to the bank moving to larger premises on the west side of Charing Cross. There its usefulness continued, and it developed as a venue, facilitating the formation of cross-connections. Scots were helped to meet fellow Scots in furtherance of money-making pursuits, whether as individuals or in partnership with other associations or businesses. Meanwhile, the bank grew in wealth and respectability, its worth known about north and south of the border. Its Directors continued their forays into the 'City', into Company affairs and into insurance in particular. Participation in the Sulivan–Clive struggle of the 1760s also enlarged its image in the banking circles of London and elsewhere.

Although Andrew Drummond died in 1769, the bank continued this sort of activity into the 1770s. For example, in 1772 it began a subscription of £100,000 in support of a cash-strapped Sir George Colebrooke, the Company Chairman. Through John Davidson sums were drawn from the Duke of Buccleuch, the Earl of Selkirk, Andrew Stuart of Craigthorn, and from a John Seton and a John Campbell. Colebrooke crashed, nevertheless, largely because of his recklessness and the credit collapse of 1772–1774. And although Drummonds bank itself was not much affected – in fact it emerged with enhanced prestige – others were not so lucky; and in 1775 Colebrooke still owed Selkirk £19,959.[14]

The banker *Adriaan Hope* of Amsterdam was a cousin of the Hopetoun family and related to the Hopes of Craighall. As outlined already, he had engaged his firm in the purchase of India stock for splitting purposes during the Company elections of the 1760s and 1770s. He dealt mainly with the Johnstones and with Lauchlin Macleane, supporting the Sulivan group.

Much of his business was done through *Fordyce's* bank. His dealings also involved Sulivan himself, as well as Henry Vansittart, Thomas Lane and Sir George Amyand – all major figures in the Company Courts. He had Parliamentary links with John Hope, MP for Linlithgowshire (which was in the Hopetoun interest) who had previously spent much of his time in Holland. This same Adriaan Hope was also one of the Sulivan–Sir George Colebrooke faction in the early 1770s.[15]

5

There are more examples of Scots receiving India favours, perfectly describing the patronage system in operation, than can be properly entered into. However, again the case studies chosen here (only to 1774) present clear and uncluttered demonstration of the continued, but unobtrusive, use of this India bounty for the good of Scotland and the British nation. Those selected reflect the intricate family networks and inter-connection through marriage and kinship within the Scottish landowning and legal elites (in the main) that led to accessing the patronage system. What is more, from the several examples of great and moderate wealth brought home by individuals, these studies add to the picture of a very healthy input to the Scottish economy. They are placed here alphabetically.

Boyd and Claud Alexander were the sons of Claud Alexander of Newton, Ayrshire and Jean Cunningham; and were brought into the Company through the influence of an uncle, James Alexander and their aunt Rebecca who married a Governor of Madras. The Directors Frederick Pigou and Thomas Walpole backed their petitions for Writers posts. Walpole was at that time in business with a collateral branch of the Alexander family, the Scottish banking firm of William Alexander. The brothers were friends in India with Thomas Graham.[16]

James Beck was the nephew of James Graham of Damside, Fife. His father died when he was a young man and he was raised by his mother 'in obscurity' in Perth. He was one of four children, but the only survivor. With the backing of his uncle, James Graham, he tried to become a lawyer, but failed and went to sea as a ship's officer in 1757. On his return to Scotland a few years later, his uncle was dead and he was left with only £500–£600, the last of his father's estate.

In London he 'tried for a year to go as an officer in an Indiaman', but got nowhere. He 'danced attendance and had to be dependent on others, going between Richmond, Hampton Court and Windsor.' Finally, at Windsor he 'found a friend', John Manship, the East India Company Director, whose patronage was vital. Bombay was reached through Manship, and with his continued patronage Beck prospered. He became a particular comrade of James Cheape; and upon his return to Scotland in 1777 they renewed a friendship that proved lasting. Cheape helped him remit a fortune that he estimated himself to be worth 70,000 rupees (approximately £10,000).[17]

Alex Brodie was the 3rd son of James Brodie of Spynie, Elginshire, advocate and Sheriff of Elgin. He was forced to seek fortune elsewhere when his brother succeeded as Laird of Brodie, at a time when the family was burdened with heavily encumbered estates. His father's position and his own marriage to Elizabeth, daughter of James Wemyss of Wemyss, gave him the leverage required to get a position as a Writer to Madras in 1773.

Brodie's achievement reflects the ongoing nature of the Argathelian system after 1765, even though titularly defunct. During the free-for-all of the 1765–1774 years, his father's electoral influence could still be used to secure a Company civil service position; and at a time when these were in some demand. Through private trade and contracts he went on to amass a fortune, returning home in 1784. He became politically powerful and a supporter of Henry Dundas.

The *Honorable John Cochrane and his brother Basil* were sons of Thomas Cochrane, the 8th Earl of Dundonald. Both were appointed Writers, John in 1766 and Basil in 1769. They were recommended by their uncles, Andrew and Col. James Stuart. With the help of Andrew Stuart in particular, John Cochrane was enabled to transfer very quickly from the civil to the marine branch of the Company; and from 1773 to 1775 he was 2nd officer of the Indiaman *Bessborough*. He eventually became Deputy Commissary to the British forces in North America.

Basil Cochrane's rise in the Company was slow, illustrating how much depended upon the sort of influence given initially by his Stuart uncles. Andrew Stuart had advised him to stay in India and gain a fortune 'cleanly'; but only in 1792 did this happen, when he was made sole agent for the management and distribution of liquors for the Company's Indian army. After his return to Scotland he too became a political supporter of Dundas.

John and David Haliburton were the sons of John Haliburton of Muirhouse, a merchant in Edinburgh, and nephews of John Haliburton of Pitcur. They were both posted Writers to Madras, taking advantage of their (dead) uncle's friends there. Prior to his appointment in 1765 young John Haliburton had been apprenticed to the London–Scottish firm of *Cochrane*. His brother David joined him in Madras in 1769.

They both excelled as linguists, like their uncle, and became Persian translators. The brothers were severely neglected in the 1765–1774 period, however, through lack of patronage. This contrasts with the support and promotion of their uncle earlier; and showed that Scots abroad still needed the political patronage machine to be successful.

George Paterson was Secretary to Plenipotentiary Sir Robert Harland. He was an informant who wrote to his Scots friends at home regarding his contemporaries abroad, especially about enemies like Governor Du Pré of Madras. He angled for friendship and social intercourse with George Dempster. His Scottish contacts included: Col. Ross, Charles Smith and the two partners in the firm of *Johnson & Mackay*. They were all at Madras in 1773. He proclaimed himself a friend of Dr. William Fordyce and of Messrs. Hunter, Ramsay, Webster, Ker and Dick, all prominent in Scottish society. Lauchlin Macleane and Andrew Stuart used him to procure introductions to the Nawab of Arcot.

Alexander Pringle of Whytebank, Selkirkshire was appointed Writer to Madras in 1765. He was recommended by the Chairman for that year, Henry Crabb Boulton, a Clivite. Pringle almost certainly owed his good fortune to the patronage of his father's friend Dr. John Rutherford of Edgirstone, a neighbouring estate; and to the Duke of Buccleuch to whom the family lands at Yair (where Alex Pringle was born) had been sold.

The Pringles were surrounded by properties belonging to gentlemen with Company connections, such as Lord Elibank, his nephew John Johnstone, and Sir Gilbert Elliot. (Dr. Rutherford's own family also entered the Company's service. Robert Rutherford became a Writer in 1768 and the other son, William, was given a ship's berth). Pringle's promotion was steady but unspectacular. In 1778 he was still just a Senior Merchant in Madras. Earlier, in 1775, his father died leaving him with the responsibilities of the family and the estate. Luckily, he was able to send sufficient remittances from India to purchase back and improve the land, raising its revenues from £170 to £200 per annum. His brother, Peter Pringle, serving as a surgeon in the Company's service at Vizipatam in 1774, also sent money home.

Alex was helped by his friendship with Sulivan's relation, John Sulivan, while at Tanjore, and by the marriage of his sister to Robert Mayne. He returned home in 1790 with a moderate fortune. In doing so he realized the words penned in the 1770s: 'We shall all have enough and bye and bye be happy in reflecting on our days of distress.'[18]

Claud Russell was the son of an Edinburgh lawyer, John Russell of Braidshaw, Writer to the Signet, and his wife Mary Anderson. Using his Argathelian and legal establishment connections, Russell was able to despatch his son Claud to Madras in 1751 as a Writer. The young man went out with another Scot, Alex Davidson; and by 1756 had been Clerk of the Peace, Coroner, Mayor and then Sheriff of Madrasapatnam. By 1761 he was a Commissary at Pondicherry, and by 1771 a Madras Councillor.

Twenty years was a long time to stay healthy in an Indian climate and Russell had nobody to push his career along. He met and was friendly with Kenneth Mackenzie, nephew of John Mackenzie of Delvine, but received no favours from that source. Even in India factional strife was prevalent. It mirrored the struggles taking place in Leadenhall. From 1769 Claud Russell was an ally of Clive against Sulivan and Vansittart, and threw his weight against Sulivan in the Company elections. His Scottish friends in the shipping and in the Direction that he joined with in this antipathy to Sulivan included (temporarily) Sir James Cockburn and George Cumming.

In 1771 *Dr. John Stewart of Hampstead* was made Judge Advocate General and Secretary to the Supreme Council at Bengal, by Warren Hastings. He was the son of Henry Stewart; his brother was Henry Stewart; and he was uncle to yet another Henry, Lt. Henry Stewart of the Company's army. He had been a secret agent for Shelburne, and was closely bound to Lauchlin Macleane in the 1760s. He arrived in Bengal in 1771, recommended by Sulivan and Sir George Colebrooke, where he was immediately handed his privileged positions. He had been deeply involved in the politics and splitting of stock for votes in the 1760s; and since 1764 had been (in Sulivan's eyes) his 'bosom friend...he has my whole confidence.' Warren Hastings was asked 'to be his shield.'[19]

Unfortunately, and unknown to Sulivan and Hastings, he was double-crossing them and was close to their enemy Robinson, and their (as yet unknown) foes, Stables and the Macphersons. Stewart of Hampstead, as he was known by contemporaries in London, had fooled Sulivan by working hardest of all during the furious contest of 1769. He was also a friend of the Director John Townson and of Richard and Edmund Burke, and had acted as go-between for them with Sulivan. It was ironic that yet another enemy of Sulivan and Hastings, Philip Francis, thinking Stewart was their friend, had him dismissed using the new regulations that came into force with the Regulating Act of 1773.[20]

6

Not every Scot gained entry to a position in the Company's ranks and many were forced to go to India as free-merchants. Yet even these people, as the careers of Sir Hugh Inglis, George Smith and James Fraser make clear, had to rely on the sinews of patronage. In 1762 Claud Russell was joined in India by his cousin, *(Sir) Hugh Inglis,* later Chairman and Director of the Company. He went out using the same channels as Russell. Inglis was regarded as an 'honest man who...got a moderate fortune in Bengal'. He became a great power in India, and when he returned, backed Sulivan in the 1780s.[21]

George Smith, who was born in 1737 and died in 1789, was a native of Fordyce, near Portsoy, Banffshire. The village and land around was owned by General Abercromby of Glasshaugh, the local laird. Smith was also the nephew of Dr. Andrew Munro, Chief Medical Officer for Madras, who died there in 1757. From these connections he gained the requisite recommendations for a career in the East.

He acted as trustee for his Munro uncle and fell heir to his estate at Canton upon his death. It provided sufficient funds to send him to Europe where he trained in merchant accounts. First he was a clerk in Holland and then in Paris; then when his father, James Smith of Fordyce, died in 1767, his inheritance was enough to send him overland to the East Indies.

He settled as a free-merchant in Madras beside his Munro relations. There he married a cousin, Margarete Aurora Munro. He also prospered to such a degree that he accumulated a fortune somewhere in the region of £50,000. In his will, written when facing death on the way home, one of his bequests paid for the establishment of a school and teacher in Fordyce and an education for boys in the area named Smith. This George Smith bounty was administered for 150 years after his death.

The final choice of a young man whose career illustrates the patronage system in operation is *James Fraser* MP, who was probably the son of James Fraser, merchant and Apothecary of Golden Square, London. The elder James Fraser was a holder of India stock in 1750. He was also a kinsman of Simon Fraser, London merchant and East India Company Director, who with a home in London, a residence at Blackheath, Kent as well as one at Ness Castle, Invernesshire, illustrated the peripatetic life led by the Scottish elite.

It would appear that the operation of patronage through Simon Fraser made it possible for young Fraser to go out to India. He was supported there from London through his father, and through Simon Fraser's influence in the Company. The latter's weight was felt elsewhere in the London business world too, such as with the Maynes, who in turn recommended James Fraser to their nephews, the Grahams.

When young Fraser became a free-merchant in Bengal he used the friendship of the Grahams and the Maynes; while Simon Fraser's support of Warren Hastings' associates in the Company's contested elections resulted in the youth being put on the road to success. Through Hastings' generosity he obtained a contract in 1772 for supplying boots and other military stores. In 1782 he returned with a fortune, only to face years of litigation with the family and executors of his last partners, Col. Graham Harper and Col. Alexander Hannay (brother of Sir Samuel Hannay) over a contract for supplying elephants to the Nawab of Oude.[22]

13

Military Recruitment 1720–80

1

For generations a formidable Caledonian presence had manifested itself throughout the world, in the armies of France, Russia, Sweden and elsewhere. Prior to the Union, poverty, both of sustenance and opportunity, continued to encourage this phenomenon; and before the 1750s the presence of Scottish soldiers in India was due to this age-old adventuring spirit. Either that or they were escaping from the depressing state of affairs at home. Thus in the 1704 to 1714 period a Lt. Wallace, Ensigns Kirkbred, Sommerville and Alex Campbell were all members of Independent Companies in Madras. They were not East India Company servants but were contracted by the Presidencies as and when required.

In the following decades there are certainly more Scots to be found, particularly in Madras, but again they were usually members of independent Companies. The careers of Major David Wilson, Captains James Johnson, Alex Sutherland, Alex Fullerton, Lt. David Murray and Ensign Clarke exemplify this.[1] It was really only with the European war from 1740 to 1755 spilling east to the Presidencies that large-scale military recruitment to India was encouraged, and post-Culloden, troops such as Col. Caroline Scott and other pro-Hanoverians were drafted there. However, this early, the Walpole–Drummond–Ilay–Milton patronage system was not used.[2]

Most Scots who did go to India at this time continued to make their way to the Carnatic, the major theatre, where war against the French and their allies continued to be fought. But Scottish officers were also to be found elsewhere, such as Ensign Campbell in Bombay in 1741, and

Ensign Thomas Kirkpatrick at St. Helena that same year. A Captain Bruce was at Fort St. David in 1747.

In 1746 the Madras garrison numbered some ten officers – from all over Britain; St. David's, Pondicherry the same, although by the end of the 1750s the figure was twice as much. However, indicative of things to come, at least twelve out of the twenty-five officers in Madras during the years 1747 to 1757 were Scots.[3] In fact, the numbers of officers and soldiers in all the Company settlements doubled in these years: from 1,020 in 1747 to 2,601 in 1755. What was remarkable, however, was that by 1775 Scots on the Madras establishment alone numbered 412, an 'amazing increase in the course of a generation.'[4]

2

Such massive enrolment among all ranks really began with the Seven Years War. Ex-Jacobite soldiers were now considered acceptable. Even Lord Chancellor Hardwicke, expressed interest in raising regiments in Scotland, and in 1759 asked the Lord Advocate, Robert Dundas, his opinion on this.[5] In the early 1760s Chatham's neutral attitude towards the Scots helped too; and the machinery of conscription in the Highlands (through the Chiefs), and in the Lowlands (through the Lairds), worked to denude the country of its fighting men.[6]

Of those Scots going into the Company's forces as officers, the majority were sons of aristocrats and the upper bourgeoisie. More often than not they had become military cadets because not enough influence could be brought to bear to secure Writers positions in the civil branch. Some 510 Scottish officers who served the Company in this period are identifiable. This is not a comprehensive list, however and the total number is almost certainly much larger.[7] These individuals illustrate the sheer numbers involved and the sweep of India patronage encouraging things, most of it Government controlled. The fact that the Dukes of Argyll were to the fore in running Scotland also explains why an extraordinary number of these officers were Campbells.

The patronage provided for this clan turned into a veritable flood when promoted by Ilay and then Bute. In the 26 years from 1748 to 1774 at least forty officers from its cadet branches were recruits to the Company's military service. In several cases the contacts used by the Argathelians and the manner of recruitment is readily seen. For example: Lieutenants Alexander and Patrick Campbell of Ardchattan entered the Company's service in 1763 in classical style. Patrick, the eldest, did so through the

Bute interest, while Alexander married into the family of the Director, Thomas Rous.[8]

Another example is Sir Archibald Campbell of Inverneill. He was the 2nd son of James Campbell of Teurchan, Commissary of the Western Isles and Chamberlain of Argyll. Archibald was seconded from the British army in 1768 to be Chief Engineer in Bengal. He was a Lt.-Colonel in 1778 when he returned home with a large fortune from private trading ventures, shipyards and docks. He became MP for Stirling burghs in 1774, using his Indian wealth against Sir Laurence Dundas. After further service with the royal army in America, he was again returned to India at the request of his friend, Henry Dundas, to become, in 1785, the Governor of Fort St. George, Madras. He resigned and came back to Scotland in 1789.[9]

Col. Charles Campbell XVth of Barbreck served in the East India Company army from 1749 to 1792. His Colonel's commission in 1760 was signed by the Chairman, Laurence Sulivan – a certain mark of the patronage system in operation, progressing from Ilay through Milton to Sulivan. From 1753 he had been second in command to General Laurence. Following the siege of Madura in 1764, which he commanded, he began to accumulate money. This was reflected in Scotland where property was bought in the Isle of Bute and an estate in Argyll in 1767. He also inherited the Hartfield property through his mother. In 1767 Sulivan wanted Robert Palk, then Governor of Madras, to get him to use his money to purchase stock for splitting purposes.[10]

Captain Donald Campbell XVIth of Barbreck, eldest son and heir of Col. Charles Campbell was to benefit too. The Bute–Sulivan connection was again used to fulfil his father's wish that he enter the Company's service. His career began in 1761 and ended in 1783.[11] There seemed no end to the largesse distributed by Argyll to his clansmen. Col. Donald Campbell of Glensaddel was another. He was the brother-in-law of Col. Charles Campbell XV of Barbreck and uncle of Donald Campbell XVI of Barbreck. Like his brother-in-law, he entered the Company through Ilay's patronage, transferring from the Guards and arriving in India in 1753 aboard the *Marlborough*. In 1771 he resigned, receiving a handsome reward from the Nawab of Arcot for his services, and by 1775 was in Campbeltown where he owned several estates.[12]

Captain Donald Campbell of Castle Sween, the son of Colin Campbell and Marion MacNeill of Colonsay was another of Ilay's protégés. He served in the Royal army from 1741 to 1747 and fought at Culloden. By 1750 he was in Madras in the East India Company army. He was one of the lucky ones who arrived home safe and well; and died at Bowmore, Islay in 1795.[13]

Although it was part of His Majesty's forces, mention must be made of the arrival in India of the Duke of Gordon's 89th Foot, consisting of men drawn exclusively from Scotland. Such had been the degree of suspicion in the south after the '45, this was a remarkable breakthrough; and an indication that one of the most diminished layers of society was being brought into the new Britain. The 89th was commanded by the American, Staats Morris, husband of the Duchess of Gordon. This company of Highlanders was raised at the instigation of the Duchess, with the help of the highland chiefs, and with the Duke of Newcastle's approval. Ilay ordered them to India and the "Highland" regiment, sailed in 1759, arriving in 1760, remaining until 1763.

A total of seventy men were involved. Thirty-eight were officers, plus a Chaplain and Surgeon. There were five Companies consisting of Major Alexander Duff with fifteen other ranks; Colonel George Scott with eleven; Major Hector Munro (Duke of Gordon's) with ten; Captain George Morrison with eight; and Captain William McGillivray with twenty-six. It became the Gordon Highlanders.[14]

Although Scotland was scoured for men to fill the ranks of his Majesty's army, the influx into the Company's military arm continued. Numbers were enlarged by the many recruited from Royal forces who remained in India when their regiments disbanded. When the 89th broke up in 1763, for example, quite a few joined the Company's service.

Young Scots officers were there to get a fortune quickly and get back home again. They appear on the establishment of every Presidency in ever-increasing numbers. Sons of the Lowland Whig gentry preponderated, but their numbers were leavened by clutches of 'loyal' Highlanders, such as the Campbells; by a trickle of ex-Jacobites like Captain Alex Grant; and a collection of maverick adventurers like General Andrew Anderson and Major John Morrison.[15]

By 1759 Clive was writing home, 'I beg that you desist from recruiting so many Scotch Highland men to your service...their only concern is to quit your service within a twelve-month with a plundered fortune.'[16] He referred, of course, to the Scots officers in the Company's army, not to His Majesty's troops, whose treatment was scandalous. Mutinies broke out in the Royal regiments at the first hint that India was to be their destination.[17]

As late as 1766, however, there was still no proper military organisation or administrative structure for the recruitment of Company troops. Each man cost £10, plus one shilling per day sustenance. He was sent out untrained, unclothed, usually unfit and, in many cases diseased.[18] Yet from 1755 especially, recruitment into the Company's military service proceeded at an enormous pace. From a total of 2,601 European officers and soldiers in India in 1755, the figure rose by 1761 to 3,647 (treble the 1747 number). By 1763 this had doubled again to 6,597. The numbers increase remorselessly: to 7,141 by 1767, to 8,352 by 1768, and to 8,527 in 1770.[19]

In all this Scots were to the fore, to the extent that it has been calculated that in 1772 at least 250 of the serving 800 or more Company officers in India came from Scotland, that is, one third of the total. It is an eye-opening statistic, and one that illuminates the sheer effectiveness of the patronage machinery at work in Scotland. These young men, on the whole more needy, better educated and more aware of Indian opportunities than their English cousins, were the first to be directed towards and grasped such career opportunities.[20] Together with the 280 non-commissioned Scottish soldiers already in the Company's service at that time, the combined total of 560 meant that Scots filled one seventh of the 4,250 Europeans on the Company's military establishment.[21]

3

Several individuals carved out illustrious careers. *Col. William Baillie* and his brother, *Lt. John Baillie of Dunean*, are prime examples. William was the second eldest son of Alexander Baillie of Dunean, Invernesshire and nephew of Alexander Baillie of Dockfour. He was one of Col. Staats Morris' 89th Foot, but remained in India after the Regiment disbanded in 1763. He fought beside General Hector Munro in the 1760s and again in the campaigns of 1778 to 1782. The fortune made from a command of Sepoys was sent home via his agent John Ogilvie and through Drummond's bank. Commanders Robert Munro and William Fullarton Elphinstone were his friends and he used them to bring home diamonds and muslins. His attorney was David Mitchell of the Scots firm *Annan & Colquhoun*, which also remitted his fortune to Scotland.

William's younger brother, Lt. John Baillie, said himself that in 1768, 'Sir Alexander Grant [in London] got him out to Madras as a Cadet' in the Company's army. Grant was a major Proprietor, but was helped in his patronage of John Baillie by his relation Duncan Grant. The initiative for such assistance probably came in the first place from Duncan Grant, who was a friend of Alex Baillie (Senior), of Dunean, and of his eldest son, also called Alexander Baillie. This younger Alex Baillie spent time in London actively espousing the careers of his younger brothers: William, already in

India, and John, waiting to get out. A fellow Scot, Commander Robert Munro, of the *Hardwicke*, took John Baillie out to India where he joined his brother.[22]

However, without doubt *General Sir Hector Munro* of Novar, Rosshire was the most brilliant Scottish soldier to operate in the Indian theatre during these years. He was the first son of Hugh Munro of Novar, a merchant of Clayside, Sutherland, by Isobel Gordon, granddaughter of Sir Robert Gordon, Bart, MP of Embo, Sutherland. He started his military career as a volunteer in Louden's Regiment in 1745, later serving in the 48th foot until 1749 and then in the 31st foot.

He owed his promotion to kinship (on his mother's side) with the Duchess of Gordon. In 1756 she made him a Major in the 89th Foot, which sailed for India in 1759. When the contested elections broke out in the Company, Munro took the Sulivan side and was rewarded with command of the Company's troops in Bengal in preference to Clive's man, Major John Carnac. Munro went on to crush the native forces at the decisive battle of Baksar in 1764.

He became at once the saviour of Bengal and amassed enormous financial rewards, such as: prize money of 80,000 rupees (approximately £10,000); a substantial present from the Raja of Benares; and 2 lakhs of rupees (approximately £20,000) compensation for not being given the grant of a *Jagir* in Bengal, such as Clive had obtained.

With this fortune Munro returned home. He had succeeded his father in 1761 and now purchased the Novar estate from a cousin George Munro, then added the Muirtown estate, Elginshire. In 1766 he entered into a contested election for Inverness burghs and successfully employed his Indian wealth against the West Indian riches of his opponent, Sir Alexander Grant. He was returned for the seat in 1768 and retained it until 1802. His agent (dealing with Company, political and domestic affairs) was John Mackenzie of Delvine.

Hector Munro retained an interest in Company politics, and as a Proprietor continued to back Sulivan during the Leadenhall contests. The credit collapse of 1772 that destroyed the Company's independence, also led to the ruin of the *Ayr* bank. Munro, who had money deposited in both suffered financial loss. This stimulated his return to India in 1777 as a Major-General and Commander-in-Chief at Madras, to face French designs on India that had been resurrected by the war with the American colonists.

Munro's irascibility led him into clashes with Warren Hastings; but his military skill was undoubted. Success at Pondicherry in 1778 and

Negapatam in 1781 balanced the rare ineptitude shown against Haider Ali in 1780. He resigned his position in 1782 and on return to Scotland in 1783 proceeded to spend the regained riches on his estates.

His total wealth from India has been assessed at around £120,000. He used it to give employment to many when work was short: rebuilding Novar House, constructing Indian-styled monuments, like the one at Fyrish, Evanton; and in general demonstrating evidence of much needed public spiritedness. Unfortunately with his introduction of sheep, eviction, dislocation and depopulation followed.[23]

14

Capital Accumulation 1720–80

1

Neil Davidson has accurately stated the point developed in this chapter: 'that the most important economic consequence of the Scottish presence in India was the investment in Scotland of the wealth accumulated by the nabobs upon their return'. Also, that India had an impact upon eighteenth-century Scotland out of all proportion to the number of Scots who went there.[1] An attempt is made here to explore and justify these propositions, and also to take them further: to demonstrate that the sheer gains, uplift and excitement from such a profitable source consolidated belief, north of the border, in the concept of Britain and helped secure its future.

In 2003 Professor Devine thought that the precise scale of gains made from empire awaited more detailed research; and that 'only an interim judgement' could be delivered 'on the overall impact of these adventures on the national [Scottish] economy'. It was admitted, though, that India money, together with that from the Americas and the West Indies, might explain the rapidity of changes in Scotland by mid-century (particularly in agriculture) at a time when money was scarce.[2]

In 1994 Professor Alan Macinnes had also thought the evidence patchy; and suggested that detailed scrutiny of monies from imperial sources invested in places like Argyll was needed; although he made it clear that in Campbell-dominated Argyll at least, there was a dependence on external funding.[3] Nevertheless, despite such uncertainty and hesitation, possibly well-justified, the aim here is to project further the argument that capital, issuing in the main from India, was indeed the major factor that brought the country to life.

Some idea of the vibrancy of Scotland from mid-century onwards, which contrasts vividly with that of 1700, will place the colossal change that occurred in context. Modern research demonstrates a very interesting, multi-faceted Scotland in existence by 1774; and in the second half of the century an immense public energy manifested itself in all fields, fuelling demand and placing pressure on Scotland's traditional leaders. There had been a decisive shift in public attitudes at all levels, and a cross-fertilization of ideas. It is now accepted, for example, that in the 1760s and 1770s agricultural, commercial and industrial developments took place in Scotland that had taken two centuries of change in England. The fact that this appeared to happen from a standing start, so to speak, is part of the conundrum.

Improvements in all fields were common; and eager acceptance of English and continental models, in agriculture and commerce especially, and of the new technologies, helped make Scotland potentially more prosperous. These progressive breakthroughs in agriculture, industry and invention formed a broad front; and were harnessed to the faith in reason that blossomed with the Enlightenment. Here it is postulated that many of these startling changes – perhaps even the Enlightenment marvel itself – were stimulated by early connection with India; that the wealth that poured back from the sub-continent, together with a broadening of perception drawn from new experiences played a more than substantial part in these phenomenal changes.

Some features about Scotland leading up to the mid-century had suggested further extensive growth, if the right catalyst could be found and applied. Although the population was only around one million compared to England's five million or so in 1707, it had risen to one and a quarter million by the 1750s. This was helped by substantial Irish immigration. Also, because of good literacy standards a quality labour force had been formed, and productivity increased.

There was a greater demand for goods, services and supply – despite a slow increase in income in general. Wages were much lower than in England. However, because Scottish goods were much cheaper, they could and did reach markets home and abroad. This capacity to make goods at lower cost per unit of output was again due to advances in technology and invention, to regional and local concentration of industries and from access to the imperial and American markets.[4]

Among other potential advantages to be exploited were substantial deposits of easily worked coal, limestone and iron ore, and abundant water. Another was the topography of Scotland, with long coastal stretches and indentations suitable for cheaper water-borne transport internally and for international trade. The main employment continued to be agriculture, supplemented by hand-loom weaving of flax and wool in the main; but as the century wore on improvements in machine technology and in roads, canals and bridges took place, creating an even better infrastructure for further development. It all needed and received money from somewhere.

Scots had certainly taken advantage of the Union and used it to continue to modernise a process that had really begun following the 'Glorious Revolution' of 1688. Commercial markets were added, and gains were being made from the limited amount of Scottish capital that was invested overseas from the earliest years.[5] Yet this slow development was never enough to explain the transformation of later years.

Fortunately, internal colonisation by England had also been avoided – something that could be viewed to some extent as an (indirect) result of the implementation of India patronage. Put another way, it could be said that such a severe move was precluded by the very large involvement of the Scots elite, who by mid-century were on equal terms with the English (as opposed, for example to the Welsh and Irish) in the new commercial opportunities coming on stream – sharing in the wealth and advancement possible via the East Indies.

Everyone realised, however (particularly the Scots) that there could be no 'empire of trade' without the power of the British armed forces and the financial resources of the new state: all understood that the Royal Navy, tariffs and success in wars underpinned everything. It was soon recognised too that empire was more important for economic growth in Scotland than it was in most other regions of the British Isles.[6]

2

There were many general features encouraging the growth of capital in Scotland, some of which might be used for investment. As discussed earlier, one of these was acceptance of a dependent role within the Union. This certainly helped; and English-based capital was clearly made available because the Scots economy complemented rather than competed with the English, especially in goods like tobacco. The extension of money payments from London banks and from abroad helped regional specializations like the cattle trade and the weaving industry – especially linen. Other changes helped too: By 1727 the Board of Trustees for Fisheries and Manufactures was in operation; and landowners were gathering revenue-tax on land.

Two other factors were of immense importance. First, there survived a superlative independent legal system, whereby contracts could be secured, conveyancing managed, and disputes settled. Lawyers played a leading role in post-Union Scotland that kept them abreast of (and usually immersed in) the commercial, political and social life of the nation. Their prominence and usefulness was noted everywhere.

The other ingredient was the existence of an all-embracing banking structure, facilitating the use of these new funds. By the 1750s it was quite advanced in operation, and capital was mobilized efficiently. This in turn encouraged wealth creation. The most powerful interest groups in Scotland, particularly the Argyll group, including the Duke himself, his brother Ilay, Queensberry, and the ever solicitous Milton, had been involved in setting up the three great banks: The Bank of Scotland in 1685 (with £250,000 stock); the Royal Bank of Scotland in 1727 (with £250,000 capital); and the British Linen Bank in 1746 (with £100,000).[7]

With sizeable sums on deposit (which grew enormously as the century wore on) the banks held considerable lending power, providing loans, credits, subsidies and overdrafts. They were able to call upon funds outwith, as well as from within Scotland; and could also draw upon monies from other places. Banking assets rose from £0.27 million in 1744 to £7.46 million in 1802. Cash credits, small note issue and overdrafts were introduced. (Despite such excellent services to hand, banking machinery, it has been adjudged, was nevertheless less important at this time than the improvised 'reploughing of profits, personal and bonded loans, trading credit...and vital support from family and friends' that also went on).[8]

3

However, it was the activities of what might be termed the 'landowning-bourgeois' elite, that provides the key to understanding why such extraordinary economic and social changes took place north of the border in these years. As was normal in most societies of the time real wealth was concentrated in their hands. This rich privileged few, and even the 'moderately prosperous', might have been 'a small minority in society,' but were at the heart of the massive changes forming and which burst into life from 1750 onwards.[9]

The landed classes and their equals, a growing body of upper and middle class gentry, were the channel by which fresh capital entered Scotland from the second quarter of the eighteenth century onwards. Here it is argued that this money came overwhelmingly from the East Indies, together with distinct contributions from cotton and tobacco estates across the Atlantic, brought mainly into Glasgow via the river Clyde. Smaller amounts (legal and illegal) came from other imperial outposts, primarily the American colonies; and some from government contracts and as a result of naval and military ventures.

Scottish Landowners and gentry simply left no stone unturned in the effort to accumulate further capital, from anywhere, and seized upon market opportunities.[10] Younger sons of cadet families were actively encouraged to accrue capital through trade, as well as through the more usual law and military channels. Professor Kiernan, quoting Philip Woodruffe, puts it more poetically: 'They were "Sons of the manse, younger sons of the big house, sons of doctors or crofters" – more hardworking than the English, and free of the stereotyping gentility of English education and the "isolating crust" of convention and social ritual.'[11] They were committed to economic modernization; and used the steady injection of capital received by them throughout the century to buy and develop land, be this cash from the Indies, via West Indian sugar plantations or from the tobacco trade.

It was not just Scots from this stratum of society, domiciled in their homeland, who were affected by the urge to improve themselves. Many were ensconced in London business, many of them Jacobites. Some, like the Scot Thomas Watts, 'the principal force controlling the Sun Fire Office', had been there since the 1720s. He was a friend of the Duke of Chandos, and involved with him in speculating, particularly in India stock, for which Chandos was renowned. As well as stocks and shares, they dealt in commercial and industrial finance, a lot of it East India Company money; and Watt sent cash home to develop and improve family estates.[12]

Another factor driving the Scottish gentry was the desire for equality with, though not independence from, their southern brethren. Like these English cousins and associates, rather than stand aloof, they wished to be involved at grassroots in the new world opening up. Moreover, their sons, now officers in the British army or soldiers filling the East India Company's ranks, fought on three continents for the Hanoverians. The discrimination suffered following the '45 was placed firmly in the past, although not forgotten, fuelled as it was by the persistent anti-Scots bias of the Southern English.

There was a vigour stimulating the Scottish elite even before mid-century (perhaps involving Protestantism and a work ethic) that combined with a new found sense of going somewhere, doing something. It was reflected in changes to land holdings. Between 1688 and 1751 large, medium and small estates all increased in value – that of the large ones particularly so. By 1751 they were valued at £2,358 more than the £2,350 they were worth in 1688; the medium sized £736 more than the earlier £1,949; and the small ones £209 more than the £729 of 1688.[13]

4

Obviously such a rise in land prices suggests there was an incentive to raise purchasing capital, and the rest of the century would see this objective attained by Scottish Landowners. Such was the ensuing injection of capital (permitting the acquisition and exploitation of estates) that not only was the land market profoundly influenced, but the whole of the Scottish countryside would never be the same again.[14] Between 1760 and 1800 rural Scotland was completely transformed, the lowlands in particular, and the agricultural system once practiced upon it gone forever.

Commercial forces, and above all the capital input of the great landowners, brought about revolutionary changes. Specifically, a new social and economic order was created, fashioned by the lairds: a virtual 'rural bourgeois'. This became, to all intents and purposes, 'an embryonic capitalist farming class', one that emerged from 'the ranks of the tenantry'.

Practical changes were also soon obvious: The years between 1760 and 1815 saw immense 'improvements in agricultural productivity, rapid communications and alterations in social structure', all of which had an overwhelming effect on the rural economy.[15] A revolution was achieved by these improving lairds and new capitalist tenant farmers, and with it came the urbanisation of Scottish rural society, especially the expansion of towns and of their numbers in the later 18th century; Professor Devine's 'urbanisation accelerator'.[16] In this development, it is maintained here, India money played a substantial part.

It must be stressed that it was elite pressure that forced changes in the farming system, from subsistence living, and payment in kind, to cash payments. The ready-money needs of the landowning class pushed demand for stronger and fewer farms. This in turn produced better rentals and marketing, changes from multiple to single tenancies, alterations to market sales rather than 'in kind'. It was also easier to implement enclosures if they were single tenancies; while a smaller number of leases meant fewer tenants.

From 1750 onwards this kind of pressure increased. Many tenants were more than ready to change, as the very speed of the revolution shows. Initiative and accumulation of capital was producing prosperous and successful individuals with large land holdings, who by the 1760s formed a formidable independent farming class holding long leases (19 years plus).[17]

The 1760s and 1770s saw general enclosure and an end to infield-outfield, run-rig systems. It all amounted to social engineering on a massive scale – manners as well. The tool for the job was the 'improving lease'. Many tenants responded well and markets boomed. The upshot was that earlier returns in grain doubled and tripled, with average rises of 200–300%, a remarkable change.

Of course there were bad spots to be overcome. Lairds were losing land in the 1770s; the *Ayr* bank crashed in 1772; bad weather and poor harvests occurred in 1772–73 and 1782–83. The process of change only began again with better weather and the good markets of the 1790s; and the whole improvement movement was probably saved by the demands of the French Revolutionary and Napoleonic wars.[18]

The pattern of these changes and improvements was without doubt due to the great landowners in Scotland. The whole movement, occupying the last quarter of the 18th century, was landlord driven. 'Improving leases' were encouraged from above (by the lairds) and became common from the 1760s. It is argued here that they had new resources to invest (such as Indian money), and that this was the key to the new developments. For instance, one year in India for General Hector Munro (that embraced the battle of Baksar) secured £20,000 – equal to 38 years of income from his Highland estate.[19]

The introduction of funds of such great magnitude could only have a beneficial knock-on effect. The money was employed on improvements in expectation of greater yields, thus profits and even more riches. From the 1760s the speed of change was remarkable, due to both the interventionist role of landowners, providing finance and initiative, and to market influence.

By the 1800s there were 7,500 large landowners in Scotland (defined as paying over £2,000 Scots value in rent) who, at the expense of the lesser lairds, held half the available land. It was the most concentrated pattern in Europe and facilitated capital accumulation because basic resources were in such few hands. This small elite could change things fast, because it also had social and political authority.

The wholesale change can be seen as authoritarian in structure – from above. Incentive came usually in the form of loans that were separate from new buildings, dwellings and roads, which the lairds also paid for. Nor was all this done out of charity. To recapitulate, there were profits from rising markets and prices, and the value of the land was increasing, this is why money was so eagerly sought and invested.[20]

The application of capital to estate development is quite clearly defined and identifiable, and examples of Nabobs at work already permeate this study. There are countless other illustrations, not necessarily using Indian money. That of Sir Richard Oswald's estate near Glasgow is an example. In 1765, with the agreement of those tenants who were progressive, educated and aware, enclosures, houses, byres, dykes, lime, clover, turnips, hedges and ditches were introduced – along with improving leases.

Robert Ainslie of the Douglas estates, in order to get the 'bad old ways' eliminated, factored social features into his surveys of new farms and in re-structuring. Old customs among farmers lingered, but no mass clearances were undertaken. There was a belief that large populations and wealth were linked, and also a fear of losing help needed at harvests. Humanitarian feelings prevailed as well – it was not a matter of profits at any cost.

The plan for the Hamilton estates executed by John Burrell, from 1763 to 1785, was totally based on the laird taking financial responsibility. 'Lavish Landlord expenditure' was at the heart of Burrell's strategy. The heavy costs involved are indicated by his calculation that £4,659 investment from the laird was needed for improvements on some 27 farms (some £153 per farm). He was helped in that many of the existing tenants on the estate were eager to enclose and use improving leases. They were seldom evicted or bought out; and by using a carrot and stick strategy multiple tenancies were steadily reduced.[21]

The new social and economic order created and fashioned by the lairds gave the cutting edge required. Although the great landowners provided the capital that was invested in their estates, these 'conservative' farmers', the new 'rural bourgeois' carried through the revolutionary changes. They became indispensable in Scotland, having benefited from the reading writing and arithmetic skills gained at good Parish schools.

This new layer provided the 'pool of tenants with the capital resources and commercial enterprise to respond rapidly and energetically to the new opportunities', causing a structural change in rural agricultural life. Most important, there were always more of them desirous of good farms than there were available, which maintained pressure for change.[22]

Thus by 1800 rural Scotland had indeed changed, although the population level remained steady. The transformation was marked by the general dispossession of cottars (or small tenants), although there is no real evidence of clearances as seen in the Highlands. Nevertheless, the cottars had virtually disappeared, apart from in the north-east. They moved to urban areas, putting a strain on the Poor Law.

The disappearance of the cottars seemed to fit in with changes all round – the move to paid servants, ploughmen and horsemen, engaged for a term of six months or a year. A migrating labour force took the place once filled by cottar families. The labour for harvests and seasonal work was now provided by people from the Highlands, from Ireland and from the rural settlements, villages and small towns that had sprung up.

Landlord action can be identified as behind these changes – it was all done deliberately. A process of urbanisation that needed and used capital had been introduced. The planned villages that appeared between 1730 and 1830 illustrate this, as did the dramatic growth in small clusters of houses and small villages at road junctions and on main roads. Mining settlements sprang-up. People still worked the land, but as paid labourers; or they were weavers, miners, iron-workers and quarrymen; or smiths, farriers, wrights and shoemakers.[23] This was the immensity of the rural change brought about by the landowning elite, helped by the introduction and outlay of India money.

5

While countless examples of renewal, expansion and novelty in estate management dotted the countryside and were quite visible deep into the second half of the eighteenth century, what had also become distinctly noticeable was the serious build-up of commercial and industrial infrastructures over wide-ranging parts of Scotland. Cumulatively it constituted a massive change, and signified an era of rapid and dynamic growth. Scotland now had a booming economy, one that would have required large and regular injections of capital over a sustained period.

Professor Devine suggests that some of this did come from overseas: 'Over 40 industrial partnerships were established using colonial market funding, from coal mines to cotton mills, sugar-houses to glassworks'. Factories were built, the Monklands canal begun; deepening of the river Clyde was ongoing. All of it was 'highly capitalised.'[24] Colonial funding was clearly important here, but probably even more so was the impact in Scotland of riches from India. Examples without number exist (many given in this book) demonstrating that generally speaking these moneys had a more geographically wide-spread effect, a greater national impact, during the years 1720 to 1780, than the Glasgow and Edinburgh centred colonial money.

To those with the correct political keys to gain entry, invariably the landed elite, the East Indies provided much of the wealth so desired by the owners of countless encumbered estates and by the scions of once well-to-do families. This is illustrated by the activities of Nabobs like the Fullarton Elphinstones of Carberry, Stirlings of Keir and Haldanes of Gleneagles, who were improving the family estates even before the mid-century, using India money. Invariably there was plenty of money left over to invest.

Others were buying new property with the wealth taken from India: men like John Johnstone of Alva (and his brothers George and William) and James Cheape of Strathyrum, St. Andrews. Families like these, enriched by funds streaming in from the east, became commonplace. The patronage of the 1720s to 1750s had borne fruit; and by the early 1760s long-term remittances from India were having a major impact.

The transfer of funds to Scotland of Sir John Cumming of Altyre, and the use it was put to illustrate the point. His activities were similar to many others and exemplify how fortunes made in India and brought back to Scotland stimulated growth and progress. Cumming's money was sent home using mainly bills of exchange – normally through the English East India Company, although the French and Dutch were sometimes used. Even when his children were sent home for health reasons, they carried back gold, which for additional security he made payable to Andrew Drummond's bank in London. He continued to remit his fortune home, using Mackenzie of Delvine, where it was invested in land, property and bank stock. In addition, the wealth Cumming brought back endowed an even higher social status than the one he had held, and exemplifies what was being repeated on a wide-scale elsewhere. Illustrations of such activities and developments litter these pages.[25]

From such copious examples, and in the absence of other explanation, it seems reasonable to believe that indeed 'service in India was the most lucrative and secure imperial prospect.'[26] The 'accumulated profits' of Asian enterprises were even being used by men 'of modest means in general', who carefully re-invested. The funds were laid out for agriculture, commerce, industry and urban building – such as the new model villages mentioned. The lairds mobilized resources, continued to invest large sums on enclosures and farm houses; and were also building the communications infrastructure, the roads and bridges. More coal, lead, iron-stone and limestone pits and quarries could be opened up. Industry, which in general still had a rural base and was complementary to estate management, was being financed by them.[27]

At local level the same people invested East Indies capital in home-based trading companies, in tobacco imports, the droving of black cattle to markets, the wood-bark trade, and meal companies. To these can be added fisheries, harbour construction and dock improvements. In the Outer Hebrides this was stimulated by Captain Alexander Macleod of the Company's shipping; and the Scottish North–East Fishery was created by the Director, George Dempster.

Although the linen industry would dominate from 1760 and well into the next century, wool, silk and cotton works grew in number and importance. Returned civil servants, Claud and Boyd Alexander, began their cotton-mill at Catrine in Ayrshire, using the India wealth they had remitted home. The Erskines of Mar developed the town of Alloa and its industries. Earlier still, as we have seen, Drummond of Quarrel had introduced Flemish weavers from Picardy into Edinburgh and Leith.[28]

Other fortunes brought home via bills on the English East India Company or through diamonds carried by ships' Captains continued to be banked at Drummond's or Coutts' bank in London and thence came to Scotland where the money helped finance other new developments that were beginning to appear. There was a spin-off to other parts of the Scottish economic fabric from these injections of capital. The legal profession in particular benefited, as the papers, not to mention the estate, of John Mackenzie of Delvine testify.[29] Massive amounts, such as £55,560 of Sir Archibald Campbell of Inverneil's India money, was placed in interest-bearing loans; just under £10,000 was given over to stock; and a little under £8,000 spent on his estate.[30]

To these individuals identified can be added the many from everywhere in Britain enjoying the benefit of India money, and who were investing large sums in Scotland via vehicles such as the York Buildings Company. Others, like Sir John Clerk of Penicuik, Sir Lawrence Dundas, James Coutts, General Hector Munro; Dukes and Earls from both sides of the border, and a whole raft of East India Company Directors and Proprietors, were investors.

In the third quarter of the century more of this money was poured into growth and improvements, such as: canal networks, further expansion of the tobacco trade in Glasgow, ship-fitting yards, and various factory and deep-mining developments. More provincial banks, such as the *Ayr* bank, were instituted and were thriving, helped by the amount of cash circulating. They benefited from a 'safe' position within the ambit of the three major Scottish banks, working in harmony with them, within the greater British financial world and the London money market.[31]

Projects were commenced, some so massive they required immense capital investment, such as the building of the Forth–Clyde canal.[32] This enjoyed expenditure from both sides of the border, and the account books dealing with the project provide absolute proof that a great deal of this was money remitted from India.[33] Edinburgh New Town was begun. Even more canals, turnpikes and bridges appeared, paid for through subscription by the self same lairds. Coasts were linked with barges carrying heavy goods like coal, iron and limestone to where these were required.

The York Buildings Company can be picked out as a case study, showing how far India capital was employed north of the border. It had an important and extraordinary part to play in the economic development of eighteenth century Scotland. This firm was full of returned East India Company servants and London merchants using money that had come originally from the east. The company had begun humbly enough in 1675, its original purpose being to build and operate a water works to draw water from the Thames. The place chosen by subscribers to operate from was York House in London, thus the name. Pipes, cisterns and ponds were built to supply the people of St. James' Fields and Piccadilly.

The fortunes of this inconspicuous little business changed, however, in 1719, when a Mr. Case Billingsley and his partners bought it with the aim of changing it into a joint-stock venture. The Duke of Chandos (who features large as a Proprietor and Director of the East India Company) was Governor when it was floated in 1720. It immediately raised a colossal £1,259,000, much of it by subscribers with a 'John' Company background.

Billingsley had noted that the ministry, desperate for funds, wanted to boost money from the sale of the estates forfeited by those Jacobites 'out' in 1715. These were vast territories, incorporating the lands of the Earl Marischal, Lord Panmure, Stirlings of Keir, Threipland of Fingask and the Carnegies of Southesk, among others. The land bought in 1720 brought in rentals of £13,700; and grossed the company £16,000 per annum.

In mid-century it had become one of the great landowners north of the border, owning whole parishes; and by the 1770s it possessed even larger tracts of land. The company also bought and operated coal mines, saltpans, glass factories, limestone quarries, lead mines and iron works: smelting the ore with charcoal made from the acres of trees it bought in places like Speyside. (In 1728 Sir James Grant of Monymusk was offered £7,000 for 60,000 firs to be cut over fifteen years).

Money was invested in places like the Tranent coal field, where in 1722 the collieries there were connected by waggonways (for the first time anywhere) to the harbour at Cockenzie. Much needed cash was also invested at Prestonpans salt works; and of course large sums continued to be devoted to linking the rivers Forth and Clyde. In 1728 furnaces were erected to exploit the Abernethy forest. Trees were carried by pack-ponies north of the Cairngorms to iron mill crofts, such as the one above Nethybridge; rafts of trees were floated down the river Nethy and down the Spey to Garmouth – all financed by York Buildings Company money.

At various times it continued to have as subscribers many of the same London businessmen, including Scots, who were to be seen as Proprietors and Directors of the East India Company. Later it became involved in endless litigation in the Scottish Courts. Efforts to wind it up began with bankruptcy in the 1770s, but it was 1829 before this was finally achieved.[34]

6

There is no doubt (as the above illustrations indicate) that ever-increasing amounts of capital were entering Britain – and Scotland in particular – from the 1720s onward. However, quantifying the capital coming from the East Indies (as separate from elsewhere and from other sources) proves to be a considerable problem. Also, assessing its distinctive importance turns out to be a formidable challenge, as others have already indicated. As things stand, and with no separate figures for Scotland, even to give some indication becomes hazardous.

Isolating India capital necessarily requires that other sources of 'spare' money (sufficient to provide working capital for investment) be traced and assessed. This has proved to be impossible. For example, as yet there are no accurate figures for investment capital that might have accrued from other colonial adventures, such as those in the Americas and the Caribbean. Yet substantial sums did accumulate from trade in tobacco, cotton, transport of slaves, entrepot activities and a black market.

Another problem arises when looking elsewhere for sources of capital – the absence of purely Scottish data. British models provide figures suggesting that gross national product, gross domestic fixed capital and gross domestic investment between 1700 and 1800 saw increases (relative to each) of between 3 and 11 per cent. Yet there is no means of exactly indicating Scotland's share.

The next dilemma is how to explain the upsurge in investment specified, with once more the only information available being intrinsic to a British study. This, however, does indicate that the increase can only be accounted for by trade and commerce. And there are other indications that this was the case. It has been worked out, for example, that in the face of an increasing gross domestic capital, the contribution from agriculture (which during the years 1761–70 equated to 32.6 per cent of the total) had by 1830 fallen to 12.8 per cent. This suggests that the money increase came from some other source, or/and that capital previously spent on the land was released for use elsewhere, such as for entrepreneurship and industrialization.[35]

The British model also implies that although equal savings were made from agriculture and industry, the total reserves produced by agriculture and available for outlay elsewhere amounted to less than one fifth of the total. This might indicate that a similar figure was fashioned by industry, and that the other three fifths had to come from some other source.

It seems reasonable to postulate that the new money available (the 'three fifths') call it venture capital, was produced by a rise in savings that stemmed from overseas business; and that these sums combined profitably with the increase in quantity and quality of goods in circulation. Also, such commerce was being introduced to invigorated and growing markets, impacting on an expanding population and in turn stimulating a larger work force.[36] Unfortunately, it seems impossible to compute a parallel, separate Scottish picture, other than to say that it would certainly be on a more limited scale; and that again trade and commerce would appear to supply the answer.[37]

All of the above implies that the major flow of capital did not arise from savings based on agriculture or industry; that it is more than likely that trade and commerce did indeed generate the 'stream of profits important to industrial expansion'.[38] This can only mean from the burgeoning empires east and west. It might even be the case that two-thirds of investment employed in Britain was financed this way; that is, from non-labour income and non-agricultural activity; and that this would apply equally to Scotland.

7

Despite the seeming impossibility at present of determining every source of capital and the total accumulated for investment, a provisional model is proposed here that indicates there were substantial sums of money flowing into Scotland from the Indies; and in addition, some idea of the amounts that might have been invested from this supply during the years 1720 to 1780. Furthermore, it is suggested that the volume of capital thus provided would seem to substantiate the thesis that sufficient capital accumulation came from this quarter alone to function as a catalyst, triggering the expansion of agriculture, commerce and industry in Scotland in the second half of the century.

Such a paradigm is made possible by projecting the identified funds that a proportion of Scots brought home on to a list of those known to be in India during the years 1720 to 1780. In this way a theoretical total of capital introduced into Scotland from that source is produced. The sum can be added to in that many Directors, Proprietors and London-businessmen (only some with a Scottish connection) spent money north of the border that had originated in the East Indies. Those subscribing to the Forth–Clyde canal were typical. Also, the funds that were employed by bankers and by lawyers (like Mackenzie of Delvine) on behalf of others who had sent back their wealth from India would also tote up.[39]

In addition, it must be remembered that in India, especially in Bengal and Bombay, as well as in Hong Kong and Canton further east, the commercial links made by powerful Scots, either individually or in groups, increased from the 1720s onwards. There was never any cessation of the funds sent home; and from the mid-century onwards a veritable stream of Scottish ventures, or Scottish controlled agencies and businesses, were churning out money. Much of this found its way to Scotland directly, or through further investment in the East India Company (with returns). It has been estimated, for example, that by the mid-18th century '60 per cent of British imports regularly came from Bengal. This trade was controlled by a small number of merchant agencies. At their height, in 1803, there were twenty-three of them based in the regional capital of Calcutta, of whom the six most important were dominated by Scots'. In fact, 'at least three' of the agencies themselves were Scottish.[40]

Excellent evidence of what a Company servant might achieve in the matter of capital accumulation, especially if he benefited from powerful leverage at India House, is seen in the advice doled out by Laurence Sulivan to his son Stephen in the late 1770s. He expected and urged the youth to accumulate about 100,000 pagodas [£30–40,000] during his stay in India. He thought the minimum Stephen could afford to return home with was £20,000. But it must be kept in mind that even then it was cheaper to live in Scotland than in and around London. Sulivan calculated that Stephen would have to bring with him, initially at least, £10,000, which (he said) would give an income of £400 per annum (4%). This he knew from first-hand experience would set his son up in a good way as a gentleman of fashion, with a good house, coach, footmen and servants.[41]

By using such figures as pointers, and by means of the evidence gathered for this study alone, it seems possible to indicate some of the wealth introduced to Scotland from the East Indies in the sixty years between 1720 and 1780. Moreover, the funds depicted here would be more than adequate for life styles similar to that of Stephen Sulivan, and still leave significant money for investment.[42]

There is no basic criterion that can be used to establish what denoted a large, medium or small fortune during these years. However, exposure to countless examples of riches drawn from the east by disparate individuals has resulted in roughly definable figures. Sulivan himself came to England in 1753 with some £40,000, which he considered more than adequate.

To all intents and purposes, therefore, it would appear that a fortune of £40–100,000 was considered large – although many were three times this amount. Even £20–40,000 (as seen in Stephen Sulivan's case) was looked upon as a very respectable and comfortable sum. £10–20,000 was on the small side, but perfectly adequate, and one that would provide security, if not great affluence, for a family from an elite background. Differences, however, were astonishing. For example, John Johnstone was believed to have accumulated something like £300,000, whereas James Cheape brought back a moderate £20–25,000.

During the period in question, some 124 servants and others, such as free-merchants, are known to have come back affluent: 37 with very large fortunes (30%); 65 medium (52%); and 21 small to middling (18%).[43] It is postulated that this indication of large, medium and small fortunes actually brought to Scotland be employed to give an idea of how much India money was being brought in between 1720 and 1780.

These percentage sizes, for known fortunes, when applied to the total number of recipients of patronage revealed in this study, produce the following familiar parabolic shape: 30% of the total number of beneficiaries (1,668) would mean that 500 might have returned with large fortunes. 52% denotes that 868 might have returned with medium ones; 18% that 300 could have managed to bring back small fortunes. It is worth stressing that even if these men died abroad after accruing wealth, the estate of each would have been returned to Scotland and would have remained considerable.[44]

Two other factors would suggest that these figures are not too imaginative: First, it is extremely unlikely that any *military field officer above the rank of Colonel* who stayed alive would return with anything other than a small fortune. Secondly, it is almost certain that *Scottish commanders* would have accumulated fairly substantial riches. One voyage alone was enough for this. A great many chief mates and surgeons would also have accrued reasonable riches.

Ninety-six tons were authorised for the crew on an outward trip in ships of 755 tons or more. Fifty-six tons went to the commander. (As indicated earlier, if the ship was registered at 499 tons, he had 25 tons on the outward journey and 15 homeward). Eight tons were allocated to the

1st mate, six each to the 2nd mate and surgeon, three tons to the purser, and one and a half shared among quartermasters, stewards and the captain's cook. Between ports in the east an 'indulgence' was also allowed of two-fifths of the tonnage, plus use of the other three-fifths if not wanted by the Company. A single voyage could yield £8,000 to £10,000, and in some cases £30,000 on the double voyage – London to Bombay or Madras, then to China and back home.[45]

Through employing the above figures some estimates can be put forward. By taking an average sum for each small fortune (say £15,000); for a medium one (around £33,000); and for a large amount (approximately £70,000); and multiplying by the personnel gauged to have received such fortunes, a sum can be arrived at that spans the 60 years between 1720 and 1780. Thus, starting with small fortunes, £15,000, multiplied by 300 recipients, gives £4,500,000; some £33,000, received by 868 individuals, amounts to £28,644,000. Large fortunes, if averaged at £70,000, enjoyed by 500 beneficiaries, would result in £35,000,000. Altogether these monies total some £68,144,000 over the 60 years.

What is certain, of course, is that a massive proportion of this (theoretical) money would not have existed. Many died in India, enough to suggest that one third of the total recipients should be disregarded. Also, of the remainder who lived, much of the money brought back would have been needed to service life-styles, free encumbered estates and pay off debts. Nevertheless, if only half of the total sum estimated here (that is approximately £34,000,000) was available for investment in one form or another, the results would be impressive.

It is, of course, impossible to assess accurately the India capital that would be injected each year into the Scottish economy over 60 years, but using this model some rough calculation is possible. Investment for the 25 years up to 1745 could be expected from a little over £14 million of the £34 million. That would equate to £560,000 each year until 1745 (£14 million divided by 25 years). Investment for the 35 years up to 1780 could be expected from a little under £20 million; that would equate to £571,428 per annum until 1780 (£20 million divided by 35 years).

From this calculation it seems possible that around a £½ million that stemmed from India was available for investment, and could have entered the Scottish economy each year. This would have become progressively more after 1745, probably nearer £¾ million, especially when subscribers to projects like the Forth–Clyde canal, the York Buildings Company, and money from Scottish controlled agencies and businesses in India and China are considered.[46]

The improvements and changes already launched by the landed classes, and noticeable from mid-century onwards, must also be considered; and returns from capital invested earlier in the century would have come into their own. Results would have been even more spectacular after the '45. With the danger offered by Jacobitism gone, an inclination to invest and speculate would have developed. Scotland was now heavily involved in major agricultural, commercial and industrial developments, with money from earlier years still working. Even more capital was pouring in from the many Scots now established abroad and involved in commerce, remittance of fortunes and agency work. As a result the growth (and with it demand) would have been greater. By 1780 investment of these monies would have created additional sums that were being pumped into the economy.

The computation is, of course, largely conjectural and is only useful in the absence of any alternative. Also, although the capital that found its way from India to Scotland must have been considerable – as indicated here – it can never be regarded on its own as a lever for industrialisation north of the border. It is lost among the other monies appearing in the Scottish economy. It is difficult to accept a single cause for such widespread change and 'progress', yet India money might be regarded as a catalyst, supplying (through the landed classes) the absolutely necessary 'spare cash' to start everything rolling.

Apart from several localized examples, it also becomes virtually impossible to see 'Indian' wealth working on its own in Scotland. The many Nabobs and others with East Indies connections certainly made an impact in their areas; but it is difficult (and perhaps at the moment unfeasible) to fully assess these individual efforts, or their cumulative effect, regionally or nationwide. However, at the very minimum it can be said that this Indian input significantly enlarged the pool of available funds, sufficient enough to be brought into the equation. In harness with such other monies it certainly generated and stimulated the revolutionary developments that took place.

In conclusion it must be stated that this study, with its named individuals and attempt to measure and assess wealth with an Indian origin that came into the country, can only be seen as a harbinger of further research. Other sources, fleetingly referred to, such as from the West Indies, also had a bearing on developments that affected Scotland, to such an extent that they deserve future scrutiny. Moreover this Indian money requires further qualification and assessment to finally judge its importance, but that must be left to another time.

Nevertheless, to contemporaries it would have been obvious – even to diehard opponents of the Union – that the open road to the East Indies, brought about through joining with England was proving a good thing, in economic terms at least. Windows of opportunity were offered to a ravenous people. In this respect the eighteenth century Indian experience, because of the knowledge, breadth of understanding, expectation and money it brought to Scotland can be interpreted as beneficial as well as bonding.

Even if this good fortune was not immediately apparent to the suffering, defenceless lower orders, the money that came trickling downwards and spread throughout the land would, in the end, give work to many. It would seem also that the wealth from India pouring into Scotland created a mighty padlock that ensured she would remain bound fast, and be part of the new 'Great Britain' well into the future.

15

Summary and Conclusions

1

The administrators examined in this study regarded the East India Company as a mechanism for unlocking political capital. This is seen specifically in the use of India patronage in Scotland between the years 1720 and 1774, for the ends of civil and parliamentary management. India patronage was used to develop the reality of a British state. It drew peoples together encouraging governmental and economic cohesion, resulting in agreement rather than discord. The Whig oligarchy in the 1720s was determined to protect the Union, still new and fragile, and it wished to strengthen the state. A successful formula was found and this was continued for six decades.

The recipients of India favours, that is, families from the right rank in Scottish society with electoral support to offer in return, quietly secreted away such advantages. They were never something boasted about, such was the nature of the agreements that made them possible. Yet, as we have seen, those involved included heads of Government, political managers in Scotland, the most powerful men in the East India Company, Scottish business exiles in London and elites from every part of Scotland.

One of the springboards for all of this was the existence of a dominant legal profession in Scotland; another was an easily managed political structure; while the East India Company was open to all would-be Proprietors. It was entering an expansionist period too, with great changes in its very structure and purpose. This opened the door somewhat to exploitation, allowing it to come under pressure from Government and its agencies.

As indicated, the use of India patronage by London ministries in favour of Scots sprang initially from fears and suspicions, which fed the opinion that stronger management was needed in Scotland. Such fears had good foundation. The commonality and many of the Scottish gentry were disillusioned with the Union and became even more restless after the '15. Popular demonstrations against London dictates were common. This was met by a Whig fear of Scottish Jacobitism sparking off an English equivalent; and probably a touch of deep-rooted phobia regarding the Scots (seen particularly in London) which flared upon sensing the quickening of the Scottish pulse.

Riots in Scotland, such as that over the Malt tax, probably the Porteous affair too, and over other deeply felt grievances, fuelled such sentiments. It was generally believed that Scotland had been 'sold' to England; that the vision of Westminster as a Parliament for Great Britain was being set aside – and with undue haste; that it was reverting to being English, and seen as such by those south of the Tweed. In truth, the Union was never regarded in England as an equal partnership.

At the time and in the years immediately afterwards, the riots were of real concern to London. Political leaders also feared that Westminster would become unstable if the quality and political direction of the Scottish peers and Members of the Commons was not vouchsafed. This was an important consideration for Walpole. The newness of the Administration in 1722 and the need to consolidate his own power-base also meant that he had to embrace the most powerful group in Scotland, the Argathelians. That is why unlimited access to patronage (from all sources) went to them in return for unswerving support and alliance in Scotland and in London.

Governments would use this patronage for much the same reasons until the mid 1760s, when the Jacobite threat was well and truly over, helped into oblivion by the use of India patronage. A sustained electoral support had been established by this date; and the integration of the two nations had progressed further, as had the Anglicisation of the Scottish aristocracy. The fact that a Scottish economic revival had begun, stimulated at least to some extent (as argued here) by India money entering the economy, eased things for both Westminster and for Edinburgh politicians.

There developed a docility and perceived harmony to Scottish internal politics that pleased Westminster and the Scottish ruling elite; and thus, even after the demise of Argathelian control in 1765, India favours continued to seep northwards. By this date India patronage had been in use some forty years. Its continuation was helped by the course of

Company politics, and cross-ties among Scots in Parliament, in the London business world and in the Company.

The incorporation by the State of this patronage was promoted by the skills and experience of a new breed of Government administrator. Men of the highest calibre, such as Charles Jenkinson and John Robinson had been involved at Westminster since the early 1760s. They were active in the implementation of North's Act. Together with Henry Dundas they would provide the competence needed by Government to regulate India patronage when it passed into ministerial hands in 1784. They were already in position before 1774, wresting control from the Company's traditional rulers.

2

The startling scale of Scottish participation in the East India Company, its shipping and business, home and abroad, during these years can be understood from a few statistics. Forty Company Directors, fifteen with direct Scottish association, patronised Scottish applicants between 1720 and 1774. Eleven did so in the 1720–42 period; fourteen between 1742 and 1765; and twenty from 1765 to 1774. At least fifty-two Scots were Proprietors of East India stock during these years: five between 1720 and 1742; thirty-one from 1742 to 1765; and thirty-one during the years 1765 to 1774. At least 1,668 Scots (and almost certainly many more) found their way to India as civil servants, military men, commanders, physicians, ships surgeons and free-merchants through being able to tap into the patronage system. A select number of these supplicants, over one hundred and sixty, are traced more fully here.[1]

But this study of India patronage, its usefulness for the political management of Scotland and for maintaining the Union, is only part of a larger tableau that makes up the Scottish–Indian connection. Mention has been made of the prominence of Scots in the economic life of the sub-continent, in the business life of London (which incorporated the East India Company), and of the financial benefits accruing to Scotland from all this. It adds up to a deep and broad, multifaceted Scottish–Indian connection in the middle years of the eighteenth century that demands further study.

To the throng of Scots who went to India between 1720 and 1774 must be added the equally large numbers concerned with them through interest, family connection and dependence. Also, ordinary soldiers, sailors and others went out in large numbers and although there are few records of their exploits, or of the money, artefacts and experiences that they brought back to Caledonia, those that survive deserve to be sought out and examined.

What is ascertained here is that around 2,000 young men from the top strata of Scottish society appeared in India during these years. Gibb said in 1937: 'Scots who left their mark [in India] are in their hundreds...yet rarely, if ever, has the influence exercised by the people of that small country upon Indian history been mentioned.'[2] This state of affairs has been slowly rectified in more recent years. However, the reverse of what Gibb says is still true. The mark left by the Indian experience on eighteenth century Scotland (as well as upon Great Britain) has still to be properly addressed.

Most calculations suggest that Scots gained about a quarter of all patronage during the years in question, which if measured on a population basis, should have really resulted in a mere eighth or ninth of the total. It was a sizable presence and the lives of those involved provide fascinating and useful insights into Scottish society at that time. Their careers and subsequent existence back home demonstrate that the India connection of these years was of major importance in stimulating political, economic and social life within Scotland. Most certainly the connection helped the coalescence of Scotland and England in all of these spheres.[3]

The final word as regards the relationship of India patronage to the political management of Scotland must concern the motive(s) for its existence; and whether it was indeed (together with financial and economic spin-offs, and the hope it gave) a vital development. At the very least it certainly helped stabilize the new state when at its most vulnerable, and ensured its sustainability. Overwhelming evidence has been given here of deliberate manipulation by Walpole, the Argathelians and their successors, as far as the inception and continuation of this particular patronage and its machinery is concerned, to achieve these very ends.

It began in a rather haphazard and informal manner and never fully materialized in any formal pronouncement, which was really only to be expected, but was very clear in the correspondence of politicians, political managers, Company officials and beneficiaries. In this it differed in no degree from any other form of patronage of the time. The Indian variety was added to other favours and sinecures, and used to preserve the fledgling British state and the pre-eminent position of its designers. The Whig oligarchy north and south of the border willingly continued in this endeavour throughout the years that followed.

The greed and the need of those whose votes were chased, dovetailed nicely with Administration's political requirements. The capital-owning classes of the period in question, with wealth mainly in the form of land, pursued courses of action that increased profits and enhanced capital. Employment of their sons in theatres such as India, which provided the best opportunity for the accretion of riches, made sense. With the satisfaction that followed, the future of the new state was assured.

It might also be said that the Scottish governing classes were lured by the promise and challenge of a new world opened up to them through Union with England. Also, among many there undoubtedly existed the belief that a strong controlling force was necessary, albeit this would operate from London. Nevertheless, it was deigned to be in their best interests and that of Scotland in the long-term to adhere to. This sentiment was re-stated in 1770 with Mackenzie of Delvine's call for a return to the Argathelian system.[4]

There is no doubt either that prestigious posts and sought-after status came to those who embraced English culture and accepted London rule; and for the Scottish elite there was undoubtedly a feeling of security involved. A final settlement of Scottish–English hostilities had been achieved; and with it preparedness for any threat from abroad. In this development the pursuit and enjoyment of India patronage had played its part.

In a sense these privileged Scots might also be considered 'victims of cultural, political and economic enslavement'; although conversion also showed pragmatism. Many of the 'indigenous Scottish elite' abandoned the mores of a long-established culture to obtain advancement for themselves, families and friends, by accepting and working towards political and social integration with their English counterparts.[5] Most became masters of both cultures, skilfully maintaining Scottish ways while utilizing the foreign culture they were grafted on to.

It would seem that Walpole married his own requirements to post-Union desires among leading, powerful Scots, by opening up all avenues of patronage to them, and particularly India patronage. He and his successors at Westminster thereby realised every objective, and especially their own continued dominance from London and the survival of a Great Britain.

In the long-term though, Scottish integration with England and the introduction of measures intended to still any active political discussion in the north, meant that Scotland entered a political sleep from which she never fully awakened during the imperial and Commonwealth eras that followed. And yet, it might be argued that the consolidation of all parts of the Kingdom spurred the united will and political strength upon which the might of the British state of the eighteenth to twentieth centuries was established. The integration of Scotland and England in this era successfully engineered the foundation of the largest combined territorial, financial and economic empire the world had ever seen.

From such a suggestively teleological point of view, manipulation of India patronage during these early years might, therefore, be thought of as being undeniably useful. The other side of the coin, of course, is that with the British Empire all but extinguished, and the cohesion it engendered gone, a reversion to the constituent parts of the United Kingdom might indeed become a reality.

Appendix

Part 1: Select list of Scots Recipients of Patronage and of Providers between 1720 and 1779

Symbols

⊤	Businessman in London	◄	Plenipotentiary
▲	Civil Service	♫	Poet
♣	Director	●	Proprietor
☼	Free-merchant	☺	Purser
♪	Hydrographer	•	Shipping
♦	Landowner	▫	Ship Owner
—	Lawyer/Political Agent	Ω	Ship's Surgeon
■	Military	□	Statesman
∞	Misc. & Untraced	♀	Surgeon
♥	Patronage Agent in London	♂	Assistant Surgeon

m	Mate	*4m*	4th Mate
1m	1st Mate	*5m*	5th Mate
2m	2nd Mate	*6m*	6th Mate
3m	3rd Mate		

B-M	Bombay Marine	W	1720–42
L-F	Large Fortune	X	1742–65
M-F	Medium Fortune	Y	1765–74
N-S	Navigation Surveyor	Z	1775–80
P	Provider, channel for patronage		
S-F	Small Fortune		

APPENDIX

- ♦ Abercrombie, Alexander WP
- ☺ Abercrombie, Thomas Y
- ∞ Abercrombie, William
- ● Abercrombie, William 2mY
- ● Abercromby, Captain Burnett X[1]
- ■ Abercromby, General Sir Ralph
- Ω Abernethy, Robert mY
- ● Adair, Captain Alex X
- ☻ Adams, John YP
- ☼ Adamson, Alexander
- ♦ Agnew, Sir James XP
- ■ Agnew, Major-General Patrick Alex
- ▲ Alexander, Boyd L-F,Y[1]
- ▲ Alexander, Claud L-F,Y[1]
- ▲ Alexander James M-F,X[1]
- ♦ Alexander, William XP
- ♦ Allardice, James, of Allardice XP
- ∞ Allardice, Mrs. Jane (nee Smart)
- Ω Allardice, Mr. Y
- ■ Alston, Lt. David Y
- ■ Alston, Captain William Y
- ♂ Anderson, Alex Z
- ■ Anderson, General Andrew X
- ♂ Anderson, Archibald[35]
- ● Anderson, Captain Archibald X
- ▲ Anderson, David[1]
- ♂ Anderson, George Z
- ♀ Anderson, Dr. James W
- ▲ Anderson, James Y[1]
- ☺ Anderson, John Y
- Ω Anderson, John Z
- Ω Anderson, Robert Z
- ● Anderson, Captain Robert Y
- ☼ Anderson, Thomas X
- ♀ Anderson, William X
- ■ Angus, James Y
- ▲ Arbuthnot, ... W
- ■ Ardloch, Lieutenant
- ■ Armstrong, Alex Y
- ■ Armstrong, Lt. Archibald Z
- ■ Armstrong, John Y
- ♀ Arnot, Thomas

- Ω Badenach, James Y
- ■ Bagshaw, Cadet Y
- ■ Baillie, Lt. Col. A.W.
- ♀ Baillie, James Z

- ▲ Baillie, James Hope S-F,Y[1]
- ■ Baillie, Lt. John X[1]
- ■ Baillie, Cadet John Y
- ♀ Baillie, Menzies X
- ■ Baillie, Lt.-Col. Robert Y
- ■ Baillie, Captain Thomas Z
- ■ Baillie, Lt. William Z[1]
- ■ Baillie, Col. William L-F,X[1]
- ♀ Baillie, William Z
- ▲ Baillie, William
- ♦ Baillie, Sir William YP[1]
- ● Baillie, Captain YP
- ▲ Baillie,... X[1]
- ▲ Baine, Duncan Andrew
- ∞ Ballantyne, Miss W
- ■ Baird, Sir David
- ♦ Baird, Sir John XP
- ● Baird, Captain John Y
- ♀ Baird, Robert W
- ∞ Baird, Mrs W
- ● Baker, Captain George X
- ♣ Baker, William WP
- ■ Balfour, Major Arthur Y
- Ω Balfour, David X
- ■♀ Balfour, Lt. Francis Y
- ▲ Balfour, John
- ● Balfour, Lewis 2mX
- ■ Balfour, Captain Sir Patrick Y
- ♀ Balfour, Thomas Y
- ▲ Balfour, Walter Y
- ☼ Balfour, William Z[19]
- ☺ Ballantyne, Andrew Z
- ● Ballantyne, Captain George Y
- Ω Ballantyne, Hugh Y
- Ω Ballantyne, Ninian X
- ∞ Ballantyne, Miss
- ☼ Bane, John
- ♀ Bannatyne, Richard Y
- ■ Bannatyne, Captain Robert X
- ▲ Barclay, Robert X
- ■ Barclay, Lt. Sir William Y
- ■ Barland, Lt. Walter Y
- ♣ Barrington, Sir Frederick Fitzwilliam XP
- ■ Barrington, Col. George X
- ● Baxter, Peter 1mZ
- ■ Bayne, Lt. Alexander
- ● Bean, James mXP[1]

APPENDIX

- ▲ Beck, James S-F,Y[1]
- ♦ Belhaven, Lord XP
- ■ Bell, Ensign Alex Y
- ☿ Berrie, William Y
- ● Bett, Alex 4mY
- ● Bigger, James m
- ■ Binny, Lt. Alex Y
- ♂ Binny, George Y
- ■ Birrell, Major David Y
- ■ Birrell, Captain George Y
- ■ Birrell, Lt. Thomas Y
- ■ Black, Captain Alex X
- Ω Black, Alex W
- Ω Blackadder, Alex mZ
- ▲ Blair, Alexander W
- ● Blair, Archibald N-SY
- ● Blair, David 3mY
- ● Blair, Eglington 5mX
- ■ Blair, Ensign John Y[26]
- ▲ Blair, Peter W
- ■ Blair, Lt. Peter Y
- ■ Blair, Ensign Robert Y
- ■ Blair, General Sir Robert Y
- ■ Blair, Captain Thomas Y
- Ω Blair, Thomas X
- ● Blair, Thomas 3mY
- ■ Blair, Colonel William Y
- ● Boddam, Captain Charles W
- ♣ Boddam, Charles M-F,YP
- ● Boddam, John 3mW
- ◉ Boddam, Hannah WP
- ▲▣ Boddam, Thomas M-F,Y
- ▲ Bogle, George
- ■ Bogle, Lt. George M-F,Y
- ▲ Bogle, Laurence Y
- ■ Borthwick, Captain Thomas
- ♀ Boswall, Dr. Alexander X
- ● Boswall, Alex 6mY
- ■ Boswall, Captain
- ● Boswell, Captain Bruce Y
- ♣ Boulton, Henry Crabb XP
- ● Bowie, Archibald 2mX
- Ω Bowie, Patrick Y
- ♀ Boyd, George Y
- ■ Boyd, Lt. Hugh
- ♣ Boyd, Sir John WP
- Ω Boyd, William Z
- ■ Bremner, Lt. John Y

- ▲ Brodie, Alexander L-F,Y[1]
- ▲ Brodie, James
- Ω Brodie, James X
- ● Brodie, Samuel 5mY
- ● Brodie, Thomas 3mY
- ■ Broughton, Major-General Edward Swift Y
- ■ Brown, Lt. Archibald
- ■ Brown, Lt. George X
- ■ Brown, Lt. John Z
- ☿ Brown, John
- ☿ Brown, Murdoch
- ■ Brown, Ensign William X[11]
- ■ Bruce, Captain George
- ■ Bruce, Captain Henry Y
- ● Bruce, John 5mZ
- ▲ Bruce, Patrick Crawford Y[1]
- Ω Bruce, Robert X
- Ω Bruce, Robert Y
- ● Bruce, Robert 4mY
- ■ Bruce, Lt.-Col. Robert Y
- ■ Bruce, Lt.-General Robert Y
- ■ Bruce, Ensign Thomas Y
- ■ Bruce, Major William Y
- ■ Bruce, Lt. William Z
- ■ Bruce, Ensign X
- ■ Bruce, Captain X
- ♣ Brydges, Jas. Duke of Chandos WP
- ● Bryson, Peter 1mY
- ∞ Buchan, Hew
- ▲ Buchan, John W
- Ω Buchanan, Archibald W
- ♀ Buchanan, Duncan X
- ■ Buchanan, Major James Y
- ◉ Buchanan, James XP
- ● Buchanan, John 3mZ
- ■ Buchanan, Captain John
- ♀ Buchanan, John Y
- Ω Buchanan, Pitcairn Y
- ■ Buchanan, Ensign William Y
- ∞ Burnes, Alexander
- Ω Burnett, Hugh X
- ♦ Burnett, James XP
- ■ Burnett, Captain James Y
- ● Burnett, James 1mY
- ■ Burnett, Lt.-Col. James
- ▲ Burnett, John X[1]

APPENDIX

- ■ Burnett, Lt.-Colonel Joseph Y
- ☻ Burnett, Thomas XP
- ☼ Burnett, Dr. Y
- ♀ Burnett, William Y
- ■ Burrington, Colonel George Y

- Ω Cairncross, Andrew Y
- Ω Cairns, Thomas X
- ■ Callander, Captain Adam Y
- ▲ Callander, Alexander X
- ■ Callander, Ensign Alexander Y
- ■ Cameron, Lt. Alexander X[6]
- ■ Cameron, Ensign Hugh Stronach W
- ● Cameron, James 4mY
- ■ Cameron, Lt. John X
- ▲ Cameron, John W
- ■ Cameron, Lt. Kenneth X
- ■ Cameron, Lt.-General William Y
- ▲ Campbell, Alexander
- ● Campbell, Alex 3mX
- ♂ Campbell, Alex Z
- ■ Campbell, Captain Alexander
- ■ Campbell, Lt. Alexander X
- □ Campbell, Archibald, Earl of Ilay WP
- ■ Campbell, Major-General Sir Archibald L-F,YP
- ■☻ Campbell, Col. Charles M- F,XP
- ■ Campbell, Lt. Colin Y
- ● Campbell, Colin 2mW
- ■ Campbell, Lt.-General David
- Ω♀ Campbell, Dr. Daniel X
- ■ Campbell, Lt. Daniel
- ■ Campbell, Captain Donald X
- ■ Campbell, Col. Donald Y
- ■ Campbell, Col. Donald M-F,X
- ■ Campbell, Captain Donald M- F,X
- ■ Campbell, Captain Dougald X
- ■ Campbell, Major-General Dugald
- ♀ Campbell, Duncan X
- ■ Campbell, Lt. Duncan
- ■ Campbell, Ensign Duncan Y
- ■ Campbell, Ensign George
- ☻ Campbell, George XP
- ■ Campbell, Captain George
- ♀ Campbell, George Y
- ■ Campbell, Major-General George

- ▲ Campbell, Hugh M-F,W[1]
- ♀ Campbell, James
- ■ Campbell, Col. James
- ♦ Campbell, James XP
- Ω Campbell, James W
- ● Campbell, James 5mZ
- □ Campbell, John, 2nd Duke of Argyll WP
- ■ Campbell, Captain John X
- ■ Campbell, Lt. John X
- Ω Campbell, John X
- ■ Campbell, Coronet John X
- ■ Campbell, Ensign John X
- ■ Campbell, Lt. John X
- ■ Campbell, Captain John (1767)Y
- ■ Campbell, Captain John (1768)Y
- ■ Campbell, Captain John (1770)Y
- ■ Campbell, Lt. John Y
- ■ Campbell, Ensign Mildmay
- ■ Campbell, Lt. Patrick X
- Ω Campbell, Patrick X
- ■ Campbell, Lt. Patrick
- ■ Campbell, Ensign Peter
- ■ Campbell, Lt. P.
- ■ Campbell, Lt. Ralph John
- ■ Campbell, Major Richard
- ■ Campbell, Lt. Robert (1753)X
- ■ Campbell, Cadet Robert (1754)X[10]
- ▲ Campbell, Thomas Dugald Y[1]
- ♀ Campbell, William
- ■ Campbell, Capt. William Y
- ■ Campbell, Ensign William Y
- ■ Campbell, Captain William
- ■ Campbell, Captain Y[28]
- ● Campbell, Captain W
- ■ Campbell, Ensign X
- ▲ Carmichael, Charles W[1]
- ♂ Carmichael, Frederick Y
- ▲ Carmichael, George W[1]
- ☺ Carmichael, John X
- ♀ Carmichael, Michael W[1]
- Ω Carmichael, Thomas X
- Ω Carnegie, Alex Y
- ▲ Carnegie, Governor David M-F,W[1]
- ▲ Carnegie, David X
- Ω Carnegie, Daniel X
- ● Carnegie, Henry 4mW

Appendix

- Carnegie, Nicholas 6mY
- Ω Carnegie, Thomas X
- Ω Carnegie, Dr.
- ▲ Carnegie,…, W
- Ω Carnegy, Alex Y
- ● Carnegy, Charles 4mX
- Ω Carnegy, David X
- ● Carr, Alex 3mX
- ■ Carstairs, Captain Peter X
- ■ Carstairs, Ensign
- ● Cathcart, Charles 4mX
- ☺ Chalmers, Alex X
- Ω Chalmers, George X
- ▲ Chalmers, William Y
- ♣ Chauncy, Richard XP
- ▲ Cheape, George Y
- ■ Cheape, Major Harry Z
- ■ Cheape, Lt. James Z
- ▲♦ Cheape, James M-F,XP[1]
- ▲♣ Cheape, Thomas M-F,YP[1]
- Ω Cheape, Thomas W
- ● Chisholme, Captain Charles Y
- ☺ Clarke, Alex X
- ●· Clarke, Captain Daniel X
- ◉ Clarke, General Duncan YP
- ● Clarke, James 1mX
- ■ Clarke, Ensign
- ■ Clearihue, Captain James X
- ■ Cleland, Ensign David Y
- ▲ Cleland, John W
- ◉ Clerk, Duncan YP[1]
- ◉♦ Clerk, Sir John XP[1]
- ◉ Clerk, Robert YP
- Ω Clugstone, Alex Grant Y
- ▲ Cochrane, The Hon. Basil L-F,Y[1]
- ■ Cochrane, Lt. George Z
- ■ Cochrane, Captain X
- ● Cochrane, John m
- ▲● Cochrane, John 2mY[1]
- Ω Cochrane, Peter Z
- ♣ Cockburn, Sir James XP[1]
- ■ Cockburn, Lt. James Y
- Ω Cockburn, James W
- ♀ Collie, James mZ
- ♣ Colebrooke, Sir George YP
- ♦ Colquhoun, James XP
- ♀ Colt, Dr… W
- ● Colville, Midshipman X[1]
- ■ Congalton, Captain Charles X
- ■ Congalton, Lt. David Y
- ● Conqueror, Peter 2mX
- ● Copper, Peter Y
- ◉ Coutts, James XP
- ♣ Coutts, Matthew Charles XP
- ▲ Coutts, Matthew W
- ◉ Coutts, Thomas XP
- ▲ Cowan, Governor L-F,W
- ■ Cowie, Cadet John Z
- ■ Cox, Captain Hiram Z
- ▲ Craig, Hew Alexander Y[1]
- ■ Craig, Lt. James Y
- ■ Craig, Ensign John Y
- ● Craig, Robert 1mX
- ■ Craig, Ensign Thomas Y
- ● Craig, Captain William W
- ♀ Craigie, John Y
- Ω■ Cranston, Lt. Andrew Y
- ● Cranston, John 2mY
- ■ Cranston, Cadet Thomas X[16]
- Ω Crawford, Gideon W
- ☺ Crawford, Hugh W
- ■ Crawford, Captain James X
- ■ Crawford, Major James Y
- Ω Crawford, John Y
- Ω Crawford, John Z
- ▲ Crawford, Quinton M-F,X[1]
- ● Crawford, Robert 5mX
- ■ Crawford, Lt. William Z
- ■ Crawford, Ensign William X
- ☼ Crawford,…
- ● Crawford,…, N-SY
- ♦ Crawfurd, George WP
- ♦ Crawfurd, Gideon WP
- ▲ Crawfurd, Henry W
- ♦ Crawfurd, John WP
- ■♂ Crawfurd, Major Moses Y
- ● Cree, Alex 2mX
- ♣ Creed, Sir James XP
- ■ Crichton, Lt. Thomas Z
- ● Crombie, Patrick 2mX
- ● Cullen, James 4mY
- ■ Cumming, Captain Alex Y
- ■ Cumming, Lt. Andrew Z
- ☼ Cumming, David
- ● Cumming, Duncan 2mX
- ● Cumming, Captain Edward Y

●♣ Cumming, Captain George M-F,WP[1]
■ Cumming, James Y
■ Cumming, Col. Sir John L-F,X[1]
■ Cumming, Captain Robert Z
♂ Cumming, Thomas Y
▲ Cumming, William X
☺ Cummings, Alex X
■ Cummings, Captain David Y
● Cummings, Captain Robert W
■ Cummings, Captain Stuart Y
● Cummings, William 5mX
● Cunningham, Alex 1mY
Ω Cunningham, Charles X
● Cunningham, Edward, 5mY
☺ Cunningham, James X
● Cunningham, James 5mZ
■ Cunningham, Major John Y[1]
● Cunningham, Ninian 1mX
Ω Cunningham, William Y
■ Cunninghame, Lt. Alex Y
■ Cuthbert, Cadet Peter Y

▲♪ Dalrymple, Alex M-F,X[1]
♦ Dalrymple, Sir Hew WP[1]
▲ Dalrymple, James X
● Dalrymple, Sir John YP
■ Dalrymple, Captain Robert Y
▲ Dalrymple, Robert
● Dalrymple, Robert 3mZ
▲ Dalrymple, William Stair X[1]
● Dalrymple, Captain William X
● Dalyell, Thomas 1mX
■ Dalziel, Ensign James Z
■ Dalziel, Lt. John
● Dalziel, Robert WP
▲ Davidson, Governor Alexander L-F,X[1]
Ω Davidson, George Y
♥ Davidson, Henry S-F,XP
♥ Davidson, John S-F,XP[1]
▲ Davidson, John S-F, (1752)X[1]
Ω Davidson, John Y
■ Davidson, Captain Robert X
Ω Davidson, William Y
♂ Davidson, ... Z
■ Davis (or Davies), Captain Peter Y
■ Deare, Lt.-Col. Charles Russell Y

■ Deare, Lt.-General George Y
♣ Decker, Sir Matthew WP[1]
▲ Dempster, Charles S-F,X
♣ Dempster, George M-F,XP[1]
Ω Dempster, George X
● Dempster, Captain John Hamilton M-F,Y
▲ Dempster, Philip S-F,X
● Dempster, Philip 1mX
Ω Dempster, William Z
● Dewar, Captain James X
☺ Dewar, James Y
♀ Dewar, James Z
▲ Dick, George X[1]
● Dick, James 3mY
▲ Dick, John X[1]
▲ Dick, Mungo Y[1]
Ω Dick, Samuel X
Ω Dick, William Z
● Dickson, Captain Alex X
■ Dickson, Lt.-General James Y
▲ Dod, John
■ Don, Lt.-Col. Patrick Z
● Donaldson, James XP
● Donaldson, James 3mY
■ Donaldson, Ensign Laurence
● Donaldson, Robert 5mZ
♣ Dorrien, John XP
● Doual, Alex 3mY
▲ Douglas, Alexander W
● Douglas, Andrew 3mW[1]
■ Douglas, Ensign Charles
● Douglas, Colin 1mY
● Douglas, Captain Francis X
● Douglas, Henry XP
▲ Douglas, James W[1]
● Douglas, James George, Earl of Morton XP
● Douglas, James 1mX
♀ Douglas, James Y
■ Douglas, Ensign John Y
☼ Douglas, John
▲ Douglas, John (1754) X
▲ Douglas, John (1759)X
Ω Douglas, John Y
■ Douglas, Lt.-Col. Patrick Y
● Douglas, Captain Sir Peter X
♀ Douglas, Dr. Robert S-F,W[1]

Appendix

- ▲ Douglas, Robert W[1]
- Ω Douglas, Robert W
- ▲ Douglas, Walter X
- ♀ Douglas, William *m*W
- ▲ Douglas, William Y
- ● Douglas, William 3*m*W
- ■ Douglas, Ensign William Y
- ■ Dow, Lt. Adam Z
- ■ Dow, Col. Alexander XP
- ● Dowell, Alex 3*m*Y
- ♣ Drake, Roger XP
- ▲ Draper, Hugh W[1]
- ☻ Drummond, Andrew L-F,WP[1]
- ● Drummond, Andrew 3*m*Z
- ■ Drummond, Ensign Charles Y
- ■ Drummond, Captain Charles Y
- Ω Drummond, David W
- ● Drummond, David 1*m*X
- ■ Drummond, Lt. Hugh Y
- ♣ Drummond, John, of Quarrel M-F,WP[1]
- ▲ Drummond, John X
- Ω Drummond, John X
- ■ Drummond, Lt. Peter Y
- ● Drummond, Captain Robert Y
- ■ Drummond, Lt. Y
- ♀ Drummond,... W
- ♦ Drummond, William WP
- ♣ Dudley, George XP
- ● Duff, Hugh 1*m*X
- ■ Duff, Lt.-Col. John Z
- ♦ Duff, Patrick XP
- ■ Duff, Major-General Patrick X
- ▲ Duff, Patrick
- ■ Duff, Captain Patrick Y
- ● Duff, Robert 3*m*Y
- ■ Duff, Lt.-Col. William Z
- ☼ Duff, William Y
- ▲ Duff, William Y
- ■ Duguid, Ensign Y[30]
- ■ Duguid, Capt. Alexander
- Ω Dunbar, James X
- ■ Dunbar, Captain James X
- ■ Dunbar, Captain William Y
- ☻ Dunbar, William XP
- Ω Duncan, Alex Y
- Ω Duncan, George Y
- ▲ Duncan, James
- ● Duncan, James 3*m*X
- ● Duncan, John 4*m*W
- Ω Duncan, John Y
- ▲ Duncan, Jonathan Y
- ■ Duncan, Lt.-Col. William Y
- ♀ Duncanson, Neil X
- ☼ Duncanson,...
- ●■ Dundas, Captain Charles MF, Y
- ● Dundas, Captain George Y
- □ Dundas, Henry, 1st Lord Melville YP[1]
- ● Dundas, Captain James X
- ☻♦ Dundas, Sir Laurence L-F, YP
- ● Dundas, Captain Philip Z
- ● Dundas, Captain Ralph Y
- ■ Dundas, Captain Thomas Y
- ♦ Dundas, Thomas XP
- ■ Durham, Ensign Hercules Y
- ● Duthy, James 1*m*Y
- ☻ Dyce, Andrew X

- ♀ Edgar, Alex W
- ● Edie, Thomas – 1*m*Z
- ▲ Edmonstone, James Y[4]
- ∞ Edmonstone, Robert
- ▲ Elliot, Alexander X[1]
- ♀ Elliot, Archibald W
- ▲ Elliot, George
- ● Elliot, Gilbert – 1*m*W
- □ Elliott, Sir Gilbert YP
- ☻ Elliott, John XP
- ● Elliot, John – 5*m*X
- ● Elliot, John – 3*m*X
- ● Elliot, John – 2*m*Z
- ● Elliot, Captain Joseph X
- ● Elliot, Philip – 3*m*X
- ● Elliot, Captain Richard W
- ♀ Elliot, Thomas Y
- ■ Elliot, Lt.-Col. William
- Ω Elliot, William W
- ■ Elliot, Captain
- ♀ Elliot, Mr. W
- ● Elphinstone, George Keith L-F,3*m*Y
- ● Elphinstone, David 1mX
- ● Elphinstone, Samuel Valentine 5*m*Y

- ☐ Erskine, Charles WP
- ■ Erskine, Ensign George Y
- ● Erskine, Hon. James XP
- ■ Erskine, Captain James Z
- ■ Erskine, Major-General John Y
- ■ Erskine, Lt. John Y
- ▲ Erskine, Robert W[33]
- ▲ Ewart, John Y
- ☻ Eyles, Sir John WP

- ●♪ Falconer, William *m*
- ■ Farquhar, Lt. Andrew Z
- ☼ Farquhar, John Y
- ■ Farquhar, Ensign Robert Y[27]
- ♀ Farquharson, William *m*W
- ● Fergus, Colin 5*m*Y
- ♀ Ferguson, Archibald Y
- ♀ Ferguson, Finlay Y
- ● Ferguson, James 5*m*Y
- Ω Ferguson, Robert X
- ☺ Ferguson, Thomas Y
- Ω Ferguson, William W
- ● Ferguson, William W[18]
- ☻ Fergusson, Sir Adam YP
- ■ Fergusson, Lt.-General Archibald Y
- ☻ Fergusson, Charles YP
- ☼ Fergusson, John
- Ω Fergusson, John *m*W
- ■ Fergusson, Lt. John Y
- ■♀ Ferrier, Ensign Alex Y
- ▲ Findlay, David
- ● Finlay, George 3*m*Z
- ■ Finlayson, Lt. John W
- ■ Finlayson, Ensign John Matthew X
- ● Fisher, Captain Benjamin X
- ▲ Fleming, Alex W
- ■ Fleming, Jacob, Ensign Y[21]
- ☼ Fleming, John Y
- ● Fleming, John Y
- ∞ Fleming, Joseph
- ♂ Fleming, William Y
- ☐♦ Fletcher, Andrew, Lord Milton WP
- ♣ Fletcher, Sir Henry YP
- ■ Fletcher, Sir Robert XP
- ☻ Fletcher, Thomas XP
- ▲ Flockhart, William X[1]
- ☺ Fogo, Alex W
- ☺ Fogo, William X
- ■ Forbes, Captain Alexander Y
- ☼ Forbes, Sir Charles
- ■ Forbes, Captain Charles Y
- Ω Forbes, Charles X
- ☐ Forbes, Duncan WP
- ● Forbes, George 1*m*Y
- Ω Forbes, George X
- ■ Forbes, Ensign James X
- ▲ Forbes, James X
- ☺ Forbes, James X
- ■ Forbes, Major-General John Y
- ● Forbes, John *m*W
- Ω Forbes, John X
- ☺ Forbes, John X
- ▲ Forbes, Thomas X
- ☻ Forbes, Sir William YP
- ♂ Forbes,...
- ▲ Forbes, Mr W[1]
- ● Forbes, Commander B-MW
- ∞ Fordyce, Rev. Francis
- ♀ Forth, Dr. William
- ■ Fothringham, Ensign Alex Z
- ☼ Fothringham, George W[1]
- ▲ Fothringham, John W[1]
- ● Fothringham John *m*
- ☺ Foulis, Charles Y
- ●☐☻ Foulis, Captain Charles L-F,WP[1]
- ■ Foulis, Cadet Charles Y
- ■ Foulis, Major George Z
- ■ Foulis, Lt. Henry Y
- ■♦ Foulis, Sir James M-F,XP[1]
- ■ Fraser, Captain Alexander
- Ω Fraser, Alex X
- ■ Fraser, Lt.-Col. Andrew Z
- ● Fraser, Archibald 1*m*X
- ■ Fraser, Captain Charles
- ● Fraser, Captain Hugh Z
- ☼☻ Fraser, James L-F,XP[1]
- ■ Fraser, Captain James Y
- ♂ Fraser, Peter Y
- ♣ Fraser, Simon YP
- ■☻ Fraser, General Simon YP
- ● Fraser, William 3*m*Z
- ●▲ Fraser, Captain (Gov.) Sir William Y
- ● Frazer, Augustine 4*m*X
- ■ Frazer, Lt. Hugh Z

Appendix

- ■ Frazer, Cadet Simon Y
- ■ Frazer, Ensign Simon Y
- ■ Frazer, Ensign Thomas Z
- ♣ Freeman, William George YP
- ■ Fullarton, Major-General John X
- ♦ Fullarton, Dr. John XP
- ♀ Fullarton, Dr. William X
- ●♣ Fullarton-Elphinstone, Captain William L-F,XP[1]
- ● Fullerton, Captain Alex Y
- Ω Fullerton, Alex W
- ■ Fullerton, Captain Alexander
- ♀ Fullerton, Isaac X
- ♀ Fullerton, John W
- ▲ Fullerton, John W
- ▲ Fullerton, John Y
- ▲ Fyfe, Richard X

- ● Gair, Alex 1mY
- Ω Galbraith, John W
- ∞ Galloway, John
- Ω Gardiner, Archibald X
- ■ Gardiner, Captain Robert Y
- ■ Gardiner, Lt. Thomas X
- ■ Gardiner, Major Thomas Z
- ♀ Gardiner, William Fullerton Z
- ▲ Gardner, Andrew W
- ● Gardyne, James 2mZ
- ■ Gavin, Lt. Alex Z
- ■ Geary, Captain Alex X
- ■ Geary, Lt. John Z
- ▫ Geddes, Alex M-F,Y
- ■ Gibson, Lt. Gilbert
- ● Gibson, Captain ... W[1]
- ♀ Gibson, William W
- ■ Gillanders, Lt.-Col. John Y
- Ω Gilchrist, Archibald W
- Ω Gilchrist, Archibald Y
- ● Gilchrist, George 4mX
- ☼ Gilchrist, John
- ♂ Gillespie, Joshua Z
- ♀ Gillies, Thomas Y
- ● Gilmour, Sir Alexander XP[1]
- ■ Glass, Lt.-Col. Andrew Z
- ▲ Gordon, Arthur X
- ▲ Gordon, Daniel X[1]
- ☺ Gordon, Edward X
- Ω Gordon, George X

- ● Gordon, George 6mZ
- ▲ Gordon, James X
- ■ Gordon, Lt.-Col. James Z
- ■ Gordon, Lt.-General John Z
- ■ Gordon, Captain John Z
- ■ Gordon, Lt. John X
- ☺ Gordon, John W
- ☺ Gordon, John X
- ● Gordon, John 3mX
- ♀ Gordon, John X
- Ω Gordon, Richard X
- ■ Gordon, Brig.-General Robert W
- ☺ Gordon, Robert X
- ♀ Gordon, Thomas mZ
- ☺ Gordon, William W
- ● Gordon, Captain William B-MW
- ● Gordon, William 4mX
- ♀ Gordon, William X
- ♀ Gordon, ...Y
- ■♀ Gordon, Ensign ... W
- ● Gorst, Samuel 1mY
- ● Gow, John 2mY
- Ω Gowdie, Dr. Walter X
- ▲ Graeme, Charles Y
- ● Graham, David 5mW[1]
- ▲ Graham, David W
- ■ Graham, Captain David
- ▲ Graham (or Graeme), George L-F,Y[1]
- ● Graham, Henry 5mZ
- ▲ Graham, James W
- ● Graham, James 5mY
- ▲ Graham, John W
- ▲ Graham John Y
- ▲ Graham, John Y
- ▲ Graham, John X
- ■▲ Graham, John X[1]
- ■▲♦ Graham, (Graeme) Major (Colonel) John L-F,XP
- ■ Graham, Ensign John Y
- ▲ Graham, (or Graeme) Thomas M-F,Y[1]
- ☺ Graham, William Z
- ■ Graham, Ensign William Y
- ∞ Graham, Miss W
- Grange, Lord XP
- ■☼ Grant, Captain Alexander X
- ●♦ Grant, Sir Alexander XP[1]

218   APPENDIX

- ■ Grant, Lt.-Col. Alexander Z
- ● Grant, Captain Charles Cathcart X
- ▲♣ Grant, Charles L-F,Y
- ♀ Grant, David Y
- ☻ Grant, Duncan YP
- ▲ Grant, Henry Y
- ■ Grant, Ensign (later Col.) Hugh X[12]
- ■ Grant, Cadet H. Y
- ▲ Grant, James Y
- ■ Grant, Major James Y
- ■ Grant, Cadet James Y
- ■ Grant, Captain (later Major) John X
- ■ Grant, Captain John X
- ■ Grant, Captain John Y
- ● Grant, John 5mZ
- ■ Grant, Major Lewis Z
- ■ Grant, Major Lewis Y
- ■ Grant, Lt.-Col. Lewis Y
- ■ Grant, Lt. Lewis
- ■ Grant, Lt.-Col. Sir Ludovick Y
- ■ Grant, Ensign Ludovick S-F,X
- ■ Grant, Ensign McGregor Y
- ■ Grant, Major Peter Y
- ■ Grant, Cadet Peter Z
- ■ Grant, Captain Robert Y
- ■ Grant, Lt. Robert Y
- ● Gray, Captain Alex Y
- Ω Gray, Alex mX
- ♀ Gray, George W
- ♀ Gray, George (Senior) M-F,XP[1]
- ▲ Gray, George (Junior) X[1]
- ☺ Gray, Joseph Y
- ▲ Gray, J.
- Ω Greig, Andrew Y
- ● Greig, Captain
- ● Grierson, Richard 6mY
- ● Grierson, William 1mX
- ■ Groat (or Grant), Lt. Donald Z
- ■ Guthrie, Lt. Alex Z
- ■ Guthrie, Lt.-Col. John Y[20]

- ♣ Hadley, Henry YP
- ● Haggey, John 1mY
- ● Haggis, Captain Charles X
- ● Haggis, Charles 5mY
- ● Haig, James 2mY
- ● Haig, John 2mY
- ● Haig, John 5mY
- ● Haig, William 4mZ
- ▲ Hairstanes, Matthew W
- ● Haldane, Captain James Alexander L-F,X[1]
- ▲ Haldane, John Y
- ● Haldane, Captain John Y
- ◘ Haldane, Mungo M-F,X
- ●☻ Haldane, Captain Robert L-F,WP[1]
- ● Haldane, Robert 6mY
- ■ Haldane, Major-General Z
- ▲ Haliburton, David Y[1]
- ▲ Haliburton, John M-F,W[1]
- ▲ Haliburton, John Gordon Y[1]
- ▲ Halkett, Alexander W[1]
- ▲ Hall, Alexander X[1]
- ● Hamilton, Captain Alex Y
- ● Hamilton, Alex 3mX
- Ω Hamilton, Alex Y
- Ω Hamilton, Charles W
- ■ Hamilton, Lt. Francis Y
- ▲ Hamilton, James X
- ● Hamilton, Captain John Z
- ● Hamilton, John 6mX
- ▲ Hamilton, John X
- ☺ Hamilton, Robert X
- ☺ Hamilton, Robert Z
- Ω Hamilton, Robert Y
- ■ Hamilton, Captain Robert X
- ■ Hamilton, Lt.-Col. Robert Y
- ■ Hamilton, Captain Robert Y
- Ω Hamilton, Thomas X
- ▲ Hamilton, Thomas X
- ▲ Hamilton, William Y[1]
- ▲ Hamilton, Mr....W[1]
- ■ Hannay, Col. Alexander Y
- ▲ Hannay, John M-F,Y
- ☼ Hannay, Ramsay M-F,Y
- ☻ Hannay, Sir Samuel L-F,YP[1]
- ● Hardie, Brice 5mX
- ■ Hardyman, Lt.-General George Y
- ☼ Hare, David
- ■ Harper, Col. Gabriel
- ▲☻ Harrison, Gov. Edward M-F,WP
- ☺ Hay, Alex W
- ● Hay, Alex 2mX
- ■ Hay, Cadet Archibald Y

Appendix

- ■ Hay, Captain Charles Y
- ■ Hay, Cadet David Y
- ● Hay, Edward Legge *1m*Y
- ● Hay, George *1m*Y
- ■ Hay, Captain George X
- Ω Hay, James W
- ☺ Hay, James Z
- ● Hay, Captain James Y
- ▲ Hay, James X
- ■ Hay, Lt. John Y
- Ω Hay, John Silvester X
- ■ Hay, Cadet Robert Y
- □ Hay, Thomas, Viscount Dupplin WP
- ▲ Hay, William X
- ▲ Hay, Mr. W
- Ω Henderson, Alex X
- ☺ Henderson, Alex Y
- ☺ Henderson, James Y
- ☺ Henderson, James Z
- ■ Henderson, Lt.-Col. John
- ☼ Henderson, John
- ☺ Henderson, John W
- Ω Henderson, John X
- Ω Henderson, John Z (1776)
- Ω Henderson, John Z (1777)
- ■ Henderson, Cadet John X[17]
- ▲ Heriot, James
- ● Hepburn, Captain George X
- Ω Hepburn, William W
- ♀ Hepburn,... W
- ■ Heron, Major Alexander
- Ω Heugh, John Z
- ■ Hind, Colonel Alex Z
- ● Home, John XP
- ● Home, Roddam *3m*Y
- ● Home, William *5m*Y
- ■ Hooke, Major Archibald X
- ● Hope, Adriaan XP[1]
- ●♣ Hope, Col. John M-F,WP
- ■ Hope, Captain Sir John X[1]
- ▲ Hope, John L-F,W[1]
- ■ Hope, Lt. Thomas Y
- ♦ Hope, Thomas XP
- ■ Hope, Cadet Sir William X[13]
- ▲● Horne, Governor John WP
- ● Hudson, Captain Charles W
- ●□ Hume, Abraham M-F,WP[1]
- ♣□ Hume, Alexander L-F,WP[1]
- ● Hume, Captain Alexander M-F,X
- ● Hume, John *1m*W
- ■ Hume, Lt. John
- ■ Hume, Lt.-Col. John Z
- ■ Hume, Lt. William
- ● Hume-Campbell, Alexander XP
- ♀ Hunter, Andrew X
- ■ Hunter, Lt. David
- ♀ Hunter, James Y
- ▲ Hunter, John
- ♀ Hunter, John W
- ☼ Hunter, John
- ● Hunter, Captain John W[1]
- ■ Hunter, Captain Patrick Y
- Ω Hunter, Robert X
- Ω Hunter, Robert X
- ♀ Hunter, Dr. Y
- ▲ Hutchinson, Governor Charles M-F
- ● Hutchinson, Captain George X
- ◘ Hutchinson, John M-F, X
- ● Hutchinson, Captain Norton W
- ● Hutchinson, Captain William L-F,W[1]
- ● Hutton, Archibald *5m*Y
- Ω Hutton, James Y
- Ω Hutton, Thomas Y
- ▲ Hyndford, Charles W
- ♦ Hyndford, Lady WP
- ■ Hyndman, Colonel Henry Y
- ▲ Hyndman, Thomas
- ∞ Hyndman, Captain

- Ω Inglis, Charles Y
- ● Inglis, Captain Cornelius X
- Ω Inglis, Cornelius W
- ☼♣ Inglis, Sir Hugh M-F,X[1]
- Ω Inglis, John X
- ● Inglis, Captain Nathaniel X
- ● Inglis, Patrick *1m*X
- Ω Inglis, Thomas X
- ♀ Inglis, William Y
- ▲ Innes, Daniel W
- ● Innes, Henry *2m*Y
- ∞ Innes, Janet (wife of Gov. Pitt)
- Ω Innes, John Y
- ☼ Innis,...& Clarke,...

Appendix

- Ω Irvine, Mr. *m*W
- ● Irwin, Thomas Y

- ☼ Jackson,... & Wedderburn,...
- ♣ James, Sir William YP
- ☼ Jameson, William
- ● Jamieson, Captain Alex X
- ☼ Johnson, James
- ■ Johnson, Captain James
- ■ Johnson, Captain William
- ⊤ Johnston, Alexander XP
- ▲ Johnstone, Alexander S-F,X
- Ω Johnston, Andrew X
- ● Johnstone, George 4*m*X
- ■ Johnstone, George Y[25]
- ●♦♣ Johnstone, George XP[1]
- ▲ Johnstone, Gideon S-F,X[1]
- ●♦ Johnstone, Sir James XP[1]
- ▲● Johnstone, John L-F,XP[1]
- ▲ Johnstone, Patrick X[1]
- ■ Johnstone, Captain Robert Y
- ☻ Johnstone, William (Pultney) L-F,XP[1]
- ■ Johnstone, Ensign Y[31]

- ■Ω☼ Keir, Captain Archibald XP
- ■ Keith, Lt. Robert Y
- ▲ Keith, Mr - W[1]
- ● Kempt, Captain Francis W
- ▲ Kennoway, John Y
- ■ Ker, Captain George Y
- ■ Ker, Ensign James Y
- ● Ker, Captain Robert X
- ■ Kerr, Ensign Charles X[8]
- ♀ Kerr, Dr. James Y
- ☻ Kerr,... YP
- ☼▲ Killican, David M-F,Y
- ■☻ Kilpatrick, Major James S-F,XP
- ■ Kilpatrick, Major Samuel Y
- Ω Kincaid, Alex X
- Ω Kincaid, John Z
- ■ Kinloch, Ensign Charles Y
- ■ Kinloch, Lt. Francis Peregrine Z
- ♀ Kinloch, Frederick Z
- ■ Kinloch, Captain George X
- ▲ Kinloch, John W
- ▲ Kinloch, John Y
- ● Kinloch, Joseph 2*m*Y

- ▲ Kinloch, William
- ▲ Kinnaird,....
- ■ Kirk, Cadet William Y
- ☻ Kirkbride, William X
- ▲ Kirkpatrick, James
- ■ Kirkpatrick, Ensign Thomas X
- ■ Kirkpatrick, Major-General William Y
- ☻ Kirkwood, Andrew X
- Ω Knox, Dr Alex X
- Ω Knox, John (Senior) W
- Ω Knox, John (Younger) X
- Ω Knox, Oliver W
- ■ Kyd, Lt.-General Alexander Z
- ■ Kyd, Lt.-Col. Robert Y

- Ω Laird, Charles Y
- Ω Laird, James Z
- Ω Laird, John X
- ● Lamb, - James *m*W[1]
- ■ Lang, Col. Ross
- ■ Lang, Lt. Thomas Y
- ☼ Lauder, James
- ● Lauder, Captain John
- ▲ Lauder, John
- ■ Lauder, Ensign William X
- ▲ Laurell, James
- ● Law, Captain X
- ● Lawrie, Henry 5*m*Y
- ● Lawson, Captain Peter X
- ■ Lawtie, Ensign George Urquhart Z
- ■ Lawtie, Lt.-Col. James Z
- ■ Lawtie, Cadet John Urquhart Z
- ■ Legertwood, Major Z
- ● Leggatt, William *m*
- ■ Leigh, Lt. Alexander
- ■ Leith, Lt.-Col. Alexander
- ● Leith, John 1*m*W
- ● Lennox, Captain Charles X
- ● Lennox, James 1*m*Y
- ● Lennox, Captain John Y
- ■ Lennox, Lt.
- ♀ Leslie, Abraham Z
- Ω Leslie, James Y
- ▲ Leslie, Lachlan X
- ▲ Leslie, Matthew Y
- ■ Leslie, Col. Matthew Y
- ☻ Leslie, William W

APPENDIX

- Ω Leslie, William X
- ▲ ● Lind, Francis YP
- ▲ Lindsay, Charles Y
- Ω Lindsay, David X
- Ω Lindsay, Francis W
- ▲ Lindsay, George Y[1]
- ● Lindsay, Captain George W
- ● Lindsay, George 1mX
- ● Lindsay, John 4mX
- ◀● Lindsay, Sir John Y[1]
- Ω Lindsay, Dr. Matthew W
- ▲ Lindsay, Robert Y[1]
- ● Lindsay, Robert 4mX
- Ω Lindsay, William W
- ● Lindsay, William m
- ▲ Lindsay, William X[1]
- ■ Lindsay, Lt.
- ☼ Lister, James W
- ■ Little, Lt. Archibald Y
- ♀ Littlejohn, Dr. Alex W
- ▲ Loch, Robert X
- Ω Lockhart, James W
- ● Lockhart, James 5mX
- ☺ Lockhart, Thomas X
- ☼ Lockhart, Thomas
- ■ Logan, Lt. James Z
- ■ Logan, Captain John Z
- ● Logie, Alex 1mY
- Ω Lorraine, Alex mZ
- ● Lowis, Captain Ninian Y
- ♣ Lyell, Henry WP
- ■ Lyon, Captain Hugh Y
- ▲ Lyon, John X

- Ω Macadam, William X
- ■ Macauley, Lt.-Gen. Colin
- ☺ Macauley, Francis Y
- ● Macauley, John 1mX
- ● McBride, Thomas 4mX
- ☺ McClary, John Y
- ■ McClintock, Captain Alex Y
- ■ McClintock, Lt. John Y
- ▲ McClintock, John Y
- ● McCondie, James 1mX
- ● MacConnachie, Captain James X
- ■ McCorkill, Lt. James Z
- ☺ MacCraken, John Y
- ∞ McCulloch, John

- Ω Macdonald, Dr. Alex X[1]
- ■ MacDonald, Ensign Alex Y
- ■ MacDonald, Lt. Alex Z
- ■ MacDonald, Cadet Charles Y
- ■ MacDonald, Lt. James X
- ♂ MacDonald, James Y
- ■ MacDonald, Lt.-General Sir John Y
- ■ MacDonald, Lt. John Y
- ■ MacDonald, Ensign John Y
- ● Macdonald, Captain John
- ∞ Macdonald, John
- ■ MacDonald, Cadet Michael Y
- ♀ MacDonald, Roderick Y
- ■ MacDonald, Rory Y
- ■ MacDonald, Lt.
- Ω MacDonnell, John X
- ● McDougal, William 6mY
- ∞ McDougal,...
- Ω McDowell, William Y
- ● McFarlane, Robert 4mX
- Ω McFarquhar, John X
- ♀ MacFie, James Z
- ■ MacFie, Lt. Thomas Z
- ■ MacGlashan, Major Alex Y
- ● MacGleshin, Captain Peter X
- ■ McGowan, Col. John Y
- ♀ MacGrath, Michael Z
- ● MacGregor, Alex m
- ● MacGregor, Captain Alpin Y
- ■ MacGregor, Captain David Y
- ■ MacGregor, Maj-General James Z
- ■ MacGregor, Lt.-Col Sir John Murray Y
- ∞ MacGregor, John Murray
- ■ MacGregor, Major Malcolm Z
- ∞ MacGregor, Peter Murray
- ■ MacGregor, Captain Robert Z
- ■ MacGregor, Captain Robert Murray Z
- ■ MacHarg, Ensign James Y
- ■ MacIntosh, Lt. Alex Y
- ☺ MacIntosh, Alex Z
- ☼ MacIntosh, Lachlan
- ● MacIntosh, Robert YP
- ● ◆ MacIntosh, William XP
- ● ■ MacIntosh, Captain William M-F,Y[1]

- ● MacIntosh, William 1mY
- ■ MacIntosh, Lt. Y
- ☺ MacIntyre, John Y
- ■ MacIntyre, Lt. J. Y
- ■ MacIntyre, Lt.-Gen. John Y
- ■ Mackay, Lt. Aeneas
- ● Mackay, David 4mY
- ■ Mackay, Lt. Donald
- ■ Mackay, Capt. Donald
- ■ Mackay, Lt. George
- ▲ Mackay, George L-F,X
- ■ Mackay, Captain Hugh X[14]
- ■ Mackay, Ensign Hugh X
- ▲ Mackay, Hector X
- ■ Mackay, Lt. Hector
- ■ Mackay, Lt. James
- ■ Mackay, Lt. Robert
- ☻ Mackay, Robert YP
- ■ Mackay, Major
- Ω McKeen, James Y
- ■ MacKelcan, Lt. John X
- ♀ MacKellar, Charles Y
- ■ Mackenzie, Major-General Sir Alex L-F,X
- ☿ Mackenzie, Alex L-F,X
- ■ Mackenzie, Ensign Bernard X
- ☿ Mackenzie, Colin M-F,X
- ■ Mackenzie, Ensign Colin Y[24]
- ∞ Mackenzie, Surveyor-Gen. Colin
- ■ Mackenzie, Capt. David Y
- ■ Mackenzie, Captain David X
- ● Mackenzie, David 5mX
- ● Mackenzie, George 4mX
- ■ Mackenzie, Lt.-Col. Jabez Y
- Ω Mackenzie, James W
- ■ Mackenzie, Lt. James Z
- — Mackenzie, John of Delvine L-F,WP[1]
- ▲ Mackenzie, John W
- ▲ Mackenzie, John
- ● Mackenzie, John 2mY
- Ω Mackenzie, Surgeon of the Fleet, John W
- ♀ Mackenzie, John X
- ☿ Mackenzie, Kenneth M-F,X[1]
- ▲ Mackenzie, Kenneth X
- ● Mackenzie, Captain Kenneth W[1]
- ∞ Mackenzie, Kenneth
- ● Mackenzie, Patrick 6mW
- ● Mackenzie, Peter 2mW
- ● Mackenzie, Captain Robert Y
- ■ Mackenzie, Lt.-Col. Robert Y
- Ω Mackenzie, William W
- ■ Mackenzie, Major William X
- ■ Mackenzie, Major
- Ω Mackleraith, Hugh W
- ♀ MacKnight, James m
- ∞ Mackrabie, A.
- ■ Mackutchin, John Y
- ■ Maclean, Lt. Alan
- ■ Maclean, Lt. Alex Y
- ■ Maclean, Lt.-Col. James
- ■ Maclean, Lt. James Z
- ■ Maclean, Lt. John
- ■ Maclean, Lt. John Z
- ■ Maclean, Captain Lachlan X
- ▲ Macleane, Henry Y
- ☻♥ Macleane, Lauchlin YP[1]
- ● Macleane, Captain Stephen Y
- ▲ MacLellan, …Y
- ● Macleod, Captain Alexander L-F,XP[1]
- Ω Macleod, Alex X
- ▲ Macleod, Alexander Y
- ■ Macleod, Lt. Alex Z
- ■ Macleod, Lt. Daniel
- ▲ Macleod, Donald Y
- ■ Macleod, Lt. Donald
- ■ Macleod, Ensign Donald Y
- ■ Macleod, Ensign Duncan X
- ● Macleod, Hector 6mY
- ■ Macleod, Captain K.
- ■ Macleod, Brigadier-General Norman Y
- ■ Macleod, Lt William X[1]
- ● McCluer, John N-SY
- Ω McMorine, Alex Y
- ● McMurdo, Douglas 1mY
- ● McMurdo, Robert 5mY
- ■ MacMurdo, Captain Robert Y
- ● McNab, Captain Angus Y
- ■ MacNab, Lt. Duncan Z
- ■ MacNab, Lt. Robert Y
- ∞ MacNaughton, William Hay
- ☺ McNeal, Alex X
- ● McNeal, Archibald 1mW

Appendix

- ● McNeal, Charles 5mX
- ● McNeal, Daniel mW
- ● McNeal, James 5mZ
- ● McNeal, Robert 3mZ
- ∞ MacNeill, Hector
- ■ Macpherson, Lt. Aeneas Y
- ■ Macpherson, Lt.-Col. Allan X
- ☺ Macpherson, David X
- ● Macpherson, James 'Fingal' S-F,YP[1]
- ▲ Macpherson, Gov. Sir John L-F,YP[1]
- ■ Macpherson, Lt.-Col. John X
- ☺ Macpherson, John Y
- ■ Macpherson, Ensign Samuel Y
- ■ Macpherson, Captain William X
- ■ Macpherson, Lt. W. C.
- ■ Macpherson, Lt.
- ∞ Macpherson, Mr. X
- ■ MacQuarrie, Ensign John Y
- Ω McQueen, John X
- ●▲● Macrae, Captain (Gov.) James L-F,WP[1]
- ● Macrae, Robert 1mX
- Ω Macrae, William X
- ● Macrae, William 4mY
- Ω MacReadie, William X
- ■ MacVeagh, Cadet Ferdinand Z
- ■ MacVicar, Lt. George Y
- ♂ Main (Mein), Alex Z
- ♀ Mair, Hugh Y
- Ω Mair, Patrick Z
- ■ Maitland, Lt.-Col. Charles Y
- ▲ Maitland, William X
- ■ Malcolm, Major John Z
- ♣ Manship, John XP
- ▲ Marjoribanks, John X
- ● Marshall, David 5mY
- Ω Mather, Alex X
- ♀ Mathewson, John Y
- ♀ Mathison, Gilbert X
- Ω Maule, Charles X
- ■ Maule, Ensign Y[29]
- ■ Maule, Captain
- ● Maxwell, Captain Arthur X
- ■ Maxwell, Lt. Francis
- ● Maxwell, George 2mX
- ☺ Maxwell, John Y
- ☼ Maxwell, John
- ■· Maxwell, Captain Patrick Y
- ■ Maxwell, Captain Robert Y
- ■ Maxwell, Lt. Robert
- Ω Maxwell, Walter X
- ■ Maxwell, Lt. Walter Z
- ■ Maxwell, Lt. William Y
- ▲ Maxwell, William Y[1]
- ● May, Alex 1mW
- ● Mayne, Robert L-F,XP[1]
- ● Mayne, Sir William L-F,XP[1]
- ☼ Menteith, ...
- Ω Menzies, Charles Y
- ■ Menzies, Lt. Charles X
- ● Metcalfe, John 4mX
- ■ Metcalfe, Major Sir Thomas Y
- ♣ Michie, John, YP[1]
- ● Milne, Alex 1mX
- ■ Milne, Ensign Alex Y
- ● Milne, Robert 3mX
- ☺ Mitchell, Alex Y
- ■ Mitchell, Captain Alexander
- ■ Mitchell, Major Archibald
- ● Mitchell, Captain Sir Charles Y
- ●◻ Mitchell, Captain David M-F,Y
- ● Mitchell, David 6mX
- Ω Mitchell, Francis X
- ■ Mitchell, Lt.-Col. James Campbell Z
- ◻ Moffatt, Andrew M-F,XP[1]
- ◻●♣ Moffatt, Captain James M-F,X[1]
- ● Moffatt, James 4mY
- Ω Moffatt, James X
- ◻ Moffatt, John Y
- ● Moffatt, John 1mX
- ● Moffatt, John S-F,1mY
- ● Moffatt, John 5mY
- ▲ Moffatt, Robert S-F,X
- Ω Moffatt, Samuel Z
- ●♣ Moffatt, William 3mX
- Ω Moffatt, William X
- ♀ Moir, William Z
- ● Moncrieff, Alex 3mX
- ♦ Moncrieff, William WP
- ▲ Moncrieff, William W
- ♣ Monson, John WP
- ● Monteith, John 4mY
- Ω Monteith, Dr. William W[1]

- ● Montgomerie, Captain Alex Y
- ● Montgomery, Captain James W
- ♦ Montgomery, Robert XP
- ●Ω Moray, John W
- Ω Morris, Alex Z
- ■ Morrison, Ensign Charles Y
- ■ Morrison, Major David X
- ■ Morrison, Captain Dennis X
- ■ Morrison, Captain George X
- ■ Morrison, Major John X
- ■ Morrison, Captain John Z
- ☺ Morrison, Richard X
- ☼ Mudie, Mr. X
- ■ Muir, Colonel Grainger X
- ▲ Muir, ...
- ∞ Muirhead, David
- ■ Munro, Captain Alex Y
- ♀ Munro, Dr. Andrew S-F,W[1]
- ♀ Munro, Dr. Duncan M-F,W[1]
- ● Munro, George 3mX
- ▲ Munro, George M-F,Y
- ♦ Munro, Captain George XP
- ■● Munro, General Sir Hector L-F,XP[1]
- ● Munro, Captain James Y
- ● Munro, James 1mX
- ♀ Munro, James mX
- ■ Munro, Lt. James Z
- ♀ Munro, Dr. John M-F,X
- ■ Munro, Ensign Robert Y
- ● Munro, Captain Robert M-F,Y
- Ω Munro, Robert X
- ▲ Munro, Robert Duncan X
- ♦ Munro, Sir Robert XP
- ● Munro, Thomas 2mY
- ♀ Munro, Walter Ross Y
- ∞ Munro, William
- ♀ Murchison, Dr. Kenneth Y
- ● Mure, Colville 2mY
- □ Mure, William YP
- ∞ Murison, William
- ▲ Murray, Alexander
- ■ Murray, Captain Alex Y
- ■ Murray, Captain Alex Z
- ♀ Murray, Andrew Y
- Ω Murray, Archibald X
- ■ Murray, Captain Charles Y
- ■ Murray, Lt. David

- Ω Murray, John W
- Ω Murray, John X
- Ω Murray, John X
- ♦● Murray, Patrick M-F,XP[1]
- ■ Murray, Lt.-Col. Peter Y
- Ω Murray, Richard W
- □ Murray, William XP
- ■ Murray, Ensign William Y
- ● Myles, Captain
- Ω Mylne, Thomas W

- ■ Nairne, Lt. Charles Y
- ● Nairne, Captain Fasham X[1]
- ■ Nairne, Lt. George Y
- ☺ Nairne, Robert X
- ● Nairne, William 2mW
- ☼ Naish,....W[1]
- Ω Nesbitt, David Y
- ● Nesbitt, James 5mW
- ▲ Newton, Andrew

- ● Ochterlony, Alex 6mY
- ■ Ochterlony, Maj-Gen. Sir David Z
- ▲ Ochterlony, James X
- ● Ochterlony, John 3mX
- ♦ Ochterlony, Mr. XP
- ■ Ogilvie, Lt. Alex Y
- ♂ Ogilvie, Charles Z
- ♂ Ogilvie, George Z
- ♦ Ogilvie, George XP
- ♦ Ogilvie, Lady Anne WP
- ■ Ogilvie, Lt. James
- ● Ogilvie, Captain James X
- ● Ogilvie, James 4mX
- ● Ogilvie, James 5mZ
- ● Ogilvie, John 5mY
- ● Ogilvie, Thomas W[1]
- ▲ Ogilvie, Thomas Y[1]
- Ω Ogilvie, William X
- ■ Ogilvie, Captain William Y
- ● Oliphant, Charles 4mX
- ● Oliphant, Christopher 3mX
- Ω Oliphant, John X
- ♀ Oliphant, Lawrence W
- ♀ Oliphant, Peter W[1]
- Ω Oliphant, William W
- ● Oliver, John 1mY

Appendix

- ▲ Orr, Willis X
- Ω Orrok, James Y
- ● Orrok, Captain Wemyss Y
- ♦ Osborne, James XP
- ● Oswald, Alex *1m*X
- ● Oswald, David Y

- ∞ Paisley,...
- ♣ Pardoe, John YP
- ■ Park, Ensign Alex Z
- ■ Parke, Captain Alex Y
- ■ Paterson, Lt. Alexander
- ▲ Paterson, George Y[1]
- ■ Paterson, Ensign William
- Ω Patterson, John X
- ☺ Patterson, John Z
- ● Patton, Captain Andrew Z
- ■ Patton, Cadet David Y
- ● Patton, William *6m*X
- ● Petrie, Captain John W
- ■ Penman, Captain David Y
- ☼■▲ Petrie, Lt. John X
- ▲ Petrie, William X
- ♣ Pigou, Frederick XP
- ● Pirie, Captain
- ● Pitcairn, Charles *3m*X
- ▲● Pitt, Gov George Morton WP
- ▲ Plenderleith, Patrick Y
- ● Preston, Captain Sir Robert L-F,XP[1]
- ▲● Pringle, Alexander L-F,YP[1]
- ■ Pringle, Captain Andrew Y
- ■ Pringle, Major-General James Y
- ☺ Pringle, James Z
- ♦ Pringle, John XP
- Ω Pringle, Patrick Y
- ♀ Pringle, Peter M-F,Y
- ▲ Proctor George Y
- ● Purdie, Robert *3m*Y
- ● Purvis, Captain Charles X

- ● Raitt, Captain Charles Z
- ▲ Raitt, Charles X[1]
- ● Raitt, John *3m*X
- ▲ Ramsay, Andrew X
- ♂ Ramsay, Charles Z
- ● Ramsay, David *5m*X
- ♀ Ramsay, Dr. George X

- ▲ Ramsay, George S-F,W[1]
- ♀ Ramsay, George W
- ▲ Ramsay, George Y
- Ω Ramsay, George Y
- ☺ Ramsay, George Y
- ● Ramsay, James *3m*X
- ● Ramsay, Malcolm *5m*X
- ■ Ramsay, Captain Richard Y
- ● Ramsay, William *m*W[1]
- ▲ Ramsden, James W
- ♀ Rankin, George Z
- ▲ Rankin, William X
- ♀ Rankin, Gabriel W[1]
- ●☼ Rannie, Captain David M-F,W[1]
- ■ Rannie, Captain Hugh Y
- ☺ Rattray, Charles Y
- Ω Rattray, Henry W
- ● Rattray, Captain James X
- ■ Rattray, Colonel John Y
- ● Rattray, John *1m*W
- ■ Rattray, Lt. William Z
- ■ Rattray, Lt.-Col. William Y
- ■ Reid, Lt.-Col. John Z
- ● Reid, Mr. *m*X
- ● Rennie, David *2m*X
- ♀ Rennie, ...Z
- ▲ Renton, John Y
- Ω Richardson, James Y
- ● Riddell, Robert *1m*Y
- ● Riddell, Captain Thomas
- ▲ Rigg, William W[1]
- ■ Rind, Major James Nathaniel Z
- ■ Ritchie, Captain John Y
- ● Robertson, Captain David M-F,W[1]
- ● Robertson, Captain George Y
- ▲ Robertson, George X
- ● Robertson, Jessamine *2m*Y
- Ω Robertson, John X
- ● Robertson, Robert *4m*W
- ● Robertson, Captain Thomas Y
- Ω Robertson, William W
- ☺ Robertson, William Y
- ● Robertson, William *2m*X
- ♀ Robinson,... W
- ■ Rochead, Thomas X[3]
- ● Rod, James *1m*W[1]
- ♀ Rollo, Robert Z
- ■ Rose, Captain Alex Y

- ♂ Ross, Andrew Z
- ☿ Ross, Andrew Y
- • Ross, Captain Andrew X
- ■ Ross, Ensign Andrew
- • Ross, Daniel N-SY
- ▲ Ross, Donald X
- ▲ Ross, George X
- • Ross, George 3mX
- ∞ Ross, Hercules
- ▲ Ross, Hugh X
- Ω Ross, James X
- ▲ Ross, James
- ▲ Ross, John X
- ■ Ross, Captain John X
- • Ross, Robert 4mY
- • Ross, William 1mX
- ▲ Ross, William
- ■ Ross, Lt.-Col. Patrick Y
- ♣ Rous, Thomas XP
- ☺ Roxburgh, Florence Y
- Ω Roxburgh, William Z
- ▲ Russell, Claud M-F,X[1]
- ▲ Russell, Sir Francis
- ♀ Russell, Francis X
- ■ Russell, Lt.-General George L-F,Y
- ∞ Russell, Hamilton
- ∞ Russell, Jane
- ● Russell, John YP
- ♂ Russell, John X
- ■ Russell, Captain Lockhart Y
- ■ Russell, Ensign Michael Y[22]
- ♀ Russell, Patrick X
- ▲ Rutherford, Robert Y
- • Rutherford, William mY

- • Sandilands, Captain Patrick B-MW[1]
- ■ Sands, Major William Y
- ♣ Savage, Robert XP
- ■ Scoon, Lt. Robert X[5]
- ■ Scotland, Captain James X
- • Scotland, James 3mX
- •■ Scott, Captain Alex M-F,X
- ▲ Scott, Andrew Y[1]
- ▲ Scott, Archibald Y[1]
- ■ Scott, Lt. Archibald Z
- ■ Scott, Col. Caroline Frederick X[1]
- ■ Scott, Lt.-Col. Charles Y
- ■ Scott, Lt. Charles X
- ■ Scott, Captain David X
- ☿♣ Scott, David YP
- ▲ Scott, George X[1]
- ▲ Scott, George W
- • Scott, Captain George Y
- ▲ Scott, Henry Y[1]
- Ω Scott, Dr. James W[1]
- ■ Scott, Captain James X
- ■ Scott, Cadet James Y
- Ω Scott, James W
- • Scott, James 4mX
- • Scott, James 4mZ
- Ω Scott, John W
- • Scott, John 2mX
- • Scott, John 4mY
- ● Scott, John YP
- ▲ Scott, John Y
- ▲ Scott, John Balliol Y[1]
- Ω Scott, John W[1]
- ♀ Scott, John X
- ■ Scott, Major John X[1]
- ♦● Scott, General John YP[1]
- ■ Scott, Lt. John Y
- ■ Scott, Cadet John Y
- ▲ Scott, Richard Y[1]
- •● Scott, Captain Robert YP
- Ω Scott, Robert W
- Ω Scott, Robert X
- • Scott, Robert 4mX
- ☺ Scott, Robert Y
- ♀ Scott, Samuel Y
- Ω Scott, Thomas X
- ■ Scott, Major Thomas Y
- • Scott, Captain William X
- Ω Scott, William X
- • Scott, William Grub 6mY
- ∞ Scott, W.
- ■ Scott, Colonel
- □ Scrope, Baron John WP
- ■ Scrymgeour, Captain John Y
- ♀ Semple, Dr. William
- ▲ Seton, Daniel X[34]
- ▲ Seton, David W
- ■ Seton, Lt. Z
- ▲ Shairp, John Y
- ▲♦ Shairp, Thomas YP[1]
- ▲ Shairp, John Y[1]

APPENDIX

- ▲ Shairp, Thomas Y[1]
- ● Shairp, Walter *m*Y[1]
- ▲ Shaw, William W
- ☿ Sibbald, James
- ● Sime, Peter *3m*Z
- ▲ Simpson, Charles
- Ω Simpson, David Y
- ● Simpson, Captain George Y
- ♀ Simpson, John Y
- ■ Simpson, Lt.-Col. Leonard Z
- ● Simpson, Peter *5m*X
- Ω Simpson, Robert Y
- ■ Sinclair, Major George Y
- ● Sinclair, Henry *5m*Y
- ● Sinclair, James *5m*W
- ● Sinclair, James *5m*X
- ■ Sinclair, Lt. James Y
- ■ Sinclair, Major James Z
- ■ Sinclair, Cadet Thomas Y
- Ω Sinclair, Robert X
- Ω Skeene, David W
- ■ Skinner, Ensign Alex Y
- ■ Skinner, Lt.-Col. Hercules Y
- ■ Skinner, Captain James X
- ■ Skinner, Lt. James Y
- ▲ Skinner, Russell X
- ■ Skinner, Ensign William Y
- ● Slater, David *3m*X
- ●■ Slater, Captain Gilbert M-F,XP
- ● Slater, Gilbert *2m*W
- ■ Smith, Cadet Alexander X[15]
- ☿ Smith, George L-F,X[1]
- ■ Smith, Captain David Y
- ● Smith, James *4m*Z
- ● Smith, Joseph *4m*Y
- ■ Smith, Ensign John X
- ■ Smith, Lt. John Hamilton Z
- ▲ Smith,... X
- ■ Sommerville, Ensign
- ■ Sparks, Captain Thomas Y
- ● Spittall, Alex *5m*X
- ▲ Stackhouse, John W
- ♀ Stark, James Z
- Ω■ Stark, Lt. John Y
- Ω Steven, Dr Thomas Y
- ■ Stevens, Major William
- ■ Stevenson, Lt. William
- ● Steward, Captain Gabriel W
- ● Steward, Captain Gabriel (1740)W
- ☺ Steward, James (1765-74)
- ● Steward, James *6m*Z
- ● Stewart, Captain Alexander X[1]
- ● Stewart, Alex *4m*Y
- ■ Stewart, Lt. Andrew Y
- ■ Stewart, Captain Archibald X
- ■ Stewart, Lt. Archibald
- ● Stewart, Archibald *1m*X
- ● Stewart, Archibald *4m*Y
- ● Stewart, Captain Charles X
- ▲ Stewart, Charles X
- ■ Stewart, Lt. Duncan Y
- ♂ Stewart, Edward Z
- ■ Stewart, Cadet Francis Y
- ☺ Stewart, Francis X
- ● Stewart, George *4m*W
- ● Stewart, Captain George X
- □♣ Stewart, Sir Gilbert WP
- ■ Stewart, Lt. Henry Y
- ● Stewart, Henry Haldane *3m*Y
- ● Stewart, James *3m*X
- ● Stewart, James *5m*Y
- ● Stewart, James *1m*Y
- ∞ Stewart, James X
- ■ Stewart, Ensign James Y
- ♀ Stewart, John Z
- ● Stewart, John *4m*X
- ● Stewart, Captain John Y
- ● Stewart, John *3m*Y
- ▲ Stewart, John X
- ▲ Stewart, John Y
- ▲ ● Stewart, Dr. John S-F,XP[1]
- ● Stewart, 'little' John XP[1]
- ● Stewart, Captain John X
- ▲ Stewart, Keith Y[1]
- ▲ Stewart, Oliver W[1]
- ● Stewart, Captain Robert Y
- Ω Stewart, Robert *m*X
- ■ Stewart, Captain Robert Y
- ■ Stewart, Captain Robert Y
- ■ Stewart, Lt. William X
- ♀ Stewart, William *m*X
- ☺ Stewart, William X
- ■ Stewart, Ensign Y[32]
- ∞ Stewart,...
- ☺☿Stirling, Archibald L-F,W[1]
- ■▲ Stirling, Ensign Henry W[1]

APPENDIX

- ☼ Stirling, Hugh M-F,X
- ♦ Stirling, James WP
- ☼ Stirling, James M-F,W[1]
- ☼ Stirling, John S-F,W[1]
- ☼ Stirling, Lewis S-F,W[1]
- ● Stirling, Captain B-MW
- ▲ Stone, John Maxwell
- ● Storar, James 1mZ
- ♀ Storey, Dr...
- ☺ Strachan, William Y
- ■ Strachan, Cadet William Y
- ■ Strachan,... X
- ● Stuart, Alex 6mX
- ◉ Stuart, Andrew XP[1]
- ● Stuart, Charles 4mZ
- ◉ Stuart, Dr. Charles YP
- ▲ Stuart, Hon. Frederick S-F,Y[1]
- ■ Stuart, Lt. Henry
- ☺ Stuart, James X
- ◉ Stuart, Sir James YP[1]
- ■ Stuart, Colonel James M-F,Y[1]
- Ω Stuart, John W
- ● Stuart, John 1mZ
- ▲ Stuart, Dr. John
- ■ Stuart, Lt.-General Robert X
- ☺ Stuart, William X
- ☼ Stuart,...
- ♦ Stuart, Lord Blantyre XP
- ■ Sturgeon, Major Richard Y
- ♣ Sulivan, Laurence XP[1]
- ■ Sumner, Lt. Edward Z
- ■ Sutherland, Lt. Aeneas X[7]
- ■ Sutherland, Captain Alexander
- ☼▲ Suttie, Charles M-F,X[1]
- ♣◉ Suttie, Sir George WP[1]
- ♀ Swanston, Alex Z
- ♀■ Swinton, Captain Archibald mX
- ■♀ Swinton, Captain John X[36]

- ∞ Tate, James
- ● Taylor, Captain Robert Y
- ● Tennent, James 2mZ
- Ω Tennent, William X
- Ω Thompson, Alex Y
- ■ Thompson, Captain Charles X
- ■ Thompson, Lt. James Stewart Y
- ♂ Thompson, Maxwell Z
- ● Thoms, William 4mY

- ● Thomson, Charles 4mY
- ● Thomson, Captain George X
- ● Thomson, James 4mZ
- ▲ Thomson, John Y
- ■ Thomson, Captain William Y
- ■ Thomson, Captain William X
- ♣ Thornton, William XP
- Ω Threipland, Dr. George W[1]
- ♀ Threipland, George W
- ● Tod, Captain Alexander Y
- ■ Todd, Ensign Charles X[9]
- ● Trail, Archibald 2mZ
- ♀ Traper, George mW[1]
- ■ Tremondo, Lt. Anthony Z
- ■ Troup, Ensign William Z
- ☺ Tulloch, Alex Y
- ▲ Tulloch, Thomas Y
- ☺ Turnbull, Gavin Y
- Ω Turnbull, Gavin Z
- ☺ Turnbull, Gilbert Y
- ● Tweeddale, Captain James Z

- ♀ Urquhart, Dr.
- ☺ Urquhart, Walter Y

- ♀ Veitch, John Y
- ● Veitch, Captain Robert X
- ● Venner, Captain Corbyn Morris Z

- ● Waddell, Captain John M-F,X
- Ω Walker, Alex Y
- Ω Walker, Andrew Y
- ■ Walker, Captain James Y
- ∞ Walker, John
- ♀ Walker, William Y
- ● Wallace, James 3mW
- Ω Wallace, Robert W
- ■ Wallace, Lt.
- ♣ Walpole, Thomas XP
- ● Watson, Alex 3mY
- ♀ Watson, Alex Z
- ● Watson, Charles 5mY
- ■ Watson, Captain James Y
- ■ Watson, Captain John S-F,X
- ▲ Watson, John X
- ● Watson, Colonel
- ■ Watson, Ensign Robert Y[23]
- ◉ Watts, Thomas M-F,W

APPENDIX

- Ω Wauch, Ronald X
- ▲ Wauchope, Patrick X
- ● Webster, Alex $2m$Y
- ▲ Webster, John X[1]
- ☐ Wedderburn, Alexander, Lord Loughborough YP[1]
- ▲ Wedderburn, Alexander L-F,W[1]
- ■ Wedderburn, Captain Charles M-F,Y
- ■ Wedderburn, General David Y
- ●■ Wedderburn, Captain Henry X
- ■ Wedderburn, Lt.-Col. John X
- ♣ Weir, (Wier) Daniel YP
- Ω Weir, John X
- ■ Welsh, Colonel Thomas Y
- ■ Wemyss, Captain John Y
- ● Wemyss, John $5m$Y
- Ω Wemyss, Walter W
- ■ Wharton, Lt.-Col. Thomas Z
- ■ White, Captain Martin X
- ● Whyte, Captain Thomas Y
- ● Wier, Dickie $4m$Y
- ♀ Williamson, Alex Z
- ● Williamson, George $3m$Z
- ● Williamson, Captain James X
- ■ Williamson, Captain James Y
- ● Wilson, Alex $1m$X
- ■ Wilson, Lt. David
- ■ Wilson, Captain George X
- ♀ Wilson, Dr. James (Senior)
- ♀ Wilson, Dr. James (Junior)
- ▲ Wilson, James Y
- ▲ Wilson, John Y
- ● Wilson, Thomas $3m$Z
- ♂ Wilson, Thomas Y
- ● Wilson, Captain W[1]
- ● Wishart, David $5m$X
- Ω Wishart, Ninian W
- Ω Wood, Alex W
- ■ Woodburn, Colonel David Y
- ♣ Woodhouse, John YP
- ♣ Wordsworth, Josias WP
- ■ Wynch, Lt. Alexander
- ▲ Wynch, George Y
- ■ Wynch, Lt. John
- ▲ Wynch, William Y

- Ω Young, Andrew W
- ● Young, Captain Robert
- ▲ Young, William L-F,X
- ∞ Yuile, Mr.[2]
- Ω Yule, John Y

Total: **1,801** names
– Less 176 Providers

= 1,625 Recipients +
43 who were also Providers
= **1,668**

Notes to Select List

Unless otherwise stated in the footnotes below, those named are to be found in the primary and secondary sources referred to in the 'Bibliography'. Most appear in: McGilvary (2), 'Patronage Profiles' section, and Appendices 1-16; Crawford, *passim*; Farrington (1) and (2), *passim*; Fawcett, *passim*; Hardy, *passim*; Hodson, *passim*; Low, *passim*; Sutton, *passim*.

1. McGilvary (2), Patronage Profiles, pp.293-377, *et. passim*.
2. Glasgow City Archives, Bogle Papers, Bo 25, George Bogle to Mary Bogle Calcutta, 24 February 1771. (Also posted on internet by Dr. A. MacKillop.)
3. N.L.S. William Pulteney Papers, Box 4: Edinburgh, John Jardine to William Johnstone 12 April 1764. (Also posted on internet by Dr. A. MacKillop.)
4. GD 219/10/1 Campbell of Succoth Papers: Archibald Edmonstone to Sir Archibald Campbell. London, 26 December 1769. (Also posted on internet by Dr. A. MacKillop.)
5 to 17. India Office Records, L/MIL/9/85: Embarkation Lists 1753–57. (Also posted on internet by Dr. A. MacKillop.)
18. University of Cambridge MSS, Mr. Ferguson's Diary of a Voyage to the Cape, Mocha, India and China, 7 June 1731–15 July 1739.
19. MacKillop (1), p. 219.
20 to 32. I.O.R. Home Miscellaneous, vol. 91, ff. 174–7, Lt. Col. Ross to H. Dundas. 'Officers on the Madras Establishment of Engineers, 1770–1794.'
33. Forrest, vol. 2, pp. 83–4; McGilvary (2), Patronage Profiles, pp. 293–377, *et. passim*.
34. McGilvary (2), 'Patronage Profiles' section; and Appendices 1–16; also Forrest, vol. 2, pp. 83–4.
35. S.R.O. GD1/495/37.
36. From Mirza Sheikh Ihtesammudin, Emissary to the Mogul Emperor. Visit to Britain in 1765, translated by Kaiser Haq; related in 'The Scotsman Weekend' for 13 July 1991.

Addenda

Where uncertainty exists over the ultimate Scots or Ulster Scots origins of some, depending upon how far back these are traced (such as with Col. John McGowan, Henry Macleane, Lauchlin Macleane, and Captain Stephen Macleane) they have been included.

The list is by no means exhaustive and is strictly limited to the period in question. Although not included, many marine and medical officers, whose names almost certainly identify them as Scottish, appear during the years 1720 to 1780. They are as follows:

Appendix

Angus (4), Annandale, Anstruther, Arbuthnot, Auchmuchty, Auld, Badenach (2), Baillie (4), Balfour (2), Bannatyne, Baxter, Begbie (4), Bethune (2), Black (2), Bruce (3), Burns (2), Carstairs (2), Christie (4), Crichton (3), Currie, Doughty (3), Geddes, Haddock (3), Hunter (2), Hutchinson (5), Jamieson (2), Kennedy (5), Kilgour (2), Kirk (2), Lesley (3), Lyon (7), Mair (3), Moir (3), Nicholson (9), Nicol (4), Plenderleith (3), Purvis (6), Russell (19), Rutherford (6), Shaw (17), Stevenson (12), Tough (2), Sutherland (7), Tait (3), Thompson (48), Walker (32), Watson (20), Watt (4), Williamson (19), Wilson (58); Total = 353.

Prior to 1720 (i.e. from the year 1600) there were only some 40 Scottish Maritime officers identified (see Farrington (2), *passim*).

From 1780 to 1834 (i.e. after the period studied here) there were an additional 1,224 (minimum) Scottish Maritime officers (including ships' surgeons).

From 1780 onwards the civil service and military arms of the Company carried ever increasing numbers of Scots.

Of the 124 fortunes documented, 37 were Large Fortunes (30%); 65 Medium Fortunes (52%); 21 were Small Fortunes (18%). Of the large fortunes known about, some were over £100,000. Several were between £100,000 and £300,000 in size. The £ (pound) of the mid-eighteenth century should be multiplied by a factor of at least 90 to give modern-day worth (i.e. 2008).

Part 2: Distribution of listed personnel between 1720 and 1780

	1720 to 1742	1742 to 1765	1765 to 1774	1775 to 1780	No dates	**Total**
providers facilitators operators	42	86	48	—	—	**176**
voyages for women	3	3	1	—	—	**7**
free-merchants	6	8	11	—	26	**51**
civil servants	53	72	79	—	36	**240**
military	2	104	239	74	93	**514**
ship commanders owners navig.surveyors	26	53	46	11	5	**141**
1st mates	7	27	19	5	—	**58**
2nd to 6th mates	21	69	74	28	7	**199**
Ships surgeons	53	75	49	29	2	**208**
Pursers	8	24	25	7	—	**64**
Medics/surgeons	23	22	34	22	11	**112**
Miscellaneous	—	—	—	—	31	**31**
Total	**244**	**543**	**626**	**177**	**211**	**1801**

Total of all positions shown between 1720 and 1780 = 1,801
(Note: This list is not exhaustive)

Short Titles and Abbreviations

Add.MSS.	Additional manuscripts kept in the Department of Manuscripts in the British Library, London.
B.L.	British Library, London
Bute MSS.	The papers of John Stuart, 3rd Earl of Bute, kept at Mountstuart, Isle of Bute.
De Bertodano Papers	Papers belonging to Mr. Martin De Bertodano De
E.P.L.	Edinburgh Public Libraries. George IV Bridge, Edinburgh
E.U.L.	Edinburgh University Library.
Hansard	*The Parliamentary History of England from the Earliest Period to the year 1803,* T. C. Hansard, W. Cobbett (eds.), (London, 1813/4).
H.M.S.C.	Historical Manuscripts Commission Reports.
I.O.L. MSS.	Manuscripts in the Asia, Pacific & Africa Collections in the British Library, London.
I.O.R.	Records of the East India Company kept in the Asia, Pacific & Africa Collections in the British Library, London.
N.L.S.	National Library of Scotland, George IV Bridge, Edinburgh.
N.L.W.	National Library of Wales, Aberystwyth.
n.p.	No pagination.
P.A.	*Public Advertiser.*
P.R.O. (London)	Public Record Office, London.
P.R.O. S.R.O.	Scottish Record Office, Register House, Edinburgh.

Notes

Preface
1. See McGilvary (2), *passim* for East India Company patronage.
2. See also Colley, *passim*.
3. Lenman (2), *passim*; Shaw, *passim*; also Kiernan, p.97.

1. Drummond: Early Life 1675–1742
1. S.R.O. GD 24/1/3, John Drummond's Will. The bulk of the material on Drummond's family has been culled from Prof. Hatton's work, which deals with Drummond's earlier career. [See Hatton (1), *passim*; Hatton (2), *passim*; and Hatton (3), *passim*]. Also Sedgwick (2); and the S.R.O. Morton and Abercairney papers.
2. I.O.R. L/AG/14/5/3 – Stock Holders, 1718–23.
3. S.R.O. GD24/Sect.1/487–487A, ff.1–86, Letters from Chandos to J. Drummond from 1717 to 1728.
4. S.R.O. GD150/3485/1, 49, 52–57.
5. Hatton (3), pp.76–78.
6. H.M.S.C. Portland iv, p.596.
7. Especially Hatton (3), pp.79, 85; also Hatton (1), *passim*; Hatton (2), *passim*; Carswell, pp.273–4.
8. H.M.S.C. Portland, vii, p.161.
9. H.M.S.C. Portland, vii, pp.9–10, *et passim*.
10. H.M.S.C. Portland, vii, p.280.
11. H.M.S.C. Portland, vii, pp.19–22; Carswell, p. 277.
12. Hatton (3), p.80; Carswell, pp.277–280.
13. Bolitho & Peel, pp.34–5; Hatton (3), pp.70, 81; H.M.S.C. Portland, vii *passim*.
14. H.M.S.C. Portland v, pp.285–7, John Drummond to Earl of Oxford, 8 May 1713. See also Hyde, pp.7–13, *et passim*; and Carswell, p.80.
15. Hatton (1), pp.89–108.
16. See also Carswell, pp.55–61, 273–284 *passim*.
17. Hatton (1), pp.89–108; Carswell, pp. 273–284 *et passim*; H.M.S.C. Portland, vii, pp. 275, 283.
18. See also Plumb (1), pp.245–377 *passim*.

19. Sedgwick (2), vol.1, pp.116, 143, 151; also Realey, pp.65–67.
20. H.M.S.C. Portland, vii, p.400, dated 14 July 1725. See also Devine (4), pp.54–55 *et passim* for background.
21. Realey, pp.65–66,140–141. See also Mitchison (1), p.36.
22. Realey, pp.65–66.
23. Realey, pp.142, 144.

2. Political and Electoral Realities 1707–74

1. See McGilvary (2), Appendices 15 & 16; and Mitchison (1), pp.301–2. £400,000 compensation was paid to Scots with the 1707 Act. 59% went to shareholders in the Darien Scheme. See also Devine (2), pp.23–27 *et passim*.
2. Until 1725 the Squadrone included 16 Lords and several of the leading gentry. Drummond acted as a bridge for people to cross over to the Argathelian side.
3. See Ferguson, W. (2), pp.134–7.
4. See Simpson, p.53.
5. Simpson, p.48; see also Plumb (2), p.244.
6. Riley (1), p.285; see also Ferguson, W. (2), p.243; Simpson, p.54; Calder, p.535.
7. *Ibid.* p.288; Simpson, p.55. See also Ferguson (2), p.143; Mitchison (1), pp.326–7.
8. Ferguson, W. (2), p.145; see also Donaldson (2), p.178; Riley (1), p.288.
9. Riley (1), p.106; see also Calder, p.535; Simpson, pp.55–6.
10. Simpson, pp.51–3. Tweeddale was Secretary of State from 1742–6; Plumb (2), pp.104–6.
11. Calder, p.682.
12. Dickson, T, (ed.), pp.81–91, *passim*; See also Cannon, p.65.
13. Cannon, pp.96–101. See also chapter 14.
14. *Ibid*, pp.82–3, 95–96.
15. *Ibid.*, p.95–6.
16. Dickson, T. (ed.), p.102.
17. See Sedgwick (2), vol.1, pp.381–404. (Six small counties had three MPs – one per two counties.)
18. Simpson, pp.66–67.
19. Sunter (1), pp.2–8, see also pp.183–223, *passim*; Murdoch (2), pp.22–23, 35; Shaw, *passim*; also Bricke, pp.157–165.
20. Dickson, T. (ed.), p.103.
21. Fergusson, J. (2), pp.121–122.
22. Whetstone, pp.4–5, 33.
23. *Ibid.* pp.4–5, 33. Most heritable jurisdictions ended in 1747.
24. Sedgwick (2), vol.1, p.381, *et passim*.
25. Fergusson, J. (2), pp.119–133.
26. Fergusson, J. (2), pp.119–133; Dickson, T. (ed.), pp.103, 105.
27. Sedgwick (2), vol.1, pp.381–404. Most of these were also Drummond's friends. See also Ferguson, W. (1), p.89. Rothes too was Drummond's friend.

3. Company and Patronage Infrastructure 1720–74

1. See Realey, p.17.
2. Sutherland (1), p.23 and pp.18–23 *passim*.

3. Sunter (1), p.515.
4. See Sedgwick (2), vol.1, *passim*; Namier & Brooke (1), vol.1, *passim*.
5. See N.L.S. Delvine papers. M.S. 1423.
6. For example: James Beck. See S.R.O. GD 240/30/Bundle 6; also McGilvary (2), p.349, on Kenneth Mackenzie.
7. For example: R. Simpson, in S.R.O. GD 156/Box 49/1/58, 74; and McGilvary (2), p.264.
8. Parker, p.111, *et passim*; see also Sunter (1), p.521; Shearer, p.208; and McGilvary (2), *passim* for Foulis, Irwin and Steven.
9. See S.R.O. GD 110/1021/1–10; and Namier & Brooke (1), vol.3, pp.495–7.
10. See N.L.S. Minto MSS. 11018, 11027.
11. Other posts gained for friends included: naval commissions, positions as gunners and boatswains; customs, treasury and excise jobs. See S.R.O. GD 110/1007, 1303.
12. See also Murdoch (2), p.267.
13. See Williams (1), vol.1, p.169; Murdoch (2), p.207.
14. See Fergusson, J. (1), pp.56–79; and Williams (1), vol.1, p.169.

4. Drummond and Management 1720–42

1. See S.R.O. GD 24/Sect.1/464/(C), f.1; and ff.482–484, *passim*.
2. He also placed people in the Africa Company's service in 1722. See S.R.O. GD 24/Sect.1/464(C), f.59, Annandale to J. Drummond, 24 January 1722; and f.72, Lady Ramsden of Byram to J. Drummond, 25 January 1724.
3. S.R.O. GD 150/3474/26, J. Drummond to Aberdour, 3 November 1733.
4. *Ibid*, f.8, J. Drummond to Aberdour, 22 August 1731.
5. S.R.O. GD 24/Sect.1/496–503A, f.5, Morton to J. Drummond, 20 July 1732.
6. S.R.O. GD 24/Sect.1/464/N–O, f.65, Gov. Pitt to J. Drummond, 29 January 1733; See also GD 24/Sect.1/487–487A, ff.488–495; GD 150/3474/1–60.
7. S.R.O. GD 24/Sect.1/488–495, ff.76–78, J. Drummond to James Drummond, 8 October 1734.
8. S.R.O. GD 24/Sect.1/464E, f.100, J. Drummond of Megginch to J. Drummond of Quarrel, 30 October 1732.
9. S.R.O. GD 150/3474/24, J. Drummond to Aberdour, 27 September 1733.
10. See S.R.O. GD 24/Sect.1/488–495, f.29, Aberdour to J. Drummond, 19 July 1733; and f.73, J. Drummond to Jas. Drummond, 7 January 1735.
11. N.L.S. MSS. 16536, ff.43, 45, 47, J. Drummond to Milton on 17 June 1727; see also letters on 12 and 15 July 1727.
12. *Ibid*. Also S.R.O. GD 150/3474/17, 37, 38, 40, J. Drummond to Aberdour, 1730–1737, *passim*. See also H.M.S.C. Portland MSS.; and Murdoch (2), p. 8.
13. S.R.O. GD 150/3474/17, 37, 38, 40, for 22 August 1732; 2 November 1734; 4 November 1734; and 19 November 1734.
14. N.L.S. MSS 16535, f.37, J. Drummond to Milton, 15 March 1733; see also f.131, J. Drummond to Milton, November 1727; MSS.16536, ff.43–52, J. Drummond to Milton, 17 June 1727, 11 July 1727, 15 July 1727; and MSS. 16556, f. 114, J. Drummond to Milton, 13 May 1734.
15. N.L.S. MSS.16536, ff.43–52, J. Drummond to Milton, 15 July 1727; see also MSS. 16538, f.172; MSS. 16553, f.35.

16. See N.L.S. MSS.16536, f.50; MSS. 16538, f.172; MSS. 16549, ff.142; MSS. 16553, f.35.
17. N.L.S. MSS. 16538, ff.17, 24; MSS. 16556, f.115; MSS. 16565, f.245.
18. S.R.O. GD 24/Sect.1/488–495, f.8, J. Drummond to W. Drummond, 14 November 1734; see also f.12.
19. S.R.O. GD 24/Sect.1/488–495, f.71, J. Drummond to Jas. Drummond, 15 August l735.
20. See S.R.O. GD 24/Sect.1/464/N–O, f.65, Gov. Pitt to J. Drummond, 29 January l733; GD 24/Sect.1/487–487A, f.127, Chandos to J. Drummond, 5 July 1733, *et passim*; GD 24/Sect.1/488–495, f.19, John to Jas. Drummond, 3 January 1736.
21. See S.R.O. Abercairney MSS. (GD 24), *passim.;* also N.L.S. MSS. 5073, ff.110, 158, J. Drummond to Ld. Erskine, 14 November 1728 and 5 June 1730; also Sedgwick (2), vol.2, pp.118–9.
22. *Ibid.*
23. *Ibid*; also Hatton (1), pp.89–108.
24. S.R.O. GD 24/Sect.1/464/C, f.110, J. Glen to J. Drummond, January 1728; f.160, Ld. Queensberry to J. Drummond, 5 July 1730; GD 24/Sect.1/464/N–O, f.8, 'Account of sale of Bulses of Diamonds', dated 8 July 1726. See also GD 24/Sect.1/482–484, *passim*; also N.L.S. MSS. 5073, f.110; and Hatton (1), pp.89–108.
25. S.R.O. GD 24/Sect.1/487–487A, f.121, Chandos to J. Drummond, 18 March 1733.
26. See S.R.O. GD 24/Sect.1/464/N–O, f.5, Ships Owners Benjamin & Christopher Lethieullier and others to J. Drummond, 15 July. 1725. Prinsep, *passim*.
27. See S.R.O. GD 24/Sect.1/464/N–O, ff.1, 18, 36, 51, 70 – letters between 1723 and 1733 to J. Drummond from Dr. Colt, Gov. George Morton Pitt, Gov. John Horne, and Gov. Cowan. See also GD 24/Sect.1/464/C, f.222; GD 24/Sect.1/487–487A, f.115; and N.L.S. MSS.16536, f.45.

5. Drummond Network 1720–42

1. See McGilvary (2), Appendices 1 and 2.
2. *Ibid.*, Appendices 1 to 3.
3. *Ibid.* See also Sedgwick (2), vol.1, pp.381–404; and S.R.O. GD 24/Sect.2/464/C, f.225, Sir Jas. Kinloch to J. Drummond, 8 September 1733.
4. *Ibid.* Appendices 3 and 4.
5. See Foster, p.16; Sedgwick (2), vol.1, pp.420, 622; vol.2, pp.14, 17, 47–48.
6. See also Sedgwick (2), vols. 1 & 2, *passim.*
7. The bulk of material used is from: S.R.O. GD 24, Abercairney Muniments; GD 110, Hamilton–Dalrymple–Papers; GD 150, Morton Papers.
8. S.R.O. GD 150/3474/24, J. Drummond to Aberdour, 29 September 1734.
9. H.M.S.C. Charles Stirling–Home–Drummond–Moray MSS. pp.153–154. See also S.R.O. GD 24/Sect.1/464/N–O, f.3, George Threipland to John Drummond, 15 August 1731, also ff.9, 15, 31 and 35 *passim*; GD 24/Sect.1/482–484, f.75, J. Drummond to W. Drummond, 27 April 1731.

10. S.R.O. GD/Sect.1/488–495, f.495, J. Drummond to W. Drummond, 4 February 1735.
11. S.R.O. GD 150/3470/9, G. Douglas to Lord Morton, 15 July 1729.
12. S.R.O. GD 24/Sect.1/464/C, ff.185–7, Sir Jas. Kinloch to J. Drummond, 5 May 1734
13. See N.L.S. MSS. 16536, f.43, John Drummond to Milton, 17 June 1727. Also S.R.O. GD 24/Sect.1/488–495, f.495; GD 150/3474/54.
14. S.R.O. GD 24/Sect.1/ 464/C, ff.116, and 196, Thos Hope of Hope Park to John Drummond, 1 June 1728 and 4 September 1732.
15. *Ibid*, f.177, Stirling of Keir to John Drummond, 6 February 1731.
16. S.R.O. GD 24 Sect.1/464/N–O, f.43, John Cleland to John Drummond, 23 January 1732.
17. S.R.O. GD 24/Sect.1/488–495, ff.76–78, J. Drummond to James Drummond, 5 October 1734. See also GD 24/Sect.1/ 464/C, f.196; f.163; GD24/Sect.1/464E, f.100.
18. S.R.O. GD 24/Sect.1/ 464/N–O, f.11, J. Lauder to J. Drummond, 26 January 1727, see also f.9; GD 24/Sect.1/464/C, ff.80; f.84; and Abercairney MSS. *passim*; Smout (3), *passim*; and Timperley (ed.), *passim*.
19. See S.R.O. GD 24/Sect.1/496–503A, f.7, Earl Morton to John Drummond, 20 July 1732; Abercairney MSS. *passim*.
20. See S.R.O. GD 24/Sect.1/464/C; GD 24/Sect.1/495; GD 150/2639; GD 150/3478/39; GD 150/3483/11; GD 24/Sect.1/ 464/N–O, f.84. See Also Love, *passim;* and Timperley (ed.), *passim*.
21. See McGilvary (2), pp.131–132, *et passim*; S.R.O. GD 150/3474/53; GD 24/Sect.1/464/N–O, ff.9, 13, 33, 61, 63–66; S.R.O. GD 24/Sect.1/464/C, f.240. See also Marshall (4), p.230, *et passim*.
22. S.R.O. GD 24/Sect.1/464/C, f.71; and f.207.
23. See S.R.O. GD 24/Sect.1/464/C, f.75, f.233; GD 24/Sect.1/464/N–O, f.23.
24. S.R.O. GD 24/Sect.1/464/E, f.90; GD 24/Sect.2/464/C, f.196. See also Riddy (1), p.5.
25. S.R.O. GD24/Sect.1/464/N–O, ff.8, 17, 19, 36, 50.
26. S.R.O. GD24/Sect.1/464/N–O, f.19, Major Roach to John Drummond, 21 January 1728.
27. Lowther invested through a native broker called Loldass, who 'made good' for them both '150,000 rupees (just under £15,000) with compound interest of 9 per cent.' S.R.O. GD 24/Sect.1/464/N–O, f.23, H. Lowther to John Drummond, 31 December 1727. See also *Ibid*, f.21; also GD 150/3483/11; GD 24/Sect.1/464/C, ff.66–68.
28. See S.R.O. GD/Sect.1/482–4/, ff.60, 87, 92, 93, 139; GD24/Sect.1 /464/N–O, ff.11, 29, 40, 41, 54, 73; GD 24/Sect.1/ 464/C, ff.179, 191, 194; GD 150/3483/2. The Mackenzie of Delvine connection was very important.
29. S.R.O. GD 24/Sect.1/464/N–O, ff.5, 13, 17, 18, 21, 36, 60–61; GD 24/Sect.1/ 464/C, f.52, f.88; N.L.S. MSS.16536, f.45. See also, Macrae, pp.235–42.
30. S.R.O. GD 24/Sect.2/464/C, f.151, Moray of Abercairney to John Drummond, 27 June 1729. See also Appendix.
31. B. L. Add. MSS. 29133; I.O.R. Writers Petitions – J/1/1–15; *P.A.* for 9 April 1763; Namier & Brooke (1), vol.2, pp.229–230; N.L.S. MSS. 10922 and 10953; Parker (1), pp.73–76, 408; Shearer, *passim*.

32. S.R.O. GD 24/Sect.1/464/N–O, f.15, Gov. Pitt to John Drummond 11 January 1728; GD 24/Sect.1/482–4, f.87, John Drummond to W. Drummond, 19 January 1731; also GD 24/Sect.1/464/C, *passim*.
33. See S.R.O. GD 24/Sect.2/464/C, *passim*; GD 24/Sect.1/482–4, *passim*. See also Appendix.
34. N.L.S. MSS. 16536, f.45, J. Drummond to Milton, 11 July 1727; See also S.R.O. GD 24/Sect.1/464/C, f.123; GD 24/Sect.1/464/N–O, f.15.
35. S.R.O. GD 24/Sect.1/464/C, f.80, P. Halkett to J. Drummond, 28 June 1725.
36. S.R.O. GD 24/Sect.1/464/N–O, f.51, J. Horne to J. Drummond, 14 March 1732. See also Appendix.
37. S.R.O. GD 24/Sect.1/464/N–O, ff.41, 43, 63–66, 75. See also Warren & Barlow, p.35. See Appendix.
38. S.R.O. GD 24/Sect.1/464/N–O *passim*; GD 150/3483/2; Love, *passim*.
39. S.R.O. GD 24/Sect.1/464/C *passim*; GD 150/3483/2 *passim*; GD 30/1582 *passim*.
40. S.R.O. GD 24/Sect.1/464/N–O, ff.41, 43, 63–66, 75. See also Warren & Barlow, p.35.
41. S.R.O. GD 24/Sect.1/464/C, f.238, Elizabeth Hyndford to J. Drummond, n.d. but 1733. See also *Ibid*, ff.55, 72, 233, 235; GD 24/Sect.1/464/N–O, ff.61, 68, 82; GD 24 Sect. 1/496–503A, f.5; GD 24/Sect.1/464/E, f.121; GD 24/Sect.1/496–503A, f.5.
42. S.R.O. GD 24/Sect.1/464/N–O, ff.56, 63–66, 70–72; S.R.O. GD 24/Sect.1/464/C, f.222; S.R.O. GD 110/980/1–2.
43. S.R.O. GD 24 Sect.2/464/C, ff.150, 235; GD18/3219; GD 24/Sect.1/482–4, *passim*.; GD 150/3483/2; N.L.S. MSS.1423, f.164. See also H.M.S.C. Charles Stirling–Home–Drummond–Moray MSS. p.155.
44. H.M.S.C. Charles Stirling–Home–Moray MSS. p.155, D. Forbes of Culloden to J. Drummond, 31 October 1729. See also *Ibid*, p.152; and S.R.O. GD 24/Sect.1/464/N–O, f.89.
45. See also Calder, pp.436, 533; and Mitchison(1), pp.326–7.
46. See N.L.S. MSS. 1666, f.200, 'Jacobite Journal;' MSS. 3188, *passim*; MSS. 5080, f.41; MSS 16647, f.16; S.R.O. GD 24/Sect.2/464/C, f.177; Namier & Brooke (1), vol.1, p.38, vol.2, pp.564–5; Marshall (4), p.3. Also Paterson (1), vol.2, p.19.
47. See Jones, pp.68–77.
48. Lenman (2), pp.176–177
49. *Ibid*.
50. S.R.O. GD 150/3485/1 and 57.

6. Operating from Scotland 1742–61

1. Shaw, p.17; Lenman (2), p.8; Realey, pp.65–66; Murdoch (2), pp.36–103 *passim*.
2. Mitchison (1), pp.333–5.
3. Youngson, p.26
4. Murdoch (2), p.67. Mentioned in *The Autobiography of Dr. Alexander Carlyle of Inveresk, 1733–1805*, p.272.
5. *Ibid.*, p.67. See also Sir James Grant's Memorial to Henry Pelham, 30 October 1765. (Mitchell Library, Glasgow, S.R. 177.)

6. See McGilvary (2) Appendices 6 to 9.
7. E.U.L. Laing MSS. vol. 2, p.384, 'Suggestions by Duncan Forbes of Culloden.'
8. See for example Simpson, p.67.
9. Simpson, p.62 and Murdoch (2), pp.63–4.
10. *Ibid*, pp.61–62; N.L.S. MSS 10781, Letterbook of Baron Maule, 1748–61. *passim*. The Letterbook shows Ilay's team at work: John Scrope, Secretary to the Treasury, Maule at the Court of Exchequer, and Charles Erskine.
11. S.R.O. GD 224/295/3/33, John Dalrymple to Charles Townshend, 5 October 1759; See Maclean (1), *passim*, for the Douglas Cause.
12. S.R.O. Argyll Muniments N.R.A.(S) 1209, Survey I, Bundle 193. See also S.R.O. R.H. 4/70, Reel 1, Bundle 55 on elections 1747–1753.
13. In 1757 Fox envisaged Newcastle as Minister for England and Ilay as Minister for Scotland. [See Simpson, p.62].
14. See Simpson, p.68; Bricke, pp.157–165.
15. Murdoch (2), p.87; Ferguson (2), pp.146–165; Lenman (2), pp. 1–30, *et passim*.
16. See N.L.S. Saltoun Papers, MSS 16501–17880, Provisional Catalogue, for career and family outline.
17. S.R.O. GD 110/947/6. Sir Hew Dalrymple to (unknown), dated 4 August 1760.
18. *Ibid.*
19. Simpson, pp.66–67; Lenman (2), pp.1–30.
20. Murdoch (2), p.20.
21. E.U.L. Laing MSS 111, 364, 'The Family of Fletcher of Saltoun' c.1780, p.47.
22. *Ibid.*
23. *Ibid.*
24. N.L.S. MSS 16660, f.204, Geo. Lind to Milton, London, 12 January 1748.
25. N.L.S. MSS 16648, f.86, Newcastle to Saltoun, 30 October 1747; Shaw, p.160.
26. N.L.S. MSS. 16627, f.8, Alex Howe to Milton, 6 March 1746.
27. See also Lenman (2), pp.176–7; Riddy (1), p.14.
28. N.L.S. MSS. 16663, f.200, dated 8 September 1748 'Jacobite Journal'; see also Riddy (1), pp.8, 10.
29. See Riddy (1), p.14.
30. See Grant (2), pp.468, 496; Riddy (1), p.14.
31. See Fraser (4), vol. 1, pp.5–6,
32. See Namier & Brooke (1), vol. 3, pp.480–1; also Maclean (1), pp.187–8. Sir James Stewart of Allanbank, son of the Solicitor–General for Scotland, had been a Jacobite exile and a political economist. He was pardoned in 1771.
33. Shaw, pp.48; also pp. 50, 87 *et passim*.
34. *Ibid.* p.47.
35. There was a darker side to his character. See Shaw, pp.153, 156; also Ramsay, pp.86–90.
36. Much has been drawn from: Shaw, pp.43–48, 147–186, *passim*; Murdoch (2), pp. 24–25; N.L.S. Fletcher of Saltoun Papers, MSS 16513–16524, 16604–16733, 16746–16753; Timperley (ed.), *passim*; Sedgwick (2), vols. 1–3, *passim*; and Namier & Brooke (1), vol. 1, pp. 469–512.
37. See N.L.S. Fletcher of Saltoun Papers, MSS. 16513–16524, 16604–16733, 16746–16753; S.R.O. GD24/Sect.1/464C, ff.185–7; Sedgwick (2), *passim*; Namier & Brooke (1), vol.1, pp.469–512; (Milton's nephews William and John

were sent to India by Drummond). See also Shaw, pp.43–48; and *The Autobiography of Dr. Alexander Carlyle of Inveresk, 1722–1805*, p.271.
38. Other invaluable friends in London were Charles Jenkinson, Patrick Crauford, MP, a Mr. Grant and a Mr. Goodchild.
39. Many of these were Scots. Until his death he was involved with at least four ships' Captains; three high–ranking officers of the Company's army; and many in the Company's civil service. He counted as friends at least five Directors, and around a dozen Proprietors. Most appear in the text.
40. The Ilay connections included five Peers, two knights and five large landowners. (See Shaw, *passim*, for these and others).
41. See Shaw, pp.43–48, 147–186 *passim*; N.L.S. Fletcher of Saltoun Papers MSS 16513–16524, 16604–16733, 16746–16753; Sedgwick (2), *passim*; Namier & Brooke (1), vol.1, pp.469–512.
42. See also Shaw, pp.43–48, 147–186.
43. As indicated earlier Drummond made Milton's relative, a Carnegie of Pittarow, Governor of Bencoolen in 1727. [N.L.S. 16536, f.43, J. Drummond to Milton, 17 June 1727; Cormack (2), pp.15–16 *et passim*.]
44. N.L.S. MSS. 16666, f.57; MSS. 16670, ff.226, 228; Namier & Brooke (1), vol. 2, pp.440–1; Riddy(1), pp.13–14; Timperley (ed.), p.21.
45. N.L.S. MSS. 16666, f.57; MSS. 16670, ff.226, 228.
46. B.L. Add. MSS. 29134, f.251, L. Sulivan to W. Hastings, 8 December 1773.
47. See for example: N.L.S. MSS. 1328, f.252; MSS. 1368, f.276; S.R.O. GD 128/4/3/13.
48. Love, vol.1, pp.177, 240, 320, 388, 407, 438, 454, 456, 550; vol.3, p.60; S.R.O. GD 93/365; GD 93/388; GD 98/391; I.O.R. Madras Civil Servants, 1764–1795; McGilvary (1), p.93, footnote 2; Timperley (ed.), pp.228, 301, 303; Sedgwick (2), vol.1, pp. 381–404; Mackenzie (2), *passim*.
49. See Records of the Royal Medical Society, Bristo Square, Edinburgh; Love, pp.550, 551.
50. Fraser (1), p.535.
51. Marshall (4), pp.120–121, 154; also N.L.S. MSS. 1423, ff.164–165.
52. Fraser (1), pp.535–545.
53. *Ibid.* p.543; also Marshall (4), pp.5, 195; Grier, vol.111, p.347; Barun Dé, pp.73–74.
54. See Timperley (ed.), pp.265, 269, 303, 322, 336; Fraser (1), pp.535–545; Riddy (1), pp.9–10.
55. *Miscellany of the Scottish History Society* (5th vol.), pp.197–290. Also Mackenzie (1), pp.613–5; Timperley (ed.), pp.264–266, 276, 302; N.L.S. MSS. 1167, f.1 and MSS. 1253–5.
56. Ferguson (2), p.94. Also N.L.S. MSS. 1131, ff.17–20; MSS. 1140, f.39; MSS. 1145, ff.62–3.
57. N.L.S. MSS. 1101, f.240. See also MSS. 1140, ff.19, 39; MSS. 1273, ff.58–60; Murdoch (2), pp.22–23.
58. Ferguson, W. (3), pp.263–283. See also N.L.S. MSS. 1273, ff.58–60, 61, 70; MSS. 1290, *passim*; MSS. 1294, ff.55–60.
59. N.L.S. MSS. 1310, f.52, J. Mackenzie to Alex MacDonald of Sleat, 21 September 1768; see also E.U.L. Laing MSS, 11,629.
60. *Ibid.*

61. N.L.S. MSS. 1337, ff.1–14, Coull to Delvine, 22 January 1758 to 12 October 1759.
62. *Ibid.*
63. *Ibid,* f.34, dated 8 April 1774.
64. *Ibid,* f.49, dated 13 December 1771.
65. *Ibid.* f.33, dated 10 January 1771.
66. N.L.S. MSS. 1423, f. 164, D. Rannie to Rev. Webster, 6 August 1760.
67. *Ibid.* f.165, D. Rannie to J. Mackenzie of Delvine, 16 August 1760; see also Riddy (1), p.11; Marshall, pp.231–232; Omand, p.217; S.R.O. GD 51/11/4.
68. N.L.S. MSS. 1328, ff.244, 246, 249, Kenneth Mackenzie to John Mackenzie on 16 January 1762, 5 February 1762 and 16 February 1762.
69. See N.L.S. MSS. 1328, ff. 254–255, 256–8, 260–263; MSS 1256, ff.136, 143–144; MSS 1368, ff.194, 276. John Mackenzie also patronised Lt. Rattray, whom he placed under the protection of Col. John Cumming.
70. N.L.S. MSS. 1256, f.7, Ann McIntosh to George Cumming, 15 May 1749.
71. N.L.S. MSS. 1256, ff.133–237, Letters from Col. (later Sir) John Cumming to John Mackenzie, from 2 February 1761 to 24 November 1777; also MSS. 1368, f.194, Coull Mackenzie to John Mackenzie, 31 March 1777; also Fawcett, p.122.
72. N.L.S. MSS. 10787, *passim*; and Mackay, p.193. See also Love, vol. 2, p.321; and N.L.S. MSS. 1256, f.174, dated 29 November 1772.
73. N.L.S. MSS. 1310, ff.33, Sir Alex. MacDonald of Sleat to John Mackenzie of Delvine, 8 July 1768.
74. N.L.S. MSS. 1310, f.38, Sir Alex. MacDonald of Sleat to John Mackenzie, 21 September 1768. See also MSS. 1165, f.52.
75. See N.L.S. MSS. 1252, ff.5, 67–68; Maclean (1), p.170.
76. See N.L.S. MSS. 1423, ff.164–5; MSS. 1297, ff.107–156, *passim*. See also Maclean (1), p.291; Mure, p.263; and Lang, pp.1–68.

7. Government: Supply and Demand 1742–61

1. See also Appendix.
2. I.O.L. MSS. Eur. D.692, Letterbook of George Gray, 1760–69. See also Marshall (4), pp.12, 194, 205–206, 237 for Gray Senior and Junior; Datta, vol.1.
3. Riddy (1), p.17, whose calculation spans the years 1760 to 1830; and Appendix.
4. See also Checkland, pp.16–17.
5. N.L.S. MSS. 10787; I.O.R. L/AG/14/5/10 for 1748–1752 Stock Ledgers. See also Bryant (1), pp.22–23.
6. Namier & Brooke (1), vol.2, p.528.
7. See McGilvary (2), pp.330–333.
8. I.O.R. Writers Petitions – J/1/1–15; N.L.S. MSS. 10787; Bolitho & Peel, *passim*; Burke (1), (1858), p.320; Namier & Brooke (1), vol.2, pp.342–343 ; *St. James' Register*, for 1765; Spencer (ed.), vol.1, p.99.
9. See Coleridge, vol.1, pp.37–39; See also Mure, vol.2, pp.73, 192; De Bertodano Papers, *passim*; Maclean (1), p.222; Namier & Brooke (1), *passim*.
10. I.O.R. Writers Petitions – J/1/1–15; Fawcett, p.176; Parker (1), pp.182–186; McGilvary (2), p.32.

11. See S.R.O. GD 224/45/28, item 5; Maclean (1), pp.187–188.
12. See N.L.S. MSS. 1337, f.40, A. Mackenzie to J. Mackenzie of Delvine, dated 2 September 1766; See also Sutherland (1), p.145, footnote 2.
13. See McGilvary (2), p.38; Parker (1), pp.55, 58.
14. See McGilvary (2), pp.193–194, *et passim*.
15. See McGilvary (2), pp.339–346, *et passim*; McGilvary (3), *passim*.
16. B. L. Add. MSS. 29133, f.533, 28 April 1773. See also McGilvary (2), pp.371–374, *et passim*; ad McGilvary (3), *passim*.
17. See N.L.S. MSS. 5400; Barun Dé, *passim*; Gurney, *passim*; McElroy, *passim*; Maclean (1), pp.41–440 *passim*; Namier & Brooke (1), vol.3, pp.495–497.
18. S.R.O. GD 24/Sect.1/464/C; GD 24/Sect.1/464/E; Anderson, vol.2, pp.489, 491, 492–495; McGilvary (1) p.17; Riddy (1), pp.5, 12; Sedgwick (2), pp.147–148; Sutherland (3) p.458; Thomson, vol.1, p.285.
19. I.O.R. Writers Petitions, 1749–95, J/1/1 – J/1/15; Bryant (1), p.41.
20. N.L.S. MSS. 16713, Milton to Ilay, 16 December 1760; and MSS. 16714, f.219, G. Dempster to Milton, 20 September 1760.
21. Fergusson (1) (ed.), p.56, also pp.56–74.
22. See McGilvary (2), pp.311–314, *et passim*; McGilvary (3), pp.76–200 *passim*.
23. McGilvary (2), pp.304–306, et passim; McGilvary (3), pp.139, 200, 252.
24. N.L.S. MSS. 1337, ff.8, A. Mackenzie to J. Mackenzie of Delvine, on 13 March 1759.
25. N.L.S. MSS. 1337, f. 11, A. Mackenzie to J. Mackenzie of Delvine, on 11 August 1759.
26. *Ibid.*
27. I.O.R. Writers Petitions, J/1/1–8; Sedgwick, vol.1, pp.381–404; Timperley (ed.), pp.101, 107, 108, 330.
28. Bute MSS. f.642, C. Stuart to Bute, London, 20 November 1761. See also I.O.R. Writers Petitions, J/1/1–8; S.R.O. RH4/reel. 14/no.7.
29. See I.O.R. L/AG/14/5/9–12, (Stockholders 1742–1762); D.N.B. vol.13, pp.406–408; and Timperley (ed.), *passim*.
30. Sedgwick (2), vol.1, p.601.
31. See McGilvary (2), pp.202–205, *et passim*.
32. *Ibid*, p.205.

8. Shipping Positions 1742–61

1. For the Shipping interest, see also: Sutherland (1), pp.36–39; Sutherland (2), p.91 *et passim;* Shearer, pp.123–168; Parker (1), 34, 394–442; McGilvary (1), pp. 33–36, 38–39; McGilvary (3), pp.2–266, *passim*. See also Sunter, pp.518–521.
2. S.R.O. GD24/Sect.1/482–p484, f.62, J. Drummond to William Drummond, 18 March 1731. See also Appendix, Part 2, 'Distribution of Personnel'.
3. Fawcett, p.24–25, 31–33; see also Parkinson, p.164, 167, 200; Sunter, p.521; Parry, p.65.
4. Fawcett, pp.29, 31, 37–38, 67–69, 73–74, 84–85, 132.
5. *Ibid.* pp.18, 96, 135–136,139–140,169; Captain Alex Hamilton, *A New Account of The East Indies,* circa 1700, *passim*; Riddy (1), pp.3–4; Love, vol.2, pp.547, 551; vol.3, pp.2, 35–37,69; Campbell, R. H., pp.38–53.
6. See S.R.O. GD 248/49/3/7.

7. See also S.R.O. GD 24/Sect.1/464 (N–P), f.19, Major Roach to John Drummond, 21 January 1728; and Appendix.
8. See Shearer, Appendix K, p.278.
9. I.O.R. L/Mar./C/651, Register of Commanders (1737–1832); also, Appendix.
10. See I.O.R. Writers Petitions, J/1/1–8, *passim*; Fawcett, pp.48–49; and Appendix.
11. See McGilvary (2), pp.214–216 *et passim*.
12. *Ibid*.
13. Ibid, pp.353–355. See also I.O.R. Writers Petitions J/1/1–15; Fawcett, *passim*; Parker (1), pp. 182–186.
14. See also Shearer, pp.35, 123–168.

9. Elections and Watersheds 1761–66

1. Simpson, p.60. See also Maclean (2), p.312.
2. Murdoch (2), p.15; See also S.R.O. Argyll Muniments, N.R.A.(S) 1209, Survey I, bundle 45.
3. Murdoch (2), pp.204–5, 211; N.L.S. MSS. 10781, f.137, Elliot; N.R.A. (S) 631, Bute Papers, Nos. 133, 134, n.p.; *Memorials of the Public Life and Character of the Rt. Hon. James Oswald of Dunniker, passim*; Sedgwick (2), *passim*.
4. Murdoch (2), pp.10–11, 14; Maclean (1), pp.351, 381, 550. See also Murray, C. de B., p.34.
5. Shaw, p.181; See also Murdoch (1), pp.214, 229; Murdoch (2), pp.99–109.
6. Murdoch (2), p.235. See also Maclean (1), p.381 Murdoch (1), pp.24, 235; Shaw, p.184; Mure, vol.2, pp.33, 80, 141, 176, 269, *et passim*.
7. Shaw, pp.184–5.
8. See N.L.S. MSS. 16715, f.1. In 1766 30 MPs were identified as Bute's Scottish followers. (See Wentworth–Woodhouse MSS. Sheffield City Library, n.p. dated 20 Dec.1766.)
9. See McGilvary (3), pp.38–72, *passim*.
10. *Ibid*. See also McGilvary (1), pp.33–46, *passim*.
11. See Appendix; and I.O.L. Writers Petitions, J/1/1–8 *passim*.
12. See Sutherland (l), pp.79, 103–4; McGilvary (1), pp.41–47; Maclean (1), p. 153.
13. See McGilvary (1), pp.63–120.
14. McGilvary (1), also pp.9, 16–17, 19, 61; I.O.R. Bombay Public Consultations, vol.18, pp.544, 562 *et passim*.
15. McGilvary (1), pp.32–35, 93.
16. See also Parker (1), *passim;* Riddy (1), p.12; Sutherland (2), p.30; Gurney, p.163.
17. For background see: McGilvary (1), pp.120–180, *passim*. For Scots pouring overseas see Appendix.
18. See McGilvary (2), *passim*.
19. See McGilvary (1), pp.76, 95, 108, 110, 114, 119, 125; and McGilvary (3). pp.51–72, 87–109 *passim*.
20. McGilvary (1), pp.151, footnote 5, and pp.160–161, 166–167, 171, 180; McGilvary (3), pp.87–146 *passim*.
21. McGilvary (1), pp.171–179, *passim*.
22. Sutherland (1), p.159, footnote 4, and pp.143, 147, 150, 165, 173–4. Also McGilvary (3), pp.87–108, 121–146 *passim*.

23. Pottle, pp.17–18.
24. *Ibid.,* pp. 29–33, 51–52, 105, 110, 300, 350; Maclean (2), pp.68, 78.
25. *Ibid.,* p.105; I.O.R. Writers Petitions, J/1/4,14, for 1761; Bute MSS. f.642; also Bute MSS. n.p., L. Sulivan to Shelburne, 24 February 1763.
26. Bute MSS. ff. 276–277; N.L.S. MSS. 16714, ff. 160–164; MSS. 16663, f.109.
27. S.R.O. GD 499/22, Dunglass MSS. vol.2, pp.499–501, Alex Hall to Sir John Hall, 4 December 1762.
28. Namier & Brooke (1), vol.3, p.500; B.L. Add. MSS. 29194, f.97; Marshall (4), p.13. See also B.L. Add. MSS. 29194, f.97.
29. D.N.B. vol.6, pp. 671–672. See also N.L.S. Minto MSS. 11018, ff.69, and 75.
30. I.O.R. Writers Petitions, J/1/4, 8 for 1760 and 1770; Maclean (1), p.435; N.L.S. Minto MSS. 11027, n.p., for 31 July 1769, and 15 July 1775.
31. Namier & Brooke (1), vol.1, p.39; Ferguson (2), pp.125, 131; Sunter, pp.532, 563.
32. Murdoch (2). p.238, see also p.256; Namier & Brooke (1), vol.1, pp.38–43; N.L.S. MSS. 17532, ff. 1–224, *passim;* and Sheffield City Libraries, Wentworth–Woodhouse MSS. n.p. 'Followers of Bedford in the Commons', dated 20 December 1766.
33. N.L.S. Saltoun MSS. SC 229, ff. 85–6; see also Murdoch (2), p.241.

10. Ministries: Company and Favours 1765–74

1. See Murdoch (2), pp. 124–8, 260–1; Lenman (2), pp.29–45.
2. Murdoch (2), pp.109–131, 232–3, 278; Simpson, p. 65. See also Namier & Brooke (1), vol.1, pp.173–5.
3. See Murdoch (2), p.262.
4. See I.O.R. Writers Petitions, *passim,* for the surge in applicants; and Appendix.
5. Scots Directors included: Charles Boddam, Sir James Cockburn, Thomas Cheape, George Cumming, George Dempster, Sir Hugh Inglis, George Johnstone, James Michie, James Moffat, William Fullerton–Elphinstone, Simon Fraser, and David Scott. See also Orme MSS. O.V.J. ff.119–133 and ff.141–160, 'Account of all Transfers of India Stock made from the 1st February 1767 to March 1767'.
6. See Brooke, pp.72–79; Norris, p.22.
7. Parker (1), p.426.
8. Sutherland (1), pp. 178–179,181; and Maclean (1), p.381.
9. Sutherland (1), p.215.
10. See McGilvary (2), p.275, footnote 1.
11. See McGilvary (2), pp.275, 349–351 *et passim.*
12. Exeter Record Office, Kennoway Documents, Palk Family/Haldon Trust, 58/9, Box 104, Item 6, L. Sulivan to Robert Palk, 13 September 1767.
13. North Riding Record Office, 'Affidavit' written and signed by Robert & Duncan Clerk, dated London, 1769.
14. See also McGilvary (3), pp.164–165.
15. See R.S.A. Minutes, vol.15 (1769–70), f.14, *passim;* and Allan, *passim.*
16. De Bertodano Papers, n.p., L. Sulivan to H. Vansittart, 28 May 1770.
17. De Bertodano Papers, n.p. L. Sulivan to H. Vansittart, 28 May, 1770; I.O.L. MSS. Eur. D. 535, R. Barwell's Letterbook, f.53.

18. See Sutherland (1), pp.219–222; Khan, pp.220–1, 231–2; and Davies, p.467.
19. De Bertodano Papers, n.p. L. Sulivan to Col. Wood, n.d. (but April 1773). See also B.L. Add. MSS. 29133, f.535; and McGilvary (3), pp.174–194.
20. See also McGilvary (3), 190–194.
21. B.L. Add.MSS. 29194, f.90, L. Sulivan to W. Hastings 28 March 1773.
22. See McGilvary (2), pp.240–242 *et passim*.
23. See James Macpherson, *The Poems of Ossian*. 1773; also Trevor–Roper, *Spectator*, for 16 March 1985.
24. See also Maclean (2), *passim;* also Namier & Brooke (1), vol. 3, pp.95–97.
25. *Ibid.* See also McGilvary (3), pp.205–262; and Appendix for Macphersons.
26. Namier & Brooke (1), vol.1, p.167; and vol.2, pp.357–361; Murdoch (2), pp.263–5.
27. Murdoch (2), pp.263–5; Namier & Brooke (1), vol.2, pp.357–361.
28. N.L.S. MSS. 10944, f.175; and N.L.S. MSS. 1078, f.1.
29. See Dwyer & Murdoch, pp.211–227.
30. Namier & Brooke, vol.2, pp.357–361; Parker (1), pp.407–408, 416.
31. See Sunter, p.537; Foley, Hayton & Maddock, *passim;* Maclean (1), pp.224, 231, 233; *The Scots Magazine,* for March 1767 and May 1767, pp. 165, 253–254.

11. Shipping Bounty 1765–74

1. Shearer, Appendix K, p.278. (See also *Ibid.* Appendix J, p.277 for ships taken up by the Company 1769–1780). See also Fawcett, pp.35–44; and Appendix.
2. Parker (1), p. 416.
3. *Ibid.* pp.415–418, 477, 481.
4. Wain, p.11; also McGilvary (2), p.370.
5. B.L. Add.MSS. 51431, f.132, Fasham Nairne to Ld. Holland, 11 December 1762.
6. Spencer, p.2; Fawcett, p.39.
7. See also Appendix.
8. I.O.R. Marine Records L/Mar/B; Riddy (1), p.3; Fawcett, pp.67, 183, 196; Spencer, p.3.
9. I am indebted to Dr. James Parker for this information. See also B.L. Add. MSS. 29133, f.563, L. Sulivan to W. Hastings, 23 May 1773; Love, vol.1, p.446.
10. Parker (1), pp.11, 182–186, 401–403, 413, 415–317, 443, 477; Maclean, p.381; Namier & Brooke (1), vol.3, p.379; E.P.L. R. Br. (Roll) XDA, 758.3.F76; Shearer, pp.183; Joslin, pp.353–355; I.O.R. Writers Petitions, J/1/1, for 1754.
11. Namier & Brooke (1), vol.3, p.362; Parker, p.416, footnote 2; Cotton, p.190; B.L. Add. MSS. 29136, L. Sulivan to W. Hastings, 15 February 1775; S.R.O. GD 1/453/Boxes 1–3.
12. Namier & Brooke (1), vol.1, p.167, vol.3, pp.94–95; Grant (2), p.468, 496; Maclean (2), pp.44, 54–55, 95; I.O.R., Marine Records L/Mar/B, for 1759; N.L.S. 1310, f.33; Fawcett, p.189; Parker (1), p.418, 477; Riddy, p.15. His eminence was referred to by a jealous rival, Robert Simson. See S.R.O. GD 156/Box. 49, Bundle 1, f.62, Robert Simson to Lady Clementine Elphinstone, 12 July 1767.
13. Fraser (4), vol.1, pp.5–6; Namier & Brooke (1), vol.2, pp.400–401.
14. S.R.O. GD 156/Box 49/Bundle 2, f.23, 26 for 1755.

15. S.R.O. GD 156/Box 49/Bundle 1, f.3, Charles Elphinstone to the Hon. Chas. Elphinstone, end of August 1757. See also, Fraser (4), vol.2, pp.1–6.
16. S.R.O. GD 156/Box 49/Bundle 1, f.4, J. Hyde to Lady Clementine Elphinstone, 20 October 1770. See also ff.38 to 56 *passim;* and *Ibid,* Bundle 2, f.23, John Elphinstone to Lady Clementine Elphinstone, 7 November 1755, f.123; Earl Marischal to Lady Elphinstone, 16 October 1768; also ff.7 and 17; I.O.R. Marine Records L/Mar/B; Fraser (4), vol.1, pp.5–6, vol.2, pp.1–6; Namier & Brooke (1), vol.2, pp.400–401; Parker (1), pp.416–417; Fawcett, pp.176, 183–5; Spencer, p.5.
17. Spencer, pp.190–191, 218.
18. Fawcett, pp.183–5; Fraser (4), vol.2, pp.6–9. Fullarton of Carberry was referred to as 'one of our East Indians' by Alex Carlyle, writing to the Earl of Dalkeith on 1 November 1759 (See GD 224/295/3/10). He was also, significantly, MP for Haddington District of Burghs.
19. S.R.O. GD 156/Box 49, Bundle 1, ff.57, 58, 74, R. Simson to Lady Clementine Elphinstone, on 10 January 1766 and 26 June 1769; to Chas. Elphinstone on 12 July 1766. One of Simson's illuminating statements was to describe a 'native king' he had met on his voyage out as 'a greater wretch than a Scotch collier.'
20. Sunter, p.528.
21. *Ibid,* pp.518, 521, 539.
22. Namier & Brooke (1), *passim.*
23. B.L. Add. MSS. 29133, f,345, L. Sulivan to W. Hastings, 26 January 1773. See also Add. MSS. 29139, f.248, L. Sulivan to W. Hastings, 30 October 1777.
24. Quoted in Feiling, p.72.

12. Patrons and Recipients 1760–74

1. B. L. Add. MSS. 29136, f, 59, L. Sulivan to W. Hastings, 10 March 1775,
2. S.R.O. GD 240/30/Bundle 6/1–61, undated, but 1782. See also McGilvary (2), pp.301–302.
3. N.L.S. MSS. 1073; 1368.
4. S.R.O. GD 30/1597; GD 30/1901; GD 30/1906.
5. I.O.R. Madras Civil Servants, 1702–1775; N.L.S. MSS. 10787, 1328, 1072; Fawcett, p.134; Love, vol.1, p.556; Spencer (ed.), vol.1, p.171.
6. Allan, p.62; Maclean, (2), pp.157–159.
7. Omand (ed.), p.114.
8. N.L.S. MSS. 1165, f, 57, H. Dundas to John Mackenzie of Delvine, n.d. but 1768.
9. See McGilvary (2), pp. 318–320 *et passim;* also McGilvary (3), pp. 191–275 *passim.*
10. S.R.O. GD 29/2057/7, William Berrie to George Graham, 10 September 1774.
11. See McGilvary (2), pp.325–330, *et passim.* See also McGilvary (3), pp. 212, 220, 221.
12. S.R.O. GD 29/2122/4, R. Mayne to John Graeme, 11 January 1775.
13. *Ibid.*
14. See McGilvary (2), pp. 316–318 *et. passim.*
15. See McGilvary (2), pp. 337–338 *et passim;* Buist, pp.3–21 *et passim;* McGilvary (3), pp.125–178 *passim.*

16. See McGilvary (2), pp.293–294. Also Ch.14.
17. GD 240/41/5/1–2, Memorial dated 11 November 1782. See also GD 240/30/Bundle 6/1–61 passim; GD 240/41/5/1. Copy of James Beck's Will, dated 1777.
18. S.R.O. GD 246/46/1, A. Pringle 'European Letterbook 1776–78'. See also McGilvary (2), pp. 298–299; 303–304; 334–335; 359–360; 361–363, *et. passim*.
19. See B. L. Add. MSS. 29151, ff.167–169, L. Sulivan to W. Hastings, 19 October 1781; also 29153, f.515, L. Sulivan to W. Hastings, 16 April 1773. See also McGilvary (2), pp.365–366; 375–376, *et. passim*.
20. See I.O.L. MSS. Philip Francis Papers, f.53, no.13, P. Francis to D'Oyly, 25 August 1775; Copeland (ed.), vol.2, p.357. See also McGilvary (3), pp.163, 188, 205–6, 223, 258, 265.
21. I.O.R. Court Book, vol.93, pp.642–643 for 6 October 1784. See also McGilvary (2), pp. 365–366.
22. See McGilvary (2), pp.322–323, 369. For the sheer number of Scots involved see Appendix I.O.R. Writers Petitions – J/1/1–15; McGilvary (2), pp. 292–377 *passim*.

13. Military Recruitment 1720–80

1. Love, vol.1, pp.128–9, 157–8, 196, 205, 212, 387, 547, 549; Warren & Barlow, p.36; Campbell, Major Sir D., pp.1, 228; Nightingale, p.19.
2. See Bryant (1), *passim*. The Appendix illustrates how few military personnel were despatched prior to the 1750s.
3. Love, *passim*; Campbell, Major Sir D., *passim*; N.L.S. Minto MSS. 11041, Item 8.
4. Love, vol.3, p.75. See also Appendix.
5. Omand, p.161.
6. See Calder, p.677; and Bryant (1), p.23.
7. See Appendix. It is thought that this equated to approximately one third of the total officer establishment at this time. See Bryant (1), pp.23–24 *et passim*.
8. Bryant (1), pp.27, 31.
9. Namier & Brooke (1), vol. 2, pp.179–180; Campbell, Major Sir D., pp.27–31; Riddy (1), p.3; B.L. Add. MSS. 29166, f.123, L. Sulivan to W. Hastings, 20 August 1784; S.R.O. GD 1/6/3, and GD 1/6/8; Love, vol. 1, p.19; Macinnes, p.26; MacKillop (1), *passim*.
10. Campbell, Major Sir D., pp.50–54; Love, vol.1, pp.486, 556, 588; H.M.S.C. Palk MSS. p.63, f.4; p.64; p.82, note 2 and p.240, no.237, R. Palk to the Nawab of the Carnatic, n.d. but circa March 1774.
11. Campbell, Major Sir D., pp.93–98.
12. *Ibid*, pp.88–92.
13. *Ibid*, pp.83–88.
14. See McGilvary (2), Appendix 9.
15. See Murdoch (2), p.277; Bryant (1), pp.23–28; and McGilvary (2), Appendices 6–10.
16. Quoted in Riddy (1), p.2.
17. See Bryant (1), p.25; S.R.O. GD 128/4/3/4, Col. William Baillie Younger, of Dunain, to his father, Ft. St. George, 10 June 1763. He expected to return

home just as needy as when he came out, 'a poor reward for scorching in the sun.'
18. See S.R.O. GD 224/45/38/Item 3.
19. See N.L.S. MSS. 11041, Item 8.
20. See McGilvary (2), 'Patronage Profiles' and Appendices 6–10 for examples. See also Appendix. Also Bielenberg, p.223 and Holmes, pp.223, 236 for comparison with Irish officers.
21. See Bryant (1), p.23; and Appendix, Part 2.
22. S.R.O. GD 128/1/1/1–26; GD 128/1/3/1–6; GD 128/4/3/2/1–59; GD 128/1/4; Feiling, p.249; Love, vol.3, p.75.
23. See McGilvary (2), pp.355–357; also, McGilvary (3), pp.76, 252; MacKillop (2), pp.246–255.

14. Capital Accumulation 1720–80

1. Neil Davidson, part of the speech given at the Word Power Books Fringe Festival on 15 August 2004, posted on the internet.
2. Devine (3), pp.334, 336.
3. Macinnes, p.27.
4. See Devine (6), pp.41–42, 44. See also Devine (5) p.401, where he says that 'urbanisation' in agriculture and everything else, was 'the dynamic'.
5. Devine, Lee & Peden, (eds.), pp.6–9.
6. Devine (3), pp.328–329.
7. Lee, pp.100–128.
8. Devine, Lee & Peden, (eds.), p.47.
9. Devine, Lee & Peden, (eds.), p.9.
10. See Devine, Lee & Peden, (eds.), p.47; and Devine (5), pp.406, 408
11. Kiernan, p.106. See also Macinnes, p.26.
12. Cummings, pp.48–49, 53, 58.
13. Macinnes, p.10 and pp.1–43, *passim*.
14. Devine, Lee & Peden, (eds.), pp.32–33. Note the effect of over a hundred tobacco magnates purchasing estates in the west of Scotland.
15. Devine (8), pp.1–18; and pp.19–34. Prior to 1707 Scotland was popularly identified with feuds, poverty, economic backwardness and religious intolerance: Glencoe, Darien, Covenanters, 'the killing times', the poor 1690s.
16. Devine (8) p.166; pp.165–6 *passim*.
17. Devine (8), pp.35–59.
18. Devine (8), p.60–78.
19. MacKillop (2), p.239.
20. Devine (8), pp.60–78.
21. *Ibid*. pp.79–83.
22. *Ibid*. pp.60–78; 165–6. It is possible that this class, all good tenants and good farmers, benefited from India money via ships' mates and pursers (perhaps of a more middling social stature) returning with capital.
23. *Ibid*. pp.111–136; 137–165.
24. Devine (3), pp.331–332.
25. See McGilvary (2), pp.292–377, 'Patronage Profiles', especially on John Cumming; and Appendices, *passim*. See also Appendix.

26. Cummings, p.23; also p 26.
27. Devine, Lee & Peden, (eds.), pp.33, 46–50.
28. See McGilvary (2), pp.292–377; and Devine, Lee & Peden, (eds.), pp.14, 35. See also Appendix. The Alexander family was immortalized by Burns in the 'Bonny Lass of Ballochmyle'. Claud Alexander was joined by David Dale in the Catrine works.
29. See McGilvary (2), pp.172–183, 292–377. See also Appendix.
30. Macinnes, p.26.
31. See Cannon, pp.96–101.
32. See Foley, Hayton & Haddock, Appendices 2–4 *et passim*. Subscribers to the Forth–Clyde canal construction, from 13th May to 16th October 1767.
33. *Ibid*. This lists at least 20 Proprietors and/or East India Company Directors.
34. Murray, D, pp.3–111, *passim*; Cummings, pp.47, and pp.43–61, *passim*; Lythe & Butt, pp.112, 175, 189; Mitchison (1), p.328; Youngson, pp.30, 206; Timperley (ed.), *passim*. For Chandos see Chapter 1.
35. Crafts, p.122. The G.N.P. for Britain rose from £57.5 million in 1720 to £64.1 million in 1740; a rise of 11.5% – linked to the 0.30% population rise. (Jubb, p.121).
36. See also Crafts, pp.73, 78.
37. See *Ibid*, p.9. 'Estimates of economic growth (in the eighteenth century)...are bound to be in the nature of controlled conjecture rather than definitive evidence'.
38. *Ibid*, p.123 also p.125.
39. See McGilvary (2), pp.292–377, and Appendices. See also Devine (2), pp.23–40 *passim*; Devine (3) pp.336, that the 'imperial factor' may have explained where the money for agricultural change came from; also *Ibid*., pp.300, 320–322, 328–337, 341–342. See also Appendix.
40. Neil Davidson, part of the speech given at the Word Power Books Fringe Festival on 15 August 2004, posted on the internet. See also Devine (3), p.52.
41. De Bertodano Papers, n.p., Laurence Sulivan's 'Letterbook' to his son Stephen Sulivan, February 1778.
42. See Appendix; McGilvary (2), 'Patronage Profiles' and Appendices; Fawcett, pp.31–37.
43. See Appendix.
44. See Appendix.
45. See Fawcett, p.33, and Farrington (2), Introduction.
46. See Appendix. Also McGilvary (2), pp.292–377, *passim*.

15. Summary and Conclusions

1. See also McGilvary (2), *passim*; and Appendix.
2. Gibb, p.182
3. See also Appendix; Graham, I. C. C., pp.185–189. Prior to 1750 Writers Petitions are scanty; military figures given are for officers not other ranks. See also Mitchison (1), p.344.
4. See also Murdoch (2), p.11.
5. Hechter, pp.103–4.

Bibliography

Primary Manuscript Sources

British Library, London
 B.L. Add.MSS. 5143, 5147, 29133 to 29137, 29139, 29141, 29143, 29147, 29149 to 29151, 29153, 29156, 29166, 29194, 51398, 51431, 51434
Bury St. Edmunds & West Suffolk Record Office
 423/447
Bute Papers, Mountstuart, Rothesay
 ff.276–7; 642; 643
De Bertodano Papers
 MSS. belonging to Mr. Martin De Bertodano. The Papers of Laurence Sulivan. No pagination. (Copies held by G. K. McGilvary)
Edinburgh Public Libraries
 R.Br. (Roll) XDA,758.3.F.76
Edinburgh University Library
 Laing MSS. 11, 73, 77,477; Laing MSS. 111,364; Laing MSS. No.77 Div.2; Strachey MSS
Exeter Record Office
 Kennoway Documents: Palk Family/Haldon Trust. 58/9, Box 104
 Hotson MSS. Papers belonging to Mr. Jack Hotson, Edinburgh
India Office Library, London
Manuscripts.
 Johnstone letters – Eng MSS. No.162; Eur.MSS. Photo No.63; Letterbook of John Spencer–Eur.302/1; Letterbook of George Paterson–Eur.319/4; The Correspondence of Charles Forbes–Eur.D.100; Letterbook of Robert Barwell–Eur.D.535; Letterbook of George Gray–Eur.D.691; A Mackrabie's Journal of a Voyage to the East Indies, 1774–Eur.E.25; Madras Letterbook of Claud Russell– Eur.E.276; Philip Francis Papers– Eur.E.379/4, Eur.E.379/8; Orme MSS.O.V.J

Records
  Bengal Civilians – 0/6/21 to 0/6/29; Bombay Civilians – 0/6/32 to 0/6/35; Bombay Civil Servants – 0/6/36 to 0/6/37; Bombay Public Consultations, vol.18; Court Books, vols. 76, 93; European Inhabitants Bombay 1719–0/5/31; European Inhabitants Madras 1702–178092.0/5/29; General Court Minutes, vols. 3, 5; Home Miscellaneous Series, vol.82; Madras Civilians – 0/6/30 to 0/6/31; Madras Civil Servants, 1702–1775; Marine Records L/Mar/B; L/Mar./C/644; L/Mar./C/651 (Register of Commands 1737–1832); Personal Records – 0/6/14; Records of Fort St. George, Madras (Diary and Consultation Books); Stock holders and Stock purchased 1718 to 1761 – L/AG/14/5/3–12;
  Writers Petitions – J/1/1–15

Mitchell Library, Glasgow
  Sir James Grant's Memorial to Henry Pelham, 30 Oct. 1745. On raising a Highland Regiment for the King's service.–593220/SR.177

National Library of Scotland, Edinburgh
  Small Collections – MSS. 1006, 1026
  Melville Papers – MSS. 1054, 1055, 1060, 1062, 1069, 1072 to 1074, 1078
  Lauriston Castle Collection: Delvine Papers – MSS.1131, 1136, 1137, 1140, 1145, 1147, 1150, 1165, 1167, 1174, 1240, 1247, 1249, 1252 to 1256, 1262, 1273, 1290, 1294, 1297, 1306, 1310, 1328, 1329, 1337, 1364, 1368, 1423, 1481
  Jacobite Papers – MSS. 1694
  Forbes of Culloden Papers – MSS. 2967
  Drummond of Balhaldie Papers – MSS. 3186 to 3189
  Mure of Caldwell Correspondence – MSS. 4944
  Erskine Murray Correspondence – MSS. 5073, 5080, 5082
  Stuart Stevenson Papers: Castlemilk and Torrance Muniments – MSS. 5321, 5330
  Andrew Stuart Papers – MSS. 5346, 5388, 5391, 5400, 8250, 8251, 8256, 8278, 8280, 8352
  Haldane Papers – MSS. 6044, 6102, 6104
  Yester Papers – MSS. 7044, 7046, 7059, 7097
  John Maule's Letterbook, 1748–61 – MSS.10781
  John Davidson of Stewartfield's Letterbook – MSS.10787
  Letters of James Begbie to Thomas Graham – MSS.10872
  Graham of Airth Papers – MSS. 10876, 10878, 10919, 10922, 10942, 10944, 10953 Minto Papers – MSS. 11001 to 11005, 11018, 11027, 11041
  Saltoun Papers – 16513 to 16524, 16535, 16536, 16538, 16543, 16544, 16545,16549, 16553, 16556, 16560, 16565, 16604, 16625, 16628, 16647, 16648, 16653, 16659, 16660, 16662 to 16664, 16666 to 16673, 16713 to 16717, 16746 to 16753, 16747,17532

National Register of Archives
  N.R.A.(S) 631 – The Louden Papers, bundle 3 for 1754, 2 for 1759, 2 and 5 for 1768–71
  N.R.A.(S) 1209 – Argyll Muniments. Survey 1, bundles 45, 193

N.R.A.(S) 1256 – John Murray (Macgregor) Bundle 797. (Held in Strathclyde Regional Archives, Glasgow)
The Bute Papers: Nos. 29, 64, 65; The Shelburne/Henry Fox Correspondence, Nos. 56, 57. (Held in West Register House, Edinburgh)

National Library of Wales, Aberystwyth
Powis MSS: Clive Papers

North Riding Record Office
Affidavit by Robert and Duncan Clerk in 1769

The Public Record Office, London
Chatham MSS – 30/8/56

The Scottish Record Office, Edinburgh
J. & F. Anderson, W.S., Edinburgh. Robert Preston of Woodford Papers – GD1/453/Boxes 1–3
Murison (Morrison) Family Papers, Banffshire, at Troup – GD1/825
Diary of Alex Pringle of Whitebank, 1754 – GD1/808/1/3–4
Articles of Agreement. Sir W. Johnstone: S. Sea Stock.– GD2/39; GD2/412
Clerk of Penicuik Muniments – GD18/3219; GD18/5218; GD18/5408
Bught Collections – GD23
Abercairney Muniments – GD24/1/23; GD24/Sect.1/464C; GD24/Sect.1/464 E; GD24/Sect.1/464 N–O; GD24/Sect.1/482–484; GD24/Sect.1/487–487A; GD24/Sect.1/488–495; GD24/Sect.1/496–503A; GD24/Sect.2/464C
Graham Papers, Kinross House – GD29/32; GD29/1865 to 1871; GD29/2053; GD29/2055 to 2058; GD29/2061; GD29/2069; GD29/2071; GD29/2121 to 2135; GD29/2171, GD29/2174
Shairp of Houston Papers – GD30/1582; GD30/1597; GD30/1707; GD30/1901; GD30/1906.
Elibank Papers – GD32/24/11/25–27, 31,34–57
Melville Castle Muniments – GD51/11/4
Mackay of Bighouse Papers – GD87/33–34
Munro of Foulis Papers – GD93/365; GD93/388
Douglas Collection – GD98/391
Hamilton–Dalrymple of North Berwick Papers – GD110/947/6; GD110/963; GD110/975; GD110/980; GD110/987;GD110/1007; GD110/1021/1–17; GD110/1026; GD110/1134; GD110/1149; GD110/1189; GD110/1303
Fraser–Mackintosh Collection – GD128/1/1/1–26; GD128/1/2; GD128/1/3/1–6; GD128/1/4; GD128/4/3/2/1–59; GD128/4/3/4; GD128/4/3/13, 19, 22, 23
North Esk Papers – GD130/Box 11
Morton Papers – GD150/2639; GD150/3466/1–14; GD150/3470/1–9; GD150/3474/1–60; GD150/3475/1–26; GD150/3477/1–19; GD150/3478/1–45; GD150/3479/1–29; GD150/3483/1–30; GD150/3484/1–21; GD150/3485/1–76; GD150/3490/1–62
Graham of Fintry Muniments – GD151/8/26; GD151/12/2, 8–10; GD151/13/36–37

Elphinstone Muniments – GD156/49/1–95; GD156/49/Bundle 2/1–123; GD156/49/Bundle 3
Buccleuch Papers – GD224/43; GD224/45; GD224/46; GD224/295/1–43; GD224/296/4; GD224/297/3; GD224/925/2; GD224/925/4
Bruce & Kerr, W.S., Haldane Papers – GD240/Box 26/Bundle 5; GD240/30/Bundle 6/1–61; GD240/41/5/1–2
Shepherd & Wedderburn, W.S. – GD242/Box 40/2/14–19
Hope, Todd & Kirk, W.S. – GD246/25/1; GD246/46/1; GD246/89
Seafield Muniments – GD248/49/2/12–13; GD248/49/3; GD248/49/3/7; GD248/50/1/1,10; GD248/50/1/19; GD248/50/2/65; GD248/50/3; GD248/50/5/3; GD248/50/10; GD248/51/2; GD248/61/1/55; GD248/63/1/8; GD248/63/1/29; GD248/229/5/1; GD248/783; GD248/784

Microfilm – (West Register House, Edinburgh)
R.H. 4, reel 14; R.H. 4/70., reel 1 Bundle 55; R.H. 4/98, reel 1, Appendix 25; R.H. 4/98, reel 8; R.H. 4/98, reel 10; R.H. 4/151

Sheffield City Library
Wentworth–Woodhouse MSS. The Correspondence of Charles 2nd Marquis of Rockingham. R.1–1443

Strathclyde Regional Archives, Glasgow
Argyll Papers –TD 40
Stirling of Keir Papers – TD 368/3
Argyll Correspondence – TD 574, 575, 589, 600

Acts of Parliament
Geo. III, c.9

Selected Printed Works

(All books below are cited by *author's surname*. If an author has more than one work quoted, then *the surname is followed by a number* [in sequence] distinguishing each particular work. Authors with the same surname are differentiated by their initials.)

Adam, Sir C. E. (ed.), *View of the Political State of Scotland in the Last Century*. (1887)
Allan, D. C. C., 'The Contest for the Secretaryship 1769–70', (Studies in the Society's Archives xxxvi–xxxvix), in *Journal of the Royal Society of Arts*, vols. 112–113. (August–December 1964).
Allardyce, A. (ed.), *Scotland and Scotsmen in the Eighteenth Century, from the Manuscripts of John Ramsay esquire, of Ochtertyre*. 2 vols. (1888)
Anderson, W., *The Scottish Nation: Biographical History of the People of Scotland*. 3 vols. (1861)
Barun De', 'Henry Dundas and the Government of India (1773–1801). A Study in Constitutional Ideas'. (Oxford University D.Phil. Thesis, 1961)
Berg, J. & Lagercrantz, B., *Scots in Sweden*. (1962)
Bielenberg, A, 'Irish Emigration to the British Empire 1700–1914', in Bielenberg, A. (ed.), *The Irish Diaspora*. (2000)
Bolitho, H. & Peel, D., *The Drummonds of Charing Cross*. (1963)
Brady, F. (1), *Boswell's Political Career*. (1965)

____(2), ' "So fast to ruin". The personal element in the collapse of Douglas, Heron And Co.', in *Ayrshire Archaeological and Natural History Society for 1973*, Ayrshire Collections, vol. 11, no.2

Bricke, M. S., 'The Pelhams v Argyll 1747–1748', in *Scottish Historical Review*, no.61

Bremner, D., *The Industries of Scotland.* (1969)

Brooke, J., *The Chatham Administration.* (1956)

Bryant, G. J. (1), 'Scots in India in the Eighteenth Century', in *Scottish Historical Review*, vol. lxiv, 1, no.177, April 1985

____(2), 'The East India Company and its Army 1600–1778.' (Ph.D. thesis, London 1975)

____(3), 'Officers of the East India Company's Army in the Days of Clive and Hastings', in Patrick Tuck, *The East India Company 1600–1858.* vol.5. (1998)

Buddle, A. with Rohatgi P. & G. Brown, I. G., *The Tiger and the Thistle: Tipu Sultan and the Scots in India, 1760–1800.* (1999)

Buist, N. G., *At Spes Non Fracta: Hope & Co. 1770–1815.* (1974)

Bullock, J. M., *Territorial Soldiering in North–East Scotland, 1759–1814.* (1914)

Burke, Sir B. (1), *Landed Gentry*, 1848, 1858, 1875, 1925, 1939 editions

____(2), *Peerage and Baronetage*, 1959 edition

Cage, R. A. (ed.), *The Scots Abroad: Labour, Capital, Enterprise, 1750–1914.* (1984)

Cain, A.M., The *Cornchest for Scotland, Scots in India.* (1986)

Calder, A., *Revolutionary Empire, the Rise of the English–Speaking Empires from the Fifteenth Century to the 1780s.* (1981)

Campbell, Major Sir D., *Records of Clan Campbell in the Military Service of the Honourable East India Company, 1600–1858.* (1925)

Campbell, R. H., *Scotland since 1707, the Rise of an Industrial Society.* (Oxford 1971).

Cannon, J., *The Whig Ascendancy.* (1981)

Carlyle, A., *The Autobiography of Dr. Alexander Carlyle of Inveresk, 1722–1805.* (1910)

Carmichael, E. K., 'Jacobitism in the Scottish Commission of the Peace, 1707–1760', in *Scottish Historical Review*, vol. lviii, 1: no.165, Apr. 1979

Carswell, J., *The South Sea Bubble.* (1960)

Carter, J. J., 'The Making of Principal Robertson in 1762: Politics and the University of Edinburgh in the second half of the eighteenth century', in *Scottish Historical Review*, vol. 49, for 1970

Checkland, S. G., *Scottish Banking: A History 1695–1973.* (1925)

Christie, I. R., *The Fall of North's Ministry 1780–1782.* (1958).

Cockayne (ed.), G.E.C. Complete Baronetage, 6 vols. (1900–1909)

Colebrooke, Sir G., '*Retrospection' or Reminiscences Addressed to my son Henry Thomas Cole–Brooke Esquire*, 2 vols (1898)

Coleridge, E. H., *The Life of Thomas Coutts, Banker*, 2 vols. (1920)

Colley, L., *Britons: Forging the Nation 1707–1837.* (1992)

Copeland, T. W. (ed.), *The Correspondence of Edmund Burke.* vols.1, 2, 4, 5. (1958)

Cormack, A. A. (1), *An Historic Outline of the George Smith Bounty, (Fordyce Academy).* (1952)

____(2), *The Carnegie Family in Gothenburg.* (1942)

Coxe, W., *Memoirs of the Administration of the Rt. Hon. H. Pelham.* 2 vols. (1829)

Crafts, N. F. R., *British Economic Growth during the Industrial Revolution.* (1985)

Cranmer–Bying, J. L., *An Embassy to China.* (1962)

Crawford, D. G, *Roll of the Indian Medical Service 1615–1930*. (1930)
Crawfurd, G., *Shire of Renfrew*. (1818)
Cruickshanks, E., 'The Political Management of Sir Robert Walpole 1720–42'; in Black, J. (ed.), *Britain in the Age of Walpole*. (1984)
Cummings, A. J. G., 'The Business Affairs of an Eighteenth Century Lowland Laird: Sir Archibald Grant of Monymusk 1696–1778'; in *Scottish Elites: Proceedings of the Scottish Historical Studies Seminar, University of Glasgow*. (1994)
Daiches, D. (1), *The Paradox of Scottish Culture: The Eighteenth Century Experience*. (1964)
____(2), *Scotland and the Union*. (1977)
Davidson, N., *Discovering the Scottish Revolution 1692–1746,* (2003)
Datta, K. K., Sinha, H. N, Sethi, R. R., Srinivasachari, C. S., Bhargava, K. D. (eds.), *Fort William – India House Correspond*ence, vols. 1–6. (Delhi 1957 to 1960)
Davies, A.M., *Clive of Plassey*. (1939)
Dé, B., 'Henry Dundas and the Government of India (1773–1801). A Study in Constitutional Ideas'. (Oxford University D.Phil. thesis, 1961)
Devine, T. M. (1), *The Tobacco Lords*. (1975)
____(2), 'The Union of 1707 and Scottish Development', in *Scottish Economic and Social History,* vol.5, for 1985
____(3), *Scotland's Empire*. (2003)
____(4), *The Scottish Nation 1700–2000*. (1999)
____(5), 'Scotland,' in Floud, R., & Johnson, P., *Cambridge Economic History of Modern Britain*. (2004)
____(6), 'Capital', in Devine, T. M., Lee, C. H. & Peden, G. C. (eds.), *Transformation of Scotland: the economy since 1700*. (2005)
____(7), 'Anglo–Scottish Relations from 1603 to 1900', in *Proceedings of the British Academy,* vol.127. (2005)
____(8), *The Transformation of Rural Scotland: Social Change and the Agrarian Economy 1660–1815*. (1999)
Devine, T. M., Lee, C. H. & Peden, G. C. (eds.), *Transformation of Scotland: the economy since 1700*. (2005)
Devine, T. M. & Young, J. R. (eds.), *Eighteenth Century Scotland: New Perspectives*. (1999)
Dickinson, H., *Walpole and the Whig Supremacy*. (1973)
Dickson, P. G .M, *The Financial Revolution in England*. (1967)
Dickson, T. (ed.), *Scottish Capitalism: Class, State and Nation from before the Union to the Present*. (1980)
Dickson, W. K. (ed.), 'Letters to John Mackenzie of Delvine, Advocate, one of the Principal Clerks of Session, from the Rev. Alex. Monroe, D.D., Principal of Edinburgh University, 1690–1698', in *Miscellany of the Scottish History Society*. (5th vol.) (1933)
(The) Dictionary of National Biography 26 vols. (1885–1901)
(The Oxford) Dictionary of National Biography, vol.53. (2004)
Dodwell, E. & Miles, J. S., *Alphabetical List of Officers of the Indian Army, 1760–1837*. (1838)
Dodwell, H. H., *The Nabobs of Madras*. (1926)
Donaldson, G. (1), *The Scots Overseas*. (1966)

____(2), *Scotland: The Shaping of a Nation.* (1980)
Donaldson, G. & Morpeth, R., *Who's Who in Scottish History.* (1973)
Donnelly, T., 'The Economic Activities of the Aberdeen Merchant Guild, 1750–1790', in *Scottish Economic and Social History,* vol. 1, 1981
Dwyer, J., Mason, R. A., Murdoch, A. (eds.), *New Perspectives on the Politics and Culture of Early Modern Scotland.* (1982)
Dwyer, J. & Murdoch, A., 'Paradigms and Politics: Morals, Manners and the Rise of Henry Dundas, 1770–1784', in (eds.) Dwyer, J, Mason, R. A., Murdoch, A., *New Perspectives on the Politics and Culture of Early Modern Scotland.* (1982)
Edwardes, M., *Warren Hastings: King of the Nabobs.* (1976)
Elliot (Lady) of Stobs & Elliot Sir A., 11th Bart. of Stobs, *The Elliots.* (1974)
Farrington, A. (1), *East India Ships' Journals and Logs 1600–1834.* (1999)
____(2), *A Biographical Index of the East India Maritime Officers 1600–1834.* (2000)
Fawcett, Sir C. (ed.), *East Indiamen: The East India Company's Maritime Service, by Sir Evan Cotton.* (1949)
Feiling, K., *Warren Hastings.* (1954)
Feinstein, C. H., 'Capital Accumulation and the Industrial Revolution', in Floud, R & McLoskey, D. (eds.), *The Economic History of Britain since 1700,* vol.1. (1981)
Ferguson, J. P. S., *Scottish Family Histories held in Scottish Libraries.* (Edinburgh 1960).
Ferguson, W. (1), Dingwall Burgh Politics and the Parliamentary Franchise in the Eighteenth Century, in *Scottish Historical Review,* vol.38 (Oct. 1959), no.126
____(2), *Scotland 1689 to the Present.* (1968)
____(3), The Electoral System in the Scottish Counties before 1832, in *Miscellany Two, of the Stair Society,* (1984)
Fergusson, J. (ed.) (1), *Letters of George Dempster to Sir Adam Fergusson 1756–1811.* (1934)
____(2), 'Making Interest in Scottish County Elections', in *Scottish Historical Review,* xxvi, 1947
Floud, R., & Johnson, P., *Cambridge Economic History of Modern Britain.* (2004)
Foley, A. L., Hayton, P., Maddock, P. J., 'The Forth–Clyde Canal. From its Inception to its Completion 1762–1794'. (Edinburgh University Undergraduate Thesis, 1971)
Forrest, Sir G. W., *Selections from the Letters Despatches and other State Papers preserved in the Bombay Secretariat, Home Series.* 2 vols. (1887)
Foster, J., *Members of Parliament, Scotland 1757–1882.* (1882)
Fraser, Sir W. (1), *The Stirlings of Keir and Cawdor.* (1858)
____(2), *Chiefs of Grant.* (1883)
____(3), *The Annandale Family Book of the Johnstones, Earls and Marquises of Annandale.* 2 vols. (1894)
____(4), *The Elphinstone Family Book of The Elphinstones, Balmerino and Coupar.* 2 vols. (1897)
Fry, H. J., *Alexander Dalrymple (1737–1808) and the Expansion of British Trade.* (1970)
Fry, M. (1), *Patronage and Principle.* (1987)
____(2), *The Dundas Despotism.* (1992)
____(3) 'A Commercial Empire: Scotland and British Expansion in the Eighteenth Century, in Devine T. M. & Young J. R. (eds.), *Eighteenth Century Scotland: New Perspectives.* (1999)

Furber, H. (1), *Henry Dundas, 1st Viscount Melville, 1742–1811.* (1931)
___(2), 'The East India Directors in 1784', in, *J. of Modern History.* vol.5, (1933)
___(3), *John Company at Work.* (1948)
Fyfe, J. G. (1), *Selected Diaries and Memoirs, 1550–1746.* (1928)
___(2), *Selected Diaries and Memoirs, 1746–1843.* (1942)
Gardner, B., *The East India Company.* (1971)
Gentleman's Magazine, vol.34 of 1764
Gibb, A. D., *Scottish Empire.* (1937)
Gill, C., *Merchants and Mariners of the Eighteenth Century.* (1961)
Gleig, G. R. (1), *The Life of Robert 1st Lord Clive,* (1848)
___(2), *Memoirs of The Life of the Rt. Hon. Warren Hastings,* 3 vols. (1841)
Graeme, L. G., *'Or And Sable'. A Book of the Graemes and Grahams.* (1903)
Graham, E. M., *The Oliphants of Gask.* (1910)
Graham, I. C. C., *Colonists from Scotland.* (1972)
Grant, I. F. (1), *The Economic History of Scotland.* (1934)
___(2), *The Macleods, The History of a Clan, 1200–1956.* (1959)
Gray, J. M. (ed.), *Memoirs of the Life of Sir John Clerk of Penicuik, Baronet, Baron of the Exchequer, Extracted by himself from his own Journals, 1676–1755.* (1892)
Grier, S.C., *The Letters of Warren Hastings to his Wife.* (1905)
Gurney, J. D., 'The Debts of the Nawab of Arcot, 1763–1776. (Oxford University D.Phil. Thesis 1968)
Hadley, W. (ed.), *Horace Walpole's Selected Letters.* (1963)
Haldane, Sir J. A., *The Haldanes of Gleneagles.* 2 vols. (1929)
Hamilton, Captain A., *A New Account of the East Indies.* (circa 1700)
Hansard, T. C. & Cobbett, W., (eds.), *The Parliamentary History of England From the Earliest Period to the Year 1803.* (1813–14)
Hardy, C., *Register of The East India Company's Shipping.* (1799)
Hatton, R. M. (1), 'John Drummond of Quarrel', in *Scottish Historical Review,* vol.38 (October 1959), no. 126.
___(2), 'John Drummond of Quarrel', in *The Scottish Genealogist,* vol. xvii, no.3, (1970)
___(3) 'John Drummond in, 'The War of the Spanish Succession: A Merchant Turned Diplomatic Agent', in *Studies in Diplomatic History: Essays in Memory of David Bayne Horn.* (1970)
Hatton, R. M. & Anderson, M. S. (eds.), *Studies in Diplomatic History: Essays in Memory of David Bayne Horn.* (1970)
Hechter, M., *Internal Colonialism: The Celtic Fringe in British National Development, 1530–1966.* (1975)
Hodson, V. C. P., *List of the Officers of the Bengal Army 1758–1834.* 4 vols. (1927)
Holmes, M. 'The Irish And India: Imperialism, Nationalism, Internationalism', in Bielenberg, A. (ed.), *The Irish Diaspora.* (2000)
Hyde, M. H., *John Law: The History of an Honest Adventurer.* (1948)
Insh, G. P., *The Company of Scotland Trading to Africa and The Indies.* (1932)
Johnstone, C. L., *History of the Johnstones, 1191–1909.* (1909)
Jones, C., 'Godolphin: The Whig Junto and the Scots: A new Lords Division List for 1709', in *Scottish Historical Review,* vol. 58 (1979)
Jones, G. H., *The Main Stream of Jacobitism.* (1954)

Joslin, D. M., 'London Private Bankers: 1720–1785', in Essays in *Economic History*, vol.2, (ed) E. M. Carus–Wilson. (1966)
Jubb, M., 'Economic Policy and Economic Development'; in Black, J. (ed.), *Britain in the Age of Walpole*. (1984)
Judd, G. P., *Members of Parliament 1734–1832*. (1955)
Keith, T., 'Municipal Elections in the Royal Burghs of Scotland. From The Union to the Passing of the Scottish Burgh Reform Bill in 1833', in *Scottish Historical Review*, xiii (1916)
Khan, A. M., 'Muhammed Reza Khan, Naib Nazim and Naib Diwan of Bengal, 1756–1775'. London University Ph.D. Thesis (1966)
Kiernan, V., 'Scottish Soldiers and the conquest of India' in Simpson, G. (ed.), The Scottish Soldier abroad, 1247–1967. (1992)
Kinsley, J. (ed.), *Alexander Carlyle, Anecdotes and Characters of the Times*. (1973)
Laing MSS., H.M.S.C.
Lang, A., *The Companions of Pickle*. (1898)
Lee, C.H., 'Establishment of the Financial Network', in Devine, T. M., Lee, C. H. & Peden, G. C. (eds.), *Transformation of Scotland: the economy since 1700*. (2005)
Lenman, B. (1), *The Jacobite Risings in Britain 1689–1746*. (London 1980).
____(2), *Integration, Enlightenment and Industrialisation, Scotland, 1746–1832*. (1981)
____(3), 'A Client Society: Scotland between the '15 and the '45'; in Black, J. (ed.), *Britain in the Age of Walpole*. (1984)
Love, H. D., *Vestiges of Old Madras 1640–1800*. 4 vols. (1913)
Low, C. R., *History of the Indian Navy 1613–1863*. vol.1. (1877)
Lythe, S. G. E. & Butt, J., *An Economic History Of Scotland 1100–1939*. (1975)
Macaulay MSS., H.M.S.C.
McElroy, G., 'Col. James Stuart and the Coup against Lord Pigot'. (Unpublished article)
McGilvary, G. K. (1), 'The Early Life and Career of Laurence Sulivan, 1713–1765'. M.Litt. Thesis. (Edinburgh University, 1978)
____(2), 'East India Patronage and the Political Management of Scotland, 1720–1774'. Ph.D. Thesis. (The Open University, 1989)
____(3), *Guardian of the East India Company: The Life of Laurence Sulivan*. (2005)
____(4), 'Post–Union Scotland and the Indian Connection', *Cencrastus*, 37 (summer 1990)
Macinnes, A., 'Landowners, Land use and Elite Enterprise in Scottish Gaeldom: From Clanship to Clearance in Argyllshire 1688–1858'; in *Scottish Elites: Proceedings of the Scottish Historical Studies Seminar, University of Glasgow*. (1994)
Mackay, A., *The Book of Mackay*. (1906)
Mackenzie, A. (1), *History of the Mackenzies*. (1894)
____(2), *History of the Munros of Foulis*. (1898)
Mackenzie, Sir A. M. (1), *Memoirs of Delvine*. (1901)
____(2), 'Scotland and the Empire: India', in *S.M.T. Magazine and Scottish Country Life*, vol. xxxi, no.6. (June 1943)
____(3), (ed.) *Scottish Pageant 1707–1802*. (1950)
Mackenzie, W. C., *The Highlands and Islands of Scotland*. (1969)
Mackie, J. D., *A History of Scotland*. (1966)

MacKillop, A. (1), 'Fashioning a British Empire: Sir Archibald Campbell of Inverneil and Madras', 1785–9, in Idem and Murdoch, S., (eds.), *Military Governors and Imperial Frontiers c.1600–1800.* (2003)

____(2), 'The Highlands and the Returning Nabob: Sir Hector Munro of Novar', in Harper, M., (ed.), *Emigrant Homecomings: The Return Movement of Emigrants, 1600–2000.* (2005)

MacKillop, A & Murdoch, S. (1), *Fighting for Identity: Scottish Military Experience 1550–1900.* (2002)

____(2), *Military Governors and Imperial Frontiers 1600–1800.* (2003) McLaren, M., *British India and British Scotland, 1780–1830: Career Building, Empire Building and a Scottish School of Thought on Indian Governance.* (2001)

Maclean, J. N. M. (1), *Reward is Secondary: The Life of a Political Adventurer and an Inquiry into the Mystery Of "Junius".* (1963)

____(2), 'The Early Political Careers of James 'Fingal'' Macpherson (1736–1796) and Sir John Macpherson, Bart. (1744–1821)'. (Edinburgh University Ph.D. Thesis, 1967)

Maclean, V., *"Much Entertainment". A Visual and Culinary Record of Johnson and Boswell's Tour of Scotland in 1773.* (1973)

Macpherson, J, *The Poems of Ossian.* (1773)

Macpherson, W. C., *Soldiering in India 1764–1787.* (1928)

Macrae, Rev. A., *History of the Clan Macrae.* (1899)

Malcolm, Sir J, *The Life of Robert Lord Clive,* 3 vols. (1836)

Marshall, P. J. (1), *Problems of Empire: Britain and India 1757–1813.* (1968)

____(2), 'The Bengal Commercial Society of 1775: Private British Trade in the Warren Hastings Period', in *Bulletin of The Institute of Historical Research,* vol. xlii (1969)

____(3), 'British Expansion in India in the Eighteenth Century; A Historical Revision', in *History,* vol.60. (1975)

____(4), *East India Fortunes – The British in Bengal in the Eighteenth Century.* (1976)

____(5), (ed.), 'The Eighteenth Century', in *The Oxford History of the British Empire,* vol.2. (1998)

Mason, J., 'Conditions in the Highlands after the 'Forty–Five', in *Scottish Historical Review,* xxvi (1947)

Matheson, C., *The Life of Henry Dundas, first Viscount Melville, 1742–1811.* (1933)

Mathieson, W. L., *The Awakening of Scotland. A History from 1747–1797.* (1910)

Memorials of the Public Life and Character of the Rt. Hon. James Oswald of Dunniker. (1825)

Menery, G., *The Life and Letters of Duncan Forbes of Culloden.* (1936)

Millar, A. H., *Historical and Descriptive Accounts of the Castles and Mansions of Ayrshire.* (1885)

Miscellany of the Scottish History Society (5th vol.)

Mitchison, R. (1), *A History of Scotland.* (1970)

____(2), *Life in Scotland.* (1978)

____(3), *Lordship and Patronage. Scotland 1603–1745.* (1980)

Murdoch, A. J. (1), "The People Above". Politics and Administration in Mid–Eighteenth Century Scotland'. (Edinburgh University Ph.D. Thesis, 1978)

____(2), *The People Above.* (1980)

___(3), 'The Importance of being Edinburgh. Management and Opposition in Edinburgh Politics 1746–1784', in *Scottish Historical Review*, vol. lxii, no.173. (1983)

___(4), 'Lord Bute, James Stuart Mackenzie, and the government of Scotland', in K. W. Schweizer (ed.), *Lord Bute: Essays in Re-Interpretation*. (1988)

Mure, W., of Caldwell, *Selections from the Family Papers Preserved at Caldwell*. 3 vols. (1854)

Murray, Col. Hon. A. C., *The Five Sons of Bare Betty*. (1936)

Murray, C. De B., *Duncan Forbes of Culloden*, (1936)

Murray, D., *The York Buildings Company*. (1883)

Namier, Sir L. (1), *Crossroads of Power*. (1962)

___(2), *The Structure Of Politics at the Accession of George III*. 2nd edition. (1965)

___(3), *England in the Age of the American Revolution*. (1966)

Namier, Sir L. & Brooke, J. (1), *The History of Parliament, 1754–1790*. 3 vols. (1964)

___(2), *Charles Townshend*. (1964)

Nightingale, P., *Trade and Empire in Western India 1784–1806*. (1970)

Norris, J., *Shelburne and Reform*. (1963)

(The) Old Country Houses of the Old Glasgow Gentry. (1878)

Omand, G. W. (ed.), *The Arniston Memoirs: Three Centuries of a Scottish House, 1751–1838*. (1887)

Palk MSS., H.M.S.C.

Park, Sir J. B., *The Scots Peerage*. 10 Vols. (1909)

Parker, J. G. (1), 'The Directors of the East India Company, 1754–1790'. Ph.D. Thesis, (University Of Edinburgh, 1977)

___(2), 'Scottish Enterprise in India, 1750–1914', in Cage, R. (ed.), *The Scots Abroad*. (1984)

Parkinson, C. N., *Trade in the Eastern Seas, 1793–1813*. (1937)

Parry, J. H., *Trade and Dominion. The European Overseas Empires in the Eighteenth Century*. (1971)

Paterson, J. (1), *History of Ayrshire*. 2 vols. (1847)

___(2), *History and Regality of Musselburgh*. (1857)

Philips, C. H. (1), *The East India Company 1784–1834*. (1961)

___(2), *Handbook of Oriental History*. (1963)

Phillipson, N. T., 'Lawyers, Landowners and the Civil Leadership of Post–Union Scotland', in *The Juridical Review*, (1976), part 2.

Phillipson, N. T. & Mitchison, R. (eds.), *Scotland in the Age of Improvement*. (1970)

Plumb, J. H. (1), *Sir Robert Walpole: The Making of the Statesman*. (1956)

___(2), *Sir Robert Walpole: The King's Minister*. (1960)

Portland MSS., H.M.S.C.

Pottle, F. A., *Boswell's London Journal 1762–1763*. (1951)

Pringle, A., *The Records of the Pringles of the Scottish Borders*. (1933)

Prinsep, C. C., *Record of the Services of the Honourable East India Company's Civil Servants 1741–1858*. (1885)

Public Advertiser for: 9 April 1763; 14 January 1772; 5 June 1772; 19 August 1772; 14 September 1772; 19 October 1772.

Realey, C. B., *The Early Opposition to Sir Robert Walpole 1720–1774*. (1931)

Records of the Royal Medical Society. (Bristo Square, Edinburgh)

(The) Regality Club. 1st Series. (1889)

Reid, J. M., *Scotland Past and Present.* (1959)

Riddy, J. C. P. (1), " 'Shaking The Pagoda Tree'. How the Scots Came to Amazing Riches–The Union, John Company and Scotland in The Eighteenth Century'. (Unpublished Article)

____(2), 'Warren Hastings: Scotland's Benefactor', in G. Carnall & C. Nicholson (eds.), *The Impeachment of Warren Hastings.* (1989)

Riley, P. W. J. (1), *The English Ministers and Scotland, 1707–1727.* (1964)

____(2), *The Union of England and Scotland.* (1978)

____(3), *King William and the Scottish Politicians.* (1979)

Roach, J., 'The 39th Regiment of Foot and the East India Company, 1754–1757', in *Bulletin of the John Rylands Library,* vol.41, no.1. (September 1958)

Robertson, I. A., 'The Earl of Kinnoul's Bridge, the construction of the Bridge of Tay at Perth, 1763–1772', in *Scottish Economic and Social History,* vol.6. (1986)

Ross, Sir E. D. & Power, E. (eds.), *Memoirs of an Eighteenth Century Footman, John Macdonald's Travels. 1745–1779.* (1927)

Royal Society of Arts, *Guard Book,* vol.1. (The Strand, London)

Royal Society of Arts, *Minutes,* vol.15 (1769–70). (The Strand, London)

Saunders, T. B., *The Life and Letters of James Macpherson.* (1895)

Scott, K. S. M., *Scott 1118–1923.* (1910)

Scott, R. H., 'The Politics and Administration of Scotland 1725–1748. (Edinburgh University Ph.D. Thesis, 1982)

Scottish Elites: Proceedings of the Scottish Historical Studies Seminar, University of Glasgow. (1994)

Scottish Modesty Displayed, In a Series of Conversations Between an Englishman and a Scotsman. London 1778. (Edinburgh Public Library, Tract XDA 758)

Sedgwick, R., (1), (ed.) *Letters from George III to Lord Bute, 1756–1776.* (1939)

____(2), *The House of Commons 1715–1754.* 2 vols. (1970)

Shaw, J. S., *The Management of Scottish Society 1707–1764: Power, Nobles, Lawyers, Edinburgh Agents and English Influences.* (1983)

Shearer, T., 'Crisis and Change in the Development of the East India Company's Affairs, 1760–1773'. Ph.D. Thesis, (University of Oxford, 1976)

Simpson, J. M., 'Who Steered the Gravy Train', in Phillipson, N.J. & Mitchison, R. (eds.), *Scotland in the Age of Improvement, Essays in Scottish History in the Eighteenth Century.* (1970)

Smailes, H., *Scottish Empire: Scots in Pursuit of Hope and Glory.* (1981)

Smith, V. A., *Oxford History of India.* (1967)

Smout. T. C. (1), 'Scottish Landowners and Economic Growth, 1650–1850', in *Scottish Journal of Political Economy,* vol. xi, (1964)

____(2), *A History of the Scottish People 1560–1830.* (1973)

____(3), *Provost Drummond.* Edinburgh University Extra–Mural Department. (1978)

Snoddy, T. G., *Sir John Scott, Lord Scotstarvit.* (1968)

(The) Society of Writers to His Majesty's Signet. (1936)

Spear, P. (1), *The Nabobs.* (1932)

____(2), *A History Of India.* (1965)

Spencer, A. (ed.), *Memoirs of William Hickey,* 3 vols. (1913)

Steele, M., 'Anti-Jacobite Pamphleteering 1701–1720', in *Scottish Historical Review*, vol. lx, no.170. (1981)
Stewart, Col. D., *Sketches of the Character, Manners and Present State of the Highlands of Scotland, with Details of the Military Service of the Highland Regiments*. 2 vols. (1917)
Stirling–Home–Drummond–Moray MSS., H.M.S.C.
Stirling–Maxwell of Keir MSS., H.M.S.C.
Stuart, M., Sc*ottish Family History*. (1930)
Stuart, M. M. (1), 'With the Brittania and the Hindostan', in *South East Asian Review*, vol.7, no.4 (July 1974)
____(2), 'Lying Under the Company's Displeasure', in *South Asian Review*, vol.8, No.1 (October 1974)
____(3), 'In Djudgement of Djanson'. (Unpublished Article)
Stuart–Wortley, E. (ed.), *A Prime Minister and his Son. From The Correspondence of the 3rd Earl of Bute and of Lt. Gen. The Hon. Sir Charles Stuart, K.B*. (1925)
Sunter, R. M. (1), 'Stirlingshire Politics 1707–1832'. (Edinburgh University Ph.D. Thesis, 1971)
____(2), *Patronage and Politics in Scotland 1707–1832*. (1986)
Sutherland, L. S, (1), *The East India Company In Eighteenth–Century Politics*. 2nd edition, (1962)
____(2), *A London Merchant 1695–1774*. (1933)
____(3), 'Lord Shelburne and East India Company Politics 1766–69, in *English Historical Review*, vol.49 (1934)
____(4), 'The East India Company and The Peace of Paris', in *English Historical Review*, vol.62 (1947)
Sutherland, L. S. & Binney, J., 'Henry Fox as Paymaster General of the Forces', in *English Historical Review*, vol.70, (1955)
Sutton, J, *Lords of the East: The East India Company and its ships (1600–1874)*. (2000)
Taylor, H., 'John, Duke of Argyll and Greenwich', in *Scottish Historical Review*, xxvi, (1947)
Taylor, W. S. & Pringle, J. H. (eds.), *Correspondence of William Pitt, Earl of Chatham*. 4 vol. (mdcccxl)
Thomson, Rev. T., *A Biographical Dictionary of Eminent Scotsmen*. 2 vols. (1875)
Timperley, L. R. (ed.), *A Directory of Landownership in Scotland, c.1770*. (1976)
Trevor-Roper, H., 'The Ossian Forgeries', in *The Spectator* (16 March 1985)
Wain, J, *The Journals of James Boswell 1762–1795*. (1991)
Warren, W. H. & Barlow, N., *St. Mary's Church, Fort St. George, Madras*. (1967)
Watson, J., *The Scot of the Eighteenth Century (His Religion and his Life)*. (undated)
Watson, J. S., *The Reign of George 111, 1760–1815*. (1960)
Weitzman, S., *Warren Hastings and Philip Francis*. (1929)
Wheeler, J. T., *Annals of James Macrae Esq.: Governor of Madras 1725–31*. (1862)
Whetstone, A. E., *Scottish County Government in the Eighteenth and Nineteenth Centuries*. (1981)
Williams, B. (1), *Life of William Pitt, Earl of Chatham*. 2 vols. (1913)
____(2),*The Whig Supremacy*. 2nd Edition (1952)
Youngson, A. J.,*After The Forty–Five*. (1973)

GLOSSARY

(Signified in the text by an asterisk*)

Argathelians: Followers and supporters of the Dukes of Argyll.

Bills of exchange: Rupees were paid into a Settlement's treasury in India; the equivalent sum, in sterling, was recovered by an agent in London after the sales.

Charter parties were the signatories (ships owners as well as master) who agreed with the Company to the terms of the hire of a ship.

Country (coastal) trade was the term used to signify European commerce with Indian peoples and merchants throughout the East Indies. The normal commerce was in peppers and spices, silks and betel nut, indigo, cotton and saltpetre. This exchange was distinct from the traffic of goods to and from India and Europe carried by EastIndiamen.

Dastak: The passport or permit granted to the Company to trade.

Directors: Proprietors who owned £2,000 of Company stock chosen by ballot at the East India Company election in April of each year (until 1774).

Durbar: A court, audience or levee: executive government of an Indian state.

EastIndiamen: Company registered ships that had the monopoly of sailing from London to the East Indies and return.

Factor: The second appointment in the Company's civil service in the Settlements abroad.

Free Merchant (Free trader): European (usually British) involved in the country (or coastal) trade along the coasts of India and in the Indies in general. No commerce was allowed with Europe.

General Letters: Official communications from the Directors in London to the Presidencies; and the same from the Governor and Council of each Presidency to India House.

Jagir: This was a quit-rent paid for territory. It was 'A tenure common under Mughal rule, in which the revenues of a given tract of land along with the power of government were made over to a servant of the state. The assignment was either conditional or unconditional, usually for life, lapsing, on the holder's death, to the state.' (Philips (2), p.66)

Lakh: A sum of rupees worth approximately £12,500 in the eighteenth century.

Glossary

Leadenhall Street: Location of India House, Company headquarters.

Nabob: Derisive name given to rich returned East India Company personnel, most of whom purchased estates and became great landowners.

Pagoda: The gold coin formerly minted at Madras, named thus because of the temple device on its face.

Permanent bottoms: came to mean a vested right by owners and/or Commanders to a ship in the Company's service.

Perpetuity of Command: came to mean a vested right by a Commander to a right of command. It became a 'property' to sell, with control over appointments; a monopoly.

Proprietors: Owners of East India Stock.

Resident: East India Company chief official and representative at principal settlements within Presidencies. [After Warren Hastings, the title applied to representatives of the Governor–General at important native courts].

Rupees: In the mid–eighteenth century a rupee was worth between two and three shillings sterling.

Ryots: Indian peasant farmers.

Scottish Money (*Of Auld Extent*): When King James VI of Scotland came to the throne of England (1603) the exchange rate for Scots pounds to sterling was fixed at 12:1. The merk (worth 13 shillings and 4 pence) was mostly a unit of account, but was sporadically minted. Scottish currency was withdrawn after the Act of Union in 1707, but rents and wages, also values (mainly of agricultural produce) continued to be stated in Scottish money.

Sepoys: The name given to Indian troops.

Ships Husband: For purposes of organisation one of the owners chosen as managing-owner, agent, or, as he was usually called, 'ships husband.' He was responsible for supervising the building, fitting and sailing of the ship and had to keep complete accounts. These were incorporated into those kept by the master and purser during the voyage and presented by the ships husband at a meeting of the owners when the ship returned.

Shipping Interest: A body of ship owners, commanders, managers and agents whose main concern was to perpetuate the Company as a trading monopoly, and held strong views on state intervention. It took a decisive part, especially under the ships husband, in the election of directors.

The Signet: It controlled Sheriff-Deputes and Sheriff Clerks who in turn officiated at elections.

Squadrone: The political opposition in Scotland to the Dukes of Argyll and their followers [Argathelians].

Supercargo: He looked after the ship's manifest, handling freight charges and the purchasing and sale of goods on board. Although not one of the crew, he would have appeared on the ship's muster.

Writer: This was the lowest rank in the Company's civil service in the Presidencies abroad.

Index

Abercrombie, Alexander, 80
Abercromby, Commander Burnet, 156, 161
Abercromby, George, of Tullibody, 161
Abercromby, James, of Brucefield, 161
Abercromby, General, of Glasshaugh, 24, 175
Abercromby, Lord, 50-1, 55, 63
Aberdour, Lady, 54
Aberdour, Lord, 39-40, 42–3, 50, 52, 54, 56
Adams, John, 169
Agnew, Sir James, 80
Ainslie, Robert, 191
Albemarle, Duke of, 3, 8
Alexander, Boyd, 60, 172, 194
Alexander, Claud, (Senior) of Newton, Ayrshire, 172
Alexander, Claud, (Junior) 172, 194
Alexander, James, 172
Alexander, Mr., 65
Alexander, Rebecca, 172
Alexander, (Provost) William, 75
Alexander, William, of Edinburgh, 79
Alexander, William, banker, 172
Allardice, James, of Allardice, 80
Alloa, 194
America, 55, 68, 91, 95, 102, 165, 170, 173, 179, 188; colonists, war with, 182; Indian wars, 141; markets, 185
Americas, 68, 170, 184, 196,
Amsterdam, 1, 7–8, 102, 104

Amyand, Sir George, 171
Anderson, General Andrew, 180
Anderson, Mary (wife of John Russell of Braidshaw), 174
Anderson, Thomas, 88
Anglo-Dutch relations, 67
Angria, Maratha Admiral, 116
Ann, 115
Annan & Colquhoun, 181
Annandale, Marquis of, 24, 39, 50–1
Annexed Estates Commission, 75, 77
Anson, 156
Anson, Lord, 118
Anstruther, Sir John, 39
Anstruther family, of Balcakie, 131
Antwerp, Congress at, 5
Arbuthnot, Alexander, MP, 51
Arbuthnot, Mr., 63
Arbuthnot, family of, 49
Argathelians, 11, 15-17, 20, 26–7, 38, 43, 45, 51, 66, 72–3, 77, 82-3, 105, 122, 136–7, 152, 178, 204, 206
Argyll-Milton interest, 118–19
Arrack, trade in, 168
Asia, 157
Atholl, Duchess of, 64, 89
Atholl, Duke of, 39, 50–1, 105
Ayr, 24, 116
Ayr bank, 19, 182, 194
Ayton, Berwickshire, 96, 107

Bagshaw, Cadet, 156

INDEX

Baillie, Alex (Senior), of Dunean, 181
Baillie, Alex (Younger), of Dunean, 181
Baillie, Alexander, of Dockfour, 181
Baillie, Bethia (daughter of John Baillie), 151
Baillie, James, of Polkemet, 164
Baillie, John, of Castlecary, 151
Baillie, Lt. John, of Dunean, 95, 181
Baillie, Sir William, of Polkemet (Senior), 164
Baillie, William (Junior), 164
Baillie, Col. William, of Dunean, 181
Baillie, Captain, 87
Baillie, Commander, 154
Baird, Mrs., 63
Baird, Robert, 58
Baird, Sir John, of Newbyth, MP, 80
Baker, Commander George, 117
Baker, William, Director, MP, 104–5, 108, 164
Baker, Alderman Sir William, 36, 110–11
Baksar, battle of, 81, 182, 190
Balcarres, Earl of, 162
Balcarres, family of, 162
Ballantyne, Miss, 63
Bank of England, 28, 37, 79, 145
Bank of Scotland, 19, 187
Banque Generale (later Banque Royale), 8
Barré, Col. Isaac, 141
Barrington, 61, 116
Barrington, Col. George, 106
Barwell, Richard, 33, 168
Bathurst, Lord, 3, 10, 45
Bean, James, 96, 116
Beck, James, of Damside, 164, 172
Bedford, Duke of, 134
Bedford faction, 103
Belhaven, Lord, 79
Bell, John, of Auchtermony, 83
Bencoolen, Sumatra, 61, 64, 89, 131
Bengal Galley, 116
'Bengal Squad', 129
Bernera, 149, 154, 158–9
Berneray, 158
Berrie, William, 168
Bessborough, 173

Billingsley, Case, 195
Binney, Alexander (Younger), 52
Binney, Mr., (Senior) Provost of Forfar, 52
Bishop's Castle, constituency of, 148
'Black Hole' of Calcutta, 86, 99, 112
Blackstone, Dr. (Sir) William, 37, 105
Blair, Alexander, 58
Blair, Peter (Senior), of Edinburgh, 58
Blair, Peter (Junior), 58
Blantyre, Lord, 82–3, 92
Board of Control for Indian Affairs 1784, 30, 166
Board of Customs, 77
Board of Trustees for Fisheries and Manufactures, 19, 77, 186
Boddam village, 115
Boddam, Commander Charles (Senior), 115, 127, 154
Boddam, Charles (Younger), 115, 130, 154
Boddam, Rawson Hart, 115
Bogle, George, 87
Bogle, James, 107
'Bombay Squad', 124, 126
Boswell, James, 102, 131, 155
Boulton, Henry Crabb, 105, 132, 73
Bourchier, Governor, 57, 60
Bowmore, Islay, 180
Boyd, John, 96, 104, 138, 143
Bradshaw, Thomas, 149
Brand, Sir Thomas, 58
Brandenburgh, Elector of, 1
Braund, William, 120
Brent, Agatha van der (wife of John Drummond, of Quarrel), 1, 5–7, 56
Britannia, 116
British Linen Bank, 19, 75, 131, 187
British Privy Council, 13
Broach, 164
Brodie, Alexander, 16, 172
Brodie James, of Spynie, Elginshire, 172
Brown, John, 112
Bruce, Charles, Earl of Elgin, 119
Bruce, Sir John of Culdraines, 51, 54
Bruce, Captain, 178

Bruce-Balfour, family of, 79
Brussels, 3
Brydges, James, Duke of Chandos, 2, 4–9, 41, 45–7, 94, 188, 195
Buccleuch, Duke of, 72, 164, 166, 170–1,
Buchan, Hew, 112
Buchan, John, 65
Buchan, John, of Letham, 112
Buchanan, Agnes (1st wife of John Graham of Kernoc), 167
Buchanan, James, 109, 119
Buchanan, Lt. William, 169
Burdwan, 167
Burgoyne, General John, 145
Burke, Edmund, 103, 145, 175
Burke, family of, 143
Burke, Richard, 175
Burn, John, 55
Burnett, Eden, 55
Burnett, James, of Monboddo, 80
Burnett, Dr., 168
Burrell, John, 191
Buteshire, 49

Caithness, Lord, 79
Calcraft, John, 95, 107
Calcutta, 33, 87–8, 92, 150, 158, 198
Calcutta, 161
Cameron, John, 127
Campbell, Ensign Alex, Madras, 177
Campbell, Lt. Alex, of Ardchattan, 178
Campbell, Sir Archibald, of Inverneill, 92, 179, 194
Campbell, Archibald, 1st Earl of Islay, (3rd Duke of Argyll) 8, 11, 14–17, 21, 24–6, 41–2, 44–5, 50, 55, 62, 69, 71–7, 79–80, 84, 93, 100, 103–5, 108, 110–11, 121–2, 126, 136-37, 178-80, 187
Campbell, Col. Charles xvth of Barbreck, 143, 151, 179
Campbell, Colin, of Colonsay, 179
Campbell, Daniel, of Shawfield, 105
Campbell, Captain Donald, xvith of Barbreck, 179
Campbell, Col. Donald, of Glensaddel, 179
Campbell, Donald, of Castle Sween, 179
Campbell, Hugh, 46, 57-8
Campbell, James, of Restalrig, 79
Campbell, James, of Teurchan, 179
Campbell, John, 171
Campbell, John, 2nd Duke of Argyll, 4, 6, 8–11, 14, 15–17, 19, 21, 24, 26, 39, 41, 43–5, 49–50, 68, 105, 118–19, 121, 136, 178, 187
Campbell, Lord Frederick, 134
Campbell, Lt. Patrick, of Ardchattan, 178
Campbell, Richard, of Arkinch, 73
Campbell, Commander, 116
Campbell, Ensign, Bombay 177
Campbell of Cawdor, 24
Campbell clan, 93, 178, 180, 184
Campbells, Dukes of Argyll, 14, 24, 72, 154, 178
Campbell family, of Burnbank, 79
Campbell and Bruce bank, 79
Campbeltown, 179
Canton, 160, 175, 198
Cape of Good Hope, 142
Caribbean, 162, 196
Carlyle, Dr. Alexander, of Inveresk, 101, 105
Carmichael, Charles, 62, 64
Carmichael, George, 64
Carmichael, Michael, 64
Carnac, Major John, 182
Carnatic, 144, 150, 177
Carnegie, Andrew, 106
Carnegie, Governor, James, 61
Carnegie, Margaret, of Pittcarow, 78
Carnegie, Mr. (Jacobite), 53
Carnegie, Mr., of Southesk, 79
Carnegie family, of Southesk, 49, 95
'Carriage' contract (carpentry work), 168
Carteret, Lord, 70–1
Castels and Wheatley, 87
Cathcart, Lord, 50–1, 55, 63
Catrine, Ayrshire, 194
Cattle trade, 18, 44, 186, 193

INDEX

Cavendish, Lord, 70, 126
Chalmers, Mr, of Errol, 118
Chancerie, Mr., 36, 104, 111
Chandler, Dr. Samuel, 107
Charing Cross, 4, 96, 170
Charlton, 115
Charteris & Menteith, 168
Chatham-Sulivan relationship, 91
Cheape, George (Senior) of Prestonpans, 78, 163
Cheape, George (Younger), 164
Cheape, James (Senior) merchant in Leith, 164
Cheape, James (Younger), later of Strathyrum St. Andrews, 79, 163–64, 172, 193, 199
Cheape, Thomas, 89, 98, 140 148, 163–64
Chesterfield, Lord, 53
China, 28, 61, 115, 149, 160, 168–69, 200; silk, 168
Chittagong, 82
Clarke, Commander Daniel, 115
Clarke, General Duncan, 141
Clarke, Ensign, 177
Clavering, General Sir John, 33, 101
Cleland, John, 55, 63
Clerk, Duncan, 89, 110, 142-43, 152
Clerk, Henry, 98
Clerk, Sir John, of Penicuik, 39, 65, 79, 89, 98, 194
Clerk, Robert, 89, 142–3, 152
Clerk, family of, 51, 89, 143
Clive, 157
Clive, Lord Robert, 31–2, 60, 88, 100, 106, 124, 126, 128–9, 139, 141–2, 144–5, 147–9, 155, 158, 162, 174, 180, 182; *jagir*, 130
Clive–Sulivan feud, 32, 129, 138–9, 142, 171
Clivites, 130, 173
Cloth, trade in, 168
Clyde, river, 192, 195
Cochrane, Basil, 173
Cochrane, Hon. John, 173
Cochrane, Thomas, 8th Earl of Dundonald, 173

Cochrane, London firm, 173
Cockburn, Archibald, of Cockpen, 86
Cockburn, Lord Henry, 86, 166
Cockburn, Sir James, of Langton, 60, 74, 77, 95, 98, 107, 130, 147, 152, 168, 174
Cockburn, William, 107
Cockburn family, of Cockpen, 89, 107
Cockburn family, of Eyemouth, 89
Cockenzie, 195
Cockermouth, 102
'Cocoa-Tree' Club, 101
Colebrooke, Sir George, 36, 60, 97, 101, 103, 105, 107, 133, 140, 144, 165, 171, 175
Colquhoun, James, 79
Colt, Dr., 47, 53, 58
Compagnie d'Occident, 8-9
Congalton, Captain Charles, 89
Conway, Lord, 103
Conyen, Gerard, 45
Copper, Peter, 161
Cotton, 156, 188, 196; mills, 192, 194
Court, Royal 4, 7, 10, 16, 18, 40, 45, 47, 69-70; of Hanover, 6; of Delegates, 77; of Chancery, 129; of Session, 134, 166
Coutts, Alex, 107
Coutts, Charles, 96, 104
Coutts, James, 109, 131, 194
Coutts, Matthew, 64
Coutts, Thomas, 109, 131, 158
Coutts, family of, 79
Coutts bank, 19, 46, 64, 96, 107, 133, 141–3, 170, 194
Coutts, and Goslings, 102
Covenanters, 11
Cowan, Governor, 47, 57–8, 62-5
Craig, Commander William, 116
Crawford, Patrick, of Auchenames, 131
Crawford, Quinton, 78, 105, 132
Crawford, Mr., of Ballingray, 83
Crawford & Duncanson, 168
Crawfurd, David, 8
Crawfurd, George, 63
Crawfurd, Gideon, 63
Crawfurd, Henry, 63

Index

Crawfurd, John, 57, 63
Cromarty, Earl of, 24–5, 83, 108
Cullen, Dr., 168
Culloden, battle of, 69, 76, 92, 122, 158, 177, 179
Cumberland, Duke of, 91, 151
Cumming, Commander George, 36, 59–60, 87, 98, 117, 141, 153–4, 162, 174
Cumming, James, 60
Cumming, Lt. Col. Sir John, of Altyre, 87, 89, 193
Cumming, Patrick, 78
Cumming, Mr., of Pitulie, 75
Cunningham, Henry, 25
Cunningham, Jean (wife of Claud Alexander (Senior), 172
Cupar, 25, 44

Dalrymple, Agnes (wife of Sir Robert Stewart), 132
Dalrymple, Alexander, 107, 111, 116, 132
Dalrymple, Sir David, Lord Hailes, 110–11
Dalrymple, Sir Hew, of North Berwick, 36–7, 39, 51, 54, 64, 74, 79, 84, 98, 110–11, 118, 132
Dalrymple, Hew (Younger), 111
Dalrymple, Hugh, of Hailes, 132
Dalrymple, Sir James, of Hailes, 102, 108, 110
Dalrymple, James, 37, 111–12
Dalrymple, John, Earl of Stair, 8, 25, 73
Dalrymple, John Hamilton, of Bargany, 111, 118
Dalrymple, John, of Culhorn, 118
Dalrymple, Lady Stair, 160
Dalrymple, Robert, 37, 111
Dalrymple, Captain Robert, 111
Dalrymple, Commander William Stair, 111, 117
Dalrymple, William Stair, 36, 98, 111
Dalrymple, of Clackmananshire, 24
Dalrymple, family of, 79, 110
Dalrymple family, of Hailes, 24, 111
Dalrymple family, of North Berwick, 51

Dalziel, General, of the Binns, 63, 119
'Dangeroux', Mr., 168
Darien Scheme, 12, 94, 115
Daseville, Monsieur M, 65
Davidson, Alex, 174
Davidson, Alex, London, 165
Davidson, Governor Alexander, 92
Davidson, Henry, of Stewartfield, 165, 170
Davidson, John, (in Scotland), 79
Davidson, John, saddlers merchant London, 87
Davidson, John, London, 87, 165
Davidson, John, of Stewartfield, 88, 95, 165–6, 170–1
Davidson, Neil, 184
Decker, Sir Matthew, 3-10, 46, 52, 57, 61, 64, 67, 93
Dempster, Charles, 106
Dempster, George (Senior), of Dunnichen, 43
Dempster, George (Junior), 36-7, 80–1, 88–9, 100, 102–3, 105–6, 110, 130–2, 140–5, 147, 152, 165, 173, 194
Dempster, George (uncle of George Dempster (Junior), 105
Dempster, John, of Dunnichen, 105
Dempster, John Hamilton, 106
Dempster, Philip, 106
Dempster, family of, 105
Deputy Keeper of the Signet, 84, 137
Deskford, family of, 73
Devine, Professor Thomas, 184, 189, 192
Devonshire, 161
Devonshire, Duke of, 90
Dewar, Commander James, 117, 127
Dick, Mr., 173
Dickson, Commander Alex, 117
Dingwall, 83
Dissenting families, 114
Don Quixote, 116
Dorrien, John, 95, 105
Douglas (legal) case, 73, 103, 147
Douglas, Alex, 127
Douglas, Andrew, 133

Douglas, Commander Francis, 87
Douglas, George, 54
Douglas, George, 12th Earl of Morton, 16, 24–5, 39–40, 43, 46, 50–1, 54, 56, 63, 65
Douglas, Henry, 107
Douglas, Sir John, 87
Douglas, John, 117, 157
Douglas, Dr. Robert, 62, 82
Douglas, Robert, 47, 57
Douglas, Walter, 119
Douglas, family of, 110
Douglas, of Roxburghshire, 24
Douglas of Gala, family of, 51
Dow, Major, (Col.) Alexander, 96, 169
Dow, Susanna (wife of Commander George Cumming, 60
Drake, Governor Roger, 112
Drake, Roger, 104, 11
Drake, 62
Drummond, Adam, banker, 158
Drummond, Agatha (wife of John Drummond of Quarrel). 1, 5–7, 56 (See also Brent, Agatha van der)
Drummond, Agatha (wife of Lord Aberdour), 56
Drummond, Andrew, 4–5, 7, 46, 56–8, 96, 170–1
Drummond, Sir George, of Blair-Drummond, 1, 54, 56
Drummond, George (son of brother James), 56
Drummond, George, Provost of Edinburgh, 56, 78, 84
Drummond, Henry, MP, of Strathallan, 96
Drummond, James, 41-2, 56
Drummond, James, of Blair-Drummond, 38, 56
Drummond, John, Writer then banker, 96, 158
Drummond, John, of Megginch, 41, 51, 54–5
Drummond, John, of Paisley, 119
Drummond, John, of Quarrel, 1–12, 15, 24–5, 30, 38–40, 42, 43, 44, 45–61, 63, 65–9, 75, 78, 80, 82, 86, 91, 93, 104–5, 110, 113–14, 116, 119, 123, 163–4, 170
Drummond, John, of Quarrel, family of, 4, 7
Drummond, Laurence, 42
Drummond, Mary (wife of James Haliburton, of Pitcur), 38, 54
Drummond, Robert, of Strathallan, 96
Drummond, William, of Grange, 38, 42–3, 45, 56, 61
Drummond, William, Viscount Strathallan, 19, 96
Drummond, Lt., 169
Drummond, Mr., Surgeon, 62
Drummond of Perthshire, family of, 51, 56
Drummond's bank, 4, 46, 56, 58, 88, 96, 128, 141, 145, 165, 170, 181, 193–4
Drumure, Laird of, 75
Du Cane, Richard, 47
Du Pré, Governor Josias, 162, 173
Duff, Major Alexander, 180
Duff, Patrick, of Premnay, 80
Duff, William, 168
Duff, of Banffshire, 24
Duke of Albany, 76, 119
Duke of Grafton, 142, 155
Dumbarton Castle, 83
Dumfries bank, 102
Duncan, Adam of Dundee, 118
Dundas, Henry, Viscount, 30, 35, 65, 73, 86, 104, 136, 146–7, 151–2, 166, 173, 179, 205
Dundas, Joanna (wife of George Dempster), 105
Dundas, Sir Laurence, 37, 89, 95, 111, 118, 128, 134, 138, 143, 146–8, 151–4, 160, 164, 179, 194
Dundas, Chief Baron Robert, of Arniston, Lord President of the Court of Session, 11, 73, 105, 122, 134, 166, 178
Dundas, Thomas of Fingask, 80, 151
Dundas, family of Arniston, 73
Dundee, 80
Dundonald, Earl of, 89
Dunicade, Lord, 54

Dunning, John, 105
Durand, John, 47
Dutch, 2-4, 7-8, 31, 94, 132, 145 banks, 7; India Company, 193

Earls of Seaforth, (Chiefs of the Mackenzies), 149, 158
Earl Talbot, 106
East India Company, 1, 4, 7, 9–12, 17, 21–2, 25–6, 28–9, 35, 37, 39, 46, 60, 64–6, 70, 77, 79–80, 82, 85, 87–8, 90–4, 96–9, 104, 106, 108–10, 113, 115, 120, 129, 132, 139, 147–9, 151, 158–61, 163–4, 172, 176–7, 179, 188, 193–6, 198, 203, 205; *Chairman*, 5, 34–5, 46, 81, 90, 93, 96, 100, 104, 107–8 111, 113, 125, 129–31, 155, 171, 173, 175, 179; *Charter*, 29–30, 125, 140; *Civil branch*, 35, 56, 62, 69, 75, 81, 87, 93, 95, 99, 111, 117, 119, 125, 161, 164–5, 172–3, 178, 194, 203, 205; *Committee of Shipping*, 35, 113 *Committee of Treasury*, 35 *Contested elections*, 31–2, 37, 60, 90, 93, 96, 99–103, 106, 120–1, 123, 125, 128, 130, 133, 136, 138, 142, 147, 155–6, 162, 167, 174, 176, 182; *Court of Directors*, 5, 29, 34–9, 41, 46–7, 60, 69, 90–1, 94, 101, 104, 109, 111, 119, 124–5, 130, 133, 136, 138–41, 143-8, 150, 152–3, 155, 164, 169–70, 174; *Deputy Chairman*, 5, 34–5, 46, 90, 93, 104, 124–5, 144, 162,; *Directors*, 1, 5, 9–10, 12, 29–30, 33–7, 40, 52, 60, 64, 79, 82, 86, 88–91, 93, 95–102, 104–16, 119–20, 124–5, 127, 130–2, 137–40, 143–8, 150, 153–5, 160–4, 167, 171–2, 175–6, 179, 194–6, 198, 205; *Free Merchants*, 35, 61–2, 65, 82, 86, 112, 154, 169, 175–6, 199, 205; *General Court of Proprietors*, 5, 29, 36, 101, 124–5, 142, 146–7, *Medical*, 35, 62, 81–2, 169, 175 *Military*, 35, 59, 81–2, 85–7, 91–3, 95–6, 102, 125–7, 134, 165, 167, 177–83, 188, 199, 205 *Proprietors*, 5, 7, 12, 29, 32, 35–7, 40, 46–7, 52, 79, 85, 91, 94–103, 105, 108, 110–1, 113–4, 116, 119–20, 125–7, 129–30, 132, 138–40, 142, 146–7, 149–50, 152, 154, 156–7, 160–1, 163–4, 181–2, 194–6, 198, 203, 205; *Shipping*, 27–8, 35, 37, 43, 59–60, 65, 86–7, 95, 100, 113, 115–20, 125, 127–8, 130, 137, 153–61, 174, 194, 205; *Shipping interest*, 1, 32, 35–6, 40, 44, 47, 60, 90, 96, 106, 113, 116–20, 124, 126, 143–4, 146, 153, 155–6, 158–9, 162, 164, 169
East Indiamen, 35, 44, 49, 55, 59, 61, 64, 76, 81, 88, 97, 111, 113–14, 116–19, 134, 142, 149, 153, 155–6, 160–1, 166, 168, 172, 173
East Indies, 13, 27, 47, 62, 68, 80, 86, 102, 155, 176, 186–8, 192–3, 196–8, 201–2
Eaton, Barrington, 47
Eckersall, John, 64
Edinburgh, 11, 20, 24, 56, 58, 64–5, 71, 74–5, 78–9, 83–4, 88, 107, 109, 123, 135, 138, 141, 149, 154–6, 158, 167, 165, 167–8, 170, 173–4, 192, 194, 204; *literary circle*, 98, 100, 132, 148; *Medical School*, 82; *New Town*, 195; *University*, 92, 105
Eglinton, Lord, 95, 122, 130-1, 167
Egremont, Lord, 128
Elections: 10, 17, 20–3, 26, 38, 42–3, 45, 50–1, 54–5, 62, 64, 66, 72–3, 75, 77, 84, 105, 133, 136, 139; *Fictitious votes*, 22; *Sheriff (or steward), power of*, 22–3; *Treating*, 22; *Voters roll (or registry)*, 23
Elections: *Burghs*, 20–5, 42, 44, 49–51, 73, 78–80, 147; Aberdeen, 24, 48; Ayr, 24, 112, 121, 147; Dumfries, 24, 109; Edinburgh, 20, 24; Elgin, 24, 95; Glasgow, 24; Inverness, 24, 182; Haddington, 24, 110; Lanark, 24; Linlithgow, 24, 107; Nairn, 93; Peebles, 24; Perth, 25, 37, 43, 54,

102, 105–06; Royal Burghs, 20, 77; Selkirk, 24; Stirling, 25, 81, 118, 151, 179; Tain, 24; Wigton, 25;
Elections: *Counties,* 20–5, 44, 49–51, 75, 80; electoral influence in, 49; freeholders, 21; Lieutenants, 23; representation, 73
Elgin, 24, 95
Elliot, Alexander, 36, 92, 133, 144
Elliot, Sir Gilbert, 36, 69, 74, 78, 86, 89, 97, 101, 107–8, 122, 126, 128, 132, 134, 137, 142, 144, 174
Elliot, Commander Richard, 61, 116
Elphinstone, Lord Charles, 39, 50, 55, 159,
Elphinstone, George Keith, 159–60
Elphinstone, John, 159
Elphinstone, Lady Clementine, 159
Elphinstone, Fullarton, Elizabeth (wife of Commander William Fullarton-Elphinstone), 161
Elphinstone, Lockhart, 159–60
Elphinstone, William Fullarton, 76, 153–4, 156, 159–61, 165, 169, 181
Elphinstone, William Fullarton, family, 160, 169, 193
Emmery, Mr., 44
Emperor Charles VI, 5
England, Edward (pirate), 59
Errol, Countess of, 64
Errol, Duke of, 7, 39, 50, 65
Erskine, Charles, Solicitor-General (then Lord Advocate), 3, 46, 50, 51, 118
Erskine, Sir Harry, 122
Erskine, Helen (wife of Commander Robert Haldane), 118
Erskine, Baron James, Lord Chief Justice Clerk, 118
Erskine, James, 25, 51, 78
Erskine, John, Earl of Mar, 14, 51
Erskine, Robert, 127
Erskine, Robert (Senior), of Carnock and Carden, 109
Erskine, Robert (Younger), of Carnock and Carden, 109
Erskine, Thomas, MP, 25, 51, 109

Erskine, Lord Thomas, 72
Erskine, Col. William, of Torrie, 83
Erskine, family of, 49, 107, 110, 118; of Kellie, 102, 131; of Mar, 194
Exchange Assurance Company, 98
Excise crisis & Bill, 16
Eyemouth, Berwickshire, 107
Eyles, Sir John, 44, 52, 60

Farquhar, John, 154
Farquharson, Mr., 160
Featherstonehaugh, Sir Matthew, 110
Fenton, Commander John, 60
Fergusson, Sir Adam, 102-3, 105–6, 149
Fergusson, John, 116
Fergusson, Mr., 64
Fife, Lord, 79
Findlater, Earl of, 24, 50-1
Findlater, family of, 73
Findlay, David, 112
Finlayson, Rev., 61
Fisher, Commander Benjamin, 117
Fisher, William, banker 97
Fisher's bank, 128, 141-2
Fisher & Younger, 97
Fisheries, 19, 77, 106, 159, 186, 194
Fleming, Alex, 127
Fleming, John (mariner), 161,
Fleming, John (merchant), 168
Fleming, John, Earl of Wigtown, 159
Fleming, Lady Clementine (wife of Lord Charles Elphinstone), 159, 161
Flemish weavers, 65, 194
Fletcher, Andrew, Lord Milton, 11, 19, 21–3, 25, 40, 42–4, 47, 49, 53, 59, 61, 69, 71–81, 83–4, 86, 89, 93, 95, 99–101, 104–10, 112, 118–9, 122, 131–4, 137–8, 154, 158–9, 165, 179, 187
Fletcher, Andrew (son of Lord Milton), 75
Fletcher, Andrew, of Saltoun (the 'Patriot'), 78
Fletcher, Sir Henry, 138
Fletcher, Robert, of Ballinshoe, 80

Fletcher, Sir Robert, 80, 92, 134, 142, 169
Fletcher, family of, 78
Flockhart, William, 105
Forbes, Duncan, of Culloden, 11, 14, 16, 24, 44, 50, 72, 75, 78-9, 122
Forbes, John, 64
Forbes, Sir William, of Edinburgh, 158
Forbes, Commander (Bombay Marine), 127
Fordyce, Dr. William, 173
Fordyce, Banffshire, 81, 175
Fordyce, Mr., banker, 97, 124
Fordyce's bank, 128, 141-3, 171
Fordyce, Grant and Co, 107
Forfar, 53, 62
Forfeited estates, 77
Forsyth, Alex, 97
Forsyth's bank, 145
Fort St. David, Pondicherry, 82, 115, 178
Fort St. George, Madras, 56-8, 63-5, 115, 150, 161, 179
Fort William, Bengal, 62-3, 92, 111, 168
Forth-Clyde canal, 194; Canal Company, 152, 198
Forth, river, 38, 195, 195
Fortrose, Lord, 50, 84
Fothringham, George, 62
Foulis, Commander Charles, 35, 116-17, 119, 127, 143, 153-4, 156-7
Foulis, Henry, of Colinton, 156
Foulis, Sir James, of Colinton, 79, 156
Foulis, Margaret (wife of William George Freeman), 157
Foulis, Mrs. (wife of Commander Charles Foulis), 157
Foulis, family of, 138, 157
Foulis-Freeman-Moffat group, 157
Fox, Henry (Lord Holland), 36, 74, 102, 122, 126, 128, 130, 143, 155
'Fragments', 148
France, 8, 177
Francis, Philip, 33, 162, 175
Fraser, James (Senior), of Golden Square, London, 176
Fraser, James (Junior) MP, 153, 169, 175-6
Fraser, Simon, 176
Fraser, Commander Sir William, 115, 158
Fraser, William (political agent), 140
Fraser, clan, 23
Fraser, family of, 110
Frederick, Sir Charles, 98
Frederick, Sir John, 98
Frederick, Sir Thomas, 47, 52, 63, 98
Frederick, family of, 104
Freeman, William George, 119, 138, 143, 154, 157
Freeman, family of, 154, 158
French, 8, 56, 150, 190; *bourse*, 9; *India Company*, 193; *language*, 98; *trade rivalry with*, 120; *war against*, 31, 92, 124, 128, 144, 177, 182
Fullarton, John, of Carberry, Mid Lothian, 161
Fullarton, William, of Carstairs, 161
Fullarton, Dr., of Carberry, 82
Fullarton, family of, 169
Fullerton, Alex (military), 177
Fullerton, Commander Alex, 168-19
Fyrish, Evanton, 183

Galloway, Earl of, 25
Gardiner, James, 8
Gardner, Andrew, 127
Garmouth, Speyside, 196
Gascoigne, Mr., 160
Generalship of the Mint in Scotland, 134
George I, 4, 65
George II, 15, 45
George III, 70, 74, 121, 132, 155
Germain, Lady Betty, 63
Gibb, A. D., 206
Gibbon, Edward, 7, 52
Gibraltar, 159
Gibson, Commander, 60
Gilmour, Sir Alexander, 94, 105-6
Glasgow, 10, 11, 24, 188, 191-2, 194
Glenbervie, Mr., Provost of St. Andrews, 54
'Glorious Revolution' of 1688, 186

Index

Godfrey, family of, 125
Godolphin, 116
Godolphin, Francis, Earl, 14
Goldsmith, Oliver, 37, 105
Golf, 88
Gombroon, 63
Gordon, Anne, (wife of Robert Dundas of Arniston, Lord President), 166
Gordon, Daniel, 105
Gordon, Duchess of, 180, 182
Gordon, Isobel (wife of Hugh Munro of Novar), 182
Gordon, James (Senior), of Ellon, 109
Gordon, James (Younger), of Ellon, 109
Gordon, Commander John, 112–16
Gordon, Sir Robert, Bart., MP, of Embo, Sutherland, 182
Gordon, Sir William, of Invergordon, 166
Gordon, Mr., 54
Gosford estate, East Lothian, 87
Goslings bank, 142
Gould, John, 46
Gower, Lord, 103
Graeme, David, 51
Grafton, Duke of, 140, 149-50
Graham, David, 58, 60
Graham, George, 167-8
Graham, James, 60
Graham, James, of Damside, Fife, 172
Graham, John, of Kernoc, 167
Graham, Colonel John, of Kinross, 80, 167, 170
Graham, John, 53, 87, 131, 133
Graham, Thomas, 60, 167-168, 172
Graham, William, of Airth, 151
Graham, Miss, 60
Graham, Mr., of Airth (the Younger), 75
Graham, family of, 89, 168–9, 176
Graham (Graeme) family, of Kinross, 92, 98
Grange, Lord, 54, 78–9
Grangemouth, 38
Grant, Sir Alexander, 80, 87, 94, 96, 108, 110, 165, 181–2

Grant, Captain Alex, 180
Grant, Charles, 96
Grant, Charles, of Knockando, 96
Grant, Commander Charles, 165
Grant, Commander Charles Cathcart, 95
Grant, Duncan, 181
Grant, Henry, 96
Grant, Sir James, of Castle Grant and Moy, 95, 112, 116
Grant, Sir James, of Knockando, 95
Grant, James, 96, 165
Grant, James, of Monymusk, 195
Grant, John, of Ballindalloch, 96
Grant, Lt. Lewis, 96
Grant, Sir Ludovick, of Knockando, 95, 131, 169
Grant, Ludovick, (son of Auchterblain), 96
Grant, McGregor, 96
Grant, Sir Patrick, 95
Grant, Colonel, 169
Grant clan, 95
Grant family: 169;
Grant of Auchterblain, 95; of Ballindalloch, 95; of Knockando, 95
Grant's bank, 142-3
Grant & Fordyce, 102
Gray, Alex, 161
Gray, George (Senior), 92
Gray, George (Younger), 92
Gray, Lord John, 83
'Great Scheme', 143
Grenville, 162
Grenville, George, 70, 111, 129–30, 134, 136, 139–40, 148
Grenville, family of, 132

Haddington, 24, 49, 79
Haggis, Commander Charles, 117, 156
Hairstanes, Matthew, 57-8
Haldane, Col. James, 119
Haldane, Commander James, 76, 117–19
Haldane, Commander James Alexander, 119

Haldane, John, of Gleneagles, 118
Haldane, Commander Robert, 76, 87, 92, 95, 116–18, 127, 134
Haldane family, of Airthrey & Gleneagles, 49–50, 76, 127, 193
Haliburton, David, 173
Haliburton, James, 39, 56
Haliburton, James, of Pitcur, 38, 43 51, 54, 56, 59
Haliburton, Jean, 56
Haliburton, John, 56, 173
Haliburton, John (Senior), 56
Haliburton, John (Junior), 56, 58, 63, 65
Haliburton, John, of Muirhouse, Edinburgh, 173
Haliburton, John, of Pitcur, 173
Haliburton, Mary (wife of James Haliburton, of Pitcur), 56
Haliburton of Pitcur, family of, 51, 56
Halkett, Alexander, 57
Halkett, Peter, 25
Halkett, Sir Peter, of Pitfirrine, 39, 51, 54, 57, 62
Halkett of Pitfirrane, family of, 49, 51 79
Hall, Alexander, 131
Hall Sir John, of Dunglass, 131
Hamilton, Commander Alexander, 115, 156
Hamilton, Lt. Francis, 169
Hamilton, Sir Hugh, of Rosehall, 83
Hamilton, Duke of, 24, 45
Hamilton, Dukes of, 103
Hamilton, Dr. William, 115
Hamilton, Mr., 54
Hamilton, Mr., of Reidhouse, 75
Hamilton–Argyll faction, 103
Hannah, 161
Hannay, Col. Alexander, 169, 176
Hannay, John, 169
Hannay, Ramsay, 169
Hannay, Sir Samuel, 102, 148, 150, 169, 176
Hannay, William, of Kirkdale, 169
Hannay, family of, 169
Hanover, 4, 6

Hanoverians, 3, 76, 99, 158, 177, 188; Army, 102; Rule, 97
Hardwicke, 182
Hardwicke, Lord Chancellor, 71, 73–5, 178
Harland, Admiral, 162
Harland, Sir Robert, 173
Harley, Lord Edward, 2–4, 52
Harley, Robert, Earl of Oxford, 2–8, 10, 14
Harley, Thomas, 4, 6
Harley, family of, 6–7
Harper, Col. Graham, 176
Harrington, 64
Harris, Barony & island of, 158–9
Harrison, Edward, 79
Harrison, Governor Edward, 5, 10, 46–7, 52, 64, 94
Harrogate, 159
Haselingfield, 118
Hastings, Warren, 33, 103, 132–3, 142, 150, 158, 162–3, 168, 175–6, 182
Hay, Alexander, 54
Hay, John, W.S., 75
Hay, Lady Margaret, 51
Hay, Margaret (wife of John Mackenzie of Delvine), 83
Hay, Thomas, of Alderston, 83
Hay, Thomas, Viscount Dupplin, Earl of Kinnoul, 3, 7, 39–40, 45–6, 50–1, 54, 79, 89, 136
Hay, Mr., 65
Hay, Mr., of Bolton, 65
Hector, 119, 160
Heiden, Jan van der, 1
Heinsius, Dutch GrandPensionary, 2
Heriot, James, (Senior) of Dirleton, 112
Heriot, James (Younger), 112
Heritable Jurisdictions, 23, 84; abolition of, 21, 92, 133
Heron, Commander George, 115
Hertford, Lord, 103
Hickey, Joseph, 160
Hill, Mr., 7
Hillsborough, 157
Hoare, Mr., 7
Hoare, Richard, 7, 52

INDEX

Holland, 2, 3, 7, 171, 175
Home, James, of Garnelshiel, 64
Home, John, 62, 78, 85, 108, 122, 132, 148
Home, Governor John, 64
Hong Kong, 198
Honiton, Devon, 159
Hope, Col. Alex, 164
Hope, Adriaan, of Amsterdam, 102, 104, 141, 171
Hope, Charles, 1st Earl of Hopetoun, 18
Hope, Col. John, MP, 164
Hope, John, MP, 171
Hope, John, 57, 92
Hope, John (of Bombay), 104, 127
Hope, John, Director, 96, 102, 104
Hope, Sir John, (later 2nd Earl of Hopetoun), 50–1, 54
Hope, Thomas, Hope Park, 54–5
Hope, Thomas, of Rankeillor, 79
Hope, Mr., Dutch Envoy, 46
Hope, of Kinrosshire, 24
Hope family, of Craighall, 171
Hope family, of Hope Park, 51
Hope bank, of Amsterdam, 9, 46, 96, 141–3, 145, 170
Hopetoun, Earls of, 18, 45, 50–1, 54, 102, 104
Hopetoun, family of, 171
Hopetoun interest, 61, 171
Horne, Governor John, 47
Hough, Commander Samuel, 125
House of Commons, 2, 15, 17, 20, 22, 32, 36, 43–6, 51, 118, 123, 145, 148, 204
House of Lords, 20, 36, 45, 71, 75 (See also Parliament & Westminster)
Howe, Commander, 160
Howe, Lady, 160
Howe, Lord, 160
Huguenot families, 114
Hume, Abraham, of Ayton, Berwickshire, 98
House of Commons, 36, 44–6, 118, 141, 148
House of Lords, 36, 45, 71

Hume, Alexander, 51, 58, 94, 96, 107, 109, 124, 148–9
Hume, Commander Alex, 117
Hume, David, 37, 105, 132, 147
Hume, Robert, of Ayton, 60, 98
Hume, family of, 97, 104, 115
Hunter, Commander John, 61, 116
Hunter, Dr., 169
Hunter, Mr., 169
Hutchinson, Commander Norton, 117
Hutchinson, Commander William, 116
Hutchinson, Colonel, 61
Hutchinson, Commander, 61
Hyde, John, 160
Haider Ali of Mysore, 144
Hyndford, Earl of, 24, 39, 50, 55
Hyndford, Lady Elizabeth, 55, 57, 62-3

Ilay–Milton patronage system, 98, 08, 111, 123
Ilay–Milton–Bute patronage system, 101
Independent Military Companies in Madras, 177
India, 95, 125–6, 128, 132, 144, 148, 157, 163, 166, 179–82, 195, 200, 207; famine of 1769, 145; India Act of 1784, 26, 166
India House, 26-7, 35, 46–8, 68, 94, 124, 128, 140–1, 145, 152, 169, 198
India patronage, 5, 9, 11, 18, 20, 23, 25–6, 30–1, 34, 36, 38–9, 44, 49–50, 55, 59, 68–70, 72, 74, 76–9, 84, 91, 93, 100, 102, 119–20, 124, 130, 132, 136–9, 142, 144, 147–8, 151–2, 154, 156–7, 165, 168–9, 178, 181, 186, 203–4, 206–8
India stock, 94
Inglis, Commander Cornelius, 117
Inglis, Commander Nathaniel, 117
Inglis, Sir Hugh, 175
Innes, Daniel, 58
Innes, Dr. Robert, 58
Innes & Clarke, 112
Inverness, 24
Irish immigration, 185
Irvine, Mr., 64

INDEX

Irving, George, 78
Irwin, Thomas, 161
Islay, island of, 179
Isle of Bute, 179

Jacobite Rebellion of 1715, 3, 13–14, 53, 59, 65, 76, 83–4, 158, 195, 204
Jacobite Rebellion of 1745, 26, 53, 67–72, 75–6, 95, 151, 158, 180, 182, 188, 201
Jacobites, 3, 10–11, 53, 66, 72,75–7, 80, 83, 85, 94, 97–9, 101–9, 122, 141, 143, 148, 154, 158–9, 163, 178, 180, 188, 195, 204
Jacobitism, 39, 53, 65–7, 71, 76, 91, 97–9, 101–2, 122, 141, 143, 148, 154, 158–9, 163, 178, 180, 188, 195, 201, 204
Jacobite Journal, 76
Jacombe, 9
Jamaica, 168
James, Sir William, 162
Janssen, Sir Theodore, 7, 52
Jenkins, Commander, 64
Jenkinson, Charles, 129, 131, 140, 146, 167, 205
John o'Groats, 78
Johnson, Captain James, 177
Johnson, Dr. Samuel, 37, 105
Johnson & Mackay, of Madras, 173
Johnston, Alex, 109, 119
Johnston, Margaret (wife of William Hannay of Kirkdale), 169
Johnston, Patrick, of Girthon, Kirkcudbright, 169
Johnstone, Alexander, 99-100
Johnstone, George, 37, 99–100, 102, 129, 141–2, 144–6, 159–60, 193
Johnstone, Gideon, 99-100
Johnstone, Sir James (Senior), 81, 99, 101, 104, 142
Johnstone, Sir James (Younger), 99
Johnstone, John, of Alva, 99–101, 129, 142, 174, 193, 199
Johnstone, Margaret (wife of Lord David Ogilvie), 99
Johnstone, Patrick, 99-100

Johnstone, William Pulteney, 99–100, 102–3, 106, 129, 132, 142–4, 157, 193
Johnstone, family of Westerhall, 80–1, 99–103, 105, 127, 129, 132, 138, 141–5, 147–8, 157, 160, 168, 171
Johnstone family, of Grange, 131
Johnstone group, 101, 106
Jones, Robert, 140
Judicature Bill of 1772, 145, 148
'Junius', 103

Kandy (Ceylon), 115
Keeper of the Great Seal in Scotland, 122
Keeper of the Signet, 21, 84, 132, 137
Keith, George, Earl Marischal, 39, 50, 64, 76, 89, 159–60, 195
Ker, Mr., 173
Kiernan, Professor Victor, 188
Killican, David, 168
Kilpatrick, Major James, 127
Kilpatrick, Captain, 143
Kincardine, 38
Kingston, family of, 79
Kinloch, Elizabeth, of Gilmerton, 79
Kinloch, Sir James, 54
Kinloch, John, 55
Kinloch, William, 55
Kinloch, family of, 50
Kirkbred, Ensign, 177
Kirkpatrick, Ensign Thomas, 178
Knox, Commander Robert, 115

Lamb, James, 61
Lambert, Sir John, 7
Lanark, 24
'Land of Cakes', 88
Lane, Commander Thomas, 125
Lane, Thomas, 171
Laurence, General Stringer, 87, 179
Law, Governor Stephen, 124
Law, John, 6-9
Law, Commander, 111
Leadenhall Street, 28, 31, 37, 92, 101, 107, 125, 129, 140, 145, 151, 164–5, 169, 174, 182

Leggatt, William, 116
Leith, 65, 84, 88, 164, 194
Lennox, Commander John, 156
Leslie, Mr., 105
Lethieullier, Benjamin, 47, 59
Lethieullier, Christopher, 47, 59
Leven, Lord, 18, 39, 50, 54
Lind, George, 78
Lind, Mr., 143
Lindsay, Sir Alex, of Evelich, Perth, 109, 162
Lindsay, Charles, 161
Lindsay, Commander George, 117, 162
Lindsay, Commander Sir John, 144, 156, 162
Lindsay, Dr. Matthew, 82
Lindsay, Robert, 162
Lindsay, William, 109, 162
Lindsay, Provost, 78
Linen goods, 44; industry, 194
Linlithgow, 24
Lisbon, 167
Lister, James, 127
Littlejohn, Dr., 57–8, 60, 62
Liverpool, 116
Loch, Robert, Writer to the Signet, 109
Lockhart, George, 11
London, 108
London financial market, 28, 97
London (Fire) Assurance Company, 97, 160
Lord Anson, 117
Lord Chancellor, 13, 147
Lord Holland, 155
Lord Mansfield, 76, 149, 154, 158–9
Lord Register, 108
Lords of the Bedchamber, 71
Louden, Earl of, 18
Lovat, Lord, 16, 23
Low Countries, 9 (See also Holland)
Lowther, Sir Henry of Swillington, 52, 57–8, 64
Lowther, Sir James, Earl of Lonsdale, 102
Lowther, William, 57
Lowther, family of, 64
Lyell, Henry, 5, 46, 59
Lyon, Elizabeth (Mrs. Robert Fletcher), 80
Lyon, John, 89
Lyon, William, of Carse, 80

MacDonald, Alexander, 154
Macdonald, Alexander, of Sleat, Skye, 76, 84, 88, 158
Macdonald, Sir James, 86, 131
Macdonald, family of, 89, 158; of Sleat, 158
Macinnes, Professor Alan, 184
MacIntosh, Lt. Alex, 169
MacIntosh, Lydia (wife of Sir Patrick Grant), 95
MacIntosh, Commander William, 156, 162
MacIntosh, William, of Auchintully, 106
MacIntosh, William, of Borlum, 95
MacIntosh and Hannay, 119
Mackay, George, 106
Mackay, George, of Skibo, 88, 165
Mackenzie, Major–General Sir Alex, of Coull, 85, 87, 89, 92, 97, 108
Mackenzie, Alex (shipbuilder at Calcutta), 87
Mackenzie, Alexander, 83
Mackenzie, Colin, 86
Mackenzie, George, 84, 86–7, 108
Mackenzie, James Stuart, 69, 71, 75, 105, 122–3, 132, 134
Mackenzie, John (Senior), 83
Mackenzie, John, 57, 148
Mackenzie, John, of Delvine, 26, 58, 78–9, 83–9, 98, 106, 108, 137, 151, 157–9, 165–6, 174, 182, 194, 207
Mackenzie of Delvine, family of, 51
Mackenzie, Sir Kenneth, of Cromarty, 39, 51
Mackenzie, Kenneth (later Lord Fortrose), 51
Mackenzie, Kenneth, of Lincoln's Inn, 97
Mackenzie, Commander Kenneth, 87
Mackenzie, Kenneth, 58, 86–7, 165, 174
Mackenzie, Commander Robert, 168

INDEX

Mackenzie, Major William, 127
Mackenzie, of Seaforth, 24
Mackenzie, Mr., of Scotsburn, 87
Mackenzie clan, 83
Mackenzie, family of, 89, 158
Maclean, Helen (wife of Commander Alex Macleod), 158
Maclean, family of, 158
Macleane, Henry, 142
Macleane, Lauchlin, 76, 89, 101, 128, 133, 140–1, 143–4, 148, 150–1, 155, 162, 165, 171, 173, 175
Macleane, Commander Stephen, 142, 155
Macleod, Commander Alexander, 76, 117, 149, 154, 156, 158, 194
Macleod, Donald, of Bernera, 149, 158
Macleod, Donald, of Grisernish, 60
Macleod, Janet (wife of Rev. Dr. John Macpherson, 149
Macleod, Captain Norman, of Unish, 158
Macleod, clan, 158
Macleod, family of, 158
MacNeill, Marion (wife of Colin Campbell of Colonsay), 179
Macpherson, Andrew, of Invertromie, 148
Macpherson, James 'Fingal', 128, 131, 140–1, 147–51, 159, 169, 175
Macpherson, Rev. Dr. John, of Sleat, Skye, 149
Macpherson, Sir John, 88, 128, 140, 142, 144, 147–8, 150, 159, 169, 175
Macpherson, Mr., 127
Macrae, Commander & Governor James, 43, 46-7, 53, 57–9, 116
Madeira, 164
Madrasapatnam, 174
Madura, 179
Mahim, 127
Malt tax, 111, 204
Mansfield, Earl of, 73, 92, 103, 109, 118, 120, 122, 128, 137, 140, 144, 148, 153, 157, 159, 162, 166
Manship, John, 164, 172
Mar, Earl of, 3, 71

March, Earl of, 24
Marchmont, Earl of, 18, 85, 108, 122, 137
'Marine society', 127
Marlborough, 158, 179
Marlborough, Duke of, 6, 8, 45
Marquis of Hamilton, 156
Maule, John, 24, 52
Maule, Baron William, Earl of Panmure, 52, 72, 78–9, 159, 195
Maxwell, Commander Arthur, 115
Maxwell family, of Annandale, 131
Mayne, Helen (wife of John Graham of Kernoc), 167
Mayne, Robert, of Powie Logie, Clackmananshire & London, 98, 128, 167, 169–70, 174
Mayne, William, of Powie Logie, Clackmananshire, 167
Mayne, Sir William, of Powie Logie, Clackmananshire & London, 86, 98, 128, 167
Mayne, family of, 138, 168–9, 176
Mayne & Barn, 167
Mayne & Needham, 167, 169, 176
McAuley, Provost, 78
McCulloch, John, 65
McGillivray, Captain William, 180
Melville, Povost, 44
Messrs Crawford & Duncanson, 168
Middleton, George, 79
Middleton, Colonel John, 79
Middleton, family of, 79
Midnapore, 168
Military Recruitment, 177–83
Millar, George, 44
Mills, Sir Thomas, 120
Mir Qasim, Nawab of Bengal, 1763, 32
Mirror newspaper, 151
Mississippi schemes, 6
Mitchell, Andrew, 67
Mitchell, David, 181
Mocha, 58
Moffatt, Andrew, 37, 97, 117, 119–20, 127, 140, 153, 157
Moffatt, Commander James, 97, 109, 117, 119–20, 127, 153–4

INDEX

Moffatt, John, 119, 127, 157
Moffatt, Martha (wife of Charles Bruce, Earl of Elgin), 119
Moffatt, Robert, 109, 119
Moffatt, family of, 97, 115, 120, 155, 157–8
Moffat–Foulis–Freeman Shipping interest, 157–8
Moncrieffe, Sir David, 73
Moncrieffe, William, 55, 61
Monklands canal, 192
Monson, Colonel George, 33
Monson, John, 46
Monson, Commander William, 58
Monson, Mr., 5
Montague, 116
Monteith, William, 63
Montgomery, Robert, 79
Montrose, Duke of, 71, 82–3
Moray, Earl of, 24
Moray, James, 13th Laird of Abercairney, 40, 50, 54, 59, 62
Moray, John, 59
Morris, Col. Staats, 180–1
Morrison, Captain George, 180
Morrison, Major John, 180
Morse, Frances (wife of Rawson Hart Boddam), 115
Morse, Nicholas, 115
Morse–Vansittart, family of, 154
Morse & Monson, 57
Motte, Thomas, 168
Mudie, Commander, 159
Mudie, Mr., 87
Mughal Empire, 31
Munro, Dr. Alexander, 82
Munro, Dr. Andrew, 81, 175
Munro, Andrew, 62
Munro, Dr. Duncan, of Obsdale, 81
Munro, Captain George, of Foulis, 81
Munro, George, 81, 182
Munro, General Sir Hector, of Novar, 81, 89, 97, 134, 180–2, 190, 194
Munro, Hugh, merchant, 182
Munro, Dr. John, 127
Munro, Dr. John, of Culcairn, 81,
Munro, Margarete Aurora (wife of George Smith), 176
Munro, Sir Robert, of Foulis, 51, 81, 84
Munro, Commander Robert, 81, 181–2
Munro, Robert Duncan, 81
Munro, Major-General Sir Thomas, 81
Munro, family of Foulis, Tain, 24, 50, 80–1, 176
Mure, Baron William, of Caldwell, 69, 71, 75, 103, 122, 132, 134
Murray, Alexander, 4th Lord Elibank, 99
Murray, Amelia (wife of Sir Alex Lindsay), 162
Murray, Barbara (wife of Sir James Johnstone, Senior), 99
Murray, David, Viscount Stormont, 162
Murray, Lt. David, 177
Murray, Lord George, 122
Murray, George, Lord Elibank, 83, 89
Murray, General James, 101
Murray, James, of Broughton, 105
Murray, John, hereditary Sheriff of Selkirkshire, 24
Murray, Patrick, 89, 99–101, 109–10, 127, 129, 131, 138, 141, 155, 160, 169, 174
Murray, Mr. (Jacobite), 53
'Mushroom' Family, 151
Musselburgh, 65, 79, 86
Myreton, Sir Andrew, of Gogar, Edinburgh, 102
Myreton, Elizabeth (wife of Archibald Stuart, Torrance), 102

Nabobs, 18, 67, 88, 92, 133, 178, 184 191, 193, 201
Nairn, 95
Nairn, Sir David, 41
Nairne, Commander Fasham, 63, 155
Naish, Dr., of Rowen, 61
Naish, Mr., 61
Napier, Lord, 83
Navigation Acts, 115
Nawab of Arcot, 132, 142, 148–50, 162, 169, 173, 179
Nawab of Bengal, 31, 92
Nawab of Oude, 169, 176

Nawab of the Carnatic, (See Nawab of Arcot)
Negapatam, 183
Netherlands, 5–6 (See also Holland)
Nethy, river, 196
Nethybridge, 196
Newcastle, Duke of, 16, 18, 70, 73–5, 90, 105, 107, 118, 121–2, 126, 134, 180
Nimes, Isaac, 58
North, Lord, 33, 103, 136, 140, 144–7, 149–150, 152, 166, 205

Ochterlony, Mr., 82
Ogilvie, Lady Anne (wife of John, 2nd Earl of Hopetoun), 54, 61, 64
Ogilvie, David, 147
Ogilvie, Lord David, 99
Ogilvie, George, of Cullen, 79
Ogilvie, Isobel (wife of John Dempster of Dunnichen), 105
Ogilvie, James, Lord Airlie (Jacobite), 53
Ogilvie, Janet (wife of David Ogilvie), 147
Ogilvie, John, 181
Ogilvie, Thomas, 61
Ogilvie, Commander, 159
Ogilvy, John, Lord Airlie, 3, 10
Ogilvy, of Banffshire, 24
Okehampton, constituency of, 148
Old Course (St. Andrews, Fife), 164
'Old Pretender', 10, 39
'Old Trojan', 158
Oliphant, Laurence, of Gask, 63
Oliphant, Peter, 63
Oliphant of Gask, family of, 51
Opium, trade in, 168
Orkney islands, 24, 56, 80
Orkney, Earl of, 18
Orme, Robert, 141
Osborne, James, 79
'Ossianic ballads', 148
Ostend, 3
Ostend Company, 98
Oswald, David, 161
Oswald, James, 78, 112, 119, 122

Oswald, Sir Richard, 191
Outer Hebrides, 158, 194

Palk, Robert, 142, 179
Panmure, Earl of, 134
Paris, 9, 175
Parliament, 3, 10, 44, 70, 93, 105, 122, 126, 139, 147, 152, 158, 170, 204 (See also House of Commons & Westminster)
Parliamentary Inquiry 1766-67, 26, 32, 139, 142
Paterson, George, 173
Patna, 87, 168
Patriot Lords, 41, 45
Patronage, 20–1; system, 46, 52; Crown, 25; legal, 25, 72; Scottish, 20, 121; Scottish political managers, 21, 25, 60, 101, 130, 157
Paymaster-General, 6, 36, 126
Payne, John, 90, 125
Peebles, 24
Pelham, Henry, 30, 45, 70–2, 75, 105, 111
Pels of Amsterdam, bankers, 7, 9
Perpetual Entail, Law of, 19
Persian translators, 173
Perth, 44, 49, 172
Perth, Earls of, 1, 3
Peterhead, 115
Petrie, Commander John, 117
Phipps, Governor, 57
Picardy Place, Edinburgh, 65
Pigot, Governor George, 59, 80, 103, 108, 150
Pigou, Frederick, 10, 172
Pitt, Governor George Morton, 41, 47, 53, 57–60, 63–4
Pitt, William, Earl of Chatham, 70, 74, 90, 92, 105, 126, 128, 132, 136, 139, 165, 178
Pitt, William, the Younger, 26, 30
Plassey, 114
Plassey, battle of, 26, 31, 69, 114, 124
Poems of Ossian, 148
'Poker' club, 105, 132
Pondicherry, 56, 174, 182

INDEX

Pope, Alexander, 65
Porteous riots, 17, 204
Portsoy, 175
Portuguese, 31
post-1707 Union apathy, 13; shift of power, 20
Pratt, Chief Justice, 105
Preston, Mr. A., 143
Preston, Sir Charles, 157
Preston, Sir George, of Valleyfield, Perth, 157
Preston, Commander Sir Robert, 153–4, 156–7
Prestonpans, 17, 163, 195
Prince Edward, 118, 119
Prince Henry, 156
Principal Medical Officers Madras, 62, 81–2
Pringle, Alex, of Whytebank, Selkirk, 167, 173
Pringle, Charlotte (wife of Robert Mayne), 167
Pringle, John, 52, 89
Pringle, John, of Haining, 80
Pringle, John, W.S., 151
Pringle, Peter, 174
Pringle, Thomas, of Selkirk, 52
Pringle, Dr., 132
Pringle, family of, 49
Pulteney, Daniel, 100
Pulteney, Frances (wife of William Pulteney Johnstone), 100
Pulteney, William, Earl of Bath, 100

Queen Anne, 3–4
Queen Caroline, 45, 64
Queensberry, Duke of, 19, 24, 46, 50–1, 131, 137, 187

Raja of Benares, 182
Ramsay, Dr. George, 82
Ramsay, Elizabeth (See Mrs. George Drummond, of Blair–Drummond), 1
Ramsay, Elizabeth (wife of Sir Gilbert, of Bamffe Perth, 56
Ramsay, Sir Gilbert, of Bamffe, 1, 56

Ramsay, Dr. George, 82
Ramsay, George, of Bamffe, 56, 58
Ramsay, George, (son of Sir James), 107
Ramsay, Sir James, of Banff, 107
Ramsay, Thomas, of Bamffe, 51
Ramsay, Mr., 160, 173
Ramsay, Mrs, (widow of Thomas Ramsay of Bamffe), 51
Ramsay of Bamffe, family of, 51
Ramsden, James, 63
Ramsden, Sir John, of Byram, 52
Ramsden, Lady (wife of Sir John Ramsden of Byram), 52, 63
Rankeillor, family of, 51
Rankin, Gabriel, 65
Rannie, Commander David of Melville, 35, 65, 79, 83, 86, 88, 116 166
Rannie, Elizabeth (1st wife of Henry Dundas), 86, 166
Rannie, Janet (wife of Cockburn of Cockpen), 86
Rawson Hart, Mary, (wife of Commander Charles Boddam), 115
Raymond, Charles, 157
Raymond, John, 90
Raymond, family of, 157
Regulating Act of 1773, 26, 32–3, 60, 144–6, 150, 175, 205
Reid, Mr., 112
Remittances, 18, 29
Renton, John, 107
Renton, William, 107, 152
Reynolds, Joshua, 37, 105
Richmond, Duke of, 146
Richmond, Yorkshire, 148
Rigg, William, 64
Roach, Major, 58-59
Robertson, Commander David, 65
Robertson, Principal William, 105
Robertson, William, 147
Robinson, John, 62, 140, 146–7, 149, 175, 205
Rockingham, Marquess of, 105, 134, 136, 140, 143, 150–2
Rod, James, 61
Rose, Hugh, of Kilravoch, 16

Roseberry, Lord, 79
Roseneath, Provost, 73
Ross, Alex, 78
Ross, Commander Andrew, 117
Ross, George, 101, 118, 122, 157
Ross, Hugh, 87
Ross, Hugh (merchant, London), 87
Ross, Col., 173
Rothes, Earl of, 25, 49-51, 54
Rous, Thomas, 95, 105, 131, 167, 179
Roxburgh, Duke of, 10–11, 71
Royal Africa Company, 9, 46
Royal Army, 103; 31st foot, 182; 48th foot, 182; 70th Foot, 99; 89th foot, Duke of Gordon's, 95, 180, 181; Louden's regiment 182; Scots regiments, 126; The Guards, 179
Royal Bank of Scotland, 19, 75, 77, 131, 12, 187
Royal Drake, 59, 98
Royal Exchange Assurance Company, 46, 167
Royal family, 121
Royal George, 161
Royal Navy, 99, 100, 159–60, 162, 186
Royal Society of Arts, 98, 127, 144, 165
Rumbold, Governor Thomas, 101
Russell, Claud, of Braidslaw, Edinburgh, 109
Russell, Claud, 87, 165, 174–5
Russell, John, 143
Russell, John, W.S., of Braidslaw, Edinburgh, 109, 174
Russia, 177
Rutherford, Dr. John, of Edgirstone, 174
Rutherford, Robert, 174
Rutherford, William, 174

Sainthill, Mr., 111
Sandilands, Patrick, 64
Sandwich, Lord, 129, 131, 140, 146
Savage, Robert, 105
'Scotch fiddle', 88
'Scotch Highlanders', 180
'Scotch Ministry', 104
'Scotch Nation', 67
'Scotch' (Company) support, 129, 141–2, 144
Scots, Presbyterian Commanders, 114
Scott, Col. Caroline, 177
Scott, David, 78, 154, 161
Scott, Col. George, 180
Scott, George, 92, 127
Scott, Dr. James, 58
Scott, James, of Logie, 52
Scott, John, 142
Scott, Robert, 146
Scott, Commander William, 117
Scott, Col., 86, 131
Scott, of Gowanberry, 58
Scott, family of, 49; family of Gala, 51
Scott, Pringle & Cheape, 164
Scottish military cadets, 93
Scottish Privy Council, 14
Scottish Representative Peers, 16, 71, 75, 152, 166
Scottish Secretary, 14, 70
Scrafton, Luke, 130
Scrope, Baron John, 11, 14, 43–5, 50, 65, 72, 75, 78
Seaforth, Lord, 50, 84
Seaton, Commander Francis, 115
Secret Service funds, 18, 72
Secretary of State, 14, 71, 128; for the North, 2, 70, 137
Secretary of the Scottish Treasury, 14
Selkirk, 24
Selkirk, Lord, 165, 171
Seton, David, 127
Seton, John, 171
Seton, Miss (wife of James Baillie), 165
Seton, Mr., (a Baillie or Councillor), 165
Seven Years War, 70, 95, 100, 124, 128, 151, 178
Shairp, John, 165
Shairp, Thomas, of Houston House, 63, 164
Shairp, Thomas, 165
Shairp, Walter, 165
Shales, Mr., 58
Shaw, William, 127
Shawfield, Riots, 10

Shelburne, Earl of, 102, 105, 122, 128, 130–2, 139, 141, 143, 149–50, 165, 175
Shepherd, Captain John, 47
Sheriff: of Elgin, 172; of Morayshire, 108; Hereditary, 22, 24, 49, 80
Sheriff–Clerks, 21, 84
Sheriff–Deputes, 21, 84
Shetland islands, 24, 56
Signet, 14, 84
Simson, Robert, 161
Sinclair, James, 49
Sinclair, of Ulbster, 24
Sinclair, family of, 50
Skye, 154
Slaines Castle, 64
Slater, Commander Gilbert, 117, 160
Slater, Commander Robert, 153
Slaves, transport of, 196
Smith, Adam, 100, 147
Smith, Charles, 173
Smith, George, of Fordyce, 81, 175; bounty, 176
Smith, James, of Fordyce, 175
Smith, Mr., 63
'Society for the Encouragement of Arts and Sciences.', 167
Sommerville, Hugh, 58
Somerville, John, 78
Sommerville, Ensign, 177
South Sea Bubble, 9
South Sea Company, 6-8, 14, 29, 98; crash of, 38
Southern Netherlands, 5
Spey, river, 196
Speyside, 195
Spilman, Mr., 1
Squadrone, 11, 14, 16–17, 71–2, 122
St. Andrews, 54, 88
St. Clair, Sir William, 52
St. Clair, General, 86, 108
St. James' Fields, London, 195
St. John, Henry, 1st Viscount Bolingbroke, 2–4, 10
St. Kilda, 159
St Mary's church, Fort St. George, 64
Stables, John, 175

Stackhouse, John, 58
Stanhope, Earl James, 66
Steven, Thomas, 161
Stevenson, Mrs. Patricia, of Edinburgh, 64
Stevenson, Rev. William, 64
Steward, Commander Gabriel, 116
Stewart, Commander Alexander, 76
Stewart, Archibald, MP, 76
Stewart, Archibald, 165
Stewart, Archibald, of Allanbank, 97
Stewart, Charles, 101, 109
Stewart, Sir Gilbert, 46–7, 50, 59
Stewart, Lt. Henry, 175
Stewart, Henry (Senior), 175
Stewart, Henry (Younger), 175
Stewart, James, 127
Stewart, James, Attorney, 165
Stewart, Sir James, of Allanbank, Jacobite, 53, 76
Stewart, John, of Stewartfield, 61
Stewart, Baillie John, of Inverness, 76
Stewart, John (son of Archibald Stewart), 76
Stewart, Commander John, 119, 155
Stewart, John, of Buckingham Street, 130, 143–4
Stewart, John, of Hampstead, 89, 132–3, 141, 144, 162, 174–5
Stewart, John 'Jack', 165
Stewart, John, of York Buildings, 97
Stewart, John (wine merchant in the Strand), 76, 107
Stewart, 'little' John, 129, 142, 165
Stewart, Oliver, 64
Stewart, Sir Robert, of Allanbank, 97, 132
Stewart, William, 52
Stewart, William (Jacobite), 53
Stewart, Mr. of Ardshiel (Ardseal), (Jacobite), 76, 155
Stewart, family of, 79
Stewart, Royal House of, 1, 39, 53
Stirling, 25, 49, 82, 151
Stirling, Archibald, of Keir, 55, 82, 89
Stirling, Ensign Harry, 82
Stirling, Hugh, 82

Stirling, James, of Keir 'the Venetian', 82
Stirling, Jamie, 82
Stirling, John, 82
Stirling, Lewis, 82
Stirling, Margaret (wife of Andrew Stuart), 103
Stirling, Sir William, of Ardvoch, Perth, 103
Stirling family, of Keir, 51, 54, 80, 82, 82–3, 92, 103, 118, 193, 195
Stock–jobbing, 34
Stratford, Dr. Nicholas, 6
Stratford, Dr. William, 2–4, 6–7, 11
Strathmore, Earl of, 89
Stuart, Alex, Lord Blantyre, 82-3
Stuart, Andrew, 36, 73
Stuart, Andrew, of Craigthorn, 97, 100, 102, 106, 110, 128–9, 144–5, 150, 164–5, 171, 173
Stuart, Anne (wife of John Stuart of Blairhall), 164
Stuart, Archibald, of Torrance, Lanark, 102
Stuart, Charles, 82, 92, 131
Stuart, Dr. Charles, 165
Stuart, Francis, Earl of Moray, 164
Stuart, Hon. Frederick, 132–3
Stuart, Grace (wife of Thomas Cheape), 164
Stuart, Sir James, 163
Stuart, Col. James, 36, 102, 144, 164, 173
Stuart, John, Earl of Bute, 26, 36–7, 69–70, 74, 89–90, 92, 95, 100–1, 105–7, 109, 118–23, 126, 128,
Stuart, John, Earl of Bute, *continued* 130–3, 136, 140, 147–50, 154, 164, 167, 178
Stuart, John, of Blairhall, 164
Stuart, Sir John, of Castlemilk, 104
Stuart, Lady, 83
Stuart, Margaret (wife of Sir Hugh Hamilton), 83
Stuart, Marion (wife of James Stirling of Keir), 82
Stuart, Peggy (sister of Sir James Stuart), 163
Stuart, Prince Charles Edward, 102
Suffolk, Lady, 63
Sugar mill, 168
Sulivan, John, 174
Sulivan, Laurence, 32–3, 36, 60, 79, 81, 87, 89–92, 95, 100–1, 103, 106–7, 109, 120, 124, 126–31, 133, 140–52, 155–8, 162–3, 165, 167–9, 171, 174–5, 179, 182, 198
Sulivan, Stephen, 198
Sulivanites (Sulivan faction-party), 60, 96, 101, 106, 149, 152
Sulivan–Colebrooke group, 171
Sumatra, 61
Sumner & Gregory, 87
Sun Fire Assurance Company, 97, 120
'Sun Fire Office', 157, 188
Sunderland, 3rd Earl, 10, 66,
Superintending Commission of 1772, 36, 145
Superiorities, 22, 25, 39, 49–50, 66, 77, 100, 105, 133
Supervisory Commission of 1769, 144
Supreme Council Bengal, 33, 103, 146, 168
Surat, 57, 64
Sutherland, 116
Sutherland, Alex, 177
Sutherland, Earl of, 25
Suttie, Charles, 98, 111
Suttie, Sir George, 104, 111
Sweden, 177

Tain, 24, 81
Talbot, Mr., 160
Tanjore, 174
Taylor, Mr., in the Landmarket, Edinburgh, 165
Tellicherry, 111
Thames, 156
Thames, river, 115, 195
The Scottish Enlightenment, 185
'The Entailer', 118
The Hague, 8
'The Silver Club', 88
Thomson, Commander David, 115

INDEX

Thomson, Commander William, 161
Threipland, Sir David (Jacobite), 53
Threipland, George, 53, 61
Threipland family, of Fingask, 195
Tinwald, Lord, 75, 78
Tobacco, trade in, 19, 168, 186, 188, 193–4, 196
Torphicen, Lord, of Calder House, 39, 64
Townshend, Charles, 11, 45, 57, 66, 73, 139
Townson, John, 89, 175
Tranent, 195
Treasury, 30, 70, 78, 146; Commissioners, 13, 20
Triton, 160–1
'Triumvirate', 33, 150
Tryal, 118
Tullie, Timothy, 125
Tweed, river, 36, 93
Tweeddale, Marquis of, 39, 51, 65, 70–1

Union of 1707, 3–4, 13, 16, 18–19, 20, 38–9, 66–8, 76, 78, 84, 93–4, 115, 137 154, 177, 186, 202–5, 207
University of Aberdeen, 149; of Edinburgh, 92, 105; of St. Andrews, 105
Uphall, 165
Urquhart, Dr., 169
Utrecht, 3

Vansittart, Henry, 101, 143, 171, 174
Veitch, Commander Robert, 117
Vizipatam, 165, 174

Waddell, Commander John, 114
Wadsets & wadsetters (mortgagees), 23, 66, 77, 133
Wake, Governor William, 64
Wallace, Lt., 177
Walpole, 115
Walpole, Sir Robert, 9–11, 13–18, 21, 25–6, 30, 38–40, 42–5, 50–1, 55–6, 59, 65, 68, 70–1, 78, 80, 90–1, 93, 119, 121, 123, 136, 170, 204, 206, 207
Walpole, Thomas, 172
Walpole–Drummond & India patronage, 115
Walpole–Drummond–Ilay–Milton & India patronage, 177
Walpole & Company, 114
Walsh, John, 130
War of the Austrian Succession, 5
War of the Spanish Succession, 2–3
Watkins, Mr., 7
Watson, Admiral Charles, 158
Watson, Commander John, 117, 127
Watson, General, 86
Watts, Thomas, 188
Watts, William, 104, 111
Webster, Alex. D.D, 107
Webster, John, 107
Webster, Mr., 173
Wedderburn, Alex, Lord Loughborough, 102–3, 106–7, 118, 131, 140, 142, 145, 147–8, 163–4
Wedderburn, Alexander, 56–7, 59, 163
Wedderburn, Alex, 92, 118
Wedderburn, Sir Alex, 44
Wedderburn, John, of Dundee, 57
Wedderburn, Mary (wife of George Cheape), 163
Wedderburn, Mary (wife of Sir John Cumming), 87
Wedderburn, Peter, of Charter Hall, Haddington, 147
Wedderburn, Captain, 87
Wedderburn, Mr., of Pitfirrane, 87
Wedderburn family, of Gosford, 77
Weir, Daniel, 162, 169
Wemyss, Elizabeth (wife of Alex Brodie), 172
Wemyss, James, of Wemyss, 172
West Florida, 100
West Indies, 55, 61, 95, 102, 107, 38, 162, 182, 188
Westminster, 6, 14, 16, 20, 25–7, 34, 46–7, 50, 69–72, 74–5, 77–9, 91–3, 107, 112, 124, 135, 137, 165, 204–5, 207 (See also Parliament, & House of Commons)

Whigs, 3–4, 17, 24, 27, 38, 49–51, 65–6, 70–1, 76–77, 83, 85, 99, 154, 203–4, 206
Whitehall, 2, 14, 20, 137
Whyte, Commander Thomas, 161
Wigton, 25
Wilmington, Lord, 82
Wilson, Major David, 177
Wilson, Mr., 8
Winchelsea, 160
Wishaw, 115

Wombwell, Sir George, 140
Wood, Robert, 128
Woodruffe, Philip, 188
Wordsworth, Josias, 5, 46

Yair, 174
York Buildings London, 76
York Buildings Company London, 194–6
York House, 195
Young, William, 101